Derek Walters is Europe's foremost authority on Chinese astrology, respected not only for his thorough academic knowledge of the subject, but also as an actual practitioner of Chinese divination. He has written a number of authoritative and popular books on oriental divination, including *The Chinese Astrology Workbook* and the *Feng Shui Handbook.* He lives in Morecambe, Lancashire.

By the same author

THE CHINESE ASTROLOGY WORKBOOK
THE FENG SHUI HANDBOOK
CHINESE MYTHOLOGY

To the Memory of
FREDERICK WALTERS
1906–1982

THE COMPLETE GUIDE TO
CHINESE ASTROLOGY

THE MOST COMPREHENSIVE STUDY OF THE SUBJECT
EVER PUBLISHED IN THE ENGLISH LANGUAGE

DEREK WALTERS

WATKINS PUBLISHING
LONDON

This Edition published in 2005 by

Watkins Publishing
Sixth Floor, Castle House
75-76 Wells Street
London, W1T 3QH

© Derek Walters 1987

First published in 1987 by Aquarian Press
Reprinted in 2002 by Watkins Publishing

Printed and bound in Great Britain

British Library Cataloguing in Publication data available

Library of Congress Cataloguing in Publication data available

ISBN: 1 84293 111 3

www.watkinspublishing.com

CONTENTS

Acknowledgements 7

Introduction to the Third Edition 10

1. Introducing Chinese Astrology 13
2. Pentology 25
3. The Chinese Calendar 51
4. The Twenty-Eight Lunar Mansions 81
5. Early Chinese Astronomical Texts 141
6. The Astrological Treatise of Ssu Ma Ch'ien 180
7. Divination Plates and Feng Shui 239
8. Chinese Horoscopes from the Eighth to the Twentieth Centuries 271

Appendices: Tables 327

Bibliography 381

Bibliographical Appendix 402

Index 405

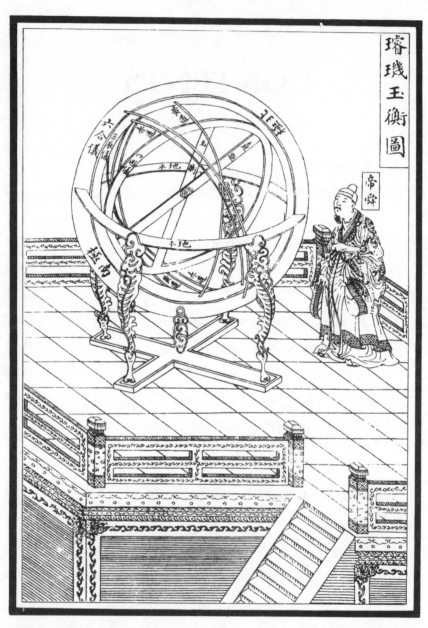

Frontispiece A late Ch'ing (late nineteenth century) impression of the Emperor Shun [2255-2205 BC] and his astronomical instrument called the 'Pearl Geared Jade Rail.' This term is now used for the armillary sphere, which is how the artist has interpreted it.

ACKNOWLEDGEMENTS

Without the help of many institutions and individuals, the writing of *Chinese Astrology* would have proved extremely difficult, if not actually impossible. Firstly, the British Library's Department of Oriental Manuscripts and Printed Books must be thanked not only for permission to reproduce examples from its unique collection, but perhaps more importantly for the considerable assistance of its friendly and helpful staff. Similarly, without the resources of the School of Oriental and African Studies, London University, and the considerable pains taken by the staff there, much valuable information would have been overlooked. The library of the Royal Asiatic Society has been a treasure trove of much original material, and I am most grateful to the Society for the many facilities which it has afforded me in the past. I am indebted, too, to the staff of the Royal Astronomical Society, London, for allowing me the use of their reference library in order to check data concerning planetary conjunctions. Certain manuscripts were made available by the East Asian History of Science Library, Cambridge, and these considerably aided my researches.

On the subject of Astronomy my thanks go firstly to Heather Couper, President of the British Astronomical Association and formerly of the Greenwich Observatory, who in a scintillating two hours there unlocked many of the mysteries of celestial geometry which had puzzled me since my schooldays. I must also acknowledge practical help given by Professor Archie Roy of Glasgow University for data relating to the precession of the equinoxes and related chronology. Particular thanks are due to Raymond Mercier, of the Faculty of Mathematical Studies, Southampton University, for his valuable suggestions which led to the dating of the horoscopes in the *I Shu Tien*.

Dr Anneliese Bulling gave me several clues regarding the

symbolism of early Chinese objects in the British Museum and the Victoria and Albert Museum, London.

Professor A. F. P. Hulsevé of Romont, Switzerland very kindly communicated to me his valuable paper *Watching the Vapours* on the mysterious subject of the aurae.

My friends Clive and Cordelia Unger-Hamilton helped me through several esoteric passages in otherwise familiar languages.

My late father, Frederick Walters, was responsible for the initial work in compiling a Chinese astrological calendar.

I am indebted to Mr Bertrand Kwong of Kowloon for pointing out that in the first edition the double-hours were calculated from midnight, when they should have been reckoned from 11pm.

Mr Osman Chung drew my attention to the importance of the Li Chün (Inauguration of Spring) and a mention of this has been incorporated.

The publication of a book such as this poses enormous difficulties for the editor and the production team, wrestling with the insertion of hundreds of Chinese characters into the text, apart from the problems of setting up tables and diagrams. My appreciation of the work done by the book's editor, Simon Franklin, must not go unrecorded.

Finally, I fear I shall never know the name of the lady, the Akela of my Wolf-Cub days, who so many years ago pointed out to me the constellations of the Great Bear, Orion, and Cassiopeia, and thus ignited a spark that was to smoulder for many years.

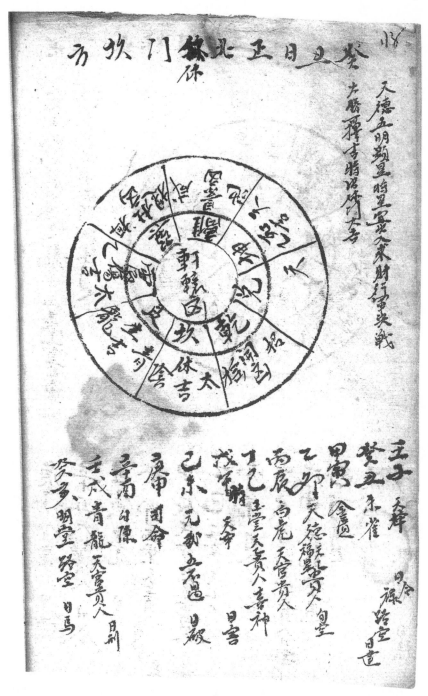

Page from a Qing dynasty manuscript of
astrological/geomantic charts (Author's collection)

INTRODUCTION
TO THE
FOURTH EDITION

If the efficacy of Chinese Astrology needed any vindication, then there is the case that when I began writing this book more than twenty years ago, I was determined that it should receive its first publication in 1984, since that year, being the first year of the coming sixty-year Chinese calendar cycle, would be an auspicious one. It is now with pleasure mixed with some astonishment that I find myself compiling a revised introduction to this, the fourth, edition of *Chinese Astrology*.

No doubt, the increasing popularity of Chinese Astrology is due in some measure to the fashionable interest in fengshui, with which Chinese Astrology is intimately bound. The Chinese hold that we have three Fates: the Heaven Fate, relating to the time we are born, (since time is measured by the movements of Celestial bodies); the Earth Fate, which derives from the place we live (that is, our fengshui), and the Human Fate, which is the way in which we behave and manage the resources bestowed upon us by Time and Location. Ironically, when planning this book, I intended to avoid discussing fengshui at any length, because by definition it is an earth-based science, not one of the 'revelations of the celestial messengers.' Similarly, I was rather dismissive of the well-known cycle of twelve animals, since these are unlikely to be Chinese in origin. But Time is a great teacher, and although it is still not possible to delve into the intriguing topic of fengshui at any length, its correlation with the Heavenly Sciences is a vital one. Similarly, although the cycle of twelve animals may not be Chinese in origin, it was an extremely felicitous invention. It is now my firm belief that the choice of the animals to represent the times of the day and months of the year, while simultaneously allegorizing the astrological qualities of their associated 'branches', was a masterstroke of ingenuity.

I always try to encourage students of fengshui and Chinese

astrology to go to the sources. This is why much of this book is devoted to translations of classical texts. These are the sources on which all other speculative interpretations have been based. The classical sources provide the reasoning behind the philosophies. In recent years, genuine indigenous Chinese astrology tends to have been swept away by a cascade of modern books by journalists and imaginative authors copying and embroidering other published works, writing to order, rather than from knowledge or experience. Sometimes the most penetrating errors are made, revealing, to the trained eye, that the author had scant first-hand familiarity with the subject.

Such basic errors of fact are not confined to popular works. It is widely believed among Chinese Science historians that the Chinese of the Han Dynasty possessed a compass in the shape of a metal plate, on which rotated a spoon made of lodestone. Such a device (intriguing copies of which can be purchased at most Chinese museums of technology) never existed. It was purely a modern conjecture based on a misinterpretation of the Chinese word for 'spoon', which also happens to be the Chinese name for the stars of the Plough, whose marker stars can be used to find true north.

Supplementing the classical texts, for the Third Edition I included a few passages taken from a later work of fiction, the *Jin Ping Mei* (usually translated as *Golden Lotus*) since it is apparent that the author must have had some familiarity (accurate or otherwise) with the technique of casting a horoscope. I urge readers to study these passages very carefully – no, even better, to acquaint themselves with the work in question. An excellent English translation by Clement Egerton was published in 1939, with the more salacious passages rendered into respectable Latin.

For those whose interests lie in astronomy rather than astrology, it is important to note that the recording of eclipses in the old Chinese histories was regarded as of great an importance as the chronicling of the enthronement and deaths of emperors. The appendix section on eclipses and prognostication is certainly of historic interest.

The original manuscript was assembled with the aid of an old-fashioned typewriter and several bottles of correcting fluid and for technical reasons it has not been possible to update the romanisation of Chinese proper names, terms and other expressions which were originally written in the now defunct Wade–Giles system of romanisation, into the now universally standard *pinyin*. The Appendix, therefore, includes a conversion table of Wade–Giles to *pinyin*, which readers familiar with only one of the two systems will find very useful. Readers of other books on Chinese astrology, fengshui, and traditional Chinese medicine are likely to encounter the occasional simplified characters which have superseded the classical script in mainland China, and a supplementary Index lists some of the commoner astronomical or calendrical terms.

The ability to read a Chinese calendar considerably reduces the time taken to convert western dates to the Chinese system, and for this reason the Appendix includes a guide to reading the Chinese *Wan Nian Li* or Ten Thousand Year Calendar. (The title is somewhat of an exaggeration, as they usually cover a mere hundred years, but this is sufficient for most lifetimes.) While it would be churlish to remove any names from the original acknowledgements, the lack of available space makes it impractical to add to it all those who have assisted me in my researches. I would, however, like to add the names of my friends Richard Tsui and Amelia Chow, Soothsayers of the Wong Tai Sin Temple in Kowloon, and to Professor Xu Zhentao of the Purple Mountain Observatory, Nanjing.

The new edition has given me an opportunity to correct a number of regrettable lapses, including the correct spelling of the town where I live, the somewhat bizarre transposition of two pages, and other occasional misdemeanors.

Thanks are certainly due to Penny Stopa of Watkins Publishing for having undertaken the considerable task of compiling the new edition.

And finally – those who have seen the original acknowledagements may recall my remark that it was my regret that I would never know the name of the Akela of my Wolf-Cub days, who sparked my interest in the stars more than fifty years ago when she pointed out to me the constellations of the Great Bear, Orion, and Cassiopeia. As a result of the publication of *Chinese Astrology*, she was at last discovered.

1.

INTRODUCING
CHINESE ASTROLOGY

This book takes a broad look at three aspects of Chinese astrology: firstly, its foundation in Chinese astronomical observation, secondly, its historical development, and thirdly, the method of interpreting the portents.

It will soon become evident that the notion of 'Chinese Astrology' is very much wider than its Western counterpart, but a book which tried to cover all of its aspects would be enormous by any standards. Indeed, even a straightforward translation of all the articles on the subject in the eighteenth century Imperial Encyclopaedia would run into several hefty volumes, since that valuable source devotes no less than *two-and-a-half thousand* chapters to the subjects of calendrical science, divination of various kinds, and what might more properly be termed 'astrology' — that is, the art (or science) of prognostication by stellar and planetary movements.

Thus, if this book were confined to aspects of astrology as the term is understood in the West, there would be, in the eyes of the Chinese practitioner, many serious omissions.

Fate Calculation or Ming Shu has a tenuous connection with astronomy being based on the Chinese lunar and solar calendars. Fengshui, though it deals with the configurations of the Earth rather than the Heavens, has its source in astronomical observation. Chinese clients expect their astrologer or fengshui practitioner to be a master of both disciplines.

I have thought it important to include a token amount of source material, particularly from the Golden Age of Chinese Astrology (the Chou and Han dynasties) since these early texts reveal what Chinese astrology was like before it was touched by Western concepts. Secondly, these texts give the reader an insight into the Chinese mind much more clearly than any summary of their main points, no matter how detailed the commentaries or interpretations. Many of these passages appear here in English for the first time, while other passages are usually only accessible in specialist libraries.

The Nature of Chinese Astrology

Several factors reveal that Chinese astronomy (and as a consequence, astrology) developed independently of studies in Western Asia and Europe. By the time that the two civilizations made contact, each side had firmly established its own principles and methods of astronomical observation. The first observation is that in Western astronomy there is an obvious nautical theme, with names of constellations such as the Whale, Fishes, Dolphin, and so on, while such maritime associations are noticeably absent from Chinese star names. Then it will become obvious that the Chinese visualise the stars being grouped into patterns quite differently; apart from the group of very bright stars which form the familiar pattern of the Plough, a Chinese star map has little in it which would be recognizable to a Western astronomer.

But the most startling difference is the method by which locations in the sky are identified. In the West, stellar positions are found by reference to the ecliptic, known to the Chinese as the Yellow Path, that is, an imaginary line through the heavens traced by the Sun (and in a broader sense, the Moon and planets also). Chinese astronomers, however, use the Celestial North Pole as a reference point, and the Celestial Equator, or Red Path, as a base line.

There may have been a good reason for this: in the Western system of observation which originated in subtropical latitudes, great importance is attached to the times of the risings and settings of the stars. In northern latitudes, the length of the twilight often means that faint stars are not seen until they have risen some way into the sky. There, it would be much more relevant to base observations on the times when stars appeared directly overhead, or at least at their highest point — i.e. an equatorial system. Such a method, based on the celestial pole star and others which are visible throughout the night and every night, would be very suitable in mountainous regions, where the horizon might be obscured by an irregular skyline.

Thus, the ecliptic (zodiacal) system used in the West is more suitable in southern regions, where the twilight is short and the terrain flat (as in desert or maritime areas) while the Chinese system is preferable in northern latitudes, where the twilight is protracted and the terrain uneven. The implication could be that Chinese astronomy-astrology had its origins in a northern mountainous region, although this is not necessarily the case. It *is* important to stress that

Chinese and Western methods developed as independently as their folklore and legends.

As a consequence of the two different observational systems, two kinds of astrological interpretation sprang up. In the West, astrology is based on the computations of the movements of planetary bodies along the ecliptic, or zodiac. In Chinese astrology, the 'lunar zodiac' has prime importance. In this the sky is divided into twenty-eight segments, each one representing a day of the moon's path through the sky. (The so-called 'Chinese zodiac', the animal cycle which begins Rat, Ox, Tiger . . . is used to enumerate the years, not the months. It is more properly called the Jupiter Cycle, on account of the fact that the planet Jupiter takes approximately twelve years to complete its circuit.) It follows that in Chinese astrology, there are many stars and constellations of importance which are irrelevant in Western astrology. Not the least of these is the Great Bear, which is the principle object of veneration by Chinese astrologers, while in Western astrology it rarely merits a mention.

To the ancient Chinese, Heavenly portents were of two kinds. There were those which happened at regular intervals, and could be predicted with accuracy; such were the rotation of the Great Bear, and the paths of the Sun and Moon. Then there were other less regularly occurring phenomena, notably eclipses. This led to two kinds of portent: those which were foreseeable regulated the order of events on earth. The other phenomena, whose appearance was less predictable, were celestial warnings. They foretold events, usually calamities, to be seen as reward or retribution for man's activity on Earth, and as all earthly action was embodied in the person of the Emperor, Heavenly portents revealed whether the Imperial Rule was in harmony with Heaven. There was no unshakeable conviction that everything was the will of Fate which could not be avoided, as, for example, is expressed in the *Oedipus* drama of Sophocles; nor on the other hand, was it believed that all circumstances were the result of one's choice of action — the view strikingly portrayed in Shakespeare's *King Lear*. For the Chinese, one's Fate lay in the blending, or 'harmony' between Heaven and Earth. Even the ancient oracle bone prophecies made the distinction by the use of two different words for 'not', one signifying that a certain result would be inadvisable, another that it would not take place at all — as of a marriage, for example.

Because Heaven revealed its intentions to mankind through its celestial phenomena, it was essential for the heavenly manifestations to be under continual surveillance, both night and day, so that the omens could be recorded, interpreted, and not least, acted upon. The Astronomical Bureau of Ssu Ma Ch'ien's time had a staff of twenty-eight, watching the stars, planets, and comets by night, and eclipses, haloes and aurae by day.

Great importance was attached to a planet's general appearance: whether its colour changed, whether its brightness was steady or flickered, or even whether it disappeared. Since everything in the sky came under the aegis of Heaven, it did not matter that these perturbations in a planet's appearance were due to meteorological conditions, all omens were sent by Heaven. But it did mean that a continual watch had to be maintained day and night, whereas Western astrologers seldom, sadly, can be bothered to look at the heavens, and instead resort to tables.

But perhaps the most revealing difference between the Chinese and the Western systems of astrology lies in the symbolism of a planet, and the interpretation of its spheres of influence. The outstanding example is the symbolism attached to the planet Venus, in the West regarded as the planet of the feminine, whereas in Chinese astrology, the Metal Planet, so-called because of its silvery whiteness, is associated with the military, and hence masculine, qualities.

The Chinese 'feminine' planet is Jupiter, the Wood Planet, associated with Spring, growth, and birth. The symbolism of the other three planets is very nearly the same in both systems of astrology, the portents being drawn by association of the planet's appearance or behaviour. Mars, because of its red colour, was the Fire Planet; Saturn, the slowest moving, was the solid Earth Planet. The swiftly moving planet Mercury was, as in the West, associated with Water and communication.

At a very early stage in the development of astrological techniques it was considered to be of paramount importance to note the direction of a particular omen. This aspect of Chinese divination is extremely ancient. In the second century BC, Ssu Ma Ch'ien noted the astrological relationships between various states and their associated directions. There are even older references to the auspiciousness or otherwise of certain directions, as for example, in the main text of the second hexagram of the *I Ching*. This certainly seems to suggest that when the *I Ching* was compiled, possibly about the second millenium BC, direction was an important divination technique. Its origins may lie in the extremely ancient art of bird prophecy. The importance of 'directionology' in Chinese divination, astrological or otherwise, cannot be stressed too strongly. Even today, at the most elementary level, the likelihood of success or failure of any aspect of

Figure 1.1 Omens drawn from the cry of birds.

business may be judged by the auspiciousness of the direction in which the process is inaugurated. Which of two suitors a girl should marry might be determined by the direction in which their abodes lie; the result of a horse race might be determined by the number which is most harmonious with the direction in which the race is run.

Allied to the directional aspect of Chinese divination is the Five Element theory. (The term 'element' has now fallen out of favour with academics, but it is as good as any other term, generally understood, and has the authority of established usage.) The Five Elements — Wood, Fire, Earth, Metal, and Water — became attached to the names of the planets, although these appear to have had their own particular technical names before the introduction of the Five Element theory. The Five Elements, concerned with the interpretation of, rather than the reason for, a planet's activity, are an essential feature in the calculation of favourable and unfavourable tendencies in a person's horoscope.

In brief, it can be said that in the matter of the techniques in setting up a horoscope, the distinguishing features of Chinese astrology are the equatorial method of planetary location; the importance of observation; the twenty-eight mansions, and the different methods of identifying and naming the constellations. In matters of philosophy, and the methods of interpreting the results, the distinguishing features of Chinese astrology lie in the differing symbolism, the importance of direction, and the use of the Five Elements.

The Sources of Chinese Astrology

The prehistory of Chinese astrology lies in the great collections of Shang Dynasty (16th-11th centuries BC) 'dragon bones' — scapulae used by ancient diviners. Although the methods of divination were not in themselves astrological, they demonstrate that the Chinese were systematically recording the heavens more than four thousand years ago. Picture signs refer to unlucky and lucky stars (for example, the graph for 'unlucky' 凶 may be a representation of the Chinese constellation Ghost Carriage: four stars with a nebula at the centre). The conclusion is that even at that time, stars must have been known by name before recorded history. A wealth of material is still being unearthed and deciphered, and among these fragmentary texts are many fascinating references to astronomical phenomena which may have had a divinatory significance.

Apart from such concrete evidence are the less tangible proofs of legend and folklore, which suggest that certain stars and

Figure 1.2b Oracle bone inscription of about 1300 BC referring to the 'Bird Star' later known as the 'Star'. (See Hsiu 25 and the Southern Palace.)

Figure 1.2a Oracle bone inscription of c.1300 BC. It has been translated as 'On the 7th day of the month, a great new star was seen, in company with the Fire Star (Antares), (See Hsiu 5, and Eastern Palace.)

constellations must have acquired their names at a very ancient date indeed. A remarkable example concerns the naming of two constellations, the Ox and the Maiden, and the siting of two bright stars known as the Ox-boy and the Weaving Maiden. As they stand at present, the bright stars are out of alignment with their respective constellations, which would not have been the case five or six thousand years ago.

Chinese Classical Sources

In China, the received classics are venerated not only for their literary and historic content, but also as sacred books. In many ways the diverse material which constitutes the classics has parallels with the collection of assorted writings which make up the Old Testament books of the Bible, both sources including historical writings, moral discourses, poetry, and descriptions of ritual and ceremonial procedures.

The core of Chinese classical literature consists of nine books, for convenience divided into five 'Ching' or canonical works, and four 'Shu' or books generally.

Figure 1.3 **The Weaving Maiden and the Ox-Boy**

The Weaving Maiden was the daughter of the Sun God, and to reward her for her skill at weaving, he married her to Keng Niu, the Ox-boy, whose herds drank from the River Han, known to us Western mortals as the Milky Way. But unhappily, once she was married, she seemed to have no further interest in her weaving, and instead gave herself over to a life of idleness. Though he loved his wife dearly, the Ox-boy was most distressed by this change in her and he too left his herds to wander the Heavens where they would. Naturally, the elder gods were very angry at the dissolute behaviour of the two young people, and it was decided to part them for ever. To this day the Ox-boy, Altair, and the Weaving Maiden, Vega, wait for each other forever separated by the River Han, he minding his herds on one side, she tending her loom on the other. Legend, however, tells that once a year thousands of magpies flock together on the seventh day of the seventh moon to form a bridge over the River Han in order that the husband and wife may meet together.

A further tale can be recounted here. Many Chinese almanacs include among their peripheral information extracts from the classics such as the twenty-four examples of filial piety. One of these is the story of Tung Yung who, too poor to pay for his father's funeral, bonded himself for ten thousand pieces of cash so that the funeral rites could be performed with all due ceremony. On his way home, he encountered a girl who announced her willingness to marry him. What was more to the point, she brought with her a dowry of three hundreds bolts of cloth. These the young man sold, and was able to redeem his bond. The young couple spent a happy month together, after which the girl told Tung that she was really Chih Nü, the Weaving Maiden, sent to Earth to reward Tung Yung for his piety. Thereupon she disappeared.

Figure 1.3 The Meeting of the Ox-Boy and the Weaving Maiden on the Borders of the Milky Way.

The five Ching are: the *I Ching* or *Chou I*, 'Book of Changes of the Chou Dynasty', the *Shu Ching*, 'Book of Documents' (equivalent to the 'Chronicles' perhaps), the *Shih Ching*, 'Book of Poetry', the *Li Chi*, 'Book of Rites', and the *Ch'un Ch'iu*, 'Spring and Autumn Annals' (this too is a kind of historical record).

The four Shu are the *Lun Yü*, usually called the 'Analects' or 'Sayings of Confucius', compiled by his disciples, the *Ta Hsüeh*, 'Great Learning', also by a disciple of Confucius, the *Chung Yung*, 'Doctrine of the Mean', ascribed to the grandson of Confucius, and the *Meng-Tzu*, 'Works of Mencius'. The oldest classical writings are generally accepted to be the *Shih Ching* and the *I Ching*. The former, the Book of Poetry, is regarded as a compilation made by Confucius. They represent a long oral tradition, and some of the verses may date from the earlier part of the Shang Dynasty (1765-1122 BC). Consequently, the astronomical references in them are of great interest to researchers. The 'Book of Changes of the Chou Dynasty' is for the main part a collection of folk-sayings and formulae of a very early date, with commentaries traditionally ascribed to Confucius, although this is not generally accepted by scholars. The texts of the 'lines' of the *I Ching* are said to be by Wen Wang and Wu Wang, and if so, date from about 1100 BC. Several passages in the *I Ching* may have an astrological symbolism which has been overlooked; see, for example, the comment regarding the lunar mansion K'ang, on page 92.

The 'Spring and Autumn Annals' record events between the eighth and fifth centuries BC; added to these are a number of astrological commentaries, based on observed events, such as the appearance of Halley's Comet in the region of the Northern Ladle (the Plough) in 613 BC, something which would only have been known from actual observation by writers at that time. It follows therefore that although the *Tso Chuan* (Commentary by Tso) and the *Kuo Yü* (Observations on the States), both ascribed to Tso Ch'iu Ming (died AD 647), did not appear in print until the eleventh century, there is a basis of reliable scientific observation in those early writings.

The *Shu Ching* (Book of Documents) includes a fascinating document, the *Yao Tien* (Edicts of the Emperor Yao), which will be discussed at length later. The *Li Chi* (Book of Rites) has an almanac which was to be the prototype of literally thousands of others, and is still quoted in the day by day guides in popular Chinese almanacs of today. The *Shih Ching* (Book of Poetry) is important for its mention of certain stars and constellations, described later in the section on the twenty-eight lunar mansions.

The four 'Books', principally concerned with moral conduct, are of lesser concern to the present work, although occasional reference may be made to them.

Non-classical Sources

Other works quoted at length in this volume include the *Shih Chi* the 'Historical Record', and the *Huai Nan Tzu* the 'Book of the Prince of Huai Nan', both of which were written in the second century BC, but based on earlier sources. The 'Historical Record' by the Grand Astrologer Ssu Ma Ch'ien was the first attempt to make a systematic history of the Chinese, and was imitated by the chroniclers of each succeeding dynasty. It contains important chapters on the sciences, including the calendar, astronomy, music, and divination by various means. The contemporaneous 'Book of the Prince of Huai Nan', derived from obviously similar sources, is a collection of essays by different authors on various occult subjects. It contains some philosophical material which Ssu Ma Ch'ien would obviously have been aware of, but did not deem worthy of inclusion in his own volume.

Among the books which provided material for both the 'Historical Record' and the 'Book of the Prince of Huai Nan' are the 'Star books' by the astronomers Shih Shen and Kan Teh, both of whom lived in the fourth century BC. Their books are no longer in existence, but fragments can be gleaned from later sources which quoted them, revealing that these astronomers had compiled catalogues of star names and positions two hundred years before any similar attempt was made in the West.

The following centuries saw a burgeoning of works on divination, including astrology and the related subject of Fate Calculation. The first few centuries of our era saw the earliest mentions of the well-known twelve-animal 'Chinese zodiac' although their origin has still not been positively identified.

A survey of the many and varied writings of the T'ang period would be beyond the limits of a single volume, but it is interesting to see that there are many T'ang fragments to be found copied in the manuscripts discovered by Aurel Stein at the beginning of this century in the cave monasteries of Tun Huang. These manuscripts remarkably, include the oldest star maps in existence. One of the major works of the T'ang period, the *Hsing Tsung*, 'Company of Stars', was added to by the Yüan dynasty astrologer Cheng Hsi Ch'eng sometime in the fourteenth century. This very important work is preserved in the Imperial Encyclopaedia of 1726, and has been a major source of information in this survey.

Figure 1.4 **The Crow in the Sun and the Hare in the Moon.**
The ancient Chinese observed and recorded sun spots two thousand years before Galileo — without the aid of a telescope. The astronomers' description of the phenomenon as like 'a large black bird' gave rise to the legend of the Crow in the Sun.

2.

PENTOLOGY

Fundamental to all forms of Chinese divination is the significance of the Five Cardinal Points. Without a thorough understanding of their symbolism it is impossible to interpret a horoscope. For this reason, the principles of the Five Cardinal Points must precede any account of the stars, planets, or astrological techniques.

The Five Cardinal Points are the Four Directions (East, South, West and North) and the Centre. Every aspect of Chinese philosophy is linked to the Five Cardinal Points: the five elements, the five planets, relationships within the family, the eight diagrams of the *I Ching*, the five senses, in fact every possible classification and category.

The earliest forms of divination were elaborations of popular oracles. Folk oracles of this kind can be found in every country. We might say, on seeing magpies, 'One for sorrow, two for joy, three for a girl, four for a boy'. Here we have a simple example of an oracle with four readings. For the Chinese, the direction from which a particular sound was heard gave the meaning of the oracle. For example, on hearing a crow, according to the time of the day, and the direction from which the sound was heard, a complex code of signals was received by the fortune-teller. If heard from the South in the early hours of the morning, the crow's cry meant that presents were going to be received, if heard mid-morning that there would be rain, if at midday, quarrelling, if in the afternoon, misfortune, or if in the evening, a lawsuit.

Although elaborate catalogues of oracle interpretations such as these were compiled as early as the second century BC (many attributed to the Han dynasty Court Wizard, T'ung Fang Shuo, whose name actually means 'Eastern Direction') the essential point here is that the tradition of using direction as a basic technique of divination was well-established by then, and obviously must have had much more ancient origins.

One of the most extraordinary books in Chinese or any other classical literature is the *I Ching* or 'Book of Changes', fragments of which are the records of oral traditions which may be six or seven thousand years old, at least. The text of the *I Ching* forms a number of layers, like geological strata, each layer representing a different period of the book's composition. Readers familiar with the *I Ching* will know that it consists of 64 diagrams of lines with accompanying text. The text may be divided, into a 'basic' text, which may vary from just a few characters to several lines of poetry, and six additional 'lines' texts, while the basic and lines text each have their own commentaries. To complete the whole work, there are additional commentaries by later writers. Tradition has it that the 'commentaries' were written at the beginning of the Chou dynasty (twelfth century BC) although it is likely that these were made later. What is not disputed is that the main texts to the diagrams, i.e. the oldest parts of the *I Ching* were assembled into something like their present form during the Chou dynasty, and that the material from which the compilation was made must have been ancient and revered even then.

Having underlined the antiquity of the main text of the *I Ching*, one or two passages from it become highly significant. Firstly, from Diagram II, K'un, the Feminine, one of the longest of all the main texts. It concludes:

Good fortune from getting friends in the South-West. In the North-East to lose friends. Peace. The auspices are fortunate.

Similarly, from the main text of Diagram XXXIX, Chien,

Fortunate the South-West; unfortunate the North-East.

The later commentaries expound the connection between the eight basic diagrams (of three lines) to the eight compass points, the symbolism, and their various attributes. More will be said about this later. The Western astrologer may wonder what all this has to do with 'astrology', which literally means the study of the stars. The Chinese astrologer, however, would wonder how it could be possible to conceive of a study of astrology without a knowledge of the Eight Trigrams, one of the foundations of fengshui theory.

Directionology
When a Chinese astrologer or soothsayer wishes to determine the likelihood of success of a particular business, the response obtained

from the oracle employed is very often expressed as a fortunate or unfortunate direction, as the examples from the *I Ching*, above, show.

A businessman might inquire from his almanac the lucky direction for the particular day when he had an important engagement. If his meeting entailed his travelling in a north-westerly direction, and North-West was the direction of the day, then he would proceed in confidence. He would also be confident that his rival, reading the same almanac, would elicit the converse information, that South-East was an unlucky direction, and that his visitor would be coming from that direction. The home-based entrepreneur would be at a psychological disadvantage, and the meeting might indeed go the way that the original inquirer wished. For that very reason, the second businessman would most likely try to postpone the meeting to a day that would be agreeable to them both. Western visitors to China soon learnt to consult the Chinese almanacs; not to find out what the future held in store for their fate and fortune, but for the sheer practical purpose of establishing the likelihood of a meeting taking place on a certain day. It would hardly be sound business practice to try and arrange a meeting on a day which the almanac warned against having dealings with strangers from the West, since the Chinese partner would in all probability just not turn up.

When a meeting was inevitable, most likely when two young people fell in love, despite the warnings of all their soothsayers, then the omens had to be cheated. Perhaps the bride was to set off to her fiance's village, which lay in a direction contrary to the best auspices of the day. There being no way in which the wedding could be postponed or brought forward, the bride's family would follow the simple expedient of setting off from the house in the wrong direction, make a detour, and arrive safe and sound.

Directionology had a very important influence in the very tangible matter of bricks and mortar. The Emperor's palace opened towards the South, and accordingly the houses of lesser mortals opened towards the North, in order to receive the beneficial presence of the Emperor. Chinese houses, and Chinese cities too, were frequently laid out on a cosmological plan which reflected the harmony of Heaven and Earth, with the residents of the city being the intermediaries between those two great forces.

But to go much further along these lines will be taking us from the realms of astrology into the sciences of the Earth: Geomancy, or as the Chinese call it, Feng Shui, meaning Wind and Water. The first thing, therefore, is to take a look at the symbolism of the directions.

The Symbolism of the Five Cardinal Points

For the purposes of Chinese astrology, it can be considered that there are Five Cardinal Points, and Eight Directions. The Centre is the fixed point, or locus, to which the others are relative. In looking at the heavens, we must remember that East and West are reversed. Looking South, the East is on one's left, the West on one's right. If the sky were then looked at as a flat map, it would show South at the bottom, North (which would be behind the observer) at the top, East on the left, and West on the right. In other words, the positions of East and West would be the reverse of a terrestial map. It is worth observing that old Chinese maps and charts usually show South at the top.

The Eight Directions are the eight compass points, North, East, South, and West, together with the intermediate points. These are dealt with in greater detail in a later section. (See page 46.)

The South   南

The Sun is predominantly in the South. During the day, the Sun is in the southern half of the sky; throughout the year, the Sun ventures further and further North as the seasons progress from Winter to Summer, but it never attains a northern position, even on the longest day, yet every day it swings round to the South. (It must be remembered that the Chinese lived almost exclusively between the Arctic circle and the tropics, and were not familiar with the phenomenon of the Midnight Sun. However, military conquests took them far South enough for a general to have noted that at the edge of the empire, the Sun cast shadows in a southerly direction on certain days.)

Thus, the South is associated with the Sun, the bringer of warmth, light, harvest, and all the good things of life generally. The Sun was at its strongest in the Summer, and consequently the Summer Solstice was regarded as the time of the year associated with South. Because fire is hot, the element which corresponds to the heat of Summer is Fire; things which are heated become red, and so Red is the colour associated with the South. Because the Emperor faces South, then South, Summer, Fire, Red, and Heat are all associated ideas. An excess of 'South' can mean fire, or drought.

The North   北

North is the opposite of South; since South represents Summer, North must represent the Winter, cold and wet. Because of the wet, North is allocated to the Water element; Winter is the season of rains.

Because Winter is a dark season, the colour associated with North is Black. Where South indicates the harvest and plenty, North symbolizes dearth. While South represents the benign influence of the Emperor, North shows the malign influence of enemies. An excess of North indicates flooding or freezing.

The East   東

Because the Sun rises in the East, this is generally taken to mean a fortunate direction. The East is associated with the inquirer, and shows the influences which are at work on the inquirer's character or business, and therefore reveal the present circumstances. Because the East is the beginning of a new day, it is associated with the beginning of the new year, and consequently its season is Spring. Because Spring is associated with the new green growth, and the blue skies after the harsh black skies of Winter, the colour associated with Spring is Green (or more correctly, a kind of bluish green). The element is Wood. A predominance of matters associated with East represents a too great a concern with the self.

The West   西

The West is the place of the setting sun. Consequently it is associated with Autumn, and the business of Autumn, which is harvesting. The fortunate side of West is therefore plenty (harvest), but the unfortunate side is the indication that everything has now been gathered in; the Winter is to come, and preparations ought to have been made for the lean times which are ahead. Because agricultural instruments (scythes, shears and the like) are made of metal, the element associated with Autumn is Metal. Just as the East represented the Self, or the subjective side, so West represents opposition, or the objective side. The West indicates opposing forces, partners, rivals, whether in business or love. Because Metal is (generally) a silvery white colour, the colour of West is White. Since the setting sun is a symbol of death and burial, the colour associated with death in China is not black, but white. The expression 'people in white garments' means, to the Chinese, the departed spirits, or ghosts.

The Centre   中

The Centre is the ground we stand on, and is stationary, whereas the four directions are 'moving'. In China, the predominant colour of the earth was the yellow loess, and so the 'Earth' colour is Yellow. The Centre represents the present time, the subject, the question itself (as distinct from the East, which represents the influences at work on the subject). Because the Centre is stationary, it represents immovable things: property and land, especially the latter.

The Seasons
As in the West, the Chinese reckon the number of seasons to be four; therefore, in order to make a correspondence between the four seasons and the Five Cardinal Points (and be an extension of the five elements) it is necessary to resort to some philosophical juggling. (In astrological terms, further confusion arises over the fact that Centre is associated with the Earth element, which is allocated to the planet Saturn.)

One of the standard ancient works on Chinese astrological theory and practice is the *Huai Nan Tzu* (The Book of the Prince of Huai Nan). This takes a notional astrological year of 360 days which is divided into five equal periods of 72 days each. The first period is Spring, belonging to the element Wood; the second season is Summer, whose element is Fire; the third is the Middle Season, whose element is Earth; and the last season, Winter, element Water. This is the most authentic of all the systems proposed for equating the seasons with the five elements. Its date has been shown to be earlier than the *Huai Nan Tzu* itself, and was in existence about a thousand years before the divinatory art of Fate Calculation sprang into existence. There are several schools of 'fate calculation'. In one, a short 'Earth' season is tacked on to the end of Summer. In another, a few days are allocated to the end of each of the conventional four seasons. There can be no doubt that both of these systems seem highly contrived and artificial and do not seem to correspond to the order of 'natural' events, on which the whole of astrological philosophy is founded. Unfortunately, the 'natural' and 'authentic' system of the *Huai Nan Tzu*, while sound in theory, is deficient in practice.

In the *Huai Nan Tzu* method, the first season begins with the day Chia Tzu [甲子] 1-I, the first day of the Chinese sixty-day cycle. (This is fully explained in a later section; see page 76ff.) The second season begins 72 days later, and will consequently begin with the day Ping Tzu [丙子] 3-I, the third season with the day Wu Tzu [戊子] 5-I, and so on. It is a great pity that this highly organized method only accounts for 360 days in the year. Later astrologers, wrestling with this problem, devised a number of complex solutions which professional astrologers still use today. The least complex of the methods is to reckon the first season starting from the first Chia Tzu (jiazi) day after the Winter Solstice. Variants of this method are used in other types of astrological and fengshui calculation, such as reckoning the Magic Square number for the day. However, most types of Fate Calculation, as will be seen later, allocate the Earth quality to the third month of each Chinese season.

A Five Season Year

For a concordance between the seasons, directions and elements which most closely follows the principles laid down by the ancient sages, Chinese authorities have devised several different, often complex, methods to solve the problems arising from a year of five seasons.

Traditionally, the four seasons are marked by solar phenomena, *and are therefore of astrological significance.* These four time-markers are the Winter Solstice, the Spring Equinox, the Summer Solstice and the Autumn Equinox. These four events are of great significance in the ancient Calendar of Rites, and we shall be looking at some attendant phenomena later. It is important to stress that the Chinese method of using these four time-markers to indicate the seasons is radically different from our own, as it is with all Chinese methods of time measurement.

The Chinese do not use markers to indicate the beginnings of time periods, but the middle point. Thus, while we regard the Winter Solstice as marking the beginning of Winter, the Chinese reckon it to indicate Mid-Winter. (Perhaps it is worth recalling that 'Mid-summer's Day' is June 24th, only three days after the Summer Solstice.)

In a five-season year, only one of these astronomical phenomena can be used to mark the beginning or the middle of the year; if for example, the Winter Solstice is used to mark the beginning of the year, then the Summer Solstice will mark the middle of the year; one of these points will be between seasons, and the other mid-season, as the diagrams will show.

The dates for the beginning of each season will therefore be one of the following alternatives:

Spring begins	5 March	or	27 January
Summer begins	17 May	or	10 April
Earth Season begins	29 July	or	22 June
Autumn begins	10 October	or	3 September
Winter begins	22 December	or	15 November

While the dates in the first list are in accordance with a northern climate, the second list may be preferred on astronomical grounds since both equinoxes then occur in their traditional positions.

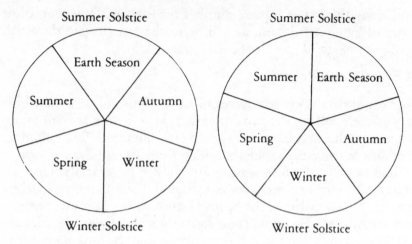

Figure 2.1

Occupations and the Seasons

A survey of occupations and social class compared with dates of birth was published in the *Guardian* newspaper for 20 March 1984. The data was obtained from a 1 in 10 sample of the then latest available census figures (1971) of the occupations of 1,461,874 men and 842,799 women who were economically active. The results, shown in graph form, are extremely significant, and well worth studying by anyone seriously interested in astrological research.

A comparison of this data with the second of the five-season schemes (described above) reveals the following general trends:

Farmers *in general* belong to the Earth season
Miners to the Water season
Chemical workers to the Water season
Electrical workers to the Wood season
Labourers, storekeepers, packers to the Earth and Metal seasons
Clerical workers to the Metal *to* Water seasons
Professional classes to the Wood *to* Fire seasons

The analysis of social groups was startling:

Social Class I peaked at the end of the Fire season, with a significant drop in the Water season
Social Class II peaked in the middle of the Fire season
Social Class III were distributed randomly, but ebbed at the Earth season

Data based on Random 1 in 10 Sampling of 1971 Census

Social Class I   Sample 80,042

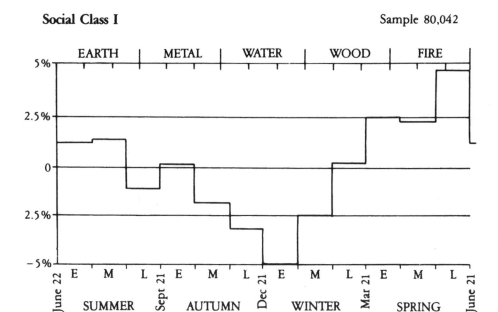

Figure 2.2

Social Class V   Sample 175,439

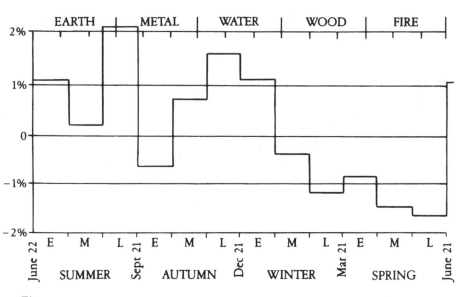

Figure 2.3

Data based on Random 1 in 10 Sampling of 1971 Census

Management and Administration

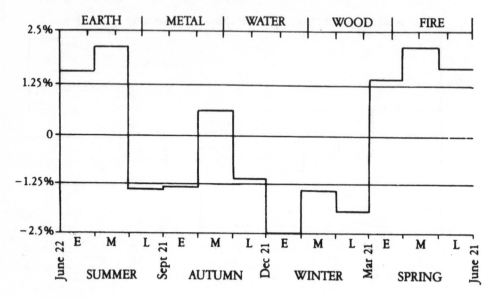

Figure 2.4

Professional Technical Workers and Artists

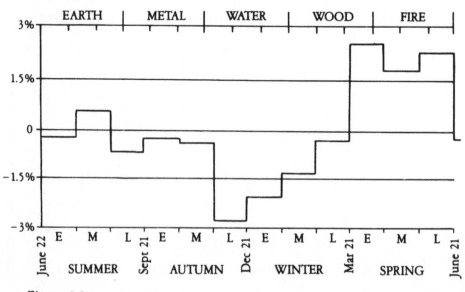

Figure 2.5

Data based on Random 1 in 10 Sampling of 1971 Census

Farmers

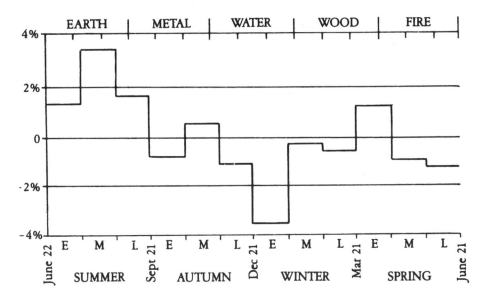

Figure 2.6

Miners

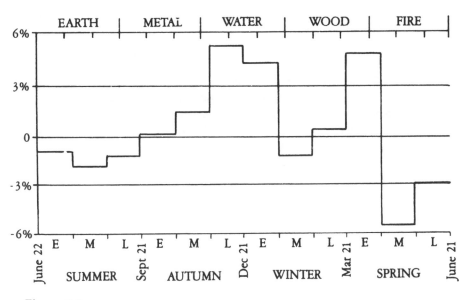

Figure 2.7

Data based on Random 1 in 10 Sampling of 1971 Census

Electrical

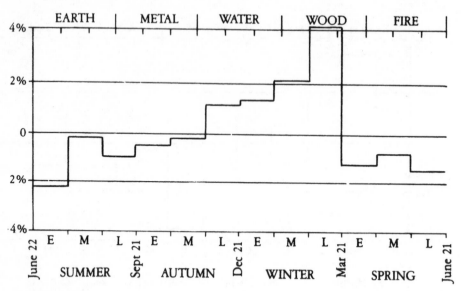

Figure 2.8

Social Class IV had a small peak in the Metal season, a greater
peak in the Water season
Social Class V spread over the Metal and Water seasons, with
a significant drop in the Fire season

The Elemental Types

In popular astrology, or Fate Calculation, predominance of certain
elements in a horoscope determines the person's character and
personality more accurately than the twelve animal types. In this
respect, the elemental attributes are akin to the 'humours' of Western
philosophy. Indeed, Chinese traditional medicine determines the
state of a person's internal order by the outward manifestation of
five elemental signs. The summary below gives the basic elemental
qualities.

Wood — Rustic, practical, casual. Creative; lover of nature and
children.

Fire — Lively, quick agile. Volatile and aggressive.

Earth — Stable, reliable. Practical, primitive, conservative.

Metal — Vigorous, progressive, acquisitive. Calculated; determined.

Water — Contemplative, attentive. Communicative, restless.

Harmony Between the Elements

It would be impossible to embark on any discussion of Chinese astrology without an understanding of the principle of the Five Elements. These are Wood, Fire, Earth, Metal and Water.

It will be seen that these correspond only partly with the Four Elements of Ancient Greek philosophy: Fire, Earth, Water, and Air. Some commentators on Chinese philosophy aver that it is incorrect to call the Chinese five principles 'elements' since strictly speaking, the Chinese principles are active agencies at work on the material constituents of the universe, while the Ancient Greeks considered their Four Elements to be the constituents of the universe itself. The distinction is questionable, and as Wu Hsing (五行) has been translated as Five Elements and understood as such for several hundred years, it seems a bit late to change.

The Mongolians, caught between East and West, and so uncertain as to whether there were Four or Five elements, made a composite of the lot: Wood, Fire, Earth, Metal, Water, plus the additional Air for good measure. Obviously, to the Mongolians, the Western concept of 'element' was no different from the Chinese one. However, the Five Elements have a much more significant role to play in Chinese astrology than the Four Elements do in the West, for the simple reason that the names of the Five Elements are also the names of the five major planets, which gave the elements their colour qualities.

Jupiter	Mars	Saturn	Venus	Mercury
木	火	土	金	水
Wood	Fire	Earth	Metal	Water

The doctrine of the Five Elements has been traced back to the Chinese philosopher Chou Yen (騶衍) fl 350-270 BC. He was either the inventor of the doctrine, or else the compiler of ideas which had been very recently introduced, since no concrete reference to the Five Elements exists before his time. Indeed, during the Han Dynasty, the term Wu Hsing (五行) was only just coming into being. Early quotations from Chou Yen speak of his referring to the 'Five Conquerors', Wu Sheng (五勝) or the 'Five Virtues', Wu Jen (五仁). Chou Yen's writings were held in high esteem during the

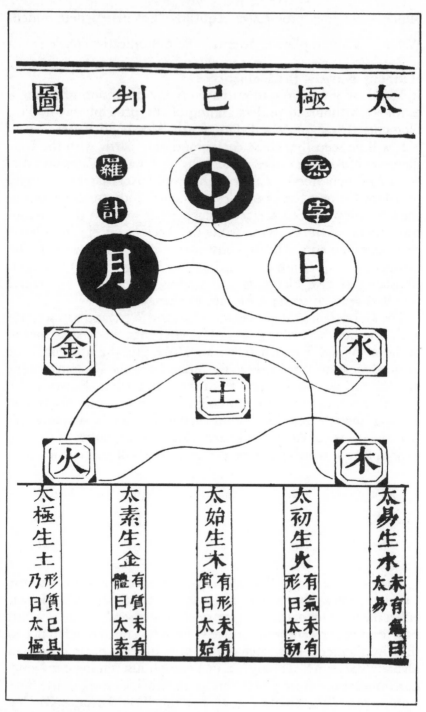

Figure 2.9 The Five Elements.

Han; they were known simply either as 'Master Chou's (Writings)', Chou Tzu (騶子) or, more significantly 'Master Chou's (Book on) Arrivals and Departures', Chou Tzu Chung Shih (騶子終始), a title which will be understood more completely in the context of the application of the doctrine of Five Elements.

One of the earliest detailed expositions of the Five Element theory dealt with the correlation of the early dynasties with the sequence of the elements; it is worthwhile paraphrasing the relevant passages from the *Lü Shih Ch'un Ch'iu* (呂氏春秋) 'The Spring and Autumn Annals of Mr Lü' (c. 239 BC):

> The birth of a new dynasty is foretold by certain signs. The reign of Huang Ti, the Yellow Emperor, was marked by the appearance of giant worms and ants, showing that the element Earth was dominant. For this reason, Earth was chosen as the emblem of the dynasty, and Yellow for the colour of the livery. Then during the reign of Yü the Great, the auspicious signs were trees which did not shed their leaves in Autumn or Winter; this revealed the element Wood to be dominant, and Green was chosen as the colour of the livery. King T'ang's dynasty (The Shang) was heralded by a bronze sword emerging from the water; so the dominant element was Metal, and the livery White. When King Wen of the Chou came to power, there was Fire in the Heavens, and Red birds assembled at the dynastic altar — thus the Fire element was dominant, and Red the colour of the livery.
>
> Therefore a dynasty whose element is Water is yet to come; its livery will be Black, and Heaven will manifest the time by signs and portent. And likewise, the Dynasty of Water will come to an end, and a new dynasty of Earth will ascend, but that time is not known to men.

We now know that the 'Water' dynasty was the Ch'in (from which the name 'China' was taken), the first time that China was united under one Emperor. In deference to the prophecy, the Ch'in adopted Black as their livery. The next dynasty — the new Earth dynasty, was the Han; later dynasties also associated themselves with manifestations of different elements, and usurping powers often drew support for their causes by proving that Heaven's Mandate was allotted, or withdrawn, in accordance with the elemental cycles.

★   ★   ★

The elements of modern chemistry are ultimate particles of matter, the entire material universe being constituted from a myriad combinations of less than a hundred prime ingredients. Modern science accords that all matter (and by consequence, all the elements) exists in four states — solid, liquid, gas, and plasma, as for example, water may exist as ice, liquid water, or steam, while the fourth state, plasma, can only exist in the nuclear furnaces of the stars or atomic laboratories.

The four element theory of Aristotlean science evolved at the same time as the five element theory of the Chinese — it is now accepted quite coincidentally. The reader will note that the order given above is the order in which the elements are associated with the seasons of the year, and in consequence, with the directions East, South, Centre, West, North, or the sequence of colours Green, Red, Yellow, White, Black. (By Green is meant a bluish-green.)

The sequence is called the 'production sequence' because this is the order in which the elements produce each other. Thus:

相生

Mutual
generation

Wood burns, producing
Fire, which leaves ash, or
Earth, from which we extract
Metal, which can be melted to
    run like
Water, which is necessary for
    the growth of . . .

Now the extraordinary thing about the five elements is that although they are all considered to be of equal weight and significance in their own right, their relationships to the other elements are quite different in the manner in which they react; in producing the next element, each element is exhausted, but in a different way. Wood is burnt up in producing fire, which itself disappears leaving the stable earth behind. Metal, whether malleable, or the forceful edge of the sword or spade, becomes quite different when melted; the metal is still there, but it has lost its strong quality, and takes on the weaker qualities of flowing water. It does not proceed further to wood of its own accord, as in the consumption of wood by fire.

In the 'destruction' sequence the differences between the elements are even more marked. These are not, as one might suppose, the reverse sequence of the production order, but another progression produced by the alternate elements in the cycle. Thus:

祖克

Mutual
annihilation

Water quenches . . .
Fire melts . . .
Metal chops . . .
Wood eats . . .
Earth drinks . . .

The five elements conquer their subordinate elements in entirely different ways. So we might find that a Water element person (or as Western astrologers might say, a person whose ruling planet was Mercury) would conquer a Fire element personality (a Mars type) by quenching his ambition. The Mars type, or, to the Chinese, the Fire element type, would conquer a Venus (Metal) type of person by constant pressure until the Metal 'melted' or was subdued. Metal would conquer the Wood situation (Jupiter) by straightforward attack. More about these relationships will be dealt with in the section on the planets themselves. (See Chapter 6).

Next, we turn to the way in which the five elements support each other. If there is a dominant element which seems set to quash the subject, or thwart the subject's interests, then there is the possibility that there may be a balancing element which maintains stability.

This may happen in one of two ways. In the first case, an element is not destroyed by a second if there is a third which destroys the second element. By looking at the table above, 'Water quenches . . . Fire melts . . . Metal' we see that if the elements Water, Fire and Metal were present, the Fire would not melt the Metal, because the Fire would be quenched by the Water. In Western astrological terms, the planets Mercury, Mars, and Venus balance each other.

There is a second way in which the destruction of an element may be prevented; this is when there is another element present which produces the element under threat. Thus, in the case of Fire, Metal and Earth, as long as there was Fire melting the Metal, there would be Earth producing more Metal, and so the Metal would not be conquered by the Fire. Thus, Fire, Metal and Earth, or the planets Mars, Venus and Saturn, would be in harmony. These relationships are shown in the diagrams below.

It will be seen from the diagram that when three planets form a conjunction of 36° they are in balance, no matter whether the conjunction is of the 'mutually controlling' or 'mutually dissolving' type. On the other hand, if three planets form a relationship which stems from a conjunction of 108° it will be seen from the diagram above that they must be in the mutually producing order, as for example, the Fire element (Mars) Earth (Saturn) and Metal (Venus).

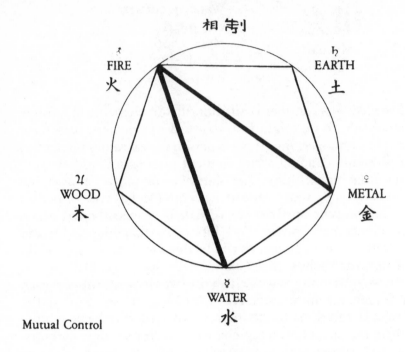

Mutual Control

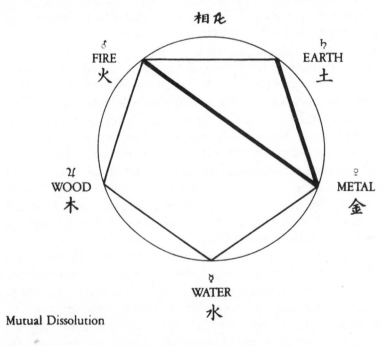

Mutual Dissolution

Figure 2.10

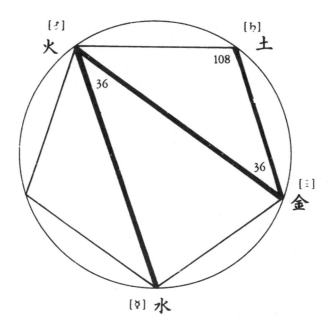

Figure 2.11

In this case, Fire is producing Earth, and Earth is producing Metal. The quantity of Metal produced is therefore increased by the production of Earth, from which the Metal is produced.

Presence of Four Elements
If four elements are present, they *must* take the form:

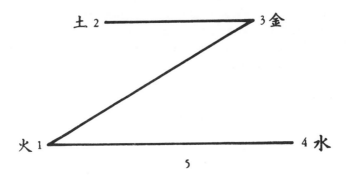

Figure 2.12

In the diagram above, Fire the first element, Earth the second, Metal the third, and Water the fourth. Wood, the fifth element, is missing. From what has gone before, we know that the three elements Water, Fire and Metal form a 'mutually controlling' triad, and the three elements Fire, Metal and Earth a 'mutually dissolving' triad. The Fire, Earth and Metal triads are mutually producing, as are the Earth, Metal, and Water triads. The net result is that it is the fourth element in the group which is dominant, being the end product of the mutually producing chain, Fire, Earth, Metal and Water. Wood is absent. Thus, in the case of four elements being present, the *final element* of the mutually producing chain is the dominant one, although all four elements will be in harmony. The fifth element, will be noticeable by default.

In ascertaining a person's character, Chinese astrologers place as much importance on those factors which are absent, as those which are present. In the diagram above, where Wood was absent, this might be regarded as a serious weakness in the character, being one who is unable to create or produce. It could mean that the person would have no heirs, or someone with a very poor 'drive' since Wood is the element of generation and growth.

It is always worth reminding ourselves that by Wood, Fire, Earth, Metal and Water, Chinese astrologers of the classical period meant the Five Planetary influences.

The typical elemental characteristics found in personalities strongly influenced by their ruling elements are summarized in the table on page 36.

The Five Palaces

From very early times, Chinese astrologers divided the sky into five 'palaces'. The Central Palace, associated with the direction Centre and the element Earth, was the area of the sky which was always visible throughout the year. For an observer at the North Pole, the whole of the sky is occupied by the Central Palace, the whole sky rotating round the observer's head throughout the year. At the equator, there is no Central Palace, since the whole of the sky rotates round a point on the horizon, and there is no significant area of the sky that is visible throughout the year.

However, for the majority of observers, there is always an area of the sky due North, somewhere between the horizon and a point directly overhead, where the sky rotates completely during the course of the day. During the Winter, those parts of the sky that are obscured by the sun's light during the day now come into prominence at night, though it must be remembered that since Winter nights are longer than Summer ones, there is more opportunity to see the greater part of the sky in the Winter, provided that the observer is prepared to watch in the early evening and in the early hours of the morning.

The Central Palace of the sky is defined by a large circle, with its Centre at the Celestial North Pole, and its circumference touching the horizon. The 'Pole Star' is very close to the Celestial North Pole, but not exactly central. With the passage of centuries, the accuracy of the Pole Star varies; although the change may not be noticeable in a lifetime, so ancient is the study of astronomy by the Chinese that twice they have re-designated certain stars as their 'pole star'. Such changes are only needed every two thousand years or so, thus indicating a history of astronomical observation dating back at least six thousand years. As in the West, the Celestial Pole is found by reference to the very dramatic group of stars in the sky which are called the Great Bear, the Big Dipper, or whatever. (The familiar pattern of a saucepan with handle, is only part of the larger constellation known as the Great Bear, and it is technically incorrect to refer to the seven major stars as such.) To the Chinese, it represented a measuring pan with a handle, and in this book we shall refer to it by the Chinese name, Northern Ladle.

Since the Northern Ladle rotates about the sky once every day, and makes a total rotation every year, it is possible to use the Ladle as a kind of celestial clock to tell the time at night. It is, of course, important to know the date, since the position of the constellation shifts by one (Chinese) degree every day (slightly less than one Western degree).

It is a very rewarding exercise to work this out for oneself. The position of the handle of the Ladle should be observed at a fixed time on a fixed date. Note the position where you are standing, and whether the handle is pointing to any geographical or architectural feature. The position moves by about one degree every four minutes (a degree in the sky is about twice the width of the full moon) or a quarter revolution every six hours. On subsequent days, the position will have shifted by one degree each day at the same time, or a quarter turn every three months.

Having established the position of the Central Palace, it now remains to divide the rest of the sky into the four directional palaces. Although these are called the North, West, South and East Palaces, they cannot, of course, refer to the actual terrestrial direction, since the sky is in constant movement. If the observer looks directly North, then the *Central* Palace will be above and in front. Part of the sky above the observer, and widening in a segment to the South, behind the observer, will be a quarter of the hemisphere which we can provisionally call another 'palace'. If this is the Southern Palace, then the Western Palace will be to the observer's left, the Eastern Palace to the Right, and the Northern Palace *underfoot*. But because the heavens are in constant motion, the Western Palace will be sinking, the Eastern Palace rising, and the Northern Palace just coming into view. Exactly which palace is where will again depend on the time of the day and the season of the year.

In astronomy (and astrology) the time of the rising of certain stars is significant. In fact, the seasons of the year were sometimes defined by the day on which certain stars rose above the horizon at certain times. Those stars lying at the southern fringes of their palaces, may come into view for only certain times on particular days in the year, and obviously such stars were regarded by ancient astrologers as being of great significance.

The Eight Directions

It might not be altogether inappropriate to close this chapter with a remark about the subdivision of the four directions into eight.

The Eight Directions are ascribed to the eight basic trigrams of the *I Ching* according to one of two systems, known as the 'Former Heaven Sequence' traditionally ascribed to the legendary Fu Hsi, and the 'Later Heaven Sequence' which is usually attributed to King Wen of the Chou dynasty. It follows that the symbolism of the Eight Directions very much depends on whether one uses the Fu Hsi or the King Wen traditions.

In the *Shuo Kua Ch'uan* (Sermon on the Eight Trigrams) commentaries of the *I Ching* the correlations between the trigrams and the eight compass points are clearly stated.

> All things proceed from Chen, Chen is the Eastern direction
> . . . Sun is the South-East; Li, brightness, is in the South. K'un
> is the Earth (*by inference the South-West*) . . . Tui corresponds
> to Autumn (*the West*) . . . Ch'ien is the North-West . . . K'an
> signifies Water, and is the trigram of the North . . . Ken is
> the trigram of the North-East . . .

The passage then continues with an elaboration of the attributes of the trigrams, and by inference, the corresponding directions. These are listed in the table on page 48.

The Correspondences of the Eight Directions according to the *Shuo Kua Ch'uan*

Chen 震	Sun 巽	Li 離	K'un 坤	Tui 兌	Ch'ien 乾	K'an 坎	Ken 艮
East	South-East	South	South-West	West	North-West	North	North-East
Eldest son	Eldest daughter	Middle daughter	Mother	Youngest daughter	Father	Middle son	Youngest son
Dragon	Fowl	Pheasant	Ox	Sheep	Horse	Pig	Dog
Thunder	Wind	Lightning The Sun	Earth	Seas	Heaven	Lakes The Moon	Mountains
Wood	Wood	Fire	Earth	Water, Metal	Metal	Water	Wood
Early Spring	Spring to Summer	Summer	Summer to Autumn	Autumn	Late Autumn	Early Winter	Winter
Young men	Merchants	Women	Multitude	Sorceresses	The King	Thieves	Officials
Feet	Thighs	Eyes	Trunk	Mouth, tongue and throat	Head	Ears	Hands, Upper limbs
Movement	Penetration	Burning	Receiving	Joy	Giving	Flowing	Stability
Roads	Business	Weaponry	Squares	Reflections	Circles	Wheels	Gates
Speed	Vegetation	Drought	Nourishment	Salt	Strength	Danger	Seeds
3	4	9	2	7	6	1	8
Jade-Green	Turquoise	Purple	Black	Red	White	White	White

The Nine Palaces

The Eight Directions, together with the Centre, are allocated to the Nine Palaces, and the Magic Square called the Lo Shu. The Emperor, according to the Rites, would occupy whatever room of his own palace was deemed to be appropriate to the season. An elaborate form of numerology based on the appropriate colours allocated to each division of the Lo Shu was devised by Chinese astrologers, examples of which can be seen in modern Chinese almanacs fundamentally no different from ninth and tenth-century almanacs found at the Lamaist monastries of Tun Huang. These are discussed more fully on page 287.

Auspices of the Eight Trigrams

The Eight trigrams play a vital role in the interpretation of Chinese horoscopes. It is important for the student of Chinese astrology to be thoroughly familiar with the various associated meanings: the relationships, activities, parts of the body and so on, in order to be able to interpret the resultant direction in the light of any question which might be posed. Their general significance is given in broad outline below.

Ch'en 震	East	3	Generation, growth. Initiative, movement. Advancement; a time to undertake new projects.
Sun 巽	South-East	4	Travel, concentration, mental activity. Good emotionally, and for business. No excessive movement, but steady progress.
Li 離	South	9	Fame; artistic accomplishment; change of residence. Good for media, publicity. Bad for keeping secrets.
K'un 坤	South-West	2	Creative, but not necessarily productive. A time to reap the benefits of former efforts.
Tui 兌	West	7	Joy; relaxation, contemplation. Accomplishment; satisfaction in achievement.
Ch'ien 乾	North-West	6	Strength and dignity; firmness of purpose. Ambition, promotion. Thrusting forward. May lead to conflict through aggression.

K'an 坎	North	1	Difficulties, obstacles. Opposition to plans. Losses, stagnation. Problems.
Ken 艮	North-East	8	Coolness; a time of ending and drawing together; finishing with one and beginning with another; internal change.
Chung	Centre	5	A peaceful period. The peak of one's achievement. Plan ahead for this period, and use the excess to store up against the future.

Diagram illustrating the relationship between the five musical tones, their corresponding elements, and the proportions of the lengths of pipes or strings to produce the required pitches. From the lowest point, in clockwise order: Gong (C) Earth, 81; Shang (D) Metal, 72; Jiao (E) Wood 64; Ji (G) Fire, 54; Yu (A) Water 48.

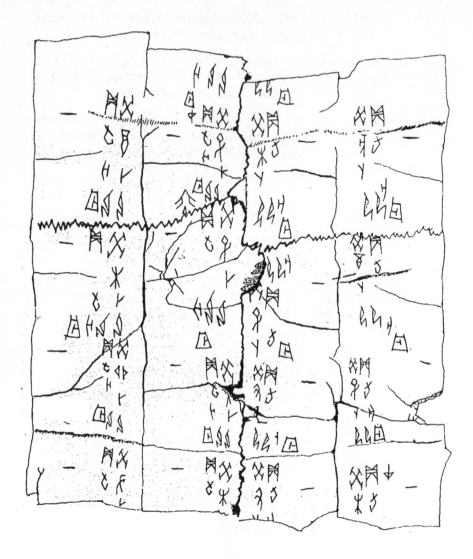

(e) Plastron of turtle inscribed with a collection of divination texts. The 'X' symbol, Stem 10, reveals that all these divinations were performed on a Tenth Stem day, suggesting that the tenth day had a sacred significance.

3.

THE CHINESE CALENDAR

The Chinese calendar is the oldest in continuous use. It is undoubtedly far more complex than the Western one, being constructed according to lunar, solar, and numerical criteria. The largest unit is the *epoch*. In the Western calendar all years are counted from a point between 31 December 1 BC, and 1 January AD 1. (There is no year 0, a fact which is occasionally overlooked.) Thus, by our reckoning, all dates before 1 January AD 1 are (as we are told in *1066 and All That*), 'counted backwards'.

The Chinese epoch is a period of 3,600 years, divided into sixty *cycles*, each of sixty years, 1984 marking the beginning of the eighteenth cycle of the second epoch since the beginning of Chinese recorded history.

Each cycle of sixty years is divided into five 'Great Years' each of twelve years. These twelve years are numbered according to a sequence of Chinese characters called *Branches*. For about a thousand years, these abstract characters have come to be known, in popular usage, as the 'twelve animals': Rat Ox, Tiger, and so on. These names are, in Chinese historical terms, comparatively recent. They are not mentioned in treatises of the first century, and in traditional Chinese calendars the animal names appear almost as an afterthought.

There are fundamental differences between Western and Chinese years. The Western year is of fixed length, varying by only one day every four years. The length of the Chinese year varies, for reasons which will be fully explained shortly. The Western year is *solar*, in that its starting point is ultimately derived from an Earth-Sun phenomenon, i.e. the length of time it takes the Earth to make a circuit of the Sun (rounded off to the nearest number of whole days).

The Chinese year, however, is lunar, in that its basic time-marker is the New Moon. (At least, in theory; it is likely that observations were taken of the first and last quarters, since the straight line of the Moon's diameter was a much more accurate marker than the New Moon, which is, of course, invisible.) A lunation taking 29½ days, Chinese months are 'little' or 'large' according to whether the month has 29 days or 30. As a result, the Chinese year is shorter than the Western one by about ten days, and because of the result of the year 'drifting' has an extra month added every few years in order to bring the calendar 'into accordance with Heaven'.

The Chinese do not customarily name the months. Although there are various fancy and poetic names (equivalent to our 'Fill-dyke' for February) the months of the year are simply known as First Month, Second Month, and so on. This means that such expressive translations as 'Tea House of the August Moon' or 'Mayflower Restaurant' reveal the imagination of the translator. In the original language, the names of these establishments would simply be 'Eighth Month Teahouse' or 'Fifth Month Flower Restaurant'.

The Solar Year

In addition to the lunar year, there is also a solar one. This is fixed to the four solar markers, the two solstices and the two equinoxes. The year is divided into twenty-four periods of fifteen or sixteen days each. These 'solar terms' are known as Ch'i, or vapours, a word which has several distinctive meanings. (See also page 236.) Their origin, as their names suggest, are essentially agricultural, as for example 'Great Heat' and 'Corn Rain'. Specifically, they represent divisions of the sun's ecliptic into twenty-four segments, each corresponding approximately to half a sign of the Western zodiac. More precisely, each term is 15° longitude measured along the horizon. These twenty-four solar terms are therefore *the closest Chinese equivalent to the zodiac of Western astrology*.

The Twenty-Four Ch'i, or Solar Periods

立 春 1.	Li Ch'un	Spring commences	Midpoint of Aquarius
雨 水 2.	Yü Shui	Rain water	Sun enters Pisces
驚 蟄 3.	Ching Chih	Insects waken	Midpoint of Pisces
春 分 4.	Ch'un Fen	Spring Equinox	Sun enters Aries
清 明 5.	Ch'ing Ming	Clear and Bright	Midpoint of Aries

穀 雨	6.	Ku Yu	Corn Rain	Sun enters Taurus
立 夏	7.	Li Hsia	Summer commences	Midpoint of Taurus
小 滿	8.	Hsiao Man	Corn sprouting	Sun enters Gemini
芒 種	9.	Mang Chung	Corn in ear	Midpoint of Gemini
夏 至	10.	Hsia Chih	Summer Solstice	Sun enters Cancer
小 暑	11.	Hsiao Shu	Little Heat	Midpoint of Cancer
大 暑	12.	Ta Shu	Great Heat	Sun enters Leo
立 秋	13.	Li Ch'iu	Autumn commences	Midpoint of Leo
處 暑	14.	Ch'u Shu	Heat finishes	Sun enters Virgo
白 露	15.	Pai Lu	White Dew	Midpoint of Virgo
秋 分	16.	Ch'iu Fen	Autumn Equinox	Sun enters Libra
寒 露	17.	Han Lu	Cold Dew	Midpoint of Libra
霜 降	18.	Shuang Chiang	Frost descends	Sun enters Scorpio
立 冬	19.	Li Tung	Winter commences	Midpoint of Scorpio
小 雪	20.	Hsiao Hsüeh	Little Snow	Sun enters Sagittarius
大 雪	21.	Ta Hsüeh	Great Snow	Midpoint of Sagittarius
冬 至	22.	Tung Chih	Winter Solstice	Sun enters Capricorn
小 寒	23.	Hsiao Han	Little Cold	Midpoint of Capricorn
大 寒	24.	Ta Han	Great Cold	Sun enters Aquarius

These twenty-four Ch'i were mentioned in 'An Account of the Travels of the Emperor Mu', a work which is even earlier than the Han dynasty. Chinese almanacs still list the dates on which the 'fortnights' commence; as they are determined astronomically, the dates of the fortnights vary slightly from year to year. A table of the dates according to the Western calendar is given in the Appendix. The dates of the Sun's entry into the various divisions of the zodiac thus include the equinoxes and solstices. There are occasional discrepancies between the Eastern and Western hemispheres however.

Twelve of the Ch'i are known as Monthly Festivals or Chieh (節). These have an importance in Fate Calculation since they are one of the factors used in determining the fatal periods. At least two of these festivals have a special significance in the Chinese social calendar.

Ch'ing Ming (Clear and Bright) generally falls on the 4th of April, and in many ways has close parallels with Easter. It is the day when family tombs are decorated and cleaned, and offerings made to the ancestors, although in the course of time, since tombs were generally situated away from the towns, it became a season for holiday-making and country excursions.

The first of the solar periods, Li Chun, the Inauguration of Spring, may occur before or after the New Year. Li Chun is always represented on the first page of traditional Chinese almanacs by the position of the Spring Ox; if it appears on one side of the farmer it shows that the Li Chun appears before the New Year, if on the other after it. Years are considered 'blind' if the year's beginning does not include the Li Chun, and such years are regarded as generally unfavourable.

The astrological significance of the Li Chun is universal, applying to humanity in general, not to any particular individual. In fact, those situations which bring universal benefit (a good harvest, for example, the consequence of which is general prosperity) are usually connected with the weather, and likewise the reverse, such as the natural calamities of drought, tempests or floods. In this sense, the auspices of the Li Chun are distinct from those omens which only affect one area of society. Usually, what is beneficial for one group of people (such as winning a battle) is poor news for others (those who lost the battle). Consequently, years beginning with the Li Chun are considered to be especially favourable for marriages, coronations, festivals, and whatever revolves on the year's harvest being good, thus stimulating general prosperity world-wide.

In the table, the first of each pair of figures (always less than 10) is the date of the Solar Month used in Fate calculation.

A final point regarding the twenty-four periods, is that they were equated (in the *Huai Nan Tzu*) with the twelve notes of the chromatic scale; the first twelve ascending, and the latter twelve descending, in pitch. Hence for each of the twenty-four periods there was a Branch, running I-XII for half the year, and XII-I for the other half.

The Chinese Month

In the Chinese calendar, the length of the month (29 or 30 days) is adjusted so that the New Moon falls on the first day of the month, and the Full Moon on the fifteenth day. In order to match certain months with the four seasons, the year begins on the first day of the New Moon after the solar term 'Great Cold', or by Western reckoning, after the Sun has entered Aquarius. New Year's Day may therefore occur on the first day of the first or second New Moon after the Winter Solstice.

The need for a simpler calendar did not escape early Chinese philosophers. As long ago as the first century a 'nonary' calendar was proposed by Yang Hsiung. (For an account of this intriguing calendar see an earlier work by the present author, the *T'ai Hsüan Ching*, pp. 33ff.)

Chinese almanacs today still include vestiges of another curious calendar which combined 28 day periods with a 13 day cycle, producing a year of 364 days. Further information on these cycles will be found in the section on the Twenty-Eight Lunar Mansions, and the Ch'ien Chu system of auspicious days.

Without the addition of extra or 'intercalary' months when needed, the Chinese calendar would slip back by thirty days, a complete month, every three years. The invention of intercalary months is credited to the time of the legendary Emperor Yao (2357-2255 BC) although it was many centuries before a systematic method of determining when the intercalary months should fall was worked out. To be precise, an extra seven months are intercalated every nineteen years, this formula being known as the 'Metonic Cycle'. In the Chinese calendar, the distribution of these extra seven months is made so that the Spring Equinox always occurs in the second month, the Summer Solstice in the fifth month, the Autumn Equinox in the eighth month, and the Winter Solstice in the eleventh month. These intercalary months always have the same number as the principal month which they follow, although the number of days in the principal month and the following intercalary one may not be the same. The first, eleventh and twelfth months are never duplicated.

With such a complex system, it would be surprising if errors did not occur from time to time; indeed, even during the Ch'ing dynasty, after it had undergone a complete revision, intercalary months were included incorrectly for the years 1669 and 1813, and accordingly corresponding adjustments had to be made. In addition to the month number, each month also bears a 'Branch', one of twelve signs used as a kind of numeral. They are discussed more fully later. The first month is not, as one might expect, given the first Branch; this is accorded to the first month before the Winter Solstice, so that the first month of the year has the third Branch, Yin (寅). This was not always the case; in the Shang Dynasty the first month of the year was designated Branch I, Tzu (子), and in the Chou dynasty it was changed to Branch II, Ch'ou (丑), thereafter the year began with the third Yin Branch month.

It is likely that these changes were made in order to adjust the year at a period of calendrical reform, so making the first month of the year occur at the beginning of Spring. There is a likely link with the sun's apparent retrograde motion through the zodiac. Readers will be familiar with the fact that during the close of the twentieth century we move into the 'Aquarian' age, the previous era of about two thousand years being the Piscean age, and the one before that, when the astronomical zodiac was devised, the Arien age; the apparent position of the Sun then coinciding with the First Point of Aries, the first sign of the zodiac, and the Spring Equinox. In the same manner, it is possible that the change in the Branch of the month represents a similar adjustment for the precession of the equinoxes.

For the sake of completeness, a list of some of the more literary ancient, or fanciful names for the months is given here, although it must be remembered that these are only used in a poetic or archaic sense.

Literary Names of the Months
The first name is the one which is given in the *Erh Ya* 爾雅, or 'Compendium of Literature', an encyclopaedia of the Chou dynasty; various poetical names follow, and finally, the hexagram of the *I Ching* with which the month is usually associated. Names of the Monthly Spirits are given in a later section, page 264.

I (一 正). Tsou (陬) Distant; Tuan (端) Beginning; Yüan (元) Chief; Ch'ing Yang (青陽) Natural Radiance; San Ho (三和) Three Harmonies; Meng Yang (孟陽) Foremost Radiance; Ch'un Wang (春王) Spring Emperor.
No. 11, T'ai (泰) Exalted.

II (二). Ju (如) Like; Hsing (杏) Apricot; Hua (花) Flower; Hua Chao (中和) Flower Dawn; Chung Ho (花朝) Central Harmony; Chung Yang (仲陽) Assistant Radiance.
No. 34, Ta Chuang (大壯) Great Flourishing.

III (三). Hsiu (寐) Resting place. T'ao (桃) Peach; T'ung (桐) Trees; Shang Ssu (上巳) Ascending Sacrifice. Ts'an (蠶) Silkworm; Han Shih (寒食) Cold Food.
No. 43, Kuai (夬) Parted Curtain.

IV (四). Yü (余) The Emperor. Huai (槐) Locust tree; Ch'ing Ho (清和) Clear Harmony; Mai Ch'iu (麥秋) Autumn Wheat.
No. 1, Ch'ien (乾) Heavenly principle.

V (五). Kao (臯) Eminent. P'u (蒲) Rushes; Liu (榴) Pomegranate; T'ien Chung (天中) Heaven Centre; Man Yüeh (滿月) Full month; Tuan Yang (端陽) Prime Radiance.
No. 44, Kou (姤) Coupling.

VI (六). Chü (且) Dignity. Ho (荷) Lotus; Fu Jih (伏日) Dog-days; Shu Yüeh (暑月) Heat of Summer; T'ien K'uang (天貺) Heaven Bestowing.
No. 33, Tun (遯) Obscurity.

VII (七). Hsiang (相) Mutually; T'ung (桐) Oil tree; Ch'iao (巧) Skill; Chung Yüan (中元) Middle Chief; Kua (瓜) Melons; Lan (蘭) Orchid.
No. 12, P'i (否) Evil.

VIII (八). Chuang (壯) Flourishing*; Kuei (桂) Cinnamon; Chung Ch'iu (中秋) Middle of Autumn; Chung Shang (仲商) Middle Tone.
No. 20, Kuan (觀) Travelling for Pleasure.

IX (九). Hsüan (亥) Sombre; Chü (菊) Chrysanthemum; Chung Yang (重陽) Important Radiance; Chi Shang (季商) Youngest Tone; Chü Ch'iu (菊秋) Autumn Chrysanthemum.
No. 23, Po (剝) Peeling.

---

*Chuang, Flourishing, is the same as the poetic name for the hexagram of the second month.
†The term 'Radiant Spring' for the middle of Autumn is the equivalent of the 'Indian Summer' of the Western temperate regions: a period of mild, balmy weather before the onset of winter.

X (十). Yang (陽) Radiance. Mei (梅) Plums; Yang Ch'un
(陽春) Radiant Spring†; Hsia Yüan (下元) Descending
Chief; Hsiao Yang Ch'un (小陽春) Little Radiant Spring.
No. 2, K'un (坤) Earth.

XI (十一). Ku (辜) Ingratitude. Chung Tung (仲冬) Secondary
Winter; Tung (冬) Winter; Ch'ang Chih (長至) Long Solstice;
Chia (葭) Bullrushes; Ch'ing Ssu (清紀) Pure Sacrifice.
No. 10, Fu (復) Return.

XII (十二). T'u (涂) Erase. La (臘) Winter Sacrifice; Chia P'ing
(喜平) Excellent Regulator; Chi Tung (季冬) Youngest
Winter.
No. 19, Lin (臨) Brinking.

Chinese Hours

The Chinese, and many other Asiatic nations, still retain the old
system of dividing the day into twelve double-hours, the midpoint
of which corresponds to the even hour of the Western clock; noon
double-hour, consequently, lasts from 11am to 1pm. In recent times
it has become customary to divide the double-hour into two, 'fore'
and 'aft', or Ch'u (初) and Cheng (正) respectively.

The double-hours, named after the 'Branches' provide another
of the Four Pillars used in Chinese Fate Calculation. It has been
estimated that the association of the double-hours with the Branches
is not earlier than 500 BC*. Much later, the double-hours were
dubbed with the names of the corresponding cyclical animals, so
that Midnight, for example, becomes the 'rat-hour'.

For completeness, it may be added that a further subdivision of
the day into a hundred K'o (刻) was the smallest unit of time until
the advent of accurate timepieces in the Ming. The K'o, of 14 minutes
24 seconds, was therefore just under a quarter-hour's length. A table
of k'o (ke) is given in the Appendix.

The Stems and Branches

We now turn to what is, for astrological purposes, the most important
aspect of the Chinese Calendar — the system of 'Stems and Branches'.

*Dr Joseph Needham in *Heavenly Clockwork*, page 201, writes: 'A passage
in the *Kuo Yü* ['Discourses on the (ancient feudal) States'], giving what
purports to be a discussion of 519 BC, indicates that by the third or fourth
century BC, at least, the twelve cyclical characters, Chih (支) had become
attached to the twelve equal double-hours.'

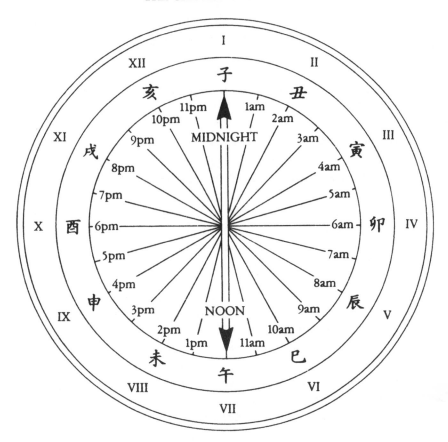

Figure 3.2 The Chinese Double-Hours
  a. The inner circle: Western hours
  b. Outer circle: The Twelve Branches,
[The Twelve Branches are represented by Roman Numerals throughout this book; ordinary figures are used for the Ten Stems.]

In addition to the lunar and solar calendars, the Chinese number their days and years according to a sixty figure cycle. Its essentials are easy to grasp, but difficult to express in simple arithmetical or alegbraic terms. Throughout this book, the convention is adopted of designating the Ten Stems by the ordinary figures 1 to 10, and the Twelve Branches by the Roman numerals I to XII. The two sequences 1 to 10 and I-XII run parallel, producing another series of 60 combinations of double signs, or 'binomes.' A glance at the table in the Appendix will make the matter clear.

It must be stressed that the twenty-two characters which form both series are *not* numbers; by themselves they have no particular value.

For example, the figure 1 in the combination 1-III has a different influence to the 1 in the combination 1-XI. Note that the sequence runs 1-I, 2-II, 3-III, etc., and not 1-I, 1-II, 1-III. Odd numbered stems always combine with odd-numbered branches, even stems with even branches, so that combinations such as 1-II, or 2-I would be impossible.

It obviously represents a very early attempt to reconcile the original decimal system of counting with a later tendency to reckon in dozens. The characters themselves are very ancient, and have been found on oracle bones of the Shang dynasty, about 1500 BC, where they are used as day reckoners. Tracing the first usage of the Stem and Branch system for hour or year reckoning is not easy. Years were anciently reckoned in the same way that still prevails in the parliamentary reports of many nations even today, that is, according to the year of accession of the reigning monarch or regime. This is the case in the *Ch'un Ch'iu* and the *Shu Ching* (the 'Spring and Autumn Annals', and the 'Book of Documents', two ancient Chinese chronicles), where all important events are dated by the Emperor's name, the year of reign, the month, day, and sexagenary characters.

The earliest use of the Twelve Branches for the names of the twelve double-hours is not much before 500 BC. As their adoption into the seemingly more sophisticated sexagenary cycle was some thousand years before this, the intriguing question is: what was the original significance of the Branches before they were recruited into the sexagenary system? The following tables of the Twelve Branch characters, give their present-day or conjectural meanings, and the auspices given in the *Huai Nan Tzu*.

I	Tzu	子	Child, son.
II	Ch'ou	丑	Clown. (Tzu 子 repeated to mean second?)
III	Yin	寅	Reverence
IV	Mao	卯	? (A constellation — the Pleiades; or the rising sun?)
V	Ch'en	辰	— (Dawn, morning; a planet; trembling; an eclipse, etc.)
VI	Ssu	巳	— (A Snake?)
VII	Wu	午	Noon (Midpoint? To oppose?)
VIII	Wei	未	Not yet (Time to rest?)

IX	Shen	申	—	(Stretch; repeat)
X	Yu	酉	Liquor	(Refreshment)
XI	Shu	戌	—	(A weapon, hence guard duty; a number?)
XII	Hai	亥	—	(Darkness?)

I	Tzu	Commencement; controlling T'ai Sui, the Great Year (of Twelve Years, i.e. the Jupiter Cycle)
II	Ch'ou	Closure; controlling the T'ai Yin (Counter-Jupiter)
III	Yin	Establishing
IV	Mao	Dividing
V	Ch'en	Filling
VI	Ssu	Equating
VII	Wu	Fixing
VIII	Wei	Regulating; controlling ruin
IX	Shen	Breaking, controlling balance
X	Yü	Danger; controlling the Tail of Tou (a reference to the 'handle' of the Great Bear)
XI	Hsu	Perfecting; controlling the Lesser Virtue
XII	Hai	Receiving; controlling Greater Virtue

Those characters which have retained a meaning suggest that they were originally names of the various offices of the day; *Tzu*, a child, means the birth of a new day; *Yin* could mean morning devotions; *Yu*, a welcome drink at the end of a day's work, and so on. But most of the characters have lost all their original meanings, and are now merely counting signs. Curiously enough, another system of names already existed:

Ming	明	Morning brightness (dawn)
Ta Ts'ai	大宋	Great assembly
Ta Shih	大食	Big Meal
Chung Jih	中日	Midday
Che	㬱	Declining Sun
Hsiao Shih	小食	Little meal

| Hsiao Ts'ai | 小宋 | Little Assembly |
| Hsi | 夕 | Midnight |

A similar list of hour names is used in descriptions of the Diviner's Board, which we shall meet in a later section:

Yeh Pan	夜半	Midnight	I	子
Chi Ming	鷄鳴	Cockcrow	II	丑
Ping Tan	平旦	Nearly Dawn	III	寅
Jih Ch'u	日出	Sunrise	IV	卯
Shih Shih	食時	Mealtime	V	辰
Yü Chung	隅中	Middle angle	VI	巳
Jih Chung	日中	Midday	VII	午
Jih Tieh	日昳	Sun declines	VIII	未
Pu Shih	晡時	Time of 'Pu'	IX	申
Jih Ju	日入	Sunset	X	酉
Huang Hun	黃昏	Yellow Dusk	XI	戌
Jen Ting	人定	Man reposes	XII	亥

The theory proposed by Dr Anneliese Bulling, the noted authority on Chinese symbolism, is that the characters for the twelve Branches are derived from the names of the monthly rites. If the names of the cyclical signs are in fact names given to divisions of the ecliptic by the moon's phases, it is possible that they were ultimately derived from names of zodiacal constellations which pre-date Babylonian influence. The most obvious candidate is Mao (卯) Branch IV, which may have been the original form of Mao (昴) the Pleiades.

Another theory, perhaps less digestible, is that the characters are symbols for the twelve animals of popular Chinese astrology; Leopold de Saussure went to elaborate lengths to show the antiquity of the twelve animal symbols. The origin of the twelve animals has still not been resolved. Perhaps the wisest comment on the subject is that of Dr Joseph Needham, in his monumental *Science and Civilisation in China* to the effect that whoever invented the system is welcome to it. But it is an intriguing point, and I would like to add a few more logs to the fire. To begin with, the question of the antiquity of the animal cycle has been confused with another issue entirely; the twelve Branches. Whether the twelve Branches were first used to designate the hours, days, months or even years, and when they were first so used is not the question; which is, when and where were *animal* names first used? Indeed, matters are not helped by one of the earlier leading authorities on the subject, Paul Pelliot, misleadingly entitling one of his papers *Le plus ancien exemple du cycle des douze animaux chez les Turcs* when it makes no mention of the twelve animals at all. But the title of the paper does raise another curious matter; the fact that the animal cycle is known to Anatolian shepherds in remote Turkey even today. How is it that this sole facet of Chinese culture should have reached right across Asia, to a people with an entirely different language, race, religion, and way of life?

The theory, which attracted very strong support, was that the animal names were in fact imported into China from the Turkic nations — perhaps the Kirghiz — instead of the other way round. The arguments against this were that the twelve *Branches* were known to be much more ancient, by perhaps two thousand years, than the earliest recorded example (quoted by Paul Pelliot) of the duodecimal system in Turkic documents. But the *Branches* are not the same as the *animals*. Here, for comparison, are the Mongolian, Kurdish and Modern Turkish names for the twelve animals. (The Tibetan forms are not given here, as the names are direct borrowings from the Chinese.)

	Chinese	*Mongolian*	*Kurdish*	*Modern Turkish*
Rat	Shu	quluğana	siçğan	sıçan
Ox	Niu	üker	ud	öküz
Tiger	Hu	bars	bars	kaplan
Rabbit	T'u	taulai	tavişğan	tavşanı
Dragon	Lung	luu	lu	ejderha
Snake	She	mogai	magr	yılan
Horse	Ma	morin	yond, hesp	at
Sheep	Yang	qonin	koy, gind	koyun
Monkey	Hou	beçin	biçin	maymun
Cock	Chi	takiya	tağuk	tavuk

	Chinese	Mongolian	Kurdish	Modern Turkish
Dog	Kou	noqai	kuti	köpek
Pig	Chu	gakai	tonguz	domuz

It can be seen that in some cases there is a resemblance between the Chinese and Turkic words (as for the rabbit, dragon and dog). But this does not indicate in which direction the animal names travelled. If the Mongolians adopted the twelve animals from the Chinese, *why did they not also adopt other Chinese astrological terms, such as the 28 lunar mansions*, well documented in the Han dynasty, at the same time? Finally, the original Mongolian list of names may have formed rhythmical triplets, which would have been used in reckoning, thus, the latter six: *morin-qonin-becin, takai-noqai-gakai*, which suggests an even older Central Asian folk-custom.

There is still the historically interesting question of the date at which the animal cycle was first used in China. Again, the problem is obscured by confusion between the Branches and the animal names. There is no mention at all of the twelve animals in Ssu Ma Ch'ien's astrological treatise written in the Han dynasty, nor do they appear in the *Chin Shu*, written some centuries later under the direction of the Emperor T'ai Tsung in about AD 635, despite the great length of the astrological chapters of this major work. But three centuries later, when by the time that the Tun Huang Monastery was in imminent danger of invasion (towards the end of the tenth century AD), the animal cycle was already well-established. A delightful drawing in a calendar of AD 978 shows the Guardian Spirits of the Twelve Branches, each wearing a hat blazoned with a badge of the head of one of the animals.

To the best of my knowledge, the oldest representations of the twelve animals are the eighth-century stone tomb guardians from Silla, Korea, one of which was exhibited at the British Museum, London, in the Spring of 1984. Since the Koreans are descendants of immigrants from Manchuria and Siberia, this provides additional evidence for the hypothesis that the animal-cycle originated in Northern Central Asia.

In literature, what may well be the earliest most complete reference to the animal cycle appears in the *Shuo Kua Ch'uan* appendix to

to the directions, seven are from the 'animal' cycle — the eighth is a pheasant. While this appears to be too strong a coincidence for

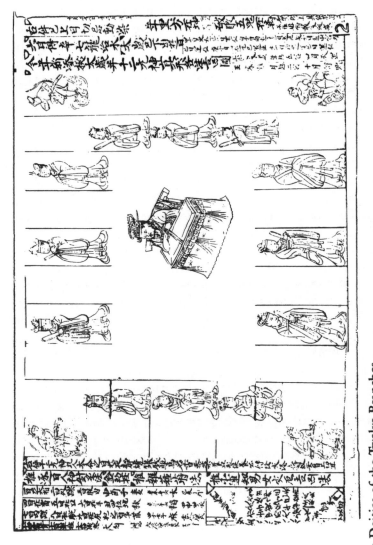

Figure 3.3 **The Deities of the Twelve Branches**
From a Tun Huang manuscript dated AD 978 (Stein 612). The deities can be recognized by the animal insignia on the headdress. The 'rat' appears bottom centre, and the remaining animal dignitaries follow in a clockwise direction. The deity centre is the T'ai Sui, the reckoner of the Years.

it not to be a definite link, it still does not reveal whether the seven animals were adopted from the *I Ching* into the cycle, or *vice versa*. It could be a comment on the date of the *Shuo Kua Ch'uan*, rather than the antiquity of the twelve animals.

Early sources of representations of the twelve animals are found on the backs of bronze mirrors, which were nearly always decorated with cosmogonic designs. The earliest of these show only the basic Chinese representation of the universe: the circle (Heaven) of the mirror being decorated with a square (Earth) shape, in which the Four Gates were represented. Later mirrors, such as those of the Hsin dynasty (AD 9-23) show the four animals of the four astrological palaces: the White Tiger, the Red Bird, the Black Tortoise, and the Azure Dragon. Before accepting this as the germ of the twelve animal cycle (because of the Tiger and the Dragon) it must be borne in mind that the Tortoise does *not* figure in the twelve animal cycle, and the Red Bird is as unlike the Cockerel as a budgerigar. I know of no bronze mirror depicting the twelve animals earlier than the T'ang (AD 620-900). This date matches the period when the twelve animals began to make their appearance in Chinese horoscopes and almanacs.

Yet curiously enough, one of the most ancient portrayals of the animals so far discovered is not just of the twelve in the cycle, but a whole zoo of thirty-six real, legendary or obscure beasts listed around the edge of a diviner's plate*, a kind of planisphere and the ancestor of the Lo P'an used by Feng Shui practitioners even today. The list of these animals is similar to, but not exactly the same as a list given in a mystical work on the Five Elements by the writer Hsiao Chi, who lived during the Sui dynasty (AD 581-618).

As a further refinement, the twenty-eight lunar mansions of Chinese astrology were also considered to have their own animals, one for each mansion, twelve of these associated with the cyclical signs.

Lists of these animals in various astrological sources agree in nearly every respect, minor discrepancies being the Hsia (a fabulous bovine animal), in place of porcupine, and the tapir (surely an odd inclusion) replacing a species of dog called 'Wang' described in the Chinese Encyclopaedia as 'small, and not very fierce'.

The thirty-six animals listed round the edge of the diviner's board fall into triads, each group of animals sharing a common feature — bovine, canine, feline, and so on. Originally each triad represented one day, the first of each triad being the morning, the second noon, and the third the evening. Those animals associated with the twelve

*Described in a later section. See page 245ff.

Comparative Table of Animal Cycles

	Thirty-Six		Twelve		Twenty-Eight		
1	Hsia	Frog			Swallow	Yen	12
2	Shu	Rat	RAT	I	Rat	Shu	11
3	Yen	Swallow			Bat	Fu	10
4	Niu	Ox	OX	II	Ox	Niu	9
5	? T'a	Otter			'Unicorn'	Hsia	8
6	? Hsia	Unicorn					
7	Fu	?			—	—	
8	Li	Cat			Leopard	Pao	7
9	Hu	Tiger	TIGER	III	Tiger	Hu	6
10	Wei	Hedgehog			Fox	Hu	5
11	T'u	Rabbit	RABBIT	IV	Rabbit	T'u	4
12	Ho	Badger			Marten	Ho	3
13	Lung	Dragon	DRAGON	V	Dragon	Lung	2
14	Ching	Whale			Scaly Dragon	Ch'iao	1
15	Yü	Fish			—	—	
16	P'iao	Pupa			—	—	
17	Chan	Cicada			Worm	Yin	28
18	She	Snake	SNAKE	VI	Snake	She	27
19	Lu	Deer			Deer	Lu	26
20	Ma	Horse	HORSE	VII	Horse	Ma	25
21	Chang	Buck			Buck	Chang	24
22	Yang	Sheep	SHEEP	VIII	Sheep	Yang	23
23	? K'uang	Wild Dog			Wild Dog	K'uang	
					(Tapir)		22
24	Yen	Goose			—	—	
25	Tan	?			—	—	
26	Yüan	Gibbon			Ape	Yüan	21
27	Hou	Monkey	MONKEY	IX	Monkey	Hou	20
28	Chih	Pheasant			Crow	Wu	19
29	Chi	Cock	COCK	X	Cock	Chi	18
30	Wu	Crow			Pheasant	Chih	17
31	Kou	Dog	DOG	XI	Dog	Kou	16
32	Wei	?			Wolf	Lang	15
33	Lang	Wolf			—	—	
34	Shih	Boar			—	—	
35	? Hsia/Chai				'Porcupine'	Yü	14
36	Chu	Pig	PIG	XII	Pig	Chu	13

Branches are not scattered at random throughout the thirty-six animals, but form a set sequence: being the middle animal of one triad, the first of the next, and the third of the next.

When the diviner's board was being designed, the *concept* of the twelve animal cycle, symmetrically arranged in that unusual way, must have been firmly established in its creator's mind; there is enough correspondence between the animals of the twenty-eight lunar mansions and the thirty-six animals of the divining board to suggest that in those places where the two sequences are out of alignment (as in the Northern Palace) then the diviner's board must be at fault. But if the triads of animals were shuffled about in order to coincide with the animals of the lunar cycle, then this would throw out the symmetrical arrangement of the twelve animals of the solar cycle. The conclusion from this observation is therefore that even though modern authorities may be in agreement with regards to the animals of the lunar cycle, they are all out of step! The ancient diviner's board is the most reliable authority, and consequently, the traditional correlation of the animals to the lunar mansions is at fault with regards to the Northern Palace.

A Practical Cycle

All the evidence for the origins of the animal cycle that has been examined so far has been literary or archaeological. But this is akin to dicussing a piece of music from the printed page without ever hearing it. When the Chinese zodiacal cycle is examined from the point of view of a practising Chinese astrologer, some surprising factors emerge. Firstly, it is apparent that the twelve animals form six distinct pairs, showing the reverse or complementary sides of some aspect of personality or actuality. Thus, the Tiger is aggressive, masculine and conquering, but the Rabbit is gentler, feminine and more diplomatic. Yet both are able to conquer, in their own distinctive manner. Although my suggestion that the twelve animals do in fact subdivide into six houses is not to be found in the classical literature, it is in full accordance with the popular interpretation of the animal signs.

House of Creativity:
The Rat creates, the Ox fulfils.
    House of Expansion:
The Tiger conquers by force, the Rabbit by diplomacy.
    House of Magic and Mystery:
The extrovert Dragon, the introvert Snake.
    House of Gender:

The masculine Horse, the feminine Sheep.
House of Technique:
The artful Monkey, the artistic Rooster.
House of Domesticity:
The Dog protects the house, the Pig the people within it.

It is also apparent that instead of being a random menagerie, many of the animals were chosen because of their familiar symbolism. Thus, when we remember that the twelve branches represented the hours of the day, and the months of the Chinese year, as well as the twelve years of the Jupiter cycle, it becomes evident that the second month in the Chinese calendar, represented by the fourth Branch, Mao, or the Rabbit, is the month which always includes the Spring Equinox. In China as in the West, the Rabbit is a universal symbol of Spring, the 'Mr Rabbit' being just as familiar to Chinese children as the Easter Bunny is to their American or European cousins. Furthermore, the Rabbit hour is dawn, when those crepuscular creatures are at their liveliest.

Similarly the Horse, perhaps the most evident symbol of masculinity, represents not just the month which includes the Summer Solstice (the Sun being the supreme Yang force) but also the noon hour, when the Sun is highest in the sky. By contrast the nocturnal Rat symbolizes the midnight hour, and by extension, the winter month which includes the Winter Solstice. The Rooster, which sounds the end of the day as well as heralding the dawn, represents the hour when the sun sets.

A word might be said here about the Cat, which some writers of popular Chinese astrology books see fit to have introduced into their version of the Chinese zodiac. From the remarks on the Rabbit symbolism outlined above, it will be evident that the Cat cannot justifiably deputize for the Rabbit. Yet it is often claimed that the two are interchangeable. No Chinese sources have ever depicted the Cat among the twelve, although the Vietnamese have substituted the Cat for the Rabbit, owing, I believe, to the fact that Rabbit in Vietnamese is homonymous with a vulgar term of abuse. Although, it must be said, I have in my possession a Tibetan calendar, which clearly depicts the fourth animal as a Cat (unless Tibetan Rabbits have long tails), it must be considered an anomaly. The official calendar, said to have been introduced into Tibet in AD 635 by Queen Wenchang, daughter of the Emperor T'ai Tsung, retained the Rabbit or Hare, as the fourth animal. In Thailand, for example, despite that country's famous feline breed, the Cat is never introduced into the calendar. Indeed, to do so could be an act of *lèse-majesté*, since the country's monarch was born in the year of the Rabbit.

If further evidence were required to emphasize the fact that the Cat may not substitute for the Rabbit, consider the fact that there are at least three existing legends to account for the absence of such a familiar animal. One of these tells that the Rat was entrusted with passing the Buddha's invitation to the Cat to be among the year markers, but that the Rat, instead of conveying the divine summons, decided to take the Cat's place, and has been honoured by inclusion in the zodiac ever since.

Personality Types

Popular astrology assigns certain personality types to each of the twelve animals of the Great Year, and modifies these by stating that the predomination of certain elements in a person's horoscope reveal the person's physical type (see page 41). There is no shortage of books on popular astrology which expound the private opinions of their authors (see, for example, bibliography, Walters (5)). For the sake of completeness, outlines of the basic twelve animal types are given below, together with tables of compatibility based on oral and written traditions.

Rat — Charming, appealing, clever. Quick-witted and sociable. Hoarders and wasters.

Ox — Methodical, routine. Dependable, sullen. Dislikes competition.

Tiger — Fiercely competitive; rash, brave, magnetic. Proud, unrestrained.

Rabbit — Gregarious, but aloof. Avoids confrontation. Benevolent, inclined to gossip. Artistic.

Dragon — Exotic, vital. Elegant, fond of the occult. Decisive, but not methodical. Over-confident, transient.

Snake — Regarded as wise, but inwardly naive. Prudent, easily scandalized. Possessive.

Horse — Sociable, prejudiced, selfish, intolerant. Fond of sport and travel.

Sheep — Fastidious, conservative, methodical. Dislikes disorder, but does not always have method.

Monkey — Audacious, insecure. Hyperactive, manic-depressive. Resents not being taken seriously. Inventive and agile.

Cock — Alert, punctual. Frank, abrasive, competitive. Shrewd and precise; extravagant.

Dog — Honest, friendly, protective and defensive. Sociable, loyal to friends, reliable.

Pig — Content, home and family loving. Practical, acquisitive, industrious.

In Fate Calculation, concordance between the Branches of the years is indicated by the angle made by the positions of the Branches round

Table of Compatibility

Key

+2 Excellent relationships	−1 Some friction
	−2 Definite antipathy
+1 Good rapport	□ Proverbially a discordant relationship
0 Disinterest	■ Proverbially an excellent relationship

	Rat	Ox	Tiger	Rabbit	Dragon	Snake	Horse	Sheep	Monkey	Cock	Dog	Pig
Rat	+1	+1	0	−1	+2	+1	−2	−1 □	+2	0		+1
Ox	+1		−1 □	+1	−1	+1	−	−1		+2	−1	
Tiger	0	−1 □				−1 □	+2	0	−1		+2	+1
Rabbit	−1	+1		+1	−	+1 ■		+2		−1	+1	+1
Dragon	+2	−1		−	0	+1		+1	+2	+2	−1	+1
Snake	+1	+1	−1 □	+1 ■	+1			+1	0	+2 □	0	−1
Horse	−2	−	+2				+1	+2			+1	
Sheep	−1 □	−1	0	+2	+1	+1	+2					+1
Monkey	+2		−1		+2	0				0	0	+1 □
Cock	0	+2		−1	+2	+2 □			0		−1 □	0
Dog		−1	+2	+2	−1	0	+1		0	+1 □		
Pig	+1		+1	+1		−1		+1	+1 □	0		

the face of the clock; opposite positions (as I and VII, midnight and noon respectively, would be incompatible; those at 'twenty-minute' positions would be harmonious.

In addition to the auspices predicted by the opposing and concordant Branches, there are several proverbs which tell of the relationships between different animals. Those in the following selection are for the most part unrelated to the 'opposite' and 'concordant' Branches. Curiously, the proverbial animosity between the cock and the snake goes against the system of 'harmonious' Branches, and indeed, against the opinions of the writers whose works on Chinese horoscopes have been consulted.

The following is a selection of 'marriage' proverbs.

When the Serpent meets the Hare, it means supreme happiness.
The Ox and Tiger quarrel ever.
An Ox can battle with two Tigers.
The Horse fears the Ox. (*Several variants.*)
When the Pig meets the Monkey, there are always tears. (*Variants.*)
The Cock and Snake are ever at odds.
When the Tiger meets the Snake, there is always a battle. (*Variants.*)
Sheep and Rat are ever at war. (*With variants.*)
The Dragon meets the Rabbit, and good luck is shattered.
Cock and Dog always end in tears.

And additionally, as warning to the household generally:

Never bring a Tigress into the house.
A Sheep for a spouse brings trouble in the house.

The Ten Stems

In popular Chinese astrology, the Ten Stems have not attained the universal familiarity of their younger companions - the twelve Branches. The stems, however, are undoubtedly much older than the branches, and found in greater frequency on oracle bones. They were originally the names of a ten-day 'week' or Hsun (Xun) 旬.

Recent research into the original characters on oracle bones shows that the most frequent character was the tenth, and this may have marked a special day for divination and sacrifice, while the modern form of the character shows two hands lifted in prayer over the symbol for Heaven.

The characters have a simple structure - the first scarcely nothing more than a marker indicating the start of the series. The second appears to be a thread, the fifth a hand holding a weapon, and the eighth a flower or herb - the modern meaning is bitter.

Just as the days of the week in the Roman and Norse calendars were named after various divinities (Sun, Moon, Mars, Mercury, Jupiter, Venus and Saturn, alternatively, Sun, Moon, Tiw, Woden, Thor, Freia, and Samh) it is likely that the ten stems were originally names of ancient deities: for example, the fifth the god of battle, the eighth of medicine, the tenth the god of divination.

Furthermore, the Shang dynasty emperors were all named after the stems, either because these were their birthday or accession days, or possibly because they were the names of deities, in the same manner than western children are given the names of saints or prophets. The custom also applied to the emperor's family - the last emperor of the Shang dynasty was the Chou Hsin (stem 8) and his concubine of ill-fame T'a Chi (stem 6).

Take care not to confuse stem 1 with branch IX (甲 申), stem 5 with branch XI (戊 戌), nor stem 6 with branch VI (己 巳).

Oracle bone script of the Ten Stems

Left to right: 甲乙丙丁戊己庚辛壬癸

The Sexagennial Cycle of Stems and Branches

From the names of the ten-day week (the Heavenly Stems) and the twelve month names (the Earthly Branches) a cycle of sixty Stem-and-Branch combinations was devised. Legend ascribes its invention to a minister of the Emperor Shang Huang Ti, and certainly, if one counts back through the cycle, it is possible to calculate its supposed date of origin, 2679 BC. Of course, this does not mean that the cycle was invented in that year, any more than our own system of dating our years from AD 1 means that our own calendar was invented in that far off era. Both calendars use a significant date in their legendary history as their starting point.

To summarize, it would appear that the earliest characters were those used for the names of the days of the ten-day week, the Ten Heavenly Stems (in Chinese the word T'ien, meaning 'Heaven', is also used for 'day'). At a later but still conjectural date, the Twelve Earthly Branches were used to denote either the months (or the hours) and were soon transferred to be used as the names of the hours (or, obviously, the months). Later, the Twelve Branches were also used to name the years of the Great Year, a custom which seems to have been in imitation of a neighbouring people to the North of China.

By extension, the Branches were also added to the names of the days, and a double-numbering system of Stems and Branches for the days gave a check on the calendar, six cycles of 60 Stem-and-Branch combinations closely approximating to the length of the Chinese year. Last of all, the Stem-and-Branch combinations were adopted for numbering the years as well. To be more precise, Stem-and-Branch numbers are to be found on oracle bones of the Shang dynasty, but Stem-and-Branch numbering of the years was not introduced until the fifth year of the rebel Emperor Wang Mang, in AD 13. Tables of Stems and Branches will be found in the Appendices.

Correlation between the Elements and Cyclical Numbers

There are several ways in which the Five Elements are deemed to correlate with the Stems and Branches. The first is the simple allocation of each pair of Stems 1/2, 3/4, 5/6, 7/8, 9/10, to the Five Elements in the following sequence: Wood, Fire, Earth, Metal, Water, i.e., the *production* order of the elements. This is the way by which the years are counted in popular astrology: wood-rat, wood-ox, fire-tiger, fire-rabbit. Of each pair, the odd numbers are said to be Yang (active, masculine, moving) and the even numbers Yin (recessive, feminine, motionless).

From this is drawn the rule: 'Heavenly Stems embrace' T'ien Kan Hsiang Ho (天千相合). It is held that a Yang Stem harmonizes with the Yin Stem which, according to its element, destroys it (see below). Such pairs are sometimes called the Husband and Wife. For example, Wood is destroyed by Metal, therefore Yang Wood harmonizes with Yin Metal.

The following shows the ten Stems, their corresponding elements, and the respective harmonizing Stem:

	Stem	Element	Polarity	Harmonizes with		
甲	1 Chia	Wood	Yang	Chi	6	己
乙	2 I	Wood produces	Yin	Keng	7	庚
丙	3 Ping	Fire	Yang	Hsin	8	辛
丁	4 Ting	Fire produces	Yin	Jen	9	壬
戊	5 Wu	Earth	Yang	Kuei	10	癸
己	6 Chi	Earth produces	Yin	Chia	1	甲
庚	7 Keng	Metal	Yang	I	2	乙
辛	8 Hsin	Metal produces	Yin	Ping	3	丙
壬	9 Jen	Water	Yang	Ting	4	丁
癸	10 Kuei	Water	Yin	Wu	5	戊

A very interesting passage from the *Kuan Tzu* (管子) 'Master Kuan's (Book)', a work of the late fourth century BC, is quoted extensively in the *Huai Nan Tzu*.*

The correlation between the day-signs, the Five Elements, and prognostications is so marked that it is not difficult to see why some commentators have ascribed the practice of Fate Calculation to the Chou dynasty.

> When we see the cyclical sign Chia Tzu (甲子)(1) arrive†, the element Wood begins its reign. If the Emperor does not bestow favours and grant rewards, but rather allows great cutting, destroying and wounding, then he will be in danger. Should he not die, then the heir apparent will be in danger, and someone of his family or consort will die, or else his eldest son will lose his life (for Spring is a time for growth, not destruction). After seventy-two days this period is over.
>
> When we see the cyclical sign Ping Tzu (丙子)(13) arrive, the element Fire begins its reign. If the Emperor now takes hurried and hasty measures, epidemics will be caused by drought, plants will die, and the people perish. After seventy-two days this period is over.
>
> When we see the cyclical sign Wu Tzu (戊子)(25) arrive, the element Earth begins its reign. If the Emperor now builds palaces or constructs pavilions, his life will be in danger, and if city walls are built (at this time) his ministers will die. (For the people should not be taken away from their harvesting.) After seventy-two days this period is over.
>
> When we see the cyclical sign Keng Tzu (庚子)(37) arrive, the element Metal begins its reign. If the Emperor attacks the mountains (by mining operations) and causes rocks to be pounded (for metallurgy) his troops will be defeated in war, his soldiers die, and he will lose his throne. After seventy-two days this period is over.
>
> When we see the cyclical sign Jen Tzu (壬子)(49) arrive, the element Water begins its reign. If the Emperor now allows the dykes to be cut, and sets the great floods in motion, his Empress or great ladies will die, birds' eggs will be found to be addled, the young of hairy animals will miscarry, and pregnant women will have abortions. After seventy-two days this period is over.

An important feature of this passage is that the Emperor was warned against actions which were sympathetic to the reigning element, rather than the contrary. For example, one should not, during the reign of Metal, practice metallurgy or during the reign of Earth, construct anything made of earth, clay, or stone. The reason for this,

*The translation is by A. Forke, published in 1925 as part of *The World Conception of the Chinese*).

†The figures in brackets are the corresponding sexagenary numbers.

probably, is that in trying to manipulate, or dominate, those elements which were in the ascendant, one would be interfering with the balance of the elements which could only reflect upon the one who had consciously upset the elemental balance.

The *Huai Nan Tzu* adds some further points, elaborating on the system. While the *Kuan Tzu* advises the Emperor, the *Huai Nan Tzu* seems to be more general in its content:

> In the time of Chia Tzu(1) action should be restrained; Herds should be enclosed, gates and barriers should be shut, and timber should not be cut.
>
> In the time of Ping Tzu(13) the worthy should be promoted and the meritorious rewarded. Nobles should be appointed (cf. the *I Ching* hexagrams III (Chun), XVI (Yü) *et passim*) and wealth distributed.
>
> In the time of Wu Tzu(25) the old and widows should be cared for, amnesties granted to prisoners, favours bestowed and goods sold.
>
> In the time of Keng Tzu(37) walls and barriers should be improved, fortifications strengthened, the 'sheep sorted from the goats', armour forbidden to troops (in case of rebellion?) officials warned and the lawless exterminated.
>
> In the time of Jen Tzu(49) close the gates of villages, search strangers thoroughly, execute offenders, close up bridges, and forbid vagrancy.

But the matters now become more detailed and specific. What happens when there is a conflict of the day sign with a period sign? The *Huai Nan Tzu* tells us:

> When (the day) Ping Tzu(13) is in (the season) Chia Tzu(1) hibernating insects come out early, and there is thunder.
>
> When Wu Tzu(25) is in Chia Tzu(1) the unborn young and unhatched eggs suffer great injury.
>
> When Keng Tzu(37) is in Chia Tzu(1) military operations will occur.
>
> When Jen Tzu(49) is in Chia Tzu(1) the Spring will be frosty.

Further prognostications may be summed up in a table, as follows:

When	Chia Tzu	Ping Tzu	Wu Tzu	Keng Tzu	Jen Tzu
Is in	甲子 (1)	丙子 (13)	戊子 (25)	庚子 (37)	壬子 (49)
Chia Tzu (1)	—	insects out early; thunder	unborn young and unhatched eggs in danger	military operations	frosty Spring

When	Chia Tzu	Ping Tzu	Wu Tzu	Keng Tzu	Jen Tzu
Is in	甲子 (1)	丙子 (13)	戊子 (25)	庚子 (37)	壬子 (49)
Ping Tzu (13)	earth-quakes	—	loud thunder	lightning	hail
Wu Tzu (25)	silkworms not formed	drought	—	calamity to the five grains	Summer cold rain frost
Keng Tzu (37)	trees and grass die and live alternately	trees and grass flourish anew	harvest may continue or fail	—	no fish
Jen Tzu (49)	Winter, but no stores	meteors fall	hiber-nating insects come out too early	Winter thunder	—

A correspondence between the Five Elements and the Twelve Branches is less easy to define since 12 is not divisible by 5. One solution was arrived at by applying the Five Elements to the seasons of the year, and making a concordance between the seasonal elements and the Branches of the months appropriate to that season. (The various ways in which the Five Elements were allotted to the four seasons has been remarked on previously, see page 31.) In one of these systems, the sixth month was accorded the element Earth, the growing season, Spring, being Wood, the hot season, Summer, Fire, the season when men harvest with sharp implements Metal, and the Winter, or wet season, Water. By allocating the elements to the Branches of the months which resulted the following concordances are obtained:

木 Wood	Spring	Yin	(III)	寅
		Mao	(IV)	卯
火 Fire	Summer	Ssu	(VI)	巳
		Wu	(VII)	午
土 Earth		Ch'en	(V)	辰
		Wei	(VIII)	未
		Hsü	(XI)	戌
		Chou	(II)	丑

金 Metal   Autumn   Shen   (IX)   申
                            You   (X)   酉

水 Water   Winter   Hai   (XII)   亥
                            Tzu   (I)   子

The *Huai Nan Tzu*, however, gives a different system for allocating the Earth Branches, although the main concordances are the same.

> (Stems) 1 and 2, (Branches) III and IV are of the element Wood;
> 3, VI, 4, and VII are Fire;
> 5, 6, and the Four Seasons are Earth;
> 7, 8, IX, X, are Metal
> 9, 10, XII, I, are Water.

Here, no Branches are allocated to Earth, but the Four Seasons are. It is possible that the inference here is that the 'Earth Season' was intended to be tacked on to the ends of the other four seasons (see above).

Summary of the Elemental Attributes

	WOOD	FIRE	EARTH	METAL	WATER
Stems, Branches	1, 2, III, IV	3, 4 VI, VII	5, 6, II, V VIII, XI	7, 8, IX, X	9, 10, I, XII
Cyclical numbers	5, 6, 19, 20, 27, 28, 35, 36, 49, 50, 57, 58	3, 4, 11, 12, 25, 26, 33, 34, 41, 42, 55, 56	7, 8, 15, 16, 23, 24, 37, 38, 45, 46, 53, 54	1, 2, 9, 10, 17, 18, 31, 32, 39, 40, 47, 48	13, 14, 21, 22, 29, 30, 43, 44, 51, 52, 59, 60
Magic Square Number	8	7	5	9	6
Musical note and corresp. mode	Soh Mixo-lydian	Lah Aeolian	Doh Ionian	Ray Dorian	Mi Phrygian
Season	Spring	Summer	—	Autumn	Winter
Direction	East	South	Centre	West	North
Colour and Star Palace	Azure Dragon	Vermilion Bird	Yellow Dragon	White Tiger	Black Tortoise

	WOOD	FIRE	EARTH	METAL	WATER
Heavenly Bodies	Stars	Sun	Earth	Lunar Mansions	Moon
Planet	Jupiter	Mars	Saturn	Venus	Mercury
Prognosticatory and Human Features					
Ministry	Agri-culture	War	State	Justice	Works
Imple-ment	Compasses	Ruler	Plumbline	Set-square	Scales
Attribute of personality	Bearing	Imagin-ation	Intellect	Eloquence	Attentive-ness
Manner	Casual	Educated	Circum-spect	Vigorous	Tranquil
Mood	Anger	Joy	Desire	Sorrow	Fear
Body	Muscles Eyes	Nerves Tongue	Circulation Mouth	Skin Nose	Skeleton Ear

Also, see the list taken from the *Yüeh Ling* on page 174.

The Four Pillars
The hour, day, month and year of one's birth (or in some old text-books, the date of one's conception) form the 'Four Pillars', the quintessence of the Chinese horoscope.

During the Sung dynasty, the criteria employed by fortune-tellers were the Stem-and-Branch for the hour and month of conception, and the day, month, and time of nativity. Because five factors were involved, this form of fortune-telling became known as the 'Five Fates' (Wu Ming). The term 'San Ming' which means 'Three Fates' is sometimes thought to refer to an old method of fortune-telling which only used three sets of criteria, although during the Han dynasty there was an expression 'San Ming She' (三命設) which meant 'three kinds of fate': the fate which followed one's behaviour, such as justice and retribution; the fate which fell despite one's behaviour, such as natural calamities; and most important of all, Cheng Ming (正命) the 'First' kind of fate, Heaven's mandate, or Destiny. This was Fate in the narrowest sense of the word. Thus, 'San Ming' came to be a term used as the title of books on fortune-telling.

From the Three Fates, and the Five Fates, there were eventually the Four Fates — the Four Pillars of Destiny as they have been called. Later philosophers had decided that the 'conception' pillar was unnecessary, and used only the criteria of the hour, day, month and year of birth. Each pillar is represented by two characters, a Stem and a Branch. For this reason the Four Pillars are sometimes known as the 'Eight Characters'. As it had long been the custom for the parents of prospective marriage partners to judge the suitability of the betrothal by comparing the sets of the 'Eight Characters' of the young couple, it eventually became a convention that when a young man wished to propose, all he need do was to send his intended a card with his name on one side and his Eight Characters on the other.

It will be remembered, however, that while the day and the year are counted according to Stem and Branch, only the Branch is used for numbering the months and the hours. The solution is given in the *San Ming T'ung Huai*. Stems for the hour and month are given in accordance with certain rules which in effect mean that two of the 'Eight Characters' are only products of the other six. Tables of Stems are given in the Appendices.

Popular Chinese astrology, which only uses the twelve 'zodiac' signs, is actually an aspect of Chinese Fate calculation, or Tzu Wei astrology, in which the Branch of the Year has been replaced by one of the twelve animal signs, and occasionally in more detailed horoscopes, with the Stem of the Year being represented by its respective elements, as in the Tibetan and Mongolian calendars.

With this distinction in mind,, we can turn away from this increasingly popular aspect of Chinese astrology, and take a step towards the understanding of the principles of authentic Chinese astrology: the interpretation of the Celestial Mandate through the ministration of Heaven's markers.

4.

THE TWENTY-EIGHT
LUNAR MANSIONS

The most significant factor pointing to the separate development of a popular Chinese astrology is the emphasis on the twenty-eight lunar mansions, and their influences on character and events. The term 'lunar mansion' or Hsiu (宿) can refer either to one of the twenty-eight constellations of the 'lunar zodiac' or to one of the twenty-eight segments of the sky containing those constellations. The constellations themselves are those which the Moon encounters on its passage through the sky.

The importance of the lunar mansions lies in the practicality of observation. Since the Sun obscures the stars in the sky, it is not possible, from direct observation, to know the position of the Sun on the ecliptic. But the Full Moon only occurs when the Moon is diametrically opposite the Sun; therefore, by knowing the position of the Full Moon in the sky, it is possible to state that the Sun must be in the opposite segment.

We shall see that the twenty-eight Hsiu were an indigenous Chinese concept. Although they are to be found in Indian and Arabian astrology, they seem to have been borrowed from China during the cultural interchange, at the time when Buddhism was first introduced into the Far East.

The first traces of personal horoscopic astrology in China reveal that the twenty-eight Hsiu were of prime importance. In *Pacing the Void,* Edward Schafer quotes the obituary of the poet Tu Mu (AD 803-852). 'My birth was in Chio (Hsiu 1). Mao (Hsiu 18, the Pleiades) and Pi (Hsiu 19, Hyades) are eight palaces away, the Palace of Sickness and Frustration; also called the Palace of the Eighth Curse. [The Seventh Curse, according to the New Method of Fate Calculation.] The Earth Star (Saturn) was there, followed by the Fire Star (Mars) and the Wood Star (Jupiter)'. The artist Yang Hsi said, 'Wood was in Chang (Hsiu 26), the eleventh from Chio, the Palace of Fortune and Virtue.' Here, it is not the meanings of the Hsiu which are paramount, but their position among the twelve 'houses' or 'palaces'.

Elsewhere, after quoting a poem by one of the greatest writers and poets of the T'ang dynasty, Han Yü (AD 768-824), Dr Schafer explains it by saying that on the day of Han Yü's birth, the Moon had been in the Hsiu Tou (Hsiu 8); the previous day in Chi (Hsiu 7) and the following day in Hsiu Niu (Hsiu 9), that is, he was born with the Moon in the Southern Ladle, the other two constellations being the Winnowing Basket and the Ox-boy. The Southern Ladle had failed him, and he was at the mercy of the Winnower, which retained the wheat, and gave out chaff. Note that two dignitaries did *not* consider it worth mentioning that Tu Mu was born in the year of the Sheep, and Han Yü in the year of the Monkey. In the formative stages of Chinese genethliacal astrology, the twenty-eight Hsiu, not the animal cycle, were the axle. Thus, long before the twelve animals gained popularity, astrologers cast horoscopes by referring to the position of the Moon with regards to the lunar constellations.

Unfortunately, it seems that at an early stage an element of expediency crept in. Finding out the particular Hsiu in which the Moon resided on the day of a person's birth requires long and difficult calculations, and a library of almanacs and ephemerides — essential for the modern practising astrologer, but beyond the means of itinerant diviners. Only the largest establishments — the monasteries and observatories — would have the kind of records to go into such astronomical detail. Accordingly, a convention was adopted of using, instead of the actual Hsiu occupied by the Moon in casting a horoscope, a *notional* Hsiu (this term, used in various places throughout this book, is an invention of my own).

Since the Moon's journey through the twenty-eight mansions takes approximately twenty-eight days, it must have seemed appropriate to allocate one of the Hsiu to each day of a twenty-eight day cycle. It is really a system of having different names for every day for four weeks. Digressing for a moment, because twenty-eight is divisible by seven, it means that each day of the Western week may have one of four 'notional Hsiu' names; thus notional Hsiu 1, 8, 15, and 22 are always Thursday; 4, 11, 18, and 25 are always Sunday. In ancient calenders such as those of the Tun Huang monastery, days of the Sun were marked in red, by the character for Sun, or the character Mi (密), which has been taken as evidence of Mithraic influence. But returning to the Hsiu, the cycle of twenty-eight notional Hsiu are as prominent in the Tun Huang calendars as they are in modern Chinese almanacs. That they rarely correspond with the actual Hsiu must be stressed very strongly; the Moon's journey through the Hsiu actually takes 27 days 8 hours (as distinct from the length of time between New Moons, which is about 29½ days). More remarkably, the divisions of the sky into the twenty-eight segments determined by the Hsiu constellations are neither regular nor equal; in fact they vary indiscriminately between just over a degree to over thirty-three degrees. Thus as the Moon actually covers about thirteen degrees each day, it follows that the Moon travels through some Hsiu in less than two hours; while it may linger for more than two days in others.

One such large constellation is the Hsiu Nan Tou (Hsiu 8) which Han Yü had so much cause to complain about. In fact he should

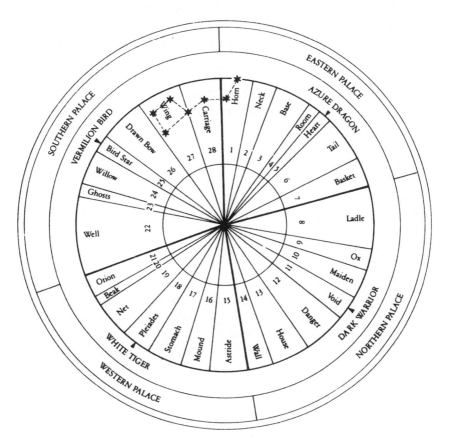

Figure 4.1 Chart showing the proportions of the segment angles of the twenty-eight Hsiu and the corresponding variation in size of the four Palaces. The view is over the Central Palace. The Hsiu constellations themselves are situated in the four directional Palaces. Note how the last star in the tail of the Great Bear indicates the segment of the first Hsiu.

have complained about his astrologer: the Moon would have taken
more than two days to traverse the Hsiu Tou; accordingly, if the Moon
entered Tou on his date of birth, it would have still been there on
the following day, and conversely, the whole of the previous day if
it had moved out of Tou on his birthday. What is more likely, is that
Han Yü's astrologer calculated his horoscope on the notional, rather
than actual Hsiu.

In casting a horoscope, therefore, the astrologer ought rightly to
consult an appropriate ephemeris to find the actual Hsiu in which
the Moon resided at the hour and date of birth; remembering that
the Moon can traverse certain Hsiu in two hours. Such calculations,
using ephemerides and conversion factors, are made extraordinarily
complex by the fact that each Hsiu is a different breadth; however,
by referring to the charts on page 344 the actual Hsiu can be found
from conventional data.

The Hsiu:
Astronomical Data

The following pages contain all the essential astronomical and
astrological data concerning the twenty-eight lunar mansions as
follows:

(a) The number of the Hsiu, according to the traditional order;
(b) The Chinese character;
(c) Its romanization;
(d) Its meaning, with supplementary interpretations if any;
(e) The Equatorial Extension, that is, the angle-width of the segment
    of the sky occupied by the constellation. This is expressed in
    (i) Chinese degrees,* according to the *Ming Yün Ta Kuan*, but
    tacitly corrected by deduction where necessary; (ii) Chinese
    degrees, according to the *Huai Nan Tzu*; (iii) modern degrees,
    according to Churyo Noda; (iv) modern degrees, the author's
    conversion of (i);
(f) Identification of the constellation, and the most prominent stars,
    usually after Gustave Schlegel, but not always;
(g) Sources before the *Huai Nan Tzu*, if any.

*The Chinese divided The Circle into 365¼°, each degree representing
one position of the sun during the course of its apparent yearly journey
through the Heavens.

The data is then followed by any remarks of interest, and the astrological symbolism and portents. These are often of necessity in two sections, the first according to the ancient astrological school, and the second according to the popular astrology of Chinese almanacs, with lucky and unlucky days, after the system of 'notional' Hsiu. Finally, the 'notional' element is given, and the horoscopic animal, explained in the section on the Twelve Branches (see page 67).

There are many differences in the portents and correspondences as expounded by the 'actual' and 'notional' Hsiu schools. The main reason for this lies in the inequality of the Hsiu segments. In the system of notional Hsiu, the Five Elements (that is, the Five Planets) and the Sun and Moon are distributed in regular order among the twenty-eight notional Hsiu; thus, the four 'Sunday' Hsiu (4, 11, 18, and 25) are always regarded as being ruled by the Sun. But since the breadths of the Hsiu are so varied it happens that an orderly distribution of the seven luminaries results in the total equatorial extension allotted to each planet being extremely irregular; for example 87° to the Wood Element (Jupiter) but only 33° to the Sun. To some extent, this imbalance is redressed by some authorities regarding Hsiu 22 (The Well) as being ruled, logically enough, by the Water Planet (Mercury) in place of Wood (Jupiter). This brings the total equatorial extensions ruled by each planet to:

Wood 54°;	Fire 54°;	Earth 56°;	Metal 33°;	Water 46°;
(Jupiter)	(Mars)	(Saturn)	(Venus)	(Mercury)

Sun 33°;   Moon 56°.

But older authorities do not distribute the planets according to such a regular system and allocate the elements (and consequently the planets) according to their astrological symbolism (as in the case just mentioned where the Well is again regarded as belonging to the element Water).

The Four Palaces
The Heavens are regarded as being divided into five 'palaces', of which the central palace, containing the Pole Star, the Great Bear and other permanently visible circum-polar stars, does not include any of the Hsiu. The remaining four palaces are those designated by the four directions, each associated with the four seasons. Originally the four

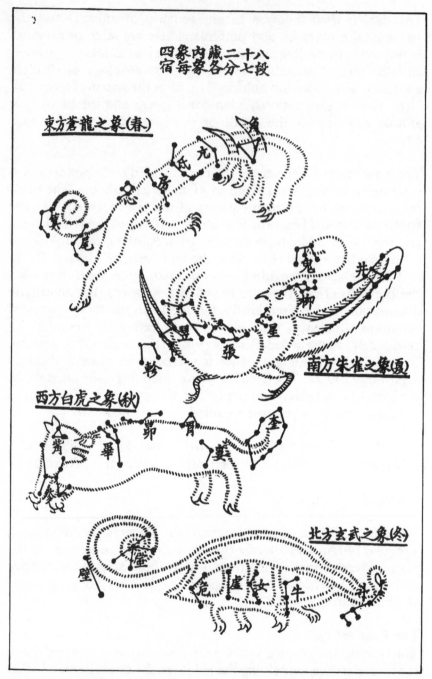

Figure 4.2   The Guardians of the Four Directional Palaces: the Green Dragon of Spring, the Vermilion Bird of Summer, the White Tiger of Autumn, and the Black Tortoise of Winter.

directional palaces were considered to be four enormous constellations, each marked by a single determinative star (described in the *Yao Tien*, q.v.). The four ancient constellations gave their names to the Four Palaces: The Green (or Azure) Dragon; the Dark Warrior (or Tortoise); the White Tiger; and the Vermilion Bird. Many of the twenty-eight Hsiu into which these four constellations were divided still bear names reminiscent of their original location.

Just as the Hsiu are irregular in size, so, perhaps surprisingly, are the four quarters of the heavens, the smallest occupying 77.22° and the broadest 109.99° of the equator. Each palace contains seven Hsiu, the ancient determinative star of each palace belonging to the central Hsiu of each seven. (The exception, Antares, now in Hsiu 5, was originally in Hsiu 4.)

The Eastern Palace 東宮   Spring 春   Wood Element 木
Hsiu 1-7
Azure Dragon 青龍 Determinative star: Huo (Antares in Scorpio) 火

Equatorial Extension: 77.22° (Less than a quadrant)

The East, in which the Sun rises, is proper to Spring, and the element Wood because it is the time of the year when things begin to grow.

The Eastern Palace was formerly the home of the mega-constellation Azure (or Green, the term not being exactly translatable) Dragon. The various Hsiu have the names pertaining to parts of the dragon's body: Head, Neck, Heart, Tail. Although the other three constellations are connected with parts of a house, these too may have originally been parts of the dragon's body. Of the twenty-eight 'lunar' animals which have been associated with the Hsiu, (see page 137) it is noteworthy that the first two are the Scaly Dragon (perhaps crocodile) and the Dragon. But this should not be taken as evidence of some connection between the animal names of the Branches and constellations and the ancient names of the Four Palaces since the lunar 'tiger' also belongs to this Palace, and not the Western Palace opposite. Nor alas do the turtle and the tortoise join in reptilian harmony; they too are allocated different domiciles.

The Northern Palace 北宮   Winter 冬   Water Element 水
Hsiu 8-14
Dark Warrior (Tortoise) 玄武 Determinative Star: Hsü (β Aquarii) 虚

Equatorial Extension: 95.07° (Just over the quadrant)

The Sun never reaches the North, so it is proper for the North to be associated with Winter; the ice, rain, and snow which are frequent in Winter makes Water the appropriate element.

The dark colour of the tortoise's shell, and its strange markings caused the tortoise to be held in reverential awe on account of the fact that the shell appeared to be a mystic map. Nevertheless, this awe did not prevent the tortoise from being sacrificed (for divination purposes) in such huge numbers that the species of tortoise became totally extinct. Other beliefs concerning the tortoise were that it led a celibate life (hence tortoises never knew their father, and 'son of a tortoise' became a euphemism for someone who did not know who their father was); their extreme longevity (if they were not caught for their carapaces) gave them a reputation for sagacity; they were also considered to be heliotropic, always turning to face the Sun, which therefore they were believed to worship. Perhaps for this reason the Tortoise was associated with the North. Turtles, as evidenced by references in the classics, were an important item of diet, but they were never eaten in the eleventh month for fear of dropsy.

The Western Palace 西宮 Autumn 秋 Metal Element 金
Hsiu 15-21
White Tiger 白虎 Determinative star: Pleiades 昴
Equatorial Extension: 82.97° (Less than a quadrant).

West being the direction in which the Sun declines, it is therefore appropriate for the Autumn. Since Autumn is the time of harvesting, when iron implements are used to cut the plants or dig the soil, Metal is the appropriate element.

The white tiger is reported to have been an actual beast; it may have been a light fawn, or even the snow leopard. Writers are quite definite about its having no stripes. Inevitably it passed into mythology, where it was credited with living a thousand years, and its fur did not turn white until five hundred of them had passed. At the beginning of February, 1986, in time for the commencement of the Year of the Tiger, two white lion cubs were born in a zoo in South Africa, a remarkable event which in ancient times would have been regarded as an auspicious omen without parallel. The constellation Tsui (the Beak, or perhaps Turtle) is regarded as the head of the Tiger, and the stars of Orion the main part of its body.

The Southern Palace 南宮 Summer 夏 Fire Element 火
Hsiu 22-28
Vermilion Bird 朱鳥 Determinative star: Niao (α Hydrae) 鳥
Equatorial Extension: 109.99° (More than the quadrant).

It is understandable that the Southern Palace should be associated with Summer, and because of the Sun's heat in Summer, with the element Fire.

What the Vermilion Bird was seems to be disputed; some authorities refer to it as the 'golden pheasant'; others to the Phoenix (not the Phoenix of Western mythology, although the name, Feng, might suggest this) and others to a kind of mythological composite bird with the front part of a swan, a scaly deer (that is, the Chi Lin, another mythical composite) for the back part of its body, the tail of a fish and the head of a serpent, with ridges on its body like a dragon, the body of a tortoise, the throat of a swallow, and the beak of a chicken.

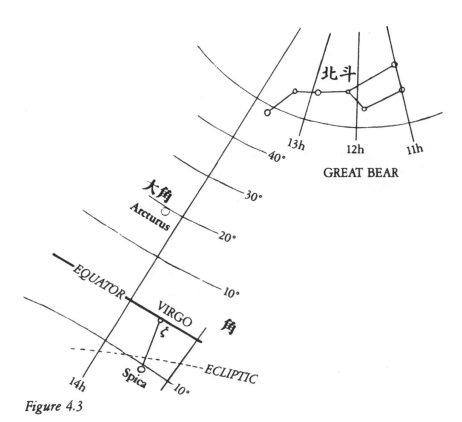

Figure 4.3

The Hsiu Pertaining to the Eastern Palace

Hsiu 1 **大角** Chio

Horn
E.E: (i) 12.70°   (ii) 12°
     (iii) 11.70°   (iv) 12.52°
ζ, α virginis (Spica)
vide Yüeh Ling

The Horn is that of the Dragon of Spring. It now only includes those two stars ζ and α virginis, but is likely to have originally included the Star Arcturus, known to the Chinese as the Great Horn, Ta Chio (大角), which was once considered to be part of the Great Bear. In fact, as can be seen from Figure 3.1, the stars of the Great Bear can be used to locate Ta Chio and Chio Hsiu. If Spica is regarded as '0', then allowing for the precession of the equinoxes of about 1° every 72 years, Spica would have marked the equinoctial position about the middle of the sixth century of the present era, and it is reasonable to suppose a change might have been made in astronomical computations at about this period.

Arcturus, on the other hand, would, by the same reckoning, have denoted the equinoxes in the middle of the fifth century BC, about the middle of the Chou dynasty.

The Dragon is often associated with rain and floods, and it may have been its calendrical appearance at a rainy season which prompted this belief. It was said that when Chio (or Ta Chio), the symbol of creation and the beginning of Spring, appeared, birds and beasts began to breed and buds burgeoned. Therefore it was held to preside over growth, creation, birth, gardening and agriculture.

Modern astrological portents: days influenced by this constellation are ideal for beginning work on construction or buying land. The head of a family can choose this day for a marriage of his children, for all who are married on the Chio day will receive great credit and standing which will put them close to the heart of the State. On the other hand, it is an unlucky day for funerals, for if they are arranged on this day there will be calamities and epidemics in the family within three years. It would be courting disaster to inspect the family vaults on this day.

Chio presages favourable rains and winds for the Spring, and rainy nights followed by cool weather in the Winter.

The particular spirit of this constellation is a genie who is able to transfix serpents with his gaze.

Lucky. Element: **Wood.** Day: **Thursday.** Planet: **Jupiter.** Animal: **Smooth Dragon.**

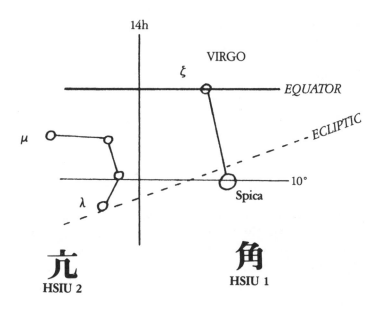

Figure 4.4

Hsiu 2 亢   K'ang   **Neck**
E.E: (i) 9.42°   (ii) 9°
(iii) 98.81°   (iv) 9.285°
λ, μ virginis
vide Yüeh Ling

The word may be taken to mean the neck of a man, or the throat of a bird; either points to its having been originally the name of part of the throat of the 'Dragon' mega-constellation. The Chinese New Year not being coincidental with the beginning of the Four Seasons, the second Hsiu is regarded as the 'New Year' constellation.

In the text of the *I Ching,* hexagram 1, the text of 'lines' 1, 2, 5 and 6 refer to the 'Dragon'. Line 5 reads:

亢龍有悔

'The Neck of the Dragon has regret'. I believe that this is in fact a clear reference to the second Hsiu. If Hui [悔] 'regret' is a substitution for Hui [晦] meaning 'eclipse', the sense becomes abundantly clear; here we have a reference to an eclipse occurring in the constellation of the Dragon's Neck.

It is possible that this passage is actually a clue to the antiquity of the *I Ching,* since a case can be made for saying that the *I Ching* was written at a time when the calendar had been adjusted to make the year begin with the Sun in the second constellation, instead of the first, which it originally did.

It was considered to preside over judgements and punishments, the release of prisoners, and even the release of animals. It is also regarded as the constellation of illness. On the first day of the first month, to counter the five injurious exhalations, it was thought to be a wise precaution to medicate oneself with the five condiments: ginger, mustard, garlic, pepper, and onion.

When the constellation shone clearly, it portended fidelity among ministers, and peace in the country.

Modern astrological portents: it is regarded as unlucky to undertake construction work on this day; if a large house is built it will fall down; a man would then lose his authority. Combats on this day result in disaster; it is like delivering the sheep to packs of wolves or driving a goat into a den of tigers. No marriages ought to be contracted on this day; nor funerals, lest someone drop dead while attending it.

It presages violent dust storms in Spring; searing heat in Summer; wind and rain in Autumn; sand storms in Winter.

The tutellary genie of this constellation is the patron deity of alchemy. **Unlucky.** Element: **Water.** Day: **Friday.** Planet: **Mercury.** Animal: **Dragon.**

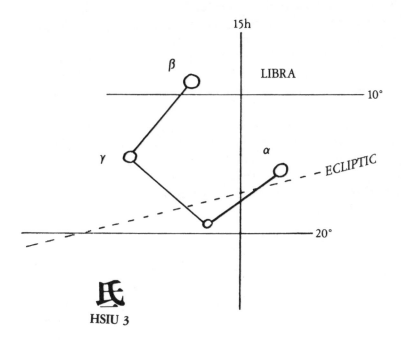

HSIU 3

Figure 4.5

| Hsiu 3 | 氐 | Ti | Base, (floor, foundation, root). |

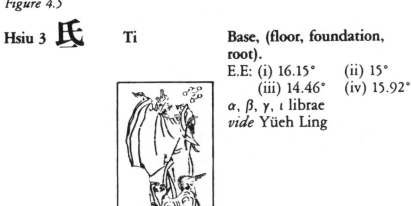

E.E: (i) 16.15°   (ii) 15°
(iii) 14.46°   (iv) 15.92°
α, β, γ, ι librae
vide Yüeh Ling

The word signifies the floor, possibly of the house in the next constellation.

It was regarded as bringing the sweet rains of Spring and the morning dew, but also the illnesses of Spring. If bright and clear, it presaged good fortune in these matters, if dull, the Spring rains would not be sweet, and illness would follow.

Modern astrological portents: the calamaties brought by this constellation are due to the failure to make proper obsequies, or pay respect to one's elders. If marriages are contracted on this day, evil men will be attracted into the house at night. If one travels by boat on this day, it will be shipwrecked. Children of any marriage contracted on this day will be poor, or suffer from being unable to express themselves, or pay attention; worse, they might be deaf and dumb.

It presages rain and wind in Spring, greater wind and rain in the Summer, even more in the Autumn, and gales and tempests in Winter.

The genie of this constellation possesses the power to fly through the air and has the secrets of magic recipes.

Unlucky. Element: **Earth.** Day: **Saturday.** Planet: **Saturn.** Animal: **Marten.**

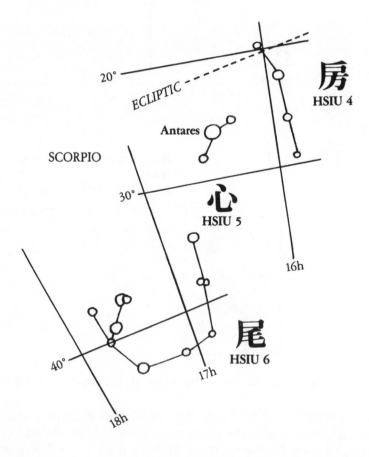

Figure 4.6

Hsiu 4 房   Fang   **Room (house, shop).**
E.E: (i) 5.41°   (ii) 5°
(iii) 5.25°   (iv) 5.33°
β, δ, π, ϱ, ν scorpionis
vide Yüeh Ling

Strictly speaking, this is the constellation which ought to contain Antares, the Fire Star of the *Yao Tien*, but owing to the shift in the Heavens over two or three thousand years, the Fire Star no longer corresponds to what is the constellation of the Spring Equinox. It represents the stomach of the Dragon.

It is the opener of that which is closed. Perhaps because of its association with the Fire Star it represents the chariot of the Sun. Its connection with the Equinox means that it is also connected with the Great Sacrifice of burnt offerings. It was formerly regarded as being the province of the planet Jupiter, and therefore, the element Wood; this is not the case with modern astrologers employing the system of 'notional' Hsiu who correlate this constellation with the Sun.

Modern astrological portents: to build today is very lucky; the happy proprietor of any building constructed on a Fang (room or house) day will be able to increase holdings, build extensions, and acquire gardens and surrounding land. It presages luxuries, happiness, longevity, and health. It is even lucky to bury today, one's ancestors being willing to assist in finding promotion, riches, and official recognition for the family. If a man takes a mistress on this day, a son will be born ere three years are out. (This was regarded as a fortunate omen, incidentally).
Lucky. Element: **varies.** Day: **Sunday.** Planet: **Sun.**
Animal: **Rabbit.**

Hsiu 5 ⼼   Hsin   **Heart**
E.E: (i) 6.18°   (ii) 5°
(iii) 4.14°   (iv) 6.09°

Antares, σ, τ scorpionis
vide Yao Tien; Hsia Hsiao
Cheng (*not* in Yüeh Ling)
Mentioned in the Shih
Ching (Book of Odes)

The (apparent) migration of Antares to this constellation has been mentioned already.

This constellation was the symbol of the Emperor, because men are the heart of Heaven and Earth, and the Emperor is the master of men.

Modern astrological portents: not a wise day to build; great misfortune; law cases result in imprisonment; it is unfavourable to those in office; it presages the necessity to sell one's property. The children of a marriage contracted on this day will be afflicted. The tutellary divinity sits in the clouds, and has the ability to transform peas into soldiers [signifying a great enemy]; and is credited with extremely swift movement [perhaps because of the narrowness of the equatorial extension, resulting in rapid transit by the Moon].
Unlucky. Element: **varies.** Day: **Monday.** Planet: **Moon.**
Animal: **Fox.**

Hsiu 6 尾   Wei

Tail
E.E: (i) 17.78°   (ii) 18°
      (iii) 18.95°   (iv) 17.525°
ε, μ, ζ, θ, ι, κ, λ, ν
scorpionis
vide Yüeh Ling

The ancient astrological significance was the heir apparent, and by extension, the women's apartments where the heir apparent would be brought up as a child. It is also regarded as that which separates

wood from water, the symbolism being a dam, or a wooden boat on which one is separated from the water. It symbolizes (again because of the association with the heir apparent) succession, and inheritances.

Modern astrological portents: this is a fortunate day for building and negotiating marriages, which will result in rich descendants. It presages the finding of hidden treasure, and promotion to high office.
Lucky. Element: **Fire.** Day: **Tuesday.** Planet: **Mars.**
Animal: **Tiger.**

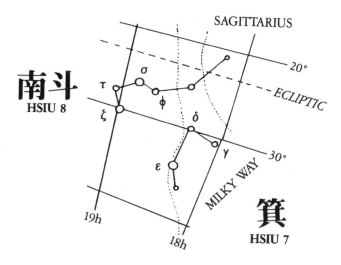

Figure 4.7

Hsiu 7 箕   Chi   **Winnowing Basket**
E.E: (i) 9.58°   (ii) 11¼°
      (iii) 10.22° (iv) 9.44°
γ, δ, ε, η sagitarii
Mentioned in the *Shih Ching* (Book of Odes)

This constellation always called the 'Winnowing Basket' in works of reference, was originally, according to the writer of the *Hsing Ching* (of unknown date) the 'dung basket.' As in many Eastern countries, dung was a valuable commodity, the only known fertilizer and a source of fuel. Its position at the tail of the dragon is self-explanatory. There was a special rite connected with the gathering and spreading of manure. The wide-mouthed basket became the symbol of a large mouth and tongue; the spreading of evil gossip and slander; malicious rumours, and by extension, adultery and harlotry. (See the reference on page 93).

Modern astrological portents: the modern significance for this constellation is quite different from the old one; it presages a year of good fortune for those who undertake new designs today, with herds of cows and horses as a reward for the industrious. New property is acquired, and the silkworms become very active. Opening a new door doubles one's fortunes, with granaries gorged with rice, and official honours being heaped on the head of the fortunate person indicated by these portents; indeed, all the family will participate in these extraordinary demonstrations of favour. The dead also may be interred with impunity.

Lucky. Element: **Water.** Day: **Wednesday.** Planet: **Mercury.**
Animal: **Leopard.**

The Hsiu Pertaining to the Northern Palace

Hsiu 8 南斗 (Nan) Tou

(Southern) Ladle or dipper
E.E: (i) 23.98°   (ii) 26°
     (iii) 26.54°   (iv) 26.63°
μ, λ, φ, σ, τ, ξ sagitarii
vide Yüeh Ling

In the *Hsing Ching* this constellation is known as the 'head of the tortoise' on account of its being the first of the 'Tortoise' constellations. Because its name is reminiscent of the Great Bear (Pei Tou) it must not be thought that this is the Little Bear, which is close to the Pole Star, and therefore even further North than the 'Northern Ladle'

as the main seven Great Bear stars are known to the Chinese. The shape, however, is reminiscent, hence the name; note, however, that it consists of six stars, instead of the Northern Ladle's seven. Its ancient astrological symbolism is based on its being likened to a liquid measure: it is the sign of recompense, satisfaction, and completion; filling up, finishing, and rewards for tasks which have been fulfilled. It is the constellation which presides over wine, wine-merchants, and makers. It is the emblem of thanksgivings to spirits for their benefactions.

Modern astrological portents: Tou is a good day for building, opening trenches, digging, and physical labour. Silkworms may be raised for great profit. This constellation indicates every kind of good fortune; officials are promoted, families enriched. The emblematic animal, the Unicorn, is not the unicorn of Western heraldry, but a creature which Gustave Doré in his monumental work translates as 'griffon'. It is the Hsia, a creature able to discriminate between right and wrong, and which destroys the wicked. Its diet, alas, includes fire, for which it has a great appetite, to the extent of gorging itself to destruction.

Lucky. Element: **Wood.** Day: **Thursday.** Planet: **Jupiter.** Animal: **Unicorn.**

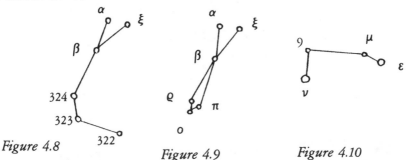

Figure 4.8   Figure 4.9   Figure 4.10

Hsiu 9 牽牛 (Ch'ien) Niu   Ox (-boy) (The Draught) Ox

E.E: (i) 7°   (ii) 8°
(iii) 7.90°   (iv) 6.90°
α, β, ξ, o, π, ϱ capricorni
Altair (α aquilae)
vide Yüeh Ling

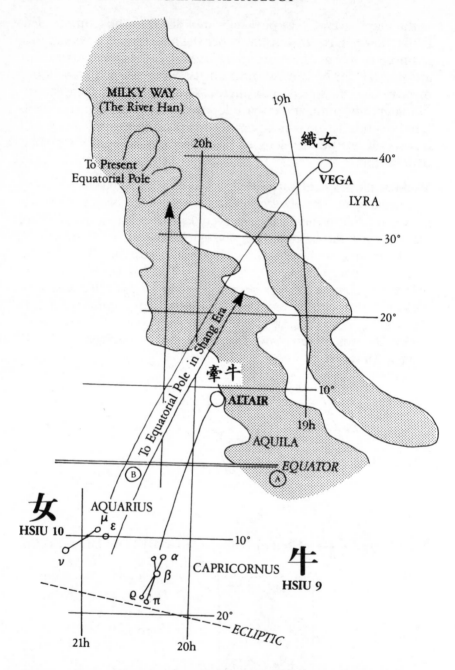

Figure 4.11 From a vantage point A on the present equator, the star Altair (the Ox Boy) is to the left of Vega (the Weaving Maiden). However in Shang times, as seen from vantage point B the position of the two stars is reversed, thus lining the two stars up with their appropriate constellations.

Hsiu 9 and 10, the Ox and the Maiden, are two of the most recurrent constellations in Chinese literature, and yet the precise identification of these constellations poses great problems. Chinese star diagrams show Hsiu 9 (very often called the *Ox-boy*, Ch'ien Niu) having six stars. These are variously identified by different authorities. That of W. F. Mayers in *A Chinese Reader's Handbook* quoting the list given in W. H. Medhurst's translation of the *Shoo King* can be discounted as an obvious misreading. Mayers gives Aries α, β, π and Sagittarius ω, A and B. This cannot be right, since Aries is so far away from Sagittarius, and what has obviously happened is that at some stage ♉ for Capricorn has been misread as ♈ Aries, although *Aries* is spelt out in full in the text. John Reeves gives Capricorn β, α, ξ plus the nebulae 323, 324, and 322. Although these match the rough shape of the constellation in Chinese star lists, the inclusion of three nebulae is doubtful. In Kuei, Hsiu 23, the presence of the nebula Praesepe is graphically described in ancient accounts. A constellation with three nebulae would surely call for further comment.

There remains Gustave Schlegel's alternative suggestion, shown in the configuration 7b, which comprises the stars listed in the heading to these notes, and which Schlegel thinks trace out the character for Ox in ancient seal-script (半).

But not one of these authorities includes the star Altair, which is germane to the whole Ox-boy and Weaving Maiden legend. (q.v. p. 19). This star, called in Chinese Ch'ien Niu (牽牛) is not far from the apotheosized Weaving Maiden (織女) the star Vega, α lyrae. Regarding the stars of Hsiu 10, the Maiden, all authorities agree with Chinese sketches of the constellation that it is the group shown in figure 8, and listed in the heading of the following notes. Now the two *stars* Ox-boy and Weaving Maiden do not immediately appear to relate to the two *constellations* Ox and Maiden. However, if the two stars are joined to the two constellations by imaginary lines, as shown in figure 6, it will be seen that both these lines run in the same direction *and point to where the equatorial pole would have been in the Shang dynasty.* This is therefore evidence for the names of the stars and the constellations having been given at a date which preceeds the date of the *Yao Tien* or any other written account, not only indicating the antiquity of Chinese astronomical observation, but that these two stars would have at one time been the determinative stars for these two constellations. Hence, Altair is the Ox-boy, and Hsiu 9 his Ox; consequently, if Vega is the Weaving Maiden, then Hsiu 10 must either be the Weaving Maiden's loom, or some other character in the story.

The imagery of the ox-boy leading his ox to pasture or market has led to the association of this constellation with roads, paths, fields, and barriers.

Modern astrological portents: such an interesting background is very badly served by its modern astrological symbolism. It presages discord, broken marriages, and the disappearance of provisions. Perhaps these woeful tidings are in commiseration for the Ox-boy, forever separated from his true love in the sky. The imagery of barriers and the ox is adopted from the ancient traditions to warn against leaving doors open, and the advent of sickness and starvation for animals.
Unlucky. Element: **Metal.** Day: **Friday.** Planet: **Venus.** Animal: **Ox.**

Hsiu 10 須女 (Hsü) Nü

(Servant) Maiden
(Sometimes known as the 'Weaving Maiden')
E.E: (i) 11.29°   (ii) 12°
      (iii) 11.82°   (iv) 11.13°
ε, μ, ν, g aquarii
vide Yüeh Ling

Because of the proximity of the Servant Maiden to the Ox-boy (q.v.), this constellation is frequently confused with that of the Weaving Maiden, Vega. The astrological symbolism is connected with the ancient custom of boys and girls sacrificing to this constellation, or rather, its guardian spirits, on the night of the Summer Solstice; it was the custom to play the flute to it to obtain wisdom, while the girls hoped to have a good dowry, and thus obtain a good husband. Perhaps because of its connection with marriage, the constellation was also regarded as presiding over the construction of houses.

Modern astrological portents: oddly, the modern portents are unfortunate, presaging disputes and quarrels among the family, and fights troubling the peace. Epidemics and illness, particularly diseases of the bowels, will follow an injudiciously arranged funeral on this day. The unlucky omens for this constellation are particularly surprising, bearing in mind that the symbolism is that of the bat, which in Chinese folklore is an emblem of good fortune.

Unlucky. Element: **Earth.** Day: **Saturday.** Planet: **Saturn.** Animal: **Bat.**

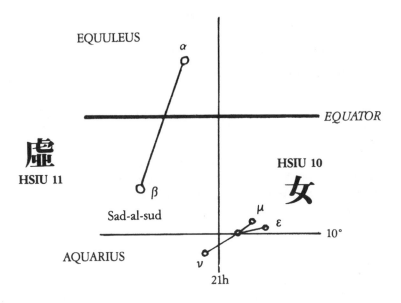

Figure 4.12

Hsiu 11 虛   Hsü   **Void**
E.E: (i) 9.13°   (ii) 10°
          (iii) 9.56°   (iv) 9.00°
β aquarii, α equulei
vide Yao Tien; Yüeh Ling

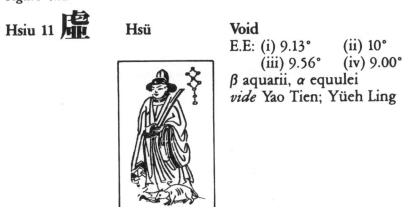

This is the determinative constellation of the Northern palace. Schlegel's opinion was that the term signifies either a tomb, a sepulchre, or some wild place; the character (虛) being composed,

possibly, of the radical 'tiger' (虎) and the North (北), suggesting
a wasteland frequented by ravenous beasts. In Arabian star-lore, β
aquarii is called *sad-al-sud* 'the fortunate one of the world'; and it
was waited for eagerly since it forecast the beginning of the rainy
season.

The ancient astrological significance is based on its funerary aspect;
it was regarded as presiding over sextons and cemeteries. It was the
bringer of storms and snow; obviously both the Arabs and the Chinese
regarded it as the harbinger of the wet season; for the former it was
a fortunate sign, for the latter less so.

Modern astrological portents: the gloomy nature of Hsü is emphasized
by modern astrologers, who take this sign to be the portent of domestic
quarrels; ill-luck awaits those who construct buildings or dig trenches:
tigers will snatch up infants and devour them, tears will stain the graves
of the newly deceased, and illnesses will afflict the family for three or
even five years; and the whole family will be plunged into ruin. The children
of marriages contracted on this day will conduct themselves badly.
Unlucky. Element: **varies.** Day: **Sunday.** Planet: **Sun.**
Animal: **Rat.**

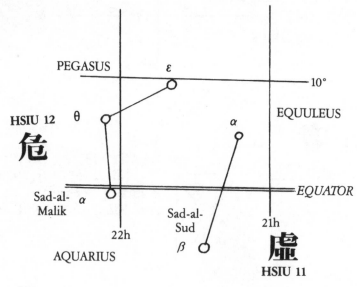

Figure 4.13

Hsiu 12 危   **Wei**

Danger (rooftop)
E.E: (i) 16.18°   (ii) 17°
      (iii) 16.64°   (iv) 15.95°
α aquarii, ε, θ pegasi
vide Yüeh Ling

The meaning of Wei is danger, although apparently, according to the *Book of Rites*, the character means 'rooftop' which the three stars resemble. As such, the name of the constellation ties in with the names of the two following constellations. Wei consists of three red stars, one of them, α aquarii, being known in Arabian astrology as *sad-al-malik* 'the fortunate one of the king' and as such, the partner of the star mentioned in Hsiu 11, above. The constellation is sometimes known as the 'Celestial Market' (one of several by this name) because, apparently, of the three day markets held at the time of the Winter Solstice. It is the sign of fortifications and earthworks, building, property, and construction. The idea of 'danger' may come from the 'danger' of being on a rooftop.

Modern astrological portents: the dangers portended by this sign are to travellers by land or water, the former being attacked on the way, the latter's ship foundering.
Unlucky. Element: **Earth.** Day: **Monday.** Planet: **Moon.**
Animal: **Swallow.**

Hsiu 13 營室 (Ying) Shih

House, pyre
E.E: (i) 18.17°   (ii) 16°
      (iii) 16.52°   (iv) 17.90°
α (Merhab) and β pegasi
vide Yüeh Ling
Mentioned in the *Shih Ching* (Book of Odes)

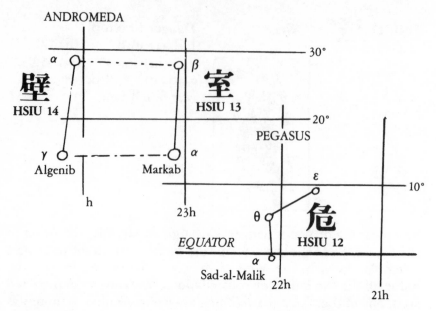

Figure 4.14

This and the next constellation were formerly the single constellation Ting (定), the Forehead, but were divided into two so that the number of constellations pertaining to Winter would be the standard seven. Present day astronomers refer to the four stars as 'The Square of Pegasus' even though one of the stars is actually in Andromeda. The character Ying (營) which frequently precedes Shih in classical references, shows a palace (宮) on which flames (火) are burning. This has been taken to represent a ceremonial pyre; a building constructed expressly for the purpose of being burnt down, in which various victims were immolated, or else a temple which contained a sacrificial fire. The modern usage of the term is 'a regulator'.

The astrological symbolism, a house full of riches, seems to suggest a house, or building, in which various sacrificial offerings were placed.

Modern astrological portents: the symbol of the House is taken to indicate that any kind of construction or building work might be carried out today, with fortunate results. All kinds of good fortune will accrue to the instigator of new ventures and schemes begun on this day. Favours are bestowed by the Emperor for good work; the family will obtain riches, and all will live in peace and concord. Heaven will shower its bounteous gifts on the fortunate person designated by this auspicious sign.
Lucky. Element: **Fire.** Day: **Tuesday.** Planet: **Mars.**
Animal: **Pig.**

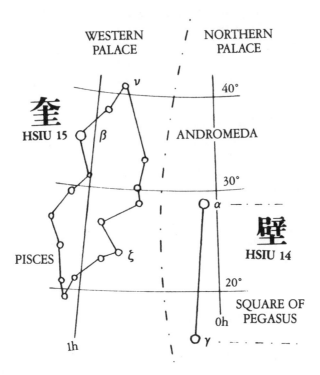

Figure 4.15

Hsiu 14 東壁 (Tung) Pi

(Eastern) Wall
E.E: (i) 9.32°   (ii) 9°
     (iii) 8.44°   (iv) 9.19°
α, andromedae, γ pegasi
vide Yüeh Ling
Mentioned (as Ting, *above*)
in *Shih Ching*

Formerly part of the constellation Ting, together with Hsiu 13 (q.v.). The ancient astrological significance was that of archives, or a state repository of some kind. The division of Ting into two constellations, one being a building, and the other its 'Eastern Wall' seems to suggest the original meaning of Ting was as some kind of Treasury, or perhaps the residence of the God of Wealth. Arising out of the meaning of repository is the constellation's presiding over literature. It is the house of exalted virtue. (Another symbolism ascribed to the constellation is quite different, considering it to be a fish's mouth from which lies issue; but this gloss, which does not match either the symbolism or the names of the two constellations, perhaps ought to be disregarded.)

Modern astrological portents: the fortunate aspects of the constellation are retained in modern astrological readings. There is ample scope for expansion by building or digging. Opening doors will bring great fortune to oneself and one's family. By being respectful (remembering one's ancestors, and making obsequies) one can gain riches and official recognition. The children born of marriages contracted today will be extremely accomplished, and bring great honour to their parents.
Lucky. Element: **Water.** Day: **Wednesday.** Planet: **Mercury.** Animal: **Porcupine.**

The Hsiu Pertaining to the Western Palace

Hsiu 15 奎   K'uei

Astride
E.E: (i) 17.70°   (ii) 16°
     (iii) 15.66°   (iv) 17.45°
η, ζ, ι, ε, δ, π, ν, μ, β andromedae;
σ, τ, L, ν, ϕ, $\varkappa$, ψ piscium
vide Yüeh Ling

The form of the constellation is supposed to resemble the sole of a shoe; it is also said to represent a man with his legs astride. Astrologically, the constellation represented the arsenal of the Emperor. The symbolism is somewhat inchoate; there are admonishments to wash old clothes and double the thickness of garments by lining them, as a precautionary measure against the oncoming cold of Winter.

Modern astrological portents: generally an unlucky day; one should not engage in construction work or riches will avoid the house. Digging will be followed by a succession of misfortunes. There is a likelihood of family quarrels and discord among acquaintances. Lawsuits are lost. Sickness takes a firm grip.

Unlucky. Element: **Wood.** Day: **Thursday.** Planet: **Jupiter.** Animal: **Wolf.**

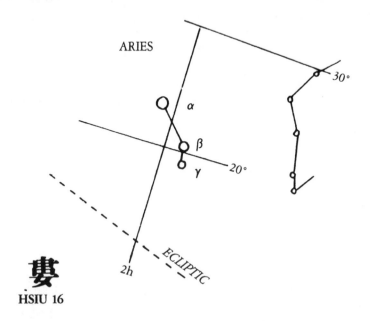

Figure 4.16

Hsiu 16 婁   **Lou**   **Mound (Bond)**

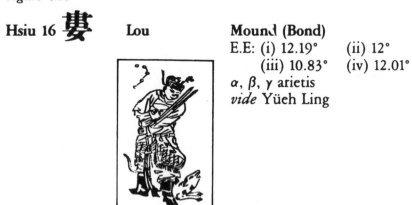

E.E: (i) 12.19°   (ii) 12°
        (iii) 10.83°   (iv) 12.01°
α, β, γ arietis
vide Yüeh Ling

This constellation is associated with the harvest, and its attendant rites and sacrifices. There was a general thanksgiving, at which the people were assembled, with much music. Because of this, the constellation is regarded as presiding over gatherings, assemblies of people, and harmony, that is, the music of many people in choirs or orchestras. It presides over reunions and meetings.

A clear aspect of the constellation denoted a good harvest and peace within the Empire.

Modern astrological portents: the happy associations of this constellation are retained by modern astrologers, who describe it as presiding over many pleasant hours of family concord. Such a day is fortunate for the construction of a triumphal arch, the opening of doors, and construction of all kinds. Children born of a marriage contracted today will fill their pockets with silver, gold, and precious stones. It is also a good day for digging trenches or opening watercourses. Men and women will spend their time in joyous abandon.

The constellation brings cool winds in Spring; mists in Summer; fine rain in Autumn; and ice in Winter.

The tutellary divinity of this constellation has the recipe for the medicine of longevity.

Lucky. Element: **Metal.** Day: **Friday.** Planet: **Venus.** Animal: **Dog.**

Figure 4.17

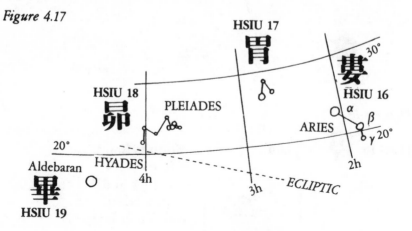

Hsiu 17 胃   Wei

Stomach
E.E: (i) 15.57°   (ii) 14°
      (iii) 15.2°   (iv) 15.35°
35, 39, 41 arietis (musca borealis)
vide Yüeh Ling

This constellation had several names, but its principal one, the Stomach, is misleading, since it actually refers to a storehouse. It was the celestial granary, or storehouse of goods harvested in the Autumn. On the other hand, in the sense of being a place where things were stored up, it acquired the sense of a prison, where men were locked up and forgotten about. Thus it became associated with punishments, imprisonment, and execution. In yet another sense, although apparently of later centuries, it became associated with the earthworks, river dredging, and the building of embankments and sea-walls against the floods of Autumn. As many constellations were known as the 'Embankment' this particular constellation was called the 'Grand Embankment.' Principally though, its two major aspects of symbolism were as a storehouse of goods, signifying riches, or on the maleficient side, imprisonment. Note that according to the ancient astrologers, the related element was Metal.

Modern astrological portents: modern astrologers ignore the 'imprisonment' aspect of Wei, and interpret it as a sign of good fortune, and the accumulation of wealth. It is regarded as lucky for both building and burial, mainly perhaps on account of its association with the Earth element. It is said that children of a marriage contracted on a Wei day will be familiars of the Emperor.
Lucky. Element: **Earth.** Day: **Saturday.** Planet: **Saturn.**
Animal: **Pheasant.**

Hsiu 18 昴   Mao   **Pleiades**
E.E: (i) 10.91°   (ii) 11°
          (iii) 10.44°   (iv) 10.75°
Pleiades
vide Yao Tien, Hsia Hsiao
Cheng (*not* in Yüeh Ling)
Mentioned in *Shih Ching*
under old name of Liu.

The name of this constellation is unique in having no other meaning. The origin of the character (昴) has been frequently discussed, and has been interpreted in several different ways; Gustave Schlegel devotes a lengthy article to the history of the character. Suffice it to mention that the phonetic part of the character Mao is the fourth of the twelve Branches; and that the same symbol appears in the character for Hsiu 24, Liu, the Willow; in fact the old name for the Pleiades was also Liu, written (畱) and the resemblance can be seen. Gliding over Schlegel's essay quickly, his view is that the essential part of the character represented a closed door surmounted by the Sun.

The ancient astrologers held that when the Pleiades flickered, it presaged an invasion by barbarians. They were regarded as the ears and eyes of Heaven, and for that reason were considered to preside over the end of criminal or judicial proceedings; if the constellation was clear and bright, it signified proceedings being dropped. It was also considered to indicate military involvement (perhaps on account of its ancient augury of invasion) and as the two aspects — criminal proceedings and military matters — both touched on untimely death, this led to the Pleiades being associated with that misfortune.

The Pleiades are the determining constellation of the Western Palace.

Modern astrological portents: very much the same symbolism is expounded by modern astrologers, who see the constellation presaging lawsuits and death within the family. The results of misjudged actions — the beginning of new construction or the digging of trenches — is regarded as heralding unhappiness, when little children will be as close to the grave as old men with long white beards. Marriages contracted today are regarded as woeful, with the separation of the partners. **Unlucky.** Element: **variable.** Day: **Sunday.** Planet: **Sun.**

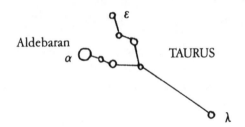

Figure 4.18

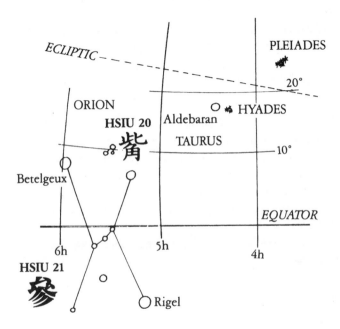

Figure 4.19

Hsiu 19 畢   **Pi**

Net
E.E: (i) 16.32°   (ii) 16°
      (iii) 17.86°   (iv) 16.09°
Hyades, α (Aldebaran), ε, δ,
γ, κ, σ, σ2, λ tauri.
vide Yüeh Ling
Mentioned in the *Shih
Ching* (Book of Odes)

Both the Hyades and the Pleiades are clusters of stars which were regarded as being the mesh of a hunting net; though it is possible that the shape of the stars of this constellation may originally have been the trident rather than the net. The game hunts were held not just for the sake of ridding the land of vermin, or even for food, but as military exercises, as various passages in the classics (such as the *Rites*) make clear.

Thus this constellation became associated with hunting, military prowess, and by extension, traitors, deserters, revolts and punishments.

The Hyades have always been associated with the rains, which were believed to be generated there. This is obviously part of another, much older, folk legend based on astronomical observation, the appearance of the Hyades coinciding, in prehistoric times, with the advent of the rains.

Modern astrological portents: the recent evaluation of the Hyades' auspices seems to recall the earlier connotation of a net catching all manner of fish and game, and therefore a fortunate sign; the less auspicious aspects of treachery and desertion have apparently been forgotten. They are regarded as fortunate for building, and for interment, the former bringing fortune, the latter honours. Long life is assured to children born of a marriage today.
Lucky. Element: **varies.** Day: **Monday.** Planet: **Moon.**
Animal: **Crow.**

Hsiu 20 觜觿 Tsui (Chui)

Beak (of the Turtle)
'To bristle up'
E.E: (i) 0.05°   (ii) 2°
      (iii) 1.47°   (iv) 0.05°
λ, 1, 2, orionis
vide Yüeh Ling

Virtually part of the constellation which follows, and usually considered to be the head of Orion, this exceptionally minute constellation would be traversed in minutes rather than days if the figures for the Equatorial Extension given in the *Ming Yün Ta Kuan* are accepted. The small triangle is thought to represent the beak of a turtle, but as the 'tortoise' belongs to the adjacent constellation, there is no likelihood that it was formerly regarded as part of that constellation — particularly as the 'Dark Tortoise' faces the other direction. It is obvious that 'the head of Orion' had to be cut off in order to make seven constellations for the Western Palace. In Ssu Ma Ch'ien's treatise, the three stars called the 'Turtle' and forming the head of the 'White Tiger' presided over flocks, herds, and people under protection.

Modern astrological portents: these seem to be entirely at variance with the ancient symbolism, presaging punishments and exile; a fatality in a Yin year (a year of the third Branch, or Tiger year), the necessity to sell property, arraignment for murder, and a death sentence. These woeful portents are of course, as with most modern portents, the results of wrongdoings which can be avoided; but they are not inescapable bonds of Fate; Tsui should be taken as a stern warning.
Unlucky. Element: **Fire.** Day: **Tuesday.** Planet: **Mars.** Animal: **Monkey.**

Hsiu 21 參   Shen

Orion (To Mix)
E.E: (i) 10.23°   (ii) 9°
(iii) 6.93°   (iv) 10.08°
α, β, γ, σ, ε, θ, x orionis,
including Betelgeux, Rigel,
Bellatrix, and three other
stars (uncertain)
vide Hsia Hsiao Cheng;
Yüeh Ling
Mentioned in the *Shih Ching* (Book of Odes)

Although Shen (參) unlike Mao (昴) has modern meanings other than being the name of this constellation, the stars of this constellation are so brilliant and recognizable that Orion is probably the most familiar star pattern in the sky. Orion properly includes the 'sword' which hangs from the hunter's belt, and the three stars of the 'head' which in Chinese astrology form Tsui, the preceeding constellation. The brightness of Orion's stars exceeds that of the Great Bear; and as it is a constellation of Winter its appearance in the early evening on a frosty night is even more spectacular.

The character for Orion is obviously a picture of the constellation, though once Orion has been decapitated, it is not clear which of the three stars is indicated by the graph. Possibly the upper star was meant, originally, to represent the brightest star in Tsui, Hsui 20. This could account for the fact that the ancient astrological portents indicate decapitation. The three strokes at the bottom of the character usually mean 'hair' and they could refer to the Great Nebula which is such a prominent feature of the constellation.

The 'Hunter' of Western astrology, and the 'Warrior' of Chinese lore, Orion presides over decapitations (see above), executions, massacres, fortresses and frontiers.

Modern astrological portents: regarded as both lucky and unlucky, according to one's actions. One source regards the constellation as bringing advantages through the Literary Star, Kuei Hsing — but this seems curious as the Literary Star actually belongs to the Northern Ladle, the main stars of the Great Bear. For those who build today, there will be rewards; beginning new ventures therefore presages success. It is not lucky for the winding up of affairs, or for burials, since these will be followed by sickness or the death of a distant relative. Nor is it a good day for marriages and betrothals which will end in separation of the parties. For other new ventures, however, dignities will be conferred. Industry is the keynote. **Variable fortune.** Element: **Water.** Day: **Wednesday.** Planet: **Mercury.** Animal: **Ape.**

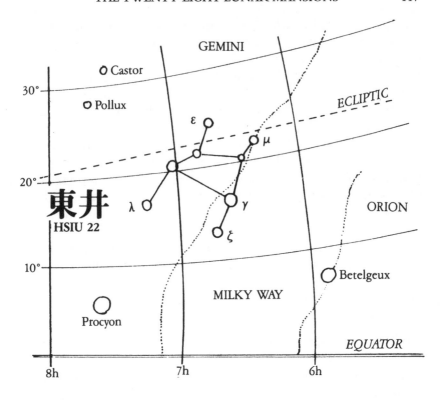

Figure 4.20

Hsiu 22 東井 (Tung) Ching

The (Eastern) Well
E.E: (i) 31,29°   (ii) 33°
      (iii) 32.60°   (iv) 30.84°
μ, ν, γ, ξ, ε, δ, ζ, λ
geminorum
vide Yüeh Ling

Following so shortly after the narrowest of the lunar mansions comes the widest of all, the Well, occupying the major segment of the largest of the palaces, and incidentally, directly opposite to the second broadest segment, that of the Southern Ladle. Frequently it is called the Eastern Well, although it is in the Southern Palace, nor is there any 'Western Well' with which it might have been confused. Since the stars do not belong to any particular direction, but rotate about the sky in the same way that the planets, Sun, and Moon do, the term 'Eastern' may therefore refer to a particular method of astronomical observation which has not yet been explained.

The 'Well' being the first of the constellations in the palace of the Vermilion Bird, this constellation is occasionally referred to, astrologically, as the Head of the Phoenix. The graph of the stars which form the constellation is so similar to that of the character Ching that is might be supposed that (井) is in fact a representation of the constellation. The most ancient forms of the script are virtually identical to the present character, usually said to be a drawing of a well-head.

Naturally, for a constellation representing a Well, it presides over Water, cleaning, ablutions, repairs, and refurbishments. The notion of cleanliness and purity is further expanded into the cleansing away of crime, expurgations, and moral uprightness; it therefore presides over law, regulations, and order.

Modern astrological portents: strictly speaking, following the regular order which operates for all the other lunar mansions, the Well should belong to the element Wood, but for reasons which have already been outlined, some authorities ascribe the element Water to the Well, and this seems sensible. The constellation too is regarded as neither particularly lucky nor unlucky, possibly because of this conflict of elemental interests. Among the many portents are the fact that it is regarded as fortunate to build, open doors, take examinations, or raise silkworms; such efforts will accrue great merit. Industrious labours in the garden, or digging ditches and watercourses, or the opening of new ways will in time bring great riches. It is also fortunate for cattle, sheep, and horses, which will grow fat and prosper. Land belonging to widows will increase in value, and bring them an income.

However, it is not regarded as fortunate to put work to one side; it is not favourable for burying, or funerals, which will result in sudden death and epidemics.

Variable fortune. Element: **Water.** Day: **Thursday.** Planet: **Jupiter.** Animal: **Tapir.**

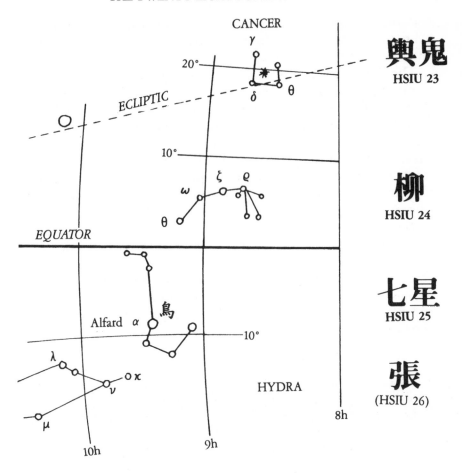

Figure 4.21

Hsiu 23 輿鬼 (Yü) Kuei

Ghosts (or, Ghostly Carriage)
E.E: (i) 2.14°   (ii) 4°
      (iii) 4.46°   (iv) 2.11°
γ, δ, ν, θ cancri, Praesepe
Described in *Hsing Ching*
(see below)

This constellation is interesting astronomically for a number of reasons, not least of which is that it is cut by the ecliptic, and therefore eclipses may take place within the actual constellation itself, rather than just the segment of the sky ruled by this Hsiu.

The 'Ghostly Carriage' is not so much an evanescent vehicle as the transport for ghosts themselves, who can be seen riding in it.

According to the *Hsing Ching*, at the centre of the constellation is 'something white like a cloud of pollen blown from willow catkins, like a cloud but not a cloud, like a star but not a star; it appears like an aura; it is the place of bodies heaped up . . .' This passage is interesting if only for allowing us a glimpse of what an 'aura' looked like (the word being Ch'i (氣) described in the section on haloes and aura on pages 222ff). In fact the ghostly inhabitant of the carriage, from which the constellation derives the name Kuei, meaning imp, demons, or Ghosts, is the nebula Praesepe. The charming description of the nebula ('like a cloud of pollen blown from willow catkins') is obviously due to the next Hsiu being the Willow. It is therefore difficult to know which imagery came first, the cloud of pollen, or the ghostly passengers. Perhaps one clue is the extreme narrowness of this particular Hsiu, the second smallest. If it were originally one constellation, that is, part of Liu, it would account for the description of the pollen blown from the Willow's catkins, and why it was such a small constellation when a new boundary might have been taken by cutting down the Well's share. If this is the case then the astrological portents, based on the 'Ghosts' image, must be of comparatively recent origin (Han rather than Chou). The box of four stars, enclosing the nebula Praesepe closely resemble the Chinese character Hsiung [凶] meaning an evil omen. This could have been the origin of the character, or perhaps the resemblance to the character suggested its malefic nature. The absence of any mention of this constellation in the Rites (the *Yüeh Ling*) also points to the possibility that the constellation acquired the name 'Ghosts' at a later date.

The constellation is regarded as presiding over departed spirits, and by extension, places where men have been killed, such as battlefields, and by further extension, horses, soldiers, and materials. In the sense of death and loss, the constellation also was regarded as the guardian spirit of buried treasures hoarded up in times of war, and thus, jewels and accumulated wealth.

Modern astrological portents: not surprisingly, this constellation is regarded as being generally unlucky, with its symbolism of death, demons, and ghosts being foremost. Doors opened today are gateways to disaster if not death. Marriages will result in women being widows longer than wives; making an enclosure presages the death of a little girl. But obsequies, and respect to one's ancestors, or the departed, will bring unusual honours to oneself and one's children.

Unlucky. Element: **Metal.** Day: **Friday.** Planet: **Venus.** Animal: **Sheep.**

Hsiu 24  **Liu**

Willow
E.E: (i) 13.20°   (ii) 15°
     (iii) 15.46°   (iv) 13.01°
δ, ε, ξ, ω, θ, ϱ, ν, σ hydri
vide Yüeh Ling

There are references to the name of this constellation in the notes on Mao (卯) (Hsiu 18) and the preceding constellation, Kuei (q.v.). There are many references to the importance of the Willow in the ancient sacrificial rites, especially those connected with the Sun. It was regarded as extremely felicitous to plant willow trees, and in those regions where willow did not grow, the fir, a symbol of longevity, was substituted in its place. Willow may have also been the original material for the sticks cast by *I Ching* diviners (there is a mention in Herodotus of Scythian soothsayers casting down willow wands) before the yarrow plant. In ceremonies where branches of willow would ordinarily be borne in procession, long canes of bamboo were carried instead in Southern regions which were too hot for the willow to grow successfully. Willow plants were also thought to ward off poisons, and it is certainly a fact that willow bark, which contains salicylic salts, was the original source of aspirin. The image of the 'weeping willow' meant that, as in the West, it was associated with funerals, and thus, portended tears.

Modern astrological portents: the unlucky portents are no doubt taken from the Willow's image of weeping. Nothing should be undertaken on this day, but somewhat surprisingly, the omens also warn against funeral ceremonies, which one would have imagined as being most appropriate to this constellation. Faults and harmful actions are followed by discord, illness and ruin.

Unlucky. Element: **Earth.** Day: **Saturday.** Planet: **Saturn.** Animal: **Buck.**

Hsiu 25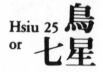
or

Niao
(Ch'i) Hsing

Bird
(Seven) Stars; (the Excellent Star)
E.E: (i) 6.40°   (ii) 7°
     (iii) 6.86°   (iv) 6.31°
α, ι, τ (1, 2,) 19, 26 hydri;
(Alfard, α hydri, is the Bird Star)
vide Yao Tien, Yüeh Ling
Pictured on oracle bones

The determinative star of this constellation is Niao, the Bird Star, which has given its name to the 'Southern Palace' as the ancient constellation Vermilion Bird. Alfard, the very bright star in Hydra, is the corresponding Western name for the star which was regarded as marking the Summer Solstice; it is one of the two oldest recorded stars in the Chinese catalogue.

After it became well established as the Bird Star, it became known simply as 'the Star' after which, because of the other stars near to it, the name 'Seven Stars' came into use.

It is regarded as presiding over bridges and fords, no doubt because it marks the Summer Solstice, it symbolized the bridge between the two halves of the year. By extension, because villains would lie in wait at bridges, it foretold brigandage and highway robbery, and dangers from attack on journeys. From the practice of gathering certain plants used as dyestuffs during the summer months, it became associated with the trade of dyeing, and by extension, with clothing and garments.

Modern astrological portents: a mixture of good and bad fortune. Building, or construction work leads to promotion. It foretells death and separation for those who bury today. If a marriage is contracted today the wife may fall into the hands of a ravisher.

Not even the Star of Confucius can dispell such portents.

Generally **unlucky.** Element: **varies.** Day: **Sunday.** Planet: **Sun.** Animal: **Horse.**

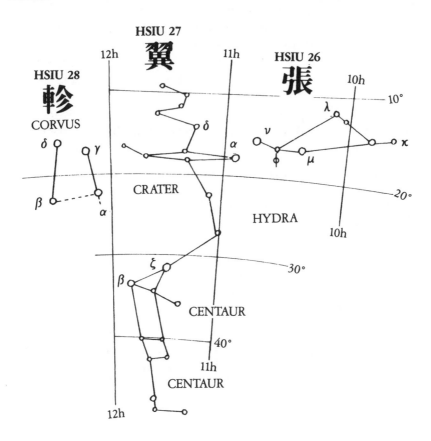

Figure 4.22

Hsiu 26 張   Chang   **Drawn Bow; Extending, spreading**

E.E: (i) 18.05°   (ii) 18°
    (iii) 17.13°   (iv) 17.79°
α, λ, μ, ν, φ hydrae

The name of this constellation has been taken to mean 'spreading', as of a net, the pattern of stars having some semblance to a spread net: The symbolism was of game collected for a feast, and therefore the constellation portended festivities. By extension, because it was the custom to give presents at such occasions, it was regarded as indicating presents; because of the cooking involved for the feast, it became associated with the kitchen, the preparation of food, and utensils.

However, the more ancient portents were that when the constellation could not be seen, it was a sign that the Emperor would become ill.

Modern astrological portents: this sign is generally favourable, right conduct being rewarded, and offering riches after a successful career, and the flourishing of one's business, symbolized by the industrious silkworm thriving happily. It is the sign of happy and harmonious relationships, and the acquiring of new property.
Lucky. Element: **varies.** Day: **Monday.** Planet: **Moon.** Animal: **Deer.**

Hsiu 27 翼   I

Wings
E.E: (i) 20.26°   (ii) 18°
    (iii) 17.74°   (iv) 19.97°
Stars of Crater, Hydra,
and Centaur
vide Yüeh Ling

This constellation represents the wing of the Bird; it is a group of a large number of stars in the vicinity of Crater and Hydra, but which have not been identified with certainty. (In the map, I have included stars of the constellation Centaurus, as these seem to match the astrological representations of the constellation better than accepted listings.) Because of the association of this constellation with the time of the Grand Assembly, when the Emperor gave a speech of praise and admonishments followed by a Grand Concert of Music, this constellation has also come to be associated with music (see Hsiu 16). The constellation of the Wing is surrounded by a great number of smaller clusters of stars, which are regarded as representing the members of the Emperor's family in attendance at the Grand Assembly.

Modern astrological portents: the modern portents are very gloomy compared with the happy picture of celebrations and music which are interpreted by ancient astrologers; the present view is of continual (chronic) illness, and calamities befalling both the spouses of anyone married on this day. Those who take to outside work this day are likely to return home to find their wives in the arms of their lovers. The day is also inauspicious for arranging celebrations to one's ancestors: it presages the child having to leave the country.

Unlucky. Element: **Fire.** Day: **Tuesday.** Planet: **Mars.** Animal: **Snake.**

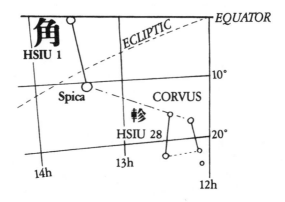

Figure 4.23

Hsiu 28 彡   Chen

The board which forms part of the construction of a carriage; a running board
E.E: (i) 18.65°   (ii) 17°
(iii) 16.76°   (iv) 18.38°
β, γ, δ, ε, [α] corvi
vide Yüeh Ling

This constellation is sometimes called 'the Celestial Carriage'. It represents the transport of tributes from foreign lands to the Emperor, thus, symbolizing the advent of wealth. It also presided over travel of all kinds and vehicles in general. Because the noise and the speed of carriages as they rolled along headlong, it was also thought that this constellation symbolized the wind, and was thus looked to for a good wind, or the end of a hurricane. There may be a more ancient connection between the symbolism of a carriage 'flying' along with the speed of the wind, and the traditional name for the Southern Palace — the Vermilion Bird.

Modern astrological portents: this constellation presages events in business which will bring great profit. Whatever is done on this day will herald fortunate returns. The construction of 'dragon' terraces will see the builder attending functions of high office, and the award of riches. Those who arrange funeral rites for their ancestors will themselves be blessed with a 'dragon child' (one of extreme talent and prowess) who will bring glory to his parents.

The same fortune is accorded to those who are judicious enough to marry on this day. This constellation is the means to official recognition. **Lucky.** Element: **Water.** Day: **Wednesday.** Planet: **Mercury.** Animal: **Worm.**

A Note Concerning the Twenty-Eight Animals of the Lunar Mansions
It has not been possible to identify all the animals of the notional Hsiu with absolute certainty; some of the mythological beasts have no exact counterpart in Western languages. The first animal, the harbinger of floods and rains, is usually translated as 'scaly dragon' to distinguish it from the 'smooth' or 'wingless' dragon of Hsiu 2, which corresponds to the 'Dragon' of the twelve cyclical animals. In English heraldry, the wingless dragon (such as appears in the arms of the Second Battalion of the Border Regiment) is known as the 'oriental dragon'. The third animal, properly called Ho or K'o, has puzzled many translators, and it appears in at least three references as 'badger' or the French 'blaireau'. Whatever this creature may be, it is certainly not a badger; as it is clearly depicted as a dog-like animal without any markings. According to the great K'ang Hsi dictionary, (狢) is erroneous for (貉), an animal much prized for its fur, and more properly translated as 'marten' of which the fur is 'sable.' Giles queries that this creature *might* be a badger in certain contexts, but the origin for this notion appears to be a misconception.* The Hsia,

* In one edition of the *Ming Yün Ta Kuan* there is a curious substitution by (茹), the mandrake plant, obviously a typographical error.

animal to Hsiu 8, is well-known in Chinese mythology, and described in the astrological notes. Here it is translated as 'unicorn' for convenience.

The Yü, the emblematic animal for Hsiu 14 is another mythical beast difficult to track down, and has been variously translated as porcupine and tapir. Neither of these terms is correct; the word is used for a species of primate. Again according to 'K'ang Hsi' the animal is the Chü Yü, or Ch'ih Yü (犰[豸]狳) and is described as a fish-like animal which pretends to be dead when attacked. The Ch'ih (豸) was itself a mythical beast, credited with the ability to tell true men from false, and was the official emblem of the Imperial Censors. Hsiu 20 and Hsiu 21 have been allocated the animals 'Monkey' and 'Ape' in that order, since this is necessary for the 'Monkey' of the 28 lunar animals to match that of the twelve cyclical ones.

Summary of the Twenty-Eight Hsiu

Hsiu of the Eastern Palace

1. Ch'io	Horn	Lucky	Wood	Thursday	Jupiter	Scaly Dragon
2. K'ang	Neck	Unlucky	Water	Friday	Mercury	Smooth Dragon
3. Ti	Base	Unlucky	Earth	Saturday	Saturn	Marten
4. Fang	Room	Lucky	Varies	Sunday	Sun	Rabbit
5. Hsin	Heart	Unlucky	Varies	Monday	Moon	Fox
6. Wei	Tail	Lucky	Fire	Tuesday	Mars	Tiger
7. Chi	Basket	Lucky	Water	Wednesday	Mercury	Leopard

Hsiu of the Northern Palace

8. Tou	Ladle	Lucky	Wood	Thursday	Jupiter	'Unicorn'
9. Niu	Ox	Unlucky	Metal	Friday	Venus	Ox
10. Nü	Maiden	Unlucky	Earth	Saturday	Saturn	Bat
11. Hsü	Void	Unlucky	Varies	Sunday	Sun	Rat
12. Wei	Danger	Unlucky	Varies	Monday	Moon	Swallow
13. Shih	House	Lucky	Fire	Tursday	Mars	Pig
14. Pi	Wall	Lucky	Water	Wednesday	Mercury	'Porcupine'

Hsiu of the Western Palace

15. K'uei	Astride	Unlucky	Wood	Thursday	Jupiter	Wolf
16. Lou	Mound	Lucky	Metal	Friday	Venus	Dog
17. Wei	Stomach	Lucky	Earth	Saturday	Saturn	Pheasant
18. Mao	Pleiades	Unlucky	Varies	Sunday	Sun	Cock
19. Pi	Net	Lucky	Varies	Monday	Moon	Crow
20. Tsui	Beak	Unlucky	Fire	Tuesday	Mars	Monkey
21. Shen	Orion	Varies	Water	Wednesday	Mercury	Ape

Hsiu of the Southern Palace

22. Ching	Well	Varies	Water	Thursday	Jupiter	Wild Dog
23. Kuei	Ghosts	Unlucky	Metal	Friday	Venus	Sheep
24. Liu	Willow	Unlucky	Earth	Saturday	Saturn	Buck
25. Niao Hsing	Bird Star	Fair	Varies	Sunday	Sun	Horse
26. Chang	Bow	Lucky	Varies	Monday	Moon	Deer
27. I	Wings	Unlucky	Fire	Tuesday	Mars	Snake
28. Chen	Carriage	Lucky	Water	Wednesday	Mercury	Worm

The Twelve Indicators of Good and Evil Fortune
Chien Ch'ü (建除)

In the early Han dynasty (about the second century BC), a cycle of twelve characters which came to be known as the Chien Ch'ü cycle (after the names of the first two characters in the sequence) was in use by diviners. They are listed in the *Huai Nan Tzu*, and examples of the sequence can be seen in the tenth century calendars from Tun Huang (although not in the calendar for AD 960); they also appear in the Manchu Imperial Calendars of the Ch'ing dynasty in Mongolian, again in Mongolian in a (probably) nineteenth century Mongolian manual of astrology, as well as in ancient Turkish texts from Turfan, a town which stood on the old route from China to the West. This makes it interesting to speculate on the origin of the Twelve Indicators, or, as they are known in Turkic, the Twelve Lords, since there appears to be a possibility that the symbols may have not been of Chinese origin, but, like the more familiar twelve animal cycle, imported from some other country to the north of China.

The Chien Ch'ü is not a simple cycle of twelve characters. Each successive sequence changes by the repetition of one of the characters in turn, according to a complex rule. Shih Sheng-Han, in his commentary to the *Fan Sheng Chih Shu* (the Book of Fan Sheng-Chih) suggests that the terdenary cycle may have been intended to run in parallel with the twenty-eight notional Hsiu to produce a year of 364 days. But as we shall see, the rules for the duplication of the characters are far more complex than would be convenient for a useful calendar and the assumption must be that the characters originally had a divinatory purpose which has remained to this day.

Mention of the Chien Ch'ü is made in Doré's *'Recherches'* (volume IV) and a list is given in Hauer's *'Handwörterbuch der Mandschusprache'*; more recently they have been listed in *'T'ung Shu — The Ancient Chinese Almanac'* by Palmer *et al* (pp.178ff). None of these sources, nor even modern Chinese astrological works, are able to give accurate directions for calculating the Chien Ch'ü sequence. It is therefore not without some importance that the following rules, determined after careful study of existing evidence, produce results which correspond to the sequences published in authentic editions of the Imperial almanacs and ancient calendars.

Rules for Determining the Twelve Indicators

The Twelve Indicators, here for ease of reference each assigned a code letter, are:

(A)	建 Chien	Establish	(G)	破 P'o	Ruin	
(B)	除 Ch'ü	Discard	(H)	危 Wei	Danger	
(C)	滿 Man	Fullness	(I)	成 Ch'eng	Completion	
(D)	平 P'ing	Even	(J)	收 Shou	Acceptance	
(E)	定 Ting	Arrange	(K)	開 K'ai	Open	
(F)	執 Chih	Grasp	(L)	閉 Pi	Shut	

The indicator for the day is found by combining the Branch of the day with the Branch of the month, but with a further, unusual refinement. It will be remembered that the Branch of the First Month is not Tzu, the first Branch, but Yin, Branch III (see page 55 for a further explanation of this point). However, the vital factor which is not always made clear in Chinese astrological manuals is that the 'month' in question is neither the Chinese lunar calendrical month nor the Western one, but the Chieh, or Monthly Festival, which is calculated according to solar positions. Thus, the 'first month' (Branch III) is consequently Li Ch'un (立春) the Beginning of Spring. It follows that the month to which Branch I pertains will be Ta Hsüeh (大雪) Great Snow, beginning (approximately) with the midpoint of Sagittarius, about 7 December. For greater accuracy concerning the dates of the Monthly Festivals, see the section on the Chieh.

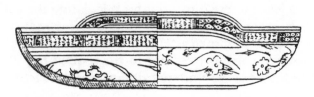

图一二　薄胎漆耳杯（Ⅰ式）（M1出土）

Table to Find the Indicator for the Day

Find the Branch for the Day according to the tables given on page 337. Cross-refer to the Monthly Festival in the table below, the resultant letter indicating the Indicator for the day. (Should the date fall on, or either side of one of the dates listed in the table, check with the more accurate list of Monthly Festival dates given on page 330ff.)

Branch of the Day Month beginning (approx.)	I 子	II 丑	III 寅	IV 卯	V 辰	VI 巳	VII 午	VIII 未	IX 申	X 酉	XI 戌	XII 亥
I	7 Dec	A	B	C	D	E	F	G	H	I	J	K	L
II	6 Jan	L	A	B	C	D	E	F	G	H	I	J	K
III	4 Feb	K	L	A	B	C	D	E	F	G	H	I	J
IV	6 Mar	J	K	L	A	B	C	D	E	F	G	H	I
V	5 Apr	I	J	K	L	A	B	C	D	E	F	G	H
VI	6 May	H	I	J	K	L	A	B	C	D	E	F	G
VII	6 Jun	G	H	I	J	K	L	A	B	C	D	E	F
VIII	8 Jul	F	G	H	I	J	K	L	A	B	C	D	E
IX	8 Aug	E	F	G	H	I	J	K	L	A	B	C	D
X	8 Sep	D	E	F	G	H	I	J	K	L	A	B	C
XI	9 Oct	C	D	E	F	G	H	I	J	K	L	A	B
XII	8 Nov	B	C	D	E	F	G	H	I	J	K	L	A

The Twelve Indicators Interpreted

From the Indicator for the day, it is possible to determine whether the day will be generally lucky or unlucky, what kinds of things one should do, and what ought to be avoided. Much of the information on daily activities is given in the almanac in other places, the source of this advice usually being the Book of Rites. The Twelve Indicators, however, provide a further guide, especially, it seems, in the matter of arranging a wedding. Here, then, are the interpretations of the Twelve Indicators. The translation of the old Chinese text is followed by an up-to-date rendering.

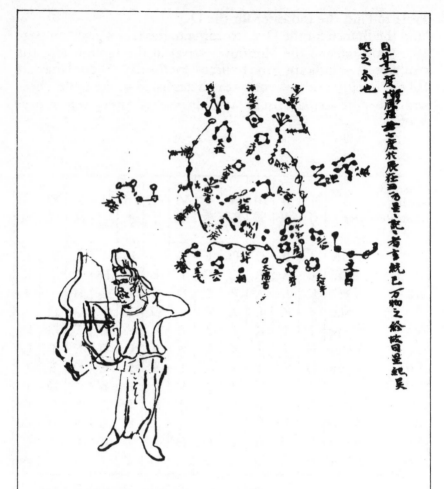

Fig. 0.0 **Star Charts from Tun Huang**
These tenth-century star charts from Tun Huang are the oldest
systematic star maps known. They are based on the catalogue of the
fifth century (AD) astronomer Ch'ien Le Chih. The principal stars,
originally described by the *Wu* Hsien over two thousand years ago
are painted in yellowed white. The additional stars listed by Shih
Shen are coloured red, and the further additions by Kan Teh are
marked in black. For a reference to these latter two astronomers, see
pages 23 and 000.

The star maps show the Northern hemisphere divided into twelve
segments, and portray the principal stars for each month, beginning
in the scroll with the twelfth month, that is the month following the
winter solstice, and so corresponding to January. The last map shows
the principal circumpolar stars, visible all year.

A 建 Chien — Establish

This day the ten thousand things are generated. Cut out garments. Pay bills. Barter and trade. Travel. Set up posts. All these things will be extremely fortunate.

But shun digging, travelling by boat, or opening stores and treasuries.

A good day for commencing new ventures, all kinds of business dealings, shopping, selling, and short commuting journeys. But avoid long journeys by air and sea, or outdoor activities, including building, gardening, or anything to do with heavy movements. Think twice before opening up stores, delving into the bank acount, or touching anything that had been saved 'for a rainy day'.

B 除 Ch'ü — Discard

Sweep away evil; this is the day of cleansing. Wash and bathe; take purgatives; such are fortunate activities.

Avoid wedding ceremonies, travel, and opening wells.

Not a good day for organized activity at all. Spring cleaning, clearing out, and general bodily maintenance are indicated. A day to consider making an appointment to see the doctor, optician, dentist, or careful consideration about health. Swimming, jogging, sporting activities are all fortunate activities, however.

C 滿 Man — Fullness

The Emperor of Heaven fills the treasuries to the brim. Organize wedding receptions; change one's residence; go on journeys; all these will be fortunate.

But shun cutting, planting, or unstopping watercourses.

A good day for big events such as weddings, receptions, conferences, important meetings. Not a day for menial tasks or jobs around the house — there are more pressing matters to be attended to today.

D　平 P'ing — Even

The day of the Official Gathering and Equal Dividing. Wedding ceremonies, change of residence, cultivating the Tao, or distempering walls, all such things are fortunate.

But avoid cutting, planting, excavating ditches or opening sluices.

Wedding receptions, conferences, and business meetings that were begun yesterday can proceed with confidence. If they have concluded, now is the time to sit back and contemplate, or make plans for future events, rather than tackle those jobs which were left outstanding — they will just have to wait a bit longer. This is the time for sitting back and taking stock.

E　定 Ting — Arrange

The Emperor of Heaven has placed everyone in their seats. The Five Grains are in abundance. Cut; plant; organize weddings; yoke the ox and the horse; dig the ground, open up wells. Avoid making accusations.

The last revellers can still carry on carousing, while the more determined can go ahead and get back to work. This is the day for all kinds of activity. Keep busy, and mind your own business; that way, everyone will get their work done quicker.

F　執 Chih — Grasp

The Emperor of Heaven administers the ten thousand things, and bestows Heaven's Blessings.

Arrange for the opening of wells, and cutting and planting, and wedding ceremonies. But avoid changing address, travel, or the opening of storehouses.

This is a day for staying in and getting work done. Domestic activity will be fortunate; but travel, moving house, and movement generally is not so bright; it is wisest to keep an eye on the purse strings too; travel may involve unexpected expense. Still, a good day for stay-at-home weddings.

G 破 P'o — Ruin

The Great Bear indicates conflicts, face-to-face arguments, and quarrels.
    This is a good day for going fishing, and punishing criminals. Other things would be unseemly.

Not a fortunate day for most things, by all accounts. Pack up and go fishing seems to be the almanac's best advice — it's going to be that kind of a day. Avoid conflicts of all kinds, not least with the law: it appears to be a good day for catching criminals.

H 危 Wei — Danger

Ascending the dangerous mountain, the wind blows fiercely: there is great peril.
    Be joyous, and drink wine. All else is little use.

Another day when everything seems to be going wrong; avoid trying to get things to work when they won't; the best course of action is to walk away from it. The old almanac's advice is to go out and get drunk!

I 成 Ch'eng — Completion

In Heaven's annals are the lives of the ten thousand things. Arrange wedding receptions, going on long journeys, digging earth. All these will be fortunate. But avoid casting aspersions.

A fortunate day for all kinds of activity, in particular for going on long journeys in which one has to stay away from home. Again, keep busy and mind your own business, and let everyone else mind theirs.

J 收 Shou — Acceptance

The Emperor of Heaven's precious treasures are received today. Open the granaries; carry on trade; enter college; arrange weddings; be active; dig the earth; all these things will be fortunate.
    Shun travel; arranging funerals; acupuncture and moxibustion.

This is the day for trading, and if necessary, for drawing on savings.

Outside activities are favoured. Arrange weddings, but funerals should be left till the day after tomorrow. A good day for studying, thinking about schooling, education, and so on. Not a good day for visiting the doctor, hospital, dentist, or clinic.

K 開 K'ai — Open

The messenger of Heaven's Emperor is out of danger. Study crafts; complete business dealings; organize wedding ceremonies; travel. Such things are fortunate.

But shun funerals and burials; other things are not wholesome.

The indications are of a recovery from illness. A good day for sending messages, receiving calls, writing letters. Business matters should be brought to a head; accounts totted up. Good also for short journeys. It is also a good day for practising skills of whatever kind: handicrafts, practising music, painting, and studying. But heavy work is not successful.

L 閉 Pi — Shut

Heaven and Earth, Yin and Yang, Open and Shut. This is the day of burial and concealment. One might set up placards, but other things are not fortunate. For most events, a day of misfortune and evil.

A day which is always printed in black in the Chinese almanacs; not a propitious day by all accounts. The only positive indications are for burials and 'establishing placards' meaning setting up memorials. It can be taken as a good day for saving (hoarding), beginning a diet, or other regime, making resolutions. Or, for more positive actions, it could be a good idea for advertising, erecting signs, writing letters, or dealing with correspondence.

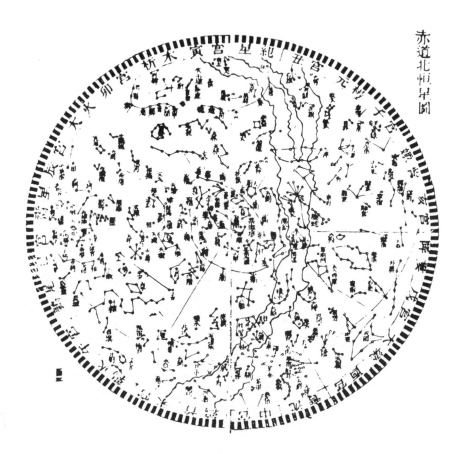

Celestial Map, showing the Celestial Equator and its relation to the
Celestial North Pole, at the centre.
The Celestial Equator is the arc in the lower half of the map.

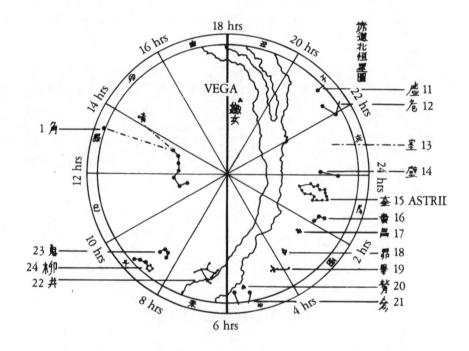

Left of centre can be seen the distinctive shape of the principal stars of the 'Great Bear.' The Milky Way runs top to bottom. Few of the other constellations have corresponding Western counterparts.

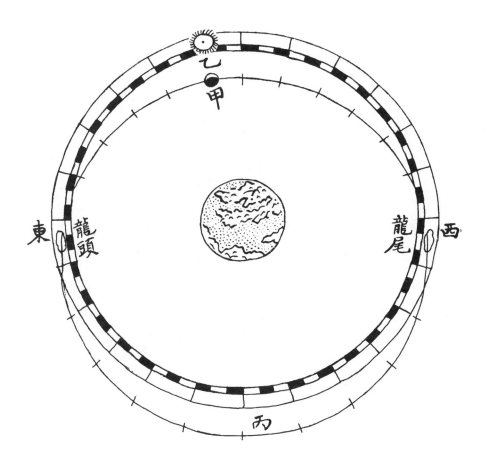

Diagram illustrating the Moons Nodes, (referred to here as the 'Head' and 'Tail' of the Dragon.)

Note. The cyclial characters Chia, I and Ping are here used to indicate features of the illustration, as (a), (b) and (c) might be used in Western books.

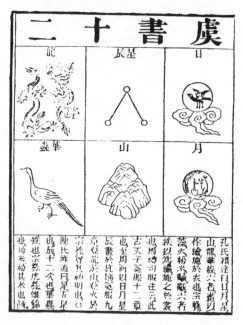

The Twelve Ritual Emblems of the Chou Dynasty. The Sun, Moon, and Stars, (symbolising Heaven) were depicted on banners; the Mountains, Dragon and Pheasant, on outer vestments; and the remaining six (ancestral vessels, duckweed, fire, grain, axe, and double bow) embroidered on inner or lower garments.

5.

EARLY CHINESE ASTRONOMICAL TEXTS

The Earliest Texts

The earlier chapters of this book have introduced the reader to the basic principles of Chinese astrology. I believe that the fullest understanding of the subject can only be obtained by studying the most authentic sources of information, and that these lie in the ancient texts themselves. Quite apart from the desirability of including source material as an aid to study, many of these passages are in fact a sheer delight to read, and give many fascinating sidelights on life in ancient China. I have included versions and commentaries on extracts from the following documents, the chronological order matching the order of length and complexity.

1. *Yao Tien* 'The Edicts of the Emperor Yao' Mythological period
2. *Hsia Hsiao Cheng* 'The Little Canon of the Hsia' Mythological period
3. *Yüeh Ling* 'Monthly Instructions' Early Chou dynasty.
4. *Huai Nan Tzu* 'The Book of the Prince of Huai Nan' Late Chou
5. The Book of Fan Sheng Chih
6. *Tien Kuan* 'The Officers of Heaven' by Ssu Ma Ch'ien, Han dynasty

The Yao Tien Calendar

Two of the oldest recorded passages dealing with Chinese astronomical observation are the *Hsia Hsiao Cheng* (the Minor Canon of the Hsia) and the *Yao Tien* (堯典), the 'Edicts of the Emperor Yao'. The dates of both of these texts are a mystery, but since the *Yao Tien* is the shorter of the two, it is dealt with here first.

The text is found in the first chapter of the *Shu Ching* (書經) the 'Book of Documents'. In essence, it is actually three separate passages which have become welded together. One is a folk-myth,

the second a series of astronomical observations, and the third a
passage on eclipses which was added at a later date in an antique
style, for reasons best known to its author.

First of all, the folk-myth. This presents, on the face of it, the edict
of the legendary Emperor Yao to his ministers, apparently six of them:
the three brothers Hsi and the three brothers Ho. They were accorded
the tasks of setting up observatories in different parts of the empire
in order to record simultaneous measurements of the sun's path (more
or less in the same way that Eratosthenes took measurements of the
sun in two locations simultaneously in order to measure the size of
the earth). Here then, is the 'Edict of Emperor Yao'.

> The Emperor Yao commanded Hsi and Ho to calculate the disposition
> of the sun, moon, stars, and planets (辰) and so manifest the seasons
> to all men.
>
> He then ordered the Younger Brother Hsi to stay with the Yü people
> at Yang Ku, there to receive the rising sun, and order the works of the
> East [taken to mean the Spring Equinox].
>
> Then he ordered Middle Brother Hsi to stay in South Chiao, there
> to attend to the [Summer] Solstice.
>
> Then he ordered the Younger Brother Ho to stay in the West at Mei
> Ku, and pay respect to the departing sun, and regulate the Autumn
> Equinox.
>
> Then he ordered Middle Brother Ho to stay in the North at Yu Tu,
> there to attend to the Winter Solstice.

Alas, this early edict to the ancestors of the Board of Astronomy is
nothing more than a confused retelling of an ancient folk-myth.
Hsi and Ho were not two families, nor did they have brothers. Hsiho,
one person, was the name of the Charioteer of the Sun — the Phaeton
of the Chinese Phoebus — and as such is to be found elsewhere in
Chinese literature.

Therefore we can pass on to the second part of the text, the
astronomical passage, which has enmeshed sinologists and
astronomers in a century of controversy. As the text is so short, the
Chinese text is given parallel with its translation.

日	中	星	鳥	'Alfard'
The day	of middle length;	the star	Niao (the Bird)	(a Hydrae)

	以	既	中	春
	by it	is regulated	the middle of Spring	

日	永	星	火	
The day	most long;	the star	Huo (the Fire Star)	(Antares)

	以	正	中	夏
	by it	is established	the middle of Summer	

夜	中	星	虛	'Sad-al-sud'
The night of the middle length;	the star	Hsü (Void)	(β Aquarii)	

	以	正	中	秋
	by it	is established	the middle of Autumn	

夜	永	星	昴
The night most long;	the star	Mao (Pleiades)	

	以	定	中	冬
	by it	is decided	the middle of Winter.	

歲	三	百	六	十	六	日
A year is	three hundred and sixty six days;					

以	閏	月	正	四	時
by	intercalary months are established the four seasons.				

Of the four stars mentioned, Hsü and Mao are the names of Hsiu 11 and 18 (q.v.) Niao Hsing, the Bird Star, is now simply known as the Star, Hsiu 25. Huo, the Fire Star, is Antares, and described in the remarks on Hsiu 4 and 5. The Bird Star and the Fire Star appear in the oracle bone text illustrated on page 19.

There has been a great deal of controversy among academics regarding the antiquity of the *Yao Tien*, proposed dates ranging over several thousand years. The methods of approach have varied from the linguistic (analyzing the significance of the verbs translated above as 'established' 'decided' and 'regulated') to theoretical astronomy. In making any suggestion regarding the origin of the *Yao Tien*, it has to be remembered that it was customary for the Chinese to use fixed points as the central marker of the time period, rather than the beginning (as with, for example, the equinoxes and the seasons, or midnight and the first double-hour).

Figure 5.1 The Emperor Yao, and the brothers Hsi and Ho.

It is therefore unlikely that 7am can be accepted as a time for making an astronomical observation. Furthermore, with regards to the time of observation, it must be remembered that observations can only be made of stars when they are actually visible: there is hardly any point in basing a theory on observations taken at 6pm in the evening or 6am in the morning, since it would not be possible to observe the skies at either of those times in the Summer — it would still be light. Consequently, it seems sensible to suppose that the observations given in the *Yao Tien* must have been made at midnight. From a simple planisphere, it is possible to see that at the present time, the Fire Star (Antares) is roughly 'central' at midnight on the night of the Summer Solstice. Therefore, it could not have been 'central' at midnight at any period in antiquity, if by 'central' is meant 'overhead'. Some other key must therefore be used to unlock this problem.

It is generally known that there are two stars in the Great Bear (The Northern Ladle) which are approximately in line with the Pole Star. The Great Bear rotates about the sky, and because it is 'circumpolar' is always visible at night in the Northern hemisphere. Indeed, during a total eclipse, it is visible in the daytime as well.

The first three stars of the 'Bear's Tail' are approximately in a straight line, after which they curve inwards. Anciently, the star Arcturus, Ta Chio, the brightest star in the Northern sky, was considered to be part of the 'Bear's Tail' but with the passage of time, this star is no longer circumpolar, and drops out of sight at certain times, and in certain seasons. When these times and seasons are can be determined by using the Bear's Tail as an astronomical clock. For example, in our present era, the first three stars of its tail will point to the left, that is westwards, at midnight on the day of the Autumn Equinox. They would also be in the same position at 6pm on the day of the Winter Solstice, and, although obscured by the light from the sun, at noon on the day of the Spring Equinox, and at 6am on the day of the Summer Solstice. Here are the four quadrature positions of the Bear's Tail for the four divisions of the day:

Direction of Bear's Tail as it *appears* in the sky	↑	←	↓	→
The direction in which it *actually* points:	South	West	North	East
The determining star:	鳥	火 (Antares)	虛	昴 (Pleiades)

Spring, 22 March	6am dawn	noon	6pm dusk	midnight
Summer, 21 June	midnight	6am day	noon	6pm day
Autumn, 21 September	6pm dusk	midnight	6am dawn	noon
Winter, 21 December	noon	6pm night	midnight	6am night

Arising out the diagram, and the astronomical timetable above, the following points can be established. Firstly, there are certain positions of the Bear's Tail which will be invisible at particular seasons; secondly, that the 6am and 6pm quadrants are sometimes night, and at other times either twilight or daytime. This is of course very relevant to the time of observation.

The next point to consider is the direction of the Bear's Tail, or rather, to establish which direction is indicated by the curve of the 'tail'. For the purposes of the diagram and the timetable above, only the stump of its tail has been considered; but in ancient times, the direction would have been shown by the end of the tail, in other words, those stars which line up with Arcturus, or Ta Chio, the 'Tip of the Horn' formerly regarded as part of the 'Northern Ladle' Pei Tou.

Now if the angle is measured between the direction shown by the stump of the Bear's Tail, and the direction shown by the 'Tip of the Horn' this angle would show by how much the earth's axis has moved (a movement resulting in what is known as the precession of the equinoxes) since the *Yao Tien* calendar was written. This angle is about 45°, so that at the rate of change of one degree every 71.6 years, the *Yao Tien* calendar would appear to have been written about 3222 years ago, i.e., *circa* 1700 BC.

I offer this date for what it is worth, because it seems to provide a much simpler solution to a problem which has puzzled scholars for more than a century. By taking in the four quadrants and the four seasons together, it obviates the vexing question of what hour of the day the observations were to be made, and whether the stars were seen as culminating (at their highest point in the sky) at 6pm, dusk, or whatever.

The Hsia Hsiao Cheng 夏小正

The second ancient document to be considered is the *Hsia Hsiao Cheng* (夏小正) or 'Minor Canon of the "Hsia" '. Hsia, which

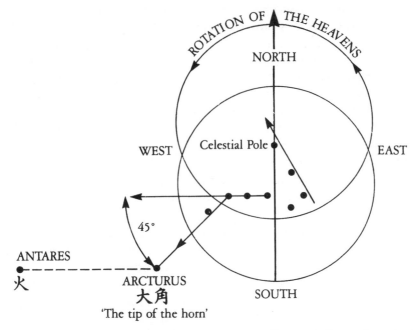

Figure 5.2 The Astronomical Clock (Schematic diagram). For explanation, see text.

means 'Summer' might be a reference to the people of the South, but it is usually taken to be a reference to the Hsia dynasty (2205 BC-1766 BC). The document is popularly, but not seriously, ascribed to the pen of Confucius (551-479 BC); Indeed it would appear to belong to a period anterior to that of the sage. Like the *Yao Tien*, the *Hsia Hsiao Cheng* has been the subject of much controversy and its date has been very difficult to determine. Although it is the longer of the two early documents, it may be older than the *Yao Tien*. Calculations based on the astronomical data contained in the *Hsia Hsiao Cheng* can only be very approximate. There are two important points to note: the first is the mention of certain constellations which are not given in the *Yao Tien*, and the possibility that certain obscure passages may refer to stars or star groups which have become known by other names.

A second important point is that there are references to observations of the stars 'at early dusk' (in the first month), 'at dusk' (in the sixth month), 'at dawn' (in the eighth month), and other places in the text. Obviously, here is ample evidence that observations were not restricted to a particular time of the day, but made continually. It would seem that this represents an alternative method of astronomical observation from that of the *Yao Tien*. The taking of observations at dusk and dawn is another indication that the *Hsia Hsiao Cheng* originated in Southern China, since it is considerably easier to observe the stars at sunset and sunrise in latitudes closer to the equator where the dusk is shorter and sharper, and the stars are more clearly seen in twilight. The northern preference for a circumpolar method of observation is due to the length of the twilight period, and the greater clarity of the stars in the higher heavens, even though it is more comfortable (for the neck muscles) to observe stars on the horizon.

The text of the *Hsia Hsiao Cheng* is met with in the *Ta Tai Li Chi*, the 'Rites of the Elder Tai', itself usually bound with the (*Hsiao Tai*) *Li Chi*, the 'Book of Rites (of the Younger Tai)'. These works, supposedly of the Former Han dynasty, were more probably compiled and edited in the first century of this era. There are, however, several pointers such as the philological and astronomical evidence which suggest an earlier date for parts of the texts. The text as a whole was incorporated into Chinese almanacs at a very early date. For example, the official almanac published by the Imperial Board of Astronomy in the Ching dynasty quotes the whole of the *Hsia Hsiao Cheng* complete. Almanacs of the present day divide the text up among the daily pages, brief quotations here and there, distinguished from the rest of the daily notes by being framed in a distinctive cartouche.

Although not all the *Hsia Hsiao Cheng* is concerned with the sciences of the heavens, some of the obscurer passages may also refer to astronomical events; as an example, the phrase 'chrysanthemums are then seen' seems to be an odd statement for the first month (January-February) even if it is translated by some other kind of flower. But the expression 'are then seen' (則見) is met with several times in the text with reference to the appearance of certain constellations in the sky. It could be therefore that the phrase refers to a star, or group of stars, which has since become known by another name.

The *Hsia Hsiao Cheng* underlines the philosophy that the works of Heaven and the Earth were forever interwoven; the Will of Heaven was manifested in the sky, and thus regulated the happenings of the Earth, whether these were the works of Nature or Man.

The calendar's curious natural history gives a further indication that the *Hsia Hsiao Cheng* originated in the South. Many of the botanical references are to plants which are to be found south of the Yang Tse, and certainly the fauna — monitors, lizards, and silkworms — are creatures which favour warmer climes.

In the *Hsia Hsiao Cheng* there are many examples of verbs being followed by the subject: 'migrate the wild geese', 'shed the muntjacks their horns'. This is not typical of Chinese, but is a feature of the Thai language, and Sino-Burmese border dialects, which may be a further indication of the document's provenance. But this may also be an antique style: the same features of word order can be found in the *Shih Ching*, The Book of Odes, generally regarded as a compilation of the oldest existing Chinese texts.

Despite attempts to date the calendar on its astronomical evidence, it has to be stressed that the actual observations are so vague that it is not even possible to date the millenium with any certainty. Those authorities who claim to have done so usually glide over several points. To begin with, the only thing which can be confidently said about the text is that it is incomplete. The absence of any astronomical observation for the twelfth month, and only the sketchiest reference to the eleventh, makes this clear enough. One can presume that the document was formerly extended, and that there were complementary astronomical references for each season of the year, as in the *Yao Tien*.

Secondly, the vagaries of the Chinese lunar calendar are such that an observation made, say, in the ninth month might correspond to the month of October in one year, late September in another, and early November in yet another year, while the various observations do not specify the date: only the approximate time of day. As has already been explained in the remarks on the *Yao Tien*, a discrepancy of only a month, (a twelfth of a circle, or thirty degrees) means an approximation of a thousand years either side!

The calculations used by sinologists and astronomers to date the text usually take the following course. At the present time, sunset occurs about 6pm on the day of the Spring Equinox, when Betelgeux, the bright star in Orion, is due South. Since, by the precession of the equinoxes, the position of the heavens alters by one month every 2,148 years, then Betelgeux would have been due South at *6pm* (not *dusk*, which would be 5pm) in the third week of February in about 250 BC. To account for the extra hour involves a further adjustment, so bringing the date to 1250 BC.

Much more important, rather than the date itself, are the constellations which are named, since their inclusion may throw some light on the antiquity of this work. Only a few star groups are identifiable: Shen (參), which is Orion; Tou (斗), later called Pei Tou, the Northern Ladle, to distinguish it from one of the lunar mansions, (Nan Tou, the Southern Ladle); Huo (火), Antares, and Mao (昴) the Pleiades, which are also met with in the *Yao Tien*. Another is the Weaving Girl (織女) Chih Nü, Vega α Lyrae, the second brightest star in the Northern Sky. Ch'en (辰) is a word which occurs frequently in old texts, and has several meanings depending on context. It is one of the cyclical numbers, (V in the series of Branches, equivalent to 7am-9am); it is used in the *Chou Li* (the Rites of the Chou) to mean 'planet', and occurs in the *Shih Chi* (Historical Records) as the name of the planet Mercury, or 'Morning Planet.' In the context of the *Hsia Hsiao Cheng*, it may mean the planet Mercury, or it could refer to some star or constellation which has not yet been identified. It has also been suggested that it refers to an eclipse of the sun.

The astronomical observations and gardening lore to one side, there remain the curious enumerations of various metamorphoses which are deemed to take place at different times of the year. For example, in the ninth month 'sparrows enter the sea and become molluscs'. Before such statements are dismissed out-of-hand as being ludicrous, it must be remembered that our own word 'barnacle' derives from the notion that these molluscs were a stage in the development of barnacle geese, the word 'barnacle' meaning 'goose' before it meant the mollusc which now bears the name.

To the ancients, such a transformation was no more remarkable than an egg turning into a chicken, or a caterpillar into a butterfly. What did astonish them was the fact that a hen could hatch out a duck's egg, or a cat act as foster mother to a pup. It was widely believed that maggots grew spontaneously from meat, and even today there are those who firmly believe that eating sugar gives one worms.

The metamorphoses therefore have to be taken at face value, without any attempt to misinterpret them. Such beliefs accounted for the disappearance of certain hibernating or migrating creatures, although oddly enough, as the document quite clearly states, the phenomena of hibernation and migration were well-known. See further references in the *Yüeh Ling*, e.g. the sixth month.

The Text of the Hsia Hsiao Cheng

The First Month . . . begins mid-January to mid-February.
1.   appear the hibernating insects,
2.   the wild geese go to their northern lands
        The northern lands are the breeding grounds of the geese, in Mongolia. They return south in the Ninth month.
3.   pheasants, drumming their wings, call,
4.   fish rise, bearing ice,
5.   the farmer binds his plough,

6. the beginning of the year is marked by the rite of ploughing,

7. in gardens, there are leeks to be seen,

8. the season has high winds,

9. the wintry sun changes the frozen wastes,

10. the field rats (?moles) come out

Later 'they turn into quails' and still later revert to their previous form.

11. the farmers get to work levelling the fields,

12. otters sacrifice fish

Otters, and bears, have a predilection for certain parts of the fish; having caught one, they would eat only the tastiest morsel, and leave the rest on the bank, which was taken by the early Chinese to be a food offering to the gods.

13. hawks now become crested hawks,

14. farmers go up to the snow line,

15. work begins in the common fields,

16. they pick rue

Rue was used as a dye, and as an insect repellant. See illustration, page 152.

17. chrysanthemums are now seen

According to the Chinese Encyclopaedia, the chrysanthemum, a native of Southern China, begins sprouting in the first month. But I suggest that this may be the name of a constellation or star; the form of the phrase is similar to other descriptions of astronomical phenomena.

18. **at early dusk, Orion is central**

Shen, Orion, is mentioned four times in the text: here, and later in lines 37, 61, and 99. The determinative star would appear to be Betelgeux.

19. **the Ladle handle points down**

Tou, the Ladle, is also referred to later in lines 77 and 90. For a description of its function as a kind of astronomical clock, see the introduction to the *Yao Tien*.

20. **willows come into bud**

'Willows budding' is appropriate for the season here, and there is no reason to suppose that the text refers to the lunar mansion, the Willow.

21. plums, apricots, and mountain peaches now blossom,

22. fruiting cyperus,

23. hens hatch chicks.

The Second Month . . . (March)

24.   working with the harrow, breaking up the ground,

25.   soon, fat lambs will no longer need their mother's care,

26.   at the 'flagstaff' there are many maidens and youths
        'Flagstaff' ceremonies are the equivalent of Maypole dances
        in Europe, although the season is earlier.

27.   on the day Ting Hai (丁亥) everyone goes to school.
        The meaning of Ting Hai is dealt with in the section on the
        calendar, page 337.

28.   sacrificing swordfish,
        See illustration, page 153).

29.   beautiful ixorae
        See illustration.

30.   they pluck the ailanthus
        That is the ailanthus glandulosa; used at sacrifices.

31.   swarms of tiny insects are tapping at their eggshells,

32.   descending swallows seek their nests,

33.   they flay eels,

34.   there are the cries of the orioles,

35.   beautiful rue
        See reference, line 16.

36.   now the panic grass can be seen, they begin to gather it.

The Third Month . . . (April)

37.   **Orion is now hidden**
        See remarks above, line 18.

38.   they gather the mulberry leaves,

39.   weeds and willows, (*or* drooping willows)

40.   butting sheep,

41.   mole-crickets now chirp,

42.   they distribute ice,

43.   they pluck the tacca

44.   young girls and boys tend the silkworm hatcheries,

45.   the matters of the silkworm farm are in hand,

46.   the sacrifice of wheat grains,

47.   in Yüeh there is a slight drought
        Yüeh is a region near Hong Kong; Kwantung, Annam. See
        also line 59.

48.   the field rats (moles) change, becoming quails,
        See references in line 10.

49.   the waving t'ung-tree and the plantain (*or* the waving
        t'ung-tree's trumpet-flowers)
        The reference may be to the tree's trumpet-like flowers, or to
        the plantain. See illustration on page 154.

50.   cooing pigeons.

The Fourth Month . . . (May)

51.   **The Pleiades are now seen**

This is the only mention of the Pleiades, which have a dominant role in the *Yao Tien* and other calendars. They must have been strategically placed, since they are usually found in the sky by reference to brighter stars, even though they form a distinctive cluster.

52.   **at early dusk, the Southern Gate**

Alpha and Beta Centauri (the Southern Gate) are two stars which just rise above the horizon at the latitude of Pekin, where they are among the remotest stars in the South, appearing for only an hour or two between the 22nd of November and the 22nd May. At sunset (8pm) on the 22nd of May they would be due South.

53.   chirping cicadas,

54.   in gardens, can apricots be seen,

55.   croaking green-frogs,

56.   **sovereign are the grasses and weeds**

Yew-weed = darnel (lolium); see illustration, page 155. It is possible that this line is a condensation of two other lines. In the Yüeh Ling (q.v.) for the fourth month the character 'Wang' (Sovereign) is followed by 'melon grows' after which come the next two characters for yew-weed and darnel, as here.

57.   **they pick hog-thistle**

See illustration, page 155.

58.   weeds obscure everything,

59.   **in Yüeh there is a great drought**

See reference above, line 47.

60.   **they catch, mount, and break in the colts.**

The Fifth Month . . . (June)

61. **Orion is now seen**
    See references above, line 18. At present, Betelgeux becomes visible in the night sky from about 5 August to 27 April.

62. gnats are abundant,

63. shrikes now call
    The sentence construction is interesting here; the word order is conventional.

64. **at this time of the year there are long days**
    This must be a reference to the Summer Solstice. Its equivalent is line 112, which oddly, appears in the tenth instead of the eleventh month. Some versions of the text include the line inserted between lines 115 and 116 in the text.

65. and, furthermore, melons,

66. the harmless cicada chirps
    'Harmless' cicada, to distinguish it from the 'poisonous' cicada, another species.

67. the rock-monitors abound. On the fifth day they congregate and at the full moon they hide.
    See illustration, page 156.

68. Burgeoning ruellia, and clematis
    See illustrations.

69. crested hawks become hawks
    See line 13.

70. the crested cicada chirps,

71. **at early dusk, the Great Fire Star is central**
    The Great Fire Star must be the Fire Star, Antares, of the *Yao Tien*. It subsequently became part of the lunar mansion Hsin, the Heart, Hsiu 5, although strictly speaking, being one of

the four determinative stars of the seasons it ought to have been part of Hsiu 4, the Room, Feng. This subject is dealt with in the section on the Hsiu.

72.   soya beans are boiled,
73.   they cook plums,
74.   they tend the vanilla plants,
75.   soya beans are boiled,
76.   they allocate the horses.

The Sixth Month . . . (July)

77.   **At dusk, the Ladle handle is exactly upright**
       See the references above, line 19.
78.   They boil peaches,
79.   the young hawks begin to seize their prey,

The Seventh Month . . . (August)

80.   Darnel, creepers, rushes,
81.   wild cats start to roam,
82.   low pools grow duckweed,
83.   bright, intense
       An expression which refers to the bright 'Indian Summer' of Autumn.
84.   duckweed, darnel,
85.   the (River) Han is contained by barriers
       Chinese commentators believe that this is a reference to the Milky Way; yet in the Ho Han Shu (the Book of the River Han) there is a description of the River, and its tendency to flood owing to the narrowness of the river mouth compared with the river upstream.
86.   Winter locusts chirp,
87.   **at early dusk, the Weaving Girl is exactly in the eastern region**

The Weaving Girl became Hsiu 10, the Maiden. See also line 114.

88.   the season has continual rain,
89.   an abundance of hog-thistles
See reference above, line 57, and illustration.
90.   **the Ladle points down; it is then dawn**
See references above, line 19.

The Eighth Month . . . (September)

91.   They slice melons,
92.   the black ones are examined,
93.   they cut open the ju-jubes,
94.   the rice-crops remain,
95.   **red birds, white birds**
A commentary suggests that the red birds are fireflies, and the white birds mosquitoes, which are apparently pursued and eaten by fireflies.
96.   **Ch'en is now hidden**
The problems in translating Ch'en have been mentioned in the introduction to the Hsia Hsiao Cheng. It has been suggested that Ch'en, in this context, may be the star Beta Corvi, which would be in keeping with the statement; possibly it refers to the planet Mercury.
97.   the deer-men go hunting,
98.   quails turn back into field rats (moles)
See further references above, line 47.
99.   **Orion is central, then it is dawn**
See references above, line 18.

The Ninth Month . . . (October)

100.   Indoors, fires,
101.   migrating wild geese
See a further reference, line 2.
102.   the Ruler of Heaven issues fire
This may mean the lighting of a temple fire, or it could be a reference to lightning storms which would be frequent at this season.
103.   ascending dark birds go into hibernation
'Black birds' = swallows.
104.   brown bears, spotted bears, panthers, martens, weasels, stoats, now go indoors.
105.   Beautiful chrysanthemums

See line 17. Here, however, chrysanthemums are appropriate
to the season. Chrysanthemum wine was supposed to guard
the drinker from disaster. See illustration below.

106.   **The King begins adorning,**
107.   **Ch'en is in conjunction with the Sun**
           See reference above, line 96. Here Ch'en cannot mean a star,
           and may either refer to an eclipse of the sun, or to a conjunction
           of the planet Mercury. Neither explanation is satisfactory,
           unfortunately.

108.   **Sparrows enter the sea and become molluscs**
           See the introduction to this section.

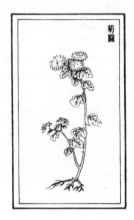

The Tenth Month . . . (November)
109.   **Polecats sacrifice animals**
           See the reference to otters, line 12. Polecats, even more curiously,
           were thought to catch animals and arrange them in the form
           of a square, the symbol of the Earth.

110.   **at early dusk, the Southern Gate is seen**
111.   **black birds skim,**
112.   **the season has long nights**
           If this is a reference to the Winter Solstice (see above, line 64)
           it is in the wrong month.

113.   **pheasants enter the sea and become irises**
           According to the Shan Hai Ching (山氵身矢) the Classic of
           Seas and Mountains, a work of the Chou or Han dynasty,
           if pheasants do not enter the sea and become irises, lascivious
           women will multiply in the country!

114.   **the Weaving Girl is exactly in the northern region, then
           it is dawn**
           See reference above, line 87.

The Eleventh Month . . . (December)

115.   The King goes hunting, (the Winter limit of the Sun)
        See the reference above, line 112.
116.   Summons to the sinews and skin, (marshalling the able-bodied)
117.   the weak man does not follow,
118.   shedding of the muntjack's horns
        This line is identical to line 123.

The Twelfth Month . . . (January)

119.   The crying of gannets,
120.   the dark colts are eager,
121.   they collect garlic bulbs,
122.   the game wardens survey the Leang Park,
123.   shedding of the muntjack's horns
        This line is identical to line 118.

The Monthly Instructions

YÜEH   LING

月   令

A later calendar, similar to the *Hsia Hsiao Cheng,* but considerably longer, is the *Yüeh Ling,* or Monthly Instructions. This exists in two versions, one of which appears in the 'Rites of Tai the Younger' (usually called the *Li Chi,* or *Li Ki*). The other version is to be found in 'The Spring and Autumn Annals of Master Lu', the *Lü Shih Ch'ün Ch'iu.* This latter work is lengthened by a considerable volume of commentary following each chapter of the *Yüeh Ling.* Since the date of Lü Shih's compilation is known to be 240 BC, it follows that the

Yüeh Ling itself must be older.

The six chapters of the *Yüeh Ling* cover the twelve months, divided into four seasons. Each season is shown to be proper to one of four of the five elements, the Earth element not being accorded a season.

The six chapters of the *Yüeh Ling* are not distributed equally among the twelve months. The first chapter deals only with the first month of Spring; chapters II, III, IV, and V are accorded two months each, and the final chapter deals with the three Winter months.

The 'Instructions' for each month begin with astronomical phenomena (discussed below) followed by a number of 'natural history' paragraphs, similar to those in the *Hsia Hsiao Cheng*. Some of these are almost identical to the earlier work, but there are occasional variations in the flora and fauna described, and a great amount of extra material. There are two places where these 'natural history' paragraphs occur, the second one being somewhat subordinate to the first. This thus provides phenomena for each of the twenty-four 'fortnights' or Ch'i of the Chinese calendar. More is said about these fortnights in the section on Jupiter in the treatise by Ssu Ma Ch'ien on page 192. The first chapter of the *Yüeh Ling*, dealing with the first month, gives the pattern for the remaining months. Repetitious data concerning the colours, sounds, and other matters appropriate to the month or season have been gathered together here in a table for easy reference. One matter of great interest is the nature of the sacrificial meal, which some think to have been the origin of the twelve animals in the 'Chinese zodiac.'

The data concerning the Earth element appears in the text as a paragraph added to the 'Instructions' for the sixth month.*

Each month's 'Instructions' refer to the constellation in which the Sun appears, and as the Sun cannot be seen at night, this is a matter which must have been calculated by default. It is possible that the apparatus known as the 'divining board' was used to establish this matter. The text also gives the equatorial constellations on the meridian at dusk and dawn. As has already been mentioned, these times vary from day to day, 4pm and 8am in Winter, 8pm and 4am in Summer. Nearly all, but not all, the Hsiu are named in the text, as well as other constellations which may have been antecedents of the Hsiu. Several Hsiu appear as meridian stars or solar mansions, but no Hsiu appears three times. Curiously enough, the Pleiades,

---

* A full translation of the *Yüeh Ling* can be found in the *Li Ki* volume of the monumental series *Sacred Books of the East*. See bibliography: Legge, J.

Hsiu 18, which play such an important role in the astronomy of the *Hsia Hsiao Cheng,* are absent from the *Yüeh Ling.*

Altogether, only five of the twenty-eight lunar mansions have not yet appeared: these are Hsiu 5, Hsin, the Heart; Hsiu 7, Chi, the Winnowing Basket; Hsiu 18, Mao, the Pleiades; Hsiu 23, Kuei, the Ghost Carriage; and Hsiu 26, Chang, the Drawn Bow. Of these, the place of Hsiu 5 is taken by the Fire Star, Ta Huo (Antares) which was formerly part of Hsiu 4 but now in Hsiu 5; Chien Hsing, the 'Determinative Star', is close to the constellations Chi (Hsiu 7) and Tou (Hsiu 8) and thus replaces Hsiu 7. It is interesting to note that this constellation should be called 'Determining' indicating that its importance was not in its prominence in the sky, but its strategic position. The constellation Hu (the Bow, of a group known as the Bow and Arrow) is a neighbour of constellations Ching (the Well) and Kuei (Ghost Carriage), Hsiu 22 and 23 respectively. These two constellations are virtually the same as the zodiacal constellations Gemini and Cancer. However, while Ching and Kuei stride the ecliptic, Hu is much more an equatorial constellation.

There does not seem to have been room to include Chang, the Drawn Bow; a glance at the second table will show why. In the region of Chang, the Hsiu which are present are not only close on each others heels, but they are repeated in the table. The name 'Drawn Bow' is so similar in meaning to that of 'The Bow' that it would seem that the concept of the determining constellation whose name was a 'bow' had shifted from one group to another.

Thus the only constellation not accounted for is Mao, the Pleiades, its absence perhaps as revealing as the dog which did not bark in the night.

The first table shows all the constellations mentioned in the opening formulae to each month of the *Yüeh Ling*; 'The Sun is in . . ., at dusk . . . is central; at dawn . . . is central.'

The second table shows, for convenience of reference, the sequence of the constellations which have been mentioned in the *Yüeh Ling.*

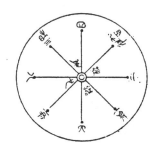

The Determining Constellations in the Yüeh Ling

MONTH	Sun in Hsiu	Central at dusk Hsiu	Central at dawn Hsiu
I	室 13 Shih, the House	參 21 Shen, Orion	尾 6 Wei, the Tail
II	奎 15 K'uei, Astride	弧 — Hu, The Bow	建 — Chien, Determiner
III	胃 17 Wei, the Stomach	七星 25 Chi Hsing, Seven Stars	牛 9 Niu, the Ox-Boy (Altair)
IV	畢 19 Pi, the Net (Hyades)	翼 27 I, the Wing	女 10 Nü, the Weaving Girl
V	井 22 Ching, the Well	亢 2 K'ang, the Neck	危 12 Wei, Danger
VI	柳 24 Liu, the Willow	火 — Huo, Antares	奎 15 K'uei, Astride
VII	翼 27 I, the Wing	建 — Chien, Determiner	畢 19 Pi, the Net (Hyades)
VIII	角 1 Chio, the Horn	牛 9 Niu, the Ox-Boy (Altair)	觜 20 Tsui, Turtle
IX	房 4 Fang, the Room	虛 11 Hsü, Void	柳 24 Liu, the Willow
X	尾 6 Wei, the Tail	危 12 Wei, Danger	七星 25 Chi Hsing, Seven Stars
XI	斗 8 Tou, the Measure	壁 14 Pi, the Wall	軫 28 Chen, the Carriage-board
XII	女 10 Nü, the Weaving Girl	婁 16 Lou, the Mound	氐 3 Ti, the Base

The Sequence of Constellations

An asterisk * indicates that the constellation is mentioned in two places.

Sun in	Central at dusk	Central at dawn	Not mentioned
1	2	3	
4	5 (a)	6*	
6*			7
8	9*	9*	
10*		10*	
	11	12*	
12*			
13	14	15*	
15*	16		
17		19*	18
19*	21 (b)	20	
22		24*	23
24*	25*	25*	26
27*	27*	28	

Note a) Place taken by Antares in Hsiu 5.
   b) Out of sequence.

YÜEH LING
月令壹

Instructions for the First Month
The first month of Spring, the sun is in Ying Shih (Hsiu 13). At dusk Shen (Hsiu 21) is central; at dawn Wei (Hsiu 6) is central.

(*Favourable*) days are Chia (甲)(Cyclical sign 1) and I (乙)(Cyclical sign 2).

Its sovereign is T'ai Hao; the presiding spirit is Chou Mang.

Its particular creatures are scaly animals.

Its corresponding note is Chio; the pitch T'ai Ch'ou. (See page 77.)

Its number is 8; its flavour sour; its odour rancid.

Its place of sacrifice is the interior door; the offering is the spleen.

The wind lessens the frost.

Hibernating insects begin to move.

Fish rise bearing ice.

The otter sacrifices fish.

The wild geese return. (*Note: no mention of 'Northern Home' as in the Hsia Hsiao Cheng*).

The Son of Heaven occupies the apartment on the left of the Ch'ing Yang. (*The Imperial Palace, where audiences were given and sacrificial rites carried out, was divided into a magic square of nine spaces. The apartment particular to the first month was the Eastern one.*)

His carriage is decorated with little bells, is drawn by an azure dragon, and carries an azure standard decorated with dragons. His garments are azure, decorated with azure gemstones. (青 *can mean sky-blue or sea-green*).

His food is corn and mutton.

Utensils are carved and decorated in relief with buds.

In this month is the rite of the inauguration of Spring.

Three days beforehand, the Grand Secretary announces to the Son of Heaven 'On such a day is the Inauguration of Spring. The Virtue of the season is seen in Wood.'

On hearing this news, the Son of Heaven gives himself to purification. The day of the Inauguration of Spring, he leads the Three Dukes, the Nine Ministers, the Princes and the Officials to meet the Spring in the Eastern suburb.

On his return, he rewards them all in court.

He orders the ministers to publish their instructions, to adjust any regulations, thank those who have done well, and bestow favours on them, and listen to the pleas of the people. Thus everyone is rewarded according to his degree. He orders the Grand Secretary to protect the laws and statutes. And to observe the passage of the Sun, the Moon, the Stars, and Planets, and the constellations where they are to be found, in order that there should be no error, and the records kept in accordance with the practice of former times.

On the day Yuan (*the first day with the Stem Hsin, 8*) the Son of Heaven prays for a prosperous year. Then, on the day Yuan Chen (*the first day with the Branch Hai*, XII) the ceremonial ploughing is performed.

The handle of the plough is put between the driver of the carriage and the guardsman in the carriage; he leads the three ministers of state, the nine other ministers, the princes and the high officers, and himself ploughs the field of the Great Sovereign. The Emperor ploughs three furrows, then the three High Ministers five furrows each, then the other ministers and the princes nine furrows each. Then the Emperor returns to his principal apartment where the Emperor offers them all refreshment, saying 'I offer you this cup in return for your exertions.'

In this month, Heaven's vapours descend and Earth's vapours ascend. Heaven and Earth are in harmony. All plants bud and grow. The Emperor orders farming to commence. Inspectors of the fields are ordered to take up residence in the lands to the East of the capital; all hedges, ditches, and borders have to be marked out and cleared.

Hills, slopes, plains and marshes have all to be inspected to determine what kinds of crops will be best suited to them. The officers must instruct and guide the people, and lead by example.

When the fields have been reviewed and marked out, the labourers can set to work without wastage.

In this month the Grand Inspector of Music is instructed to enter the colleges and rehearse the dances.

Sacrificial rites are reviewed. Orders are given for offerings to be made to the spirits of mountains, forests, waters and lakes.

It is prohibited to make an offering of female animals. (*Eggs, the unborn and the young were proscribed; females might be carrying young; see below*).

It is prohibited to cut down trees.

One must watch that nests are not destroyed; unhatched insects must not be destroyed; unborn young must not be destroyed; birds learning to fly must not be destroyed; nor young deer nor eggs. Also prohibited is the assembling of large crowds; nor are great building projects carried out. (*The reason being, that all able-bodied men should be at work in the fields ploughing and repairing fields.*)

Bones and flesh are buried.

In this month it is prohibited to take up arms; whoever takes up arms will be punished by Heaven. But it is not prohibited to defend the realm against hostilities.

Do not change the ways of Heaven; do not break off the functions of the Earth; do not confound the regularity of men's purpose.

In the first month of Spring, if the Emperor performed any

functions which are proper to the Summer, then rain would not appear in its season; plants would die quickly; and the country would be in fear.

If the works proper to Autumn are carried out, there would be a plague; boisterous winds would wreak havoc, rain would be torrential, and orach, fescue, darnel and southernwood would run wild. If the works proper to Winter were carried out, there would be destruction by flooding, snow and frost would return and the first sown seeds would not take root in the ground.

Abridgements of the 'Instructions' for months two to twelve.

In the second month . . .
Rain begins to fall,
peach trees blossom,
the oriole sings,
hawks become crested hawks.

In this month, budding plants and new growth must be carefully protected. Nourish the young and newly born; consider the welfare of orphans.

In this month, the swallows return. The day of their arrival, an ox, a ram and a pig are sacrificed to the god of marriage and birth. The Empress takes nine ladies of the second rank, and all the concubines, to dine, and gives quivers of arrows to all those who have conceived in honour of the god of birth.

(*The quiver of arrows is reminiscent of the European gods Eros and Cupid*).

In this month the equinox occurs. Thunder is heard, lightning strikes. Hibernating animals begin to move, and opening the mouths of their caves, come out into the open.

Three days before the beginning of the thunder, the herald will strike a bell, and sound the wood-blocks, and announce: 'If there are any women who have been unwise in their conduct, they will give birth to malformed children.'

At the Equinox, all weights and measures are tested, and adjusted if inaccurate.

(*This is a very significant passage. The equality of day and night is seen as a symbolic time to regulate balances, but it also served to ensure that weights and measures were tested on the same day of the year, thus helping to secure comparable environmental conditions — temperature, humidity, atmospheric pressure and so on. It has been suggested by Schlegel, in his monumental work on*

Chinese astronomy, that the constellation Libra derived its name from being the part of the zodiac occupied by the sun at the time of the equinox. As the equinoxes occur in Pisces or Leo at present, this would mean that the name of the 'balances' was given to the 'equinoctial' part of the zodiac either a thousand years ago or, at the other extreme, 13,000 years ago, when Libra would have corresponded with the Spring Equinox. As the zodiac has been recorded thousands of years before the present time, clearly the former date is untrue. But with regards to the zodiac having been invented 13,000 years ago, this is generally regarded as impossible. Schlegel, however, did propose further very intriguing evidence for his theory. But again, the question arises of when observations were made — whether the constellation was rising, or at mid-point in the heavens.

In this month, farmers rarely remain indoors. One may repair doors of wood and wicker, or rearrange the disposition of the interiors of houses. But no large undertakings which take men away from their farming duties must be put in hand.

On the first of the days denoted by the Stem 4, (Ting 丁), the Grand Inspector of Music tests students on their progress in singing, after which he offers watercress and edible seaweed to the God of Music. The Son of Heaven, the three principal ministers of State, nine other ministers, all the feudal princes, and all the Grand Officials also take part in the ceremony. On the second Ting day, the Grand Inspector of Music goes to the college to teach music.

In this month no animals are offered in sacrifice. Instead the jade ornaments Kuei and Pi are offered.

If in the second month, works proper to Summer are carried out, there will be flooding and cold winds, and armed robbery will be rife. If the business of Winter is done, the warm weather will not come nor the corn ripen and robbers will be everywhere.

If the business of Spring is carried out, the hot weather will come too soon, there will be drought, and pests pollute the grain.

In the third month . . .

the field rats (moles) change, becoming quails,
rainbows are seen,
duckweed begins to cover the water.

The Inspector of Boats must upturn all boats and inspect the bottoms five times. When they are judged to be ready, the Emperor makes his first journey by boat and offers a sturgeon in the Hinder Chamber of the Ancestral Temple, asking the gods for a good grain harvest.

The Superintendent of Public Works gives orders for all watercourses to be inspected, banks repaired, and all drains and ditches unblocked.

(There are then further instructions to the silkworm industries, and various trades inspectors.)

At the end of the month, at a suitable time, a Grand Concert is arranged, to be attended by the Son of Heaven, the three Grand Ministers, the nine other ministers, and all the feudal princes of the court. If in the third month, works proper to Winter are carried out, it will become cold, vegetation will perish, and the people will be in fear. If the business of Summer is done, plagues will trouble the people, there will be no rain, and nothing will be produced.

If the business of Autumn is done, fogs will occur, the rains will be early, and war break out.

In the fourth month . . .

肆
> green frogs croak,
> earthworms come out,
> melons ripen,
> darnel and yew weed grow.

The Son of Heaven offers pulse and chicken in sacrifice.

The Grand Inspector of Music is ordered to teach the ritual music. Fields are cleared of wild animals which might damage crops, but there must be no hunting on a big scale.

In this month, medicinal herbs are collected. Delicate plants may die.

> This is the season of the corn harvest.
> Only minor crimes are tried, and only small punishments allotted.
> Prisoners serving sentences for minor crimes are released.
> Silkworm culture is now finished.

If in the fourth month, works proper to the Autumn are carried out, there will be much rain, and crops not ripen. Frontier dwellers will be forced to take refuge in fortified positions.

If the business of Winter be done, plants will dry out, great flooding will wash away earthworks.

If the business of Spring be done, locusts will ravage the crops, the wind become violent, and flowering crops not come to fruition.

In the fifth month . . .

伍
> the mantis appears,
> the magpie cries,
> but the mynah is not heard.

The Grand Inspector of Music is ordered to repair the tambourines and the drums, tune the stringed instruments and the double-flutes, tune the large and small mouth organs, the traverse flutes, the reed instruments, and put in order the bells, the lithophones, gongs, and tiger-scraper.

It is forbidden to cut indigo, make charcoal, or put cloth out to bleach in the sun.

No customs dues are to be levied at markets. Prisoners undergoing hard labour may have their sentences lightened and their rations increased.

This month, the days are longest.

Hermits must keep to their cells; they are not to be aroused by sensual sights or sounds.

No fires are to be lit in places exposed to the South (*no doubt for fear of forest and grass fires*).

If in the fifth month, the works proper to Winter are carried out, hail will destroy the harvest, and roads become impassable.

If the business of Spring is done, grain will develop late, all kinds of locusts will appear, and famine will spread.

If the business of Autumn is done, plants will drop their leaves, fruit arrive too early, and plagues trouble the populace.

In the sixth month . . .

 the cricket sits in the walls,
young hawks begin to seize their prey,
rotting vegetation turns into glow worms.
(*It is a fact that certain fungi growing on rotten wood are luminous, and this may have led to the belief that glow-worms were generated in this way.*)

The Inspector of Fisheries orders the destruction of crocodiles, the collection of certain lizards, the collection of tortoises (*for divination*) and the collection of giant turtles (*to be eaten*).

In this month, the Inspectors of Female Labour gives order for the silk to be dyed in various colours according to the custom of ancient times. It is forbidden to deviate from these rules.

The dyes used must be of the finest quality, and care must be taken not to use inferior colours. With the silk thread are woven the fabrics for the various robes of the officials of different ranks.

No earthworks must be undertaken, nor troops sent to war, since all labour is needed for the harvest. If men are taken from their work in the fields, there will be floods. If any great undertaking is put under way, Heaven will send calamities.

Earth is central.
The days peculiar to the Earth are those with the Stems Wu and
Chi. To Earth corresponds the number 5, the sweet flavour, and the
perfumed odour . . . (*see table, page 174*).

The Emperor's sacrificial meal is beef with yellow millet.

If in the sixth month, works proper to the Spring are carried out,
the cereals in grain will fail. The multitudes will be cold, and people
leave their homes.

If the business of Autumn is carried out, hills and valleys will be
flooded, and the harvest not grow. There will be frequent accidents
to women.

If the business of Winter be carried out, there will be unseasonable
cold winds, and hawks and falcons will seize young birds.

In the seventh month . . .
> A cool wind blows,
> white frost is formed,
> the cicada chirps,
> the hawk sacrifices birds.

In this month, the generals are ordered to conscript men into military
service. The Emperor metes out punishments to the oppressor and
disobedient. He makes his desires known clearly, and listens to the
pleas of the people, even the most distant.

The Inspector of Punishments must repair the prisons, procure
shackles and fetters, prevent crimes, seek out and punish the guilty.
Judges must examine bruises, wounds, fractures, and mutilations,
in order that trials are fair and consistent, and the guilty punished
in accordance with the severity of their crimes. Heaven and Earth
both make their severity known.

The Emperor's sacrifice is dogmeat, cooked with millet.

The officers receive the taxes; walls and embankments are inspected
to prevent flooding after the heavy rains.

No new officials or posts are to be created, nor grand presents
offered.

If in the first month of Autumn, works proper to the Winter are
carried out, then the Yin force will prove too active. Insects will eat
stored grain, there will be a drought, and war devastate the country.

If the business of Spring is done, then the Yang force will
predominate, and the harvest will not produce enough grain.

If the works proper to Summer are done, then fire will ravage the country, and the people become fevered.

In the eighth month . . .

捌 A stormy wind blows,
wild geese arrive,
swallows return South.

In this month, care is given to the aged and destitute. Each one is given food, a table, and firewood.

The officials review the laws, and condemn to death those that have deserved the sentence. Heaven will send dire punishments if the judges are unjust.

This is the time to construct barricades in and out of the cities, to found new towns, dig tunnels, and construct granaries. Seeds are sown at a favourable time. The opportune moment must not be missed.

In this month the Equinox occurs. Thunder ceases; decaying forces increase, active forces decrease.

At the Equinox, weights and measures are adjusted and regulated. If in the second month of Autumn, works proper to the Spring are carried out, there will be no rain, plants and trees blossom (*when they should be fruiting*) and the country put into turmoil.

If the works proper to Summer are carried out, then drought will ruin the State, and the crops turn spindly.

If the works proper to Winter are carried out, there will be gales, and plants will die early.

In the ninth month . . .

玖 Geese call on their way South,
Sparrows dive into the Great Water and become molluscs
(*The Hsia Hsiao Cheng has 'Sea'*)
The polecat sacrifices smaller animals
(*during the tenth month in the Hsia Hsiao Cheng*).

All the harvest and tribute is now counted. The white frost begins to form and all labour in the fields ceases. Officers have orders to release men to return to their homes.

On the first Ting day, the Grand Inspector of Music receives orders to visit the colleges and test pupils on their playing of wind instruments.

All officers are allocated their duties, and the calendar for the following year is published.

In this month the king leads his officers in the hunt.

All matters to do with horses and carriages are attended to.

In this season, leaves turn yellow and fall. Wood is cut for charcoal.

If the works proper to Summer are now carried out, the country will be flooded, the Winter stores rot, and people die of pneumonia.

If the works proper to Winter are now carried out, there will be robbers, troubled frontiers, and lost territories.

If the works proper to the Spring are now carried out, men will become enfeebled, and the army weak.

In the tenth month . . .

拾

Water begins to freeze,
Pheasants enter the Great Water to become irises.
(*The Hsia Hsiao Cheng has 'Sea' here.*)
Rainbows are no longer seen.

Orders are given to the following effect: Heaven and Earth no longer work together; their ways are closed. Thus is the beginning of Winter.

The granaries have to be carefully covered. Walls are repaired. Locks and keys are examined, and surveys made of barriers and bridges.

The Emperor's sacrifice to his ancestors is pork with millet.

In this month the Grand Secretary receives the order to daub the tortoise carapaces with the blood of a sacrificial victim, to interpret the signs of the tortoise, and to interpret the divination by milfoil stalks. By this means flatterers and conspirators are revealed.

The ceremonies concerning mourning are examined and revised.

The Inspector of Public Works prepares his report. He must be careful to ensure that no-one makes or designs objects which are likely to arouse covetousness and a love of luxury. All objects must bear the name of the craftsman, so that in the case of faulty workmanship the offender can be reprimanded. The Son of Heaven prays that the following year will be propitious.

The Chiefs of Staff give orders for military exercises and manoeuvres; training the soldiers in bowmanship and chariot driving. Competitive events will be organized.

The Inspector of Fisheries will examine rivers and waterways.

If, in the first month of Winter, the works proper to Spring are carried out, the frost will not properly cover the ground, and the evil exhalations from the earth will be noxious.

If the works proper to Summer are carried out, there will be frequent gales, the weather will prove unseasonably warm and insects come out.

If the works proper to Autumn are carried out snow and ice will not arrive at the proper time. Attacks on the State will be frequent, and territory will be lost.

In the eleventh month . . .

拾　　the ice thickens,
　　　the ground splits open,
弍　　the dawn herald no longer crows,
　　　tigers begin mating.

The Rites for the year are reviewed.

Orders are given to prohibit earthworks and excavations. If ground is broken, Earth vapours will be dissipated, hibernating insects die, and epidemics spread.

In this month the Chief Eunuch receives instructions to examine all doors and fastenings, making sure that all fit properly.

Women's crafts are inspected, and they are warned against producing anything too elaborately ornamented or luxurious.

This applies to all women, of whatever rank.

In this month is the shortest day. Yin and Yang are in conflict. At the solstice trees may be cut down, bamboo gathered.

Doors are shuttered, gates closed, and prisons rebuilt. This is so that Earth and Heaven, which has stopped issuing, will be in harmony.

If, during the last month of Winter, works proper to the Summer are carried out, there will be drought, thick fog, and thunder.

If the business of Autumn be done, there will be sleet, melons will not grow to maturity, and wars break out.

If the business of Spring be done, locusts will wreak havoc, water courses will be polluted, and there will be outbreaks of scabies and leprosy.

In the twelfth month . . .

拾　　Wild geese travel northwards,
　　　magpies build their nests,
式　　pheasants cry,
　　　hens sit.

The Emperor orders Grand ceremonies to disperse plagues. He then takes a clay bull by means of which the Winter Vapours are dispersed.

Birds of prey become ferocious.

The Inspector of Fisheries declares the fishing season open. Ice is abundant, and on rivers and lakes very deep. Orders are given for the ice to be cut and stored.

Agricultural implements are repaired.

The Grand Inspector of Music is ordered to give the End of the Year Concert.

The Seasonal Attributes as Given in the Yüeh Ling

Attribute	Spring	Summer	EARTH	Autumn	Winter
Direction	東 East	南 South	中 Centre	西 West	北 North
Element	木 Wood	火 Fire	土 Earth	金 Metal	水 Water
Cyclical numbers	甲乙 1 2	丙丁 3 4	戊己 5 6	庚辛 7 8	壬癸 9 10
Emperor	太 皥 T'ai Hao	炎 帝 Yen Ti	黃 帝 Huang Ti	小 皥 Hsiao Hao	顓 頊 Chuan Hü
Guardian spirit	句 芒 Ku Meng	祝 融 Chou Yung	后 土 Hou T'u	蓐 收 Ju Shou	玄 冥 Hsüan Ming
Animal	鱗 Scaly	羽 Feathered	倮 Hairless	毛 Furry	介 Armoured
Tone	角 Chio	徵 Chih	宮 Kung	商 Shang	羽 Yü
Number	八 8	七 7	五 5	九 9	六 6
Taste	酸 Sour	苦 Bitter	甘 Sweet	辛 Musty	鹹 Salt
Smell	羶 Rancid	焦 Burnt	香 Perfume	腥 Raw	朽 Rotten
Place of sacrifice	戶 Doors	竈 Hearth	幡 Centre	門 Gates	行 Passageways
Viscera	肝 Liver	心 Heart	脾 Spleen	肺 Lungs	腎 Kidneys
Colour	青 Azure	赤 Red	黃 Yellow	白 White	黑 Black
Sacrificial Meal	羊 Mutton	雞 Chicken	牛 Beef	犬 Dog	彘 Pork

In this month, the Sun finishes its course; the Moon completes its cycle of twelve; the reckoning of days is almost ended; the Year gives way to the beginning of another. It is announced to the farmers that having completed their tasks, they are not to be given others.

The affairs for the following year are studied, and the order of work for the New Year prepared.

If in the last month of Winter, the works of the Autumn are put in hand, then there will be white frost, and a multitude of scaly creatures will appear.

If the business of Spring is done, then there will be many stillbirths and chronic illnesses, and Heaven will not be propitious.

If the works of the Summer are performed, then there will be torrential rain and the snow will not fall, the ice will melt and a thaw set in.

淮南子

The Huai Nan Tzu Treatise on Astrology

There are several other texts of the early Han period and before. Contemporary with Mencius (372-289 BC) were three famous astronomers, Shih Shen 石申, Kan Teh 甘德 and Wu Hsien 巫咸. Their star catalogues appear to have been successfully handed down, lost, restored and lost again over the dynasties. Fragments, however, are known to exist in certain extant documents: the *Chin Shu* ('Annals of the Chin Dynasty', written in the seventh century AD); the *K'ai Yuan Chan Ching* 開元占經 (The K'ai Yuan Dynasty Divination Classic) written in the eighth century AD; the *Hsing Ching* 星經 *(Star Classic) found in the Taoist Patrology under the title T'ung Chan Ta Hsiang Li Hsing Ching.* 通占大衆曆星經 Collection of Great Calendar and Star Classics; compiled in the ninth century and in a manuscript discovered at Tun Huang, dating from the late ninth/early tenth century. These older works would undoubtedly have been referred to by the compilers of all astronomical texts from the Han dynasty onwards, indirectly if not directly.

Two of the most important astronomical/astrological works, both in themselves complete treatises, were compiled during the reign of the Han Emperor Wu Ti; these are the Book of the Prince of Huai Nan, and the treatise by Ssu Ma Ch'ien, the Imperial Astrologer to the Court of Emperor Wu Ti.

In 122 BC, Liu An, the Prince of Huai Nan, grandson of the great Liu Pang (who founded the Han dynasty), and (since the Emperor Wu Ti had no heir of his own) in direct line to the throne, finally succeeded in distilling the Elixir of Life. Rather than order a minion to test the precious draught, the Prince quaffed the potion himself, lest the experiment, proving successful, should somewhat embarrassingly bestow the gift of immortality on a mere commoner. To the astonishment of his attendants, the Prince was immediately transformed and lifted heavenwards. The goblet in which the essence had been distilled fell from his grasp on to the courtyard below, whereupon investigating dogs, lapping up the few spilt dregs, were suddenly whisked aloft in the wake of their master. So, according to legend, occurred the remarkable apotheosis of the Prince of Huai Nan.

Like his uncle the Emperor, the Prince was a philosopher, gathering at his court an assembly of sages, magicians, and practisers of the arts and sciences of astrology and alchemy. His compilation of a number of treatises on both natural and supernatural topics became simply known as the *Huai Nan Tzu*, although it is more properly known by its title, the *Hung Lieh Chuan* (鴻烈傳) the 'Vast and Eminent Chronicle'. It contains what must be the oldest complete astrological treatise still extant, antedating the treatise by Ssu Ma Ch'ien, although both the Prince and the Imperial Astrologer must have drawn on the same original sources. The *Huai Nan Tzu* contains the germs of that particular Chinese form of divination known as 'Fate Calculation.'

In addition to the passages which follow, there are several other quotations from the *Huai Nan Tzu* throughout the present work, and the reader is referred to the Index.

Extracts from the Huai Nan Tzu Treatise on Astrology

(i) The tilt of the Earth

Long ago, Kung Kung rebelled against Chüan Hsü to gain the empire. He struck his head against the Imperfect Mountain and caused it to fall down. Heaven's links with the Earth were broken, and the Earth toppled over to the North-West.

That is why the Sun, Moon, and Planets are to one side, and why the Earth is bare in the South-East, and why the waters ran away to form seas.

The Tao of Heaven is circular; the Tao of Earth is square.

The Square presides over concealment; the Circle presides over brightness.

The brightness emits Ch'i, (*see the section on aura in the treatise by Ssu Ma Ch'ien for an explanation of the meanings of this term.*)

Hence Fire is the Outer force.
The concealed retained Ch'i; Hence Water is the Inner force.

(ii) The interaction of Heaven and Earth

Men's lives are reflected in the movements of Heaven.
When there is cruelty and violence, there will be violent winds.
When there are oppressive laws, there will be plagues of insects.
When the innocent are put to death, there will be a red death.
When harvesting is forbidden, there will be torrential rains.
The Four Seasons are the Annals of Heaven;
The Sun and Moon and the Messengers of Heaven;
The Stars and Planets record Heaven's seasons;
Rainbows and comets are Heaven's warnings.

(iii) The Nine Regions

These are the Nine Regions:
The Central Region is the Celestial Balance;
  its Hsiu are Chio, Kang and Ti (Hsiu 1, 2, and 3).

The Eastern Region is the Blue Heaven;
  its Hsiu are Fang, Hsin, and Wei (Hsiu 4, 5, and 6).

The North-Eastern Region is the Changing Heaven;
  its Hsiu are Chi, Nan Tou, and Ch'ien Niu (Hsiu 7, 8, and 9).

The Northern Region is the Black Heaven;
  its Hsiu are Wu Nü, Hsü, Wei, and Shih (Hsiu 10, 11, 12, and 13).

The North-Western Region is the Concealed Heaven;
  its Hsiu are Tung Pi, K'uei, and Lou (Hsiu 14, 15, and 16).

The Western Region is the Shining Heaven;
  its Hsiu are Wei, Mao, and Pi (Hsiu 17, 18 and 19).

The South-Western Region is the Vermilion Heaven;
  its Hsiu are Tsui Kuei, Shen, and Tung Ching (Hsiu 20, 21 and 22).

The Southern Region is the Fiery Heaven;
  its Hsiu are Yu Kuei, Liu, and Ch'i Hsing (Hsiu 23, 24, and 25).

The South-Eastern Region is the Yang Heaven;
  its Hsiu are Chang, I, and Chen (Hsiu 26, 27, and 28).

This is the oldest complete list of the twenty-eight Hsiu.

(iv) The Eight Winds
These are the days of the Eight Winds;
(The Eight Winds begin with the Winter Solstice; after that each
'wind' lasts for forty-five days.)

1. The Long Wind;
2. The Bright Wind;
3. The Clear and Bright Wind;
4. The Luminous Wind;
5. The Cool Wind;
6. The Gates of Heaven;
7. The Imperfect Wind;
8. The Wide and Extensive Wind.

During the Long Wind, issue minor instructions; it is a time for
delay rather than action.

During the Bright Wind, inspect boundaries and repair ground;

During the Clear and Bright Wind, issue instructions for the
maintenance of the silk industries.

During the Luminous Wind, report on efficiency and make the
Four Sacrifices.

During the Gates of Heaven, pay attention to legal matters and
put aside trifling amusements.

During the Imperfect Wind, repair public buildings and houses,
improve embankments and walls.

During the Wide and Extensive Wind, close up gates, and bridges,
and see that punishments are properly carried out.

The Book of Fan Sheng Chih [氾 朕 之]
Early texts, particularly The Monthly Ordinances, reveal a close
relationship between astronomy and agriculture. It is, of course,
understandable that given the unpredictable nature of the weather,
farmers might want some reassurance regarding the approach of the
changing seasons. Thus, in the Huai Nan Tzu, the following guidance
is given:

> Sow millet when Chang (*Hsiu 26*) is central;
> Glutinous millet and soya when Ta Huo (*Antares, Hsiu 5*) is central;
> Winter wheat when Hsü (*Hsiu 11*) is central;
> Gather fuel when Mao (*Hsiu 18*) is central.

In this respect, astronomical information, such as the culmination
of stars, or the appearance of seasonal constellations, would be a sure

indication of the passage of time. But another explanation – and a purely astrological one – must lie behind some of the precepts in an ancient agricultural manual: the *Book of Fan Sheng Chih*. This farmer-scholar, active between 32 and 7 BC, was an adviser on agriculture and other matters in Chang-an. Though much of his work was lost, a few fragments have been preserved as quotations in the writings of later commentators. Among substantially sound advice on types of soil, methods of seeding, cultivation and harvesting, are some purely astrological maxims, such as the following pieces of advice on choosing suitable dates for sowing crops, which have little to do with the progress of the seasons:

The Choice of Dates for Sowing Crops
Do not sow barley on days of the First Branch
Nor glutinous millet on days of the Second Branch
Spiked millet will not thrive on days of the Third Branch
Nor small beans when planted on days of the Fourth Branch;
Rice and Hemp are badly suited for days of the Fifth Branch;
Do not plant hard millet on days of the Seventh Branch
Soya beans on the Eighth
Nor wheat on the Eleventh.
All the nine cereals have their own particular days when they are ill-suited. This is not just idle talk, but the consequence of Nature.

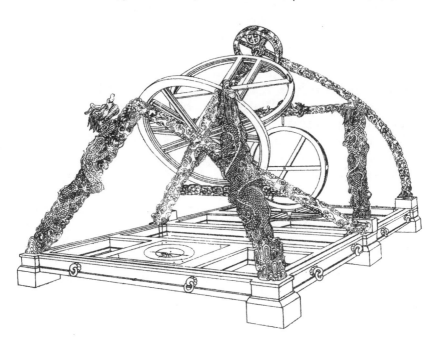

6.

THE ASTROLOGICAL TREATISE OF SSU MA CH'IEN

天官

While the Prince of Huai Nan was assembling a coterie of philosophers at his court, the Emperor, Wu Ti, was similarly engaged, but on a somewhat grander scale. In appointing Ssu Ma Ch'ien (163-85 BC) to the post of Grand Astrologer the Emperor secured one of the greatest scholars of the Han dynasty. The *Shih Chi*, or 'Historical Record', begun by Ssu Ma Ch'ien's father, Ssu Ma T'an, is a complete history of the Chinese up to that time. It was the first major undertaking of its type, and the model for all subsequent histories. Father and son collected material together from all known sources, thus preserving the details of many events which would otherwise have been lost. But the work not only deals with the relentless struggle for control of the Empire, it also gathers together a number of treatises on the sciences and the arts, among them the following treatise on the officers of the Heavens. This section, very broad in scope, calls in part on older treatises which are still extant (such as the *Huai Nan Tzu*) and others which are known to have existed but are now lost. That Ssu Ma Ch'ien selected from such works, rather than including them whole, is obvious from a comparison of Ssu Ma Ch'ien's treatise with other examples of the texts which are more detailed or broader in scope in their original versions. Later compilers of dynastic histories felt obliged to follow Ssu Ma Ch'ien's model. The *Ch'ien Han Shu*, the 'History of the Former Han Dynasty', by Ma Hsu, also had its astronomical chapter, almost identical to that of Ssu Ma Ch'ien, although a further chapter of astronomical data was added thus showing the advance in astronomical knowledge during the Former Han dynasty. It included the calculation of calendar cycles, and some tentative, if not wholly accurate, formulae for calculating eclipses.

The *Hou Han Shu*, the 'History of the Later Han Dynasty', has a mere three chapters on the astrological aspects, relating the manifestations of celestial phenomena to terrestrial events.

The next dynastic history, the *San Kuo Chih*, describing the turbulent times of the Three Kingdoms, is the only one lacking an astronomical chapter before the *Chin Shu*. This latter work's encyclopædic treatise on astronomy relies heavily on Ssu Ma Ch'ien, but the chapters which follow it, relating celestial events with political manoeuvres on the earth, provide an exhaustive apologia for astrology, with a thorough analysis of the subject. This latter work has been fully translated into English and copiously annotated by the Chinese scholar Dr Ho Peng Yoke in a recent edition which is highly recommended as a source for the study of Chinese mundane astrology.

It is not difficult to see why Ssu Ma Ch'ien should have been concerned with such disparate studies as history and astronomy. As Imperial Astrologer, subordinate only to a minister of state, it was his main commission to organise the calendar, which had become faulty. Indeed, his studies were the foundation on which all subsequent Chinese calendars have been based. To carry out this task he needed to study the annals in order to establish an accurate chronology of past events. Further, since the calendar, whether lunar or solar, is entirely dependant on its correspondance with celestial phenomena, a thorough knowledge of the mathematics of celestial movements was a prerequisite. As for the prognosticatory side of astronomy — that which we now distinguish by the name of astrology — Ssu Ma Ch'ien makes it quite clear that he believed implicitly that Heaven's Will was manifested by the movements of the celestial governors, and that the penalties for failing to respond to, or record, or even keep watch for, Heaven's portents were dire indeed.

Ssu Ma Ch'ien's life was marred by a tragic incident. In 99 BC his friend, Li Ling, was given the commission of a legion of some five thousand men to put down an uprising of some eighty thousand Hsiung Nu rebels (Mongol Tartars, or Huns). Li's legion was routed, and Li captured. To the Emperor's fury, Ssa Ma Ch'ien dared to speak in defence of the defeated hero. He was arraigned for criminally abetting a traitor, and sentenced to death. But in view of his colossal undertaking, and his duty of filial piety in completing the work begun by his father, Ssu Ma Ch'ien accepted the lesser punishment, but greater disgrace, of castration.

Some indication of the size and scope of the project may be gathered from the fact that the chapter which follows is but one of eight treatises (the others being on such diverse subjects as the calendar, music, rites, and so on) with a further 112 chapters of annals and biographies, together with detailed chronological tables of China's history.

Because of its importance, the treatise is here quoted as fully as possible, abridging only those lengthy passages in the final section of the treatise, which did not deal specifically with celestial phenomena or prognostication; there Ssu Ma Ch'ien tends to recapitulate historical and ethnographical details which are outside the scope of our subject. Occasionally where contemporary or older sources (such as the *Huai Nan Tzu*) or passages from other treatises in the Historical Record augment the information given in the treatise, additional remarks have been added in a distinguishable form.

The treatise deals with the Five Palaces, and the stars contained, distinguishing the twenty-eight Hsiu, from individual stars and other constellations — in other words, not only those which lie near the ecliptic, (that is, the zodiac, the path of the planets) or the celestial equator, but stars at the North Pole, and others on the horizon which would only be seen at certain times of the year. This feature is absent from other astrological systems, which deal almost exclusively with stars along the ecliptic. In Chinese astrology, since the non-zodiacal constellations are not subject to visitations by the planets, other means of taking prognostications were used. The importance of watching the whole sky all the time is stressed several times; any changes in the appearance of the stars had to be noted carefully. Such changes may have been in the colour, the magnitude, the brightness, or the position of the stars. Even the type of twinkling has to be observed.

Every contingency was allowed for in the list of prognostications, even for celestial movements which could never have occurred — for example, the planets visiting non-zodiacal constellations. Whatever celestial event occurred, its portents could be read from the position in the sky, the colour, the direction of movement, the length of time for which the event was seen, and even the date on which it appeared.

It was not only the Sun, Moon, Stars and Planets which revealed the Celestial Will; the portents of comets, meteors, and strangest of all 'vapours' or 'aura' are also described. What these last are has been very difficult to establish. The term seems, on the one hand, to include meteorological phenomena such as clouds, fogs, mists, and perhaps more understandably, haloes round the sun and moon. On the other hand, the text (as in other sources) takes pains to point out that the 'aura' only *resembled* such phenomena; in other words, they were not, in fact, clouds, fogs, mists, or whatever.

Finally, while it is instructive to note what the treatise contains, it is also extremely revealing to take note of what the treatise leaves out. There is no 'zodiac', nor the 'twelve animals' of popular Chinese astrology. The prophecies are almost exclusively about wars, pestilences, and harvests. There is nothing about bodily appearance, accumulation of wealth, love, marriage, children, or career. Nowhere are we told, for instance, that one planet signifies romance, or that another brings old age.

For the Heavens were concerned only with the workings of the State, not personal whims and ambitions. For that reason, no doubt, the discipline of Fate Calculation evolved, the seeds of which have already been seen in passages in the *Huai Nan Tzu* such as references to the portents of the Eight Winds, and remarks on days which had certain cyclical numbers as their 'signature'.

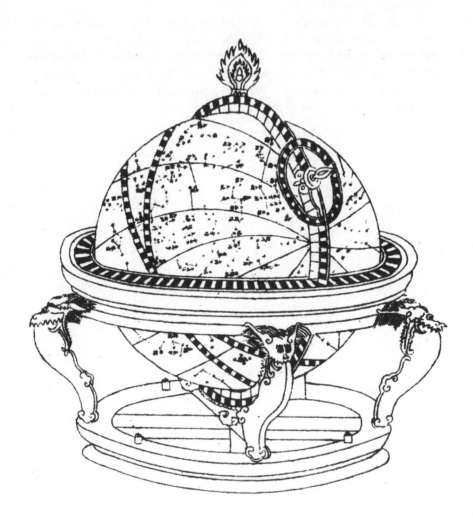

Ssu Ma Ch'ien — The Officers of Heaven

Prognostications are shown in a distinguishing format, thus.

I — The fixed stars, and their portents

The Central Palace 中宮
In the Central Palace, the brightest star is T'ien Chi (天極) Heaven's Pillar, the home of the Great Monad, T'ai I (*from which Yin and Yang are generated.*) The three stars to the side of it are San Kung (三公) the Three Lords, also called Tse Shou (子屬) the Heirs. Behind, in a curve, lie four stars; the last and brightest is Cheng Fei (正妃) the Principal Wife; the other three are ladies of the harem. Around them in a square are twelve other stars Fan Ch'en (藩臣) the Bodyguard. All these stars belong to the Purple Palace Tse Kung (紫宮) (*and therefore represent the Emperor and his family*).

In front, in a line to the right of the Northern Ladle, Pei Tou (北斗) (*the familiar stars of the Great Bear*) are three stars like a pointed hat turned to the North; because they are sometimes visible and other times not, they are called Yin Teh (陰德) Hidden Virtue or T'ien I (天一) Celestial Monad. To the East of the Purple Palace are three stars called T'ien Ch'iang (天槍) Celestial Spear. To the West of these three stars is T'ien Pei (天棓) the Celestial Flail. To the North, behind the Celestial Flail are six stars which cross the Milky Way and finish at Ying Shih (營室) the Regulator of the House, (i.e., Hsiu 15, Shih). These (six stars crossing the Milky Way) are known as Ko Tao (閣道) the Pavilion Path.

The seven stars of the Northern Ladle, Pei Tou (北斗) are the ones of which (Emperor Chuan 2513-2435 BC) said: 'The functioning of the Jade Balance shows the Seven Governments in harmony.' Star Piao (杓) the Handle is attached to the Horn of the Dragon (Hsiu 1); star Heng (衡) the Yoke leads to the centre of the Southern Ladle (Hsiu 8). The Literary Star, Kuei (魁) is supported on the head of Hsiu 21 (Orion).

6pm is indicated by the Handle, Star Piao (杓) which is found over the Mountain Hua in the South-West.

Midnight is indicated by the Yoke, Star Heng (衡) in the central region, in the land between the Yellow River and the Chi River.

6am is indicated by the Literary Star Kuei (魁) between the Sea and the sacred mountain of Shan Tung.

The stars of the Northern Ladle represent the Emperor's carriage, rotating round the centre of the universe. It governs the Four Directions, and divides Yin from Yang. It determines the Four Seasons, balances the Five Elements, regulates the divisions of time, the degrees of the sky, and many other things. Such are the stars of the Northern Ladle.

By the Literary Star, Kuei (魁) are six stars in a square called Wen Ch'ang Kung (文昌宮) the Palace of Literary Genius. The names of the individual stars are Shang Chang (上將) Chief of Staff; Tse Chang (次將) Lieutenant General; Kuei Hsiang (貴相) Honourable Counsellor [of Rites]; Ssu Ming (可命) the Controller of Fate; Ssu Chung (司中) the Controller of the Centre; [*In the Chin Shu, this is the 'Imperial Astrologer, Prognosticator and Interpreter of Strange Events'*] and Ssu Lu (司祿) the Controller of Rewards. At the centre of the Literary Star Group is the Kuei Jen Che Lao (貴人之牢) Prison of Peers. Below the Literary Star Group are six stars in pairs called San T'ai (三台) the Three Privy Counsellors.*

When the colour of the stars in the constellation San T'ai (三台) Three Counsellors in uniform, the Prince and Ministers are in harmony; but if not so, then there is opposition and dispute (within the government). While the star Fu (輔) Supporting Shaft is close and bright, the ministers under its control will be well-liked and powerful; but if it is distant and small, they will be weak and brushed aside.

At the end of Piao (杓) the Handle are two constellations. The one in the middle is Mao (矛) the Lance, sometimes called Chao Yao (招搖) the Bringer of Conflict. The outer constellation is called Tun (盾) the Shield or T'ien Feng (天鋒) Celestial Spearhead.

The fifteen stars folded into a circle are known as Chien Jen Che Lao (賤人之牢) the Prison of Paupers.

When the star at the centre of the Prison of Paupers is bright, many humble people will be put into prison. When the star is weak, the gates will be opened and prisoners released.

When T'ien I (天一) Celestial Monad, T'ien Ch'iang (天槍) Celestial Spear, Mao (矛) the Lance, and Tun (盾) the Shield sparkle and scintillate, great wars begin.

The Eastern Palace 東宮

The Eastern Palace of the Green Dragon includes the Room (Hsiu

*There is a misprint in Chavannes edition of the text.

4) and the Heart (Hsiu 5). The Heart is the 'Bright Hall' (Ming T'ang). The brightest of these stars is T'ien Wang (天王) the Heavenly King (= *Antares, the Fire Star of the Hsia Hsiao Cheng*). The stars behind it are his sons; they should not be in a straight line, if they are, the Heavenly King is out of alignment.

The House (Hsiu 4) is (?) the market. It is also called T'ien Ssu (天駟) the Celestial Four-in-Hand. The northernmost star is the right-hand horse; either side of it are the two stars called Ch'ien (鈐) the Carriage Ornament. [*These stars have several other names, discussed in Schlegel's 'Uranographie Chinoise' but only of passing importance here.*] To the North is Hsü (辖) the Axle-hub. To the North-West, a group of twelve stars is Ch'i (旗) the Banner; the four stars in the middle of the banner are T'ien Shih (天市) the Celestial Market; the other six stars are the Shih Lou (市婁) 'Market Tower'.

When the stars in the Celestial Market are numerous, there is substantial produce; but when they are few, there is a dearth.

The star to the left of the Horn (Hsiu 1) is Li (理) the Judge; the star to the right of the Horn is Chiang (將) the General; the Great Horn [*star Ta Chio (大角) = Arcturus*] is T'ien Wang Ti T'ing (天王帝廷) the Imperial Court of the Celestial King. On each side are three stars arranged like the feet of a tripod. These are the *She T'i* (攝提) or Indicators, since by a straight line from the Handle they indicate the seasons and divisions of time; thus they are the She T'i Ko (攝提格) [*the beginning of the Jupiter Cycle, q.v.*]

The stars of Hsiu 2, the Neck, are the Temple Precincts.

(Hsiu 2) presides over illnesses.

North and South are two large stars called Nan Men (南門) the Southern Gate. Next comes Hsiu 3 the Base, known as T'ien Ken (天艮) Heaven's Boundary,

which presides over epidemics

Hsiu 6, the Tail, also called Chiu Tse (九子) the Nine Sons, of which it is said

the prince and his ministers are divided against each other,

and Hsiu 7, the Winnowing Basket, also called Ao K'e (敖客) the Wandering Traveller, or K'ou She (口舌) Mouth and Tongue.

The Southern Palace 南宮

The Southern Palace of the Red Bird includes the constellations of Ch'üan (權) the Weights and Heng (衡) the Balance.

The Balance is the court of the Three Luminaries of T'ai Wei (太微) the Great Spy. (*The 'Three Luminaries' usually refers to the Sun, Moon, and other celestial bodies.*)

The twelve stars forming a guard of honour in a square are called Fan Ch'en (藩臣) the Bodyguard (*another constellation of this name*). To the West is Chiang (將) the General; to the East is Hsiang (相) the Counsellor, to the South, the four stars Chih Fa (執法) are the Directors of the Laws. At their centre is Tuan Men (端門) the Main Gate; to the left and right I Men (掖門) the Side Gate. Within the gates, the six stars are called Chu Hou (諸侯) The Company of Lords. The five stars in the middle are Wu Ti Tso (五帝坐) the Seats of the Five Emperors (*equivalent to the Five Elements*). At the back is a group of fifteen stars like a thicket called Lang Wei (郎位) the Place of the Young Lords. To the right is a bright star, Chiang Wei (將位) the Seat of the General.

If the Moon and planets enter these star groups regularly, they will leave accordingly. But if they stop by a particular star, this indicates that the Emperor will execute the corresponding minister.

The Central Seat is a portent; if the common people are rising and plotting, this is indicated by the presence of the Metal Planet (Venus) and the Fire Planet (Mars) resting there.

To the West of Fan Ch'en (藩臣) the Twelve Guardsmen are five stars, arranged North to South forming Hsiao Wei (小微) Little Spy, Shih (士) the Sage; and Ta Fu (大夫) the Great Scholar.

Stars Ch'üan, the Weights, are also known as Hsien Yüan (軒轅) Shaft and Axle, forming the body of the Yellow Dragon.

The large star at the back Nü Chu (女主) is the Queen (Regulus). The little stars at the side comprise the Harem of Royal Ladies.

When the Moon and Five Planets maintain their position in the Royal Harem, the portents are the same as for (衡) the Balance, Heng.

The Eastern Well, (Hsiu 22) is concerned with all matters pertaining to water.

Towards the West is a star called Yüeh (鉞) the Battleaxe. To the North of the Battleaxe is Pei Ho (北河) the Northern River, and to the South Nan Ho (南河) the Southern River. Between these rivers, and T'ien Ch'üeh (天闕) Heaven's Watchtower is Kuan Liang (關梁) the Barrier Beam.

The Ghostly Carriage (Hsiu 23) represents all things concerning one's ancestors.

At the centre, the 'whiteness' (the 'Praesepe' Nebula in Cancer) is Chih (質) Matter. (*The section on the Hsiu quotes another passage regarding this nebula.*)

Virtue is produced by Heng (衡) the Balance; prophecy by Huang (潢) the Lake; defeats by Yüeh (鉞) the Battleaxe; calamities by Hsiu 22, the Well; death by Chih (質) Matter.

Hsiu 24, the Willow, makes the beak of the Red Bird; it presides over trees and vegetation. Hsiu 25, the Star, (sometimes called Ch'i Hsing (七星) Seven Stars) is the throat of the Red Bird, and presides over urgent business.

Hsiu 26, the Drawn Bow, also called Su (素) Pristine Matter, symbolizes a kitchen and presides over banquets and feasts.

Hsiu 27, the Wing, presides over departed guests.

Hsiu 28, the Carriage Board, represents a carriage and presides over the winds.

To the side of Hsiu 28 is a little star, Ch'ang Sha (長沙) the Gravel Path. It does not always shine. When it does, it equals the other stars of the Carriage in brilliance.

If the five planets are found among the stars of the Carriage, then great wars break out.

To the South of the Carriage Board (Hsiu 28) are several stars called T'ien K'u Lou (天庫樓) the Celestial Treasure Tower.

The Treasury holds six carriages; if the stars are more or less than six, there is no room for both carriages and horses.

The Western Palace 西宮

The Western Palace, (*the White Tiger*) includes the constellation Hsien Ch'ih (咸池) Many Ponds, or T'ien Wu Huang (天五潢) the Five Lakes of Heaven. These lakes are Wu Ti Ch'e She (五帝車舍) the Five Imperial Carriage Sheds.

If the Fire Planet (Mars) is therein, there will be droughts; if the Metal Planet (Venus), war; if the Water Planet (Mercury), water.

In the middle are San Chu (三柱) the Three Pillars.

If the columns are not complete, wars will break out.

Astride (Hsiu 15) is called Feng Shih (封豕) the Boar, and represents canals.

The Mound (Hsiu 16) represents assembled crowds.

The Stomach (Hsiu 17) is also called T'ien Ts'ang (天倉) the Celestial Granary. To the south of it is a group of stars called Kuei Chi (層積) the Haystack.

The Pleiades (Hsiu 18) is also called Mao T'ou, (毛頭) the Tresses. These stars are the emblem of the barbarian Ho tribes.

They preside over reunions with people in white garments (i.e. with the spirits of the dead).

The Net (Hsiu 19) is called Han Ch'e (罕車) the Strange Carriage.

It represents troubles at the frontiers. It presides over hunting, arrows, and nets.

To the side of the large star is a smaller star Fu Erh (附耳) the Attentive Ear.

When the Attentive Ear is brilliant, it signifies lying subjects and plotters up to no good.

Between the Net (Hsiu 19) and the Pleiades (Hsiu 18) is T'ien Chieh (天街) the Celestial Road. To the North of it are the Yin realms; to the South of it are the Yang realms.

Orion (Hsiu 21) is the White Tiger. The three stars in a straight line are Heng Shih (衡石) the Stone Weights. Below it are three stars in a pointed formation called Fa (罰) Punishment.

They represent execution.

The three outside stars are Tso Yu Chien Ku (右左肩股) the Left and Right Shoulders and Thighs. The three little stars at an angle are called Tsui Kuei (觜觿) The (?) Turtle's Beak (or Ivory Tuning Pin). [Hsiu 20].

They form the head of the (White) Tiger, and preside over flocks, herds, and people under protection.

To the South are four stars called T'ien Ts'u (天厠) the Celestial Bedside. Below the stars of the Celestial Bedside is a star called T'ien Shih (天矢) the Celestial Arrow (or Pointer).

When the Arrow is yellow, it is a favourable omen; when white or black, it is unlucky.

To the left of it are several stars in a twisted line in three groups of nine. The first ones are called T'ien Ch'i (天旗) the Celestial Banner; the second group is called T'ien Yüan (天苑) the Celestial Garden, and the third Chiu Yu (九游) the Nine Pennants. To the East is a large star called Lang (狼) the Wolf.

When the Wolf changes colour, there will be much piracy and theft.

To the South are four stars called Hu (弧), the Bow, aimed at the Wolf. Symmetrically aligned with the Wolf is another large star Nan Chi Lao Jen (南極者人) The Old Man of the South Pole.

When the Old Man of the South Pole is visible, then there is good government and peace, but otherwise, wars break out. It is usually to be seen in southern regions at the Autumn Equinox. When Fu Erh (附耳) the Attentive Ear enters Hsiu 19, the Net, wars begin. [This is an extraordinary statement. Both Fu Erh (附耳) the Attentive Ear, and Hsiu 19, the Net, are fixed stars in relation to each other, and as a consequence, the possibility does not arise. Since the statement has also dropped out of place here, instead of being noted a few sentences back, it seems to have been added later, possibly indicating a mistaken observation made at some time, a meteor or some other light being mistaken for the Attentive Ear.]

The Northern Palace 北宮
The Northern Palace of the Dark Warrior embraces the lunar mansions Void (Hsiu 11) and Danger (Hsiu 12).

Void presides over loss of loved ones; Danger over the roofs of buildings.

To the South is a group of stars called Yu Lin T'ien Chün(羽林天軍) the Celestial Army of the Winged Forest. To the West of this army is Lei (壘) the Rampart, which is sometimes called Yüeh (鉞) the Battleaxe. At the side is a large star called Pei Lo (北落) the Northern Village.

If the Northern Village fades, it shows loss of the army. If it is bright and flashes, then becomes feeble, and the Five Planets return to the Northern Village, there will be uprisings, more particularly, in the presence of the Fire Planet (Mars), the Metal Planet (Venus) or the Water Planet (Mercury). The presence of the Fire Planet shows the annihilation of the army; the Water Planet that it will be defeated. The presence of the Wood Planet (Jupiter) or the Earth Planet (Saturn) however, show a favourable outcome.

To the East of (Hsiu 12) Danger, there are six stars arranged in pairs called Ssu K'ung (司空) the Controllers of Public Works. (This should read Ssu Ming (司命) the Controllers of Fate).

The Regulator of the House, Ying Shih (營室) (Hsiu 13) is the symbol of Ch'ing Miao (清廟) the Purification Temple. It is further known as Li Kung (離宮) the Bright Palace, and Ko Tao (閣道) the Pavilion Path.

In the middle of the Milky Way are four stars called T'ien Ssu (天駟) the Celestial Four-in-Hand. At their side is a star called Wang Liang (王良) King Excellence.

When King Excellence whips the horses, carriages and horses fill the countryside.

At the side are eight stars crossing the Milky Way. These are called T'ien Huang (天潢) the Celestial Lake. At the side of the Celestial Lake is Chiang Hsing (江星) the River Star (so called, probably, from its proximity to the Milky Way, which was known to the Chinese as the Celestial River).

When the River Star brightens, men cross the water.

The Pestle, Ch'u (杵) and Mortar, Chiu (臼) are four stars to the South of (Hsiu 12) Danger.

When P'ao Kua (匏瓜) the Gourd is occupied by a green or black planet, fish and salt are dear.

The Southern Ladle Nan Tou (南斗) represents the Ancestral Temple; to the North of it is the Marker Star; this constellation is Ch'i (旗) the Banner mentioned above. (*The Marker*, pi sagitarii, *Ch'ien Hsing (建星) was used as the starting point for the planetary cycles, more of which is said in the next section on the Jupiter Cycle.*)

The Draught Ox, Ch'ien Niu (牽牛) (Hsiu 9) represents the victim for sacrifice.

To the North of the Draught Ox is Ho Ku (河鼓) the River Drum. The big star in the River Drum represents the General-in-Chief; the stars to his left and right are his lieutenant generals. To the North of Wu Nü (婺女) the (?) Sewing-Girl (= Hsiu 10) is Chih Nü (織女) the Weaving Girl. She is the Youngest Daughter of Heaven.

II — The Five Planets and their portents

The Wood Planet, Jupiter, called The Year Star

The following section on the planet Jupiter would be unintelligible even to the astronomically minded without an explanation of some of the technical terms which are used.

Firstly, the 'Jupiter Stations'. These are divisions of the Celestial Equator into twelve parts, similar to, but not, it must be stressed, the same as, the division of the ecliptic into the twelve signs of the zodiac. They are known by the cyclical signs Tze, Ch'ou, Yin, etc. (子丑寅 . . .) and are here designated according to the convention used throughout this book by the Roman numerals I, II, III etc. Thus, the Celestial Equator is divided in two entirely different ways; first, by the twenty-eight Hsiu, and secondly, by the twelve 'stations'. Not only do these two divisions not tally, but different authorities have variously given equivalences between the lunar Hsiu and the Jupiter stations. (The reason why they are known as 'Jupiter' stations will be explained later.) A fuller account of the variations in the correspondence between the Hsiu and the stations at different periods is given in Ho Peng Yoke's translation of the *Chin Shu* Astronomical Treatise, which is a few centuries later than that of Ssu Ma Ch'ien.

Secondly, the matter of the 'Counter-Jupiter'. It is probably easier to make an analogy between the courses of the planets, and two trains travelling in the same direction. A passenger in an overtaking train often experiences the curious sensation that the slower train appears to be travelling backwards. Such is the case with Jupiter, which similarly appears to traverse the sky in the opposite direction to the Sun, although of course it does not do so — not even if one presumes the Earth to be stationary with the Sun travelling round it. Because of this curious phenomenon, early astronomers adopted the convention of a counter-Jupiter which progressed in the 'correct' direction across the sky, its movements mirroring those of the real planet.

Two sets of terms were used, one an astronomical set of terms for the positions of the real Jupiter, and a further set of 'astrological' terms for the positions of the imaginary planet.

The division of the Celestial Equator into twelve parts thus produced twelve virtually equal months, which did not correspond to the lunar months, since the latter were dependent on the progress of the Moon around the Earth, while the former were measured by the progress of the Earth around the Sun, beginning (as was seen in the last paragraph of the previous section) at the constellation known as the Marker Star. These astronomical/astrological months were each divided into two, thus producing the twenty-four 'fortnights' or 'seasons'. The term for these, Ch'i (氣) is the same as that used for 'vapours' or 'aura' dealt with in a later section. The twenty-four Ch'i are listed on pages 52-3 in the calendar section.

Jupiter takes approximately twelve years to complete its orbit of the Sun; as a consequence its progress through the twelve divisions of the Celestial Equator proceeds annually by one station every year.

Table 6.1: **The Year Names, and the Cyclical Signs**

Year	Hsiu	Name of the Jupiter station	Branch	Branch	Name of the T'ai Sui station
		The Year Star (歲星) (the planet Jupiter) moves forwards, but falls back one sign each year.		The T'ai Sui (大歲) (Counter-Jupiter) is imagined to be travelling in mirror fashion to the planet Jupiter	
1	斗 8 Southern Ladle	星紀 Hsing Chi (Year marker)	II	III	攝提格 She T'i Ko
2	女 10 Weaving Maiden	玄枵 Hsüan Hsia (Dark hollow)	I	IV	單閼 Tan O
3	危 12 Danger	娵訾 Ch'ü Tze (Bride Money)	XII	V	執徐 Chih Hsü
4	奎 15 Astride	隆婁 Hsiang Lou (Returning thread)	XI	VI	大荒落 Ta Huang Lo
5	胃 17 Stomach	大梁 Ta Liang (Large Beam)	X	VII	敦牂 Tun Tsang
6	畢 19 Net	實沈 Shih Ch'en (Fortune lost)	IX	VIII	協洽 Hsieh Hsia
7	井 22 Well	鶉首 Ch'un Shou (Quail's Head)	VIII	IX	涒灘 T'un T'an
8	柳 24 Willow	鶉火 Ch'un Huo (Quail's Fire)	VII	X	作噩 Tso O
9	軫 28 Carriage-board	鶉尾 Ch'un Wei (Quail's Tail)	VI	XI	淹茂 Yen Mao
10	氐 3 Neck	壽星 Shou Hsing (Long-life Star)	V	XII	大淵獻 Ta Yuan Hsien
11	心 5 Heart	大火 Ta Huo (Great Fire)	IV	I	困敦 K'un Tun
12	箕 7 Basket	析木 Hsi Mu (Split Wood)	III	II	赤奮若 Ch'ih Fen Jo

Thus was conceived the twelve-yearly 'Jupiter Cycle' or Great Year of twelve earthly years, which derives its terms from the position which Jupiter occupies in the Celestial Equator in any year. (Later, animal names were attached to these signs which became used to designate not only the years and months, but also the hours as well.) Jupiter was therefore called the Sui Hsing (歲星) Year Star, and 'Counter-Jupiter' the T'ai Sui (太歲) the Great Year. Within a specific context, the actual planet Jupiter became called simply the Star, and Counter-Jupiter, (as an abstract concept, rather than an astronomical body) the Year. As the text of the passage on Jupiter is very repetitious, for convenience of reference and reading the first part, dealing with the various terms used for the progress of the planet and 'year', is given in tabular form. (The text for the first of the stations is however also given as prose.)

These tables can be compared with the table given by Dr Joseph Needham on page 403 of Volume III of *Science and Civilisation in China*. It will be seen that the cyclical numbers given in Dr Needham's table do not match the ones given by Ssu Ma Ch'ien, although the year-names are the same. By the same token, the 'associated Hsiu' in Dr Needham's table are also in a different order.

The Jupiter Cycle
Table 6.1 summarizes the information given by Ssu Ma Ch'ien, for ease of reference.

These names have not been translated for the simple reason that they are untranslatable. Various suggestions have been put forward to account for these unusual names, one being that they are transliterations from the Sanskrit, but this appears to have been disproved. L. de Saussure, in *Les Origines de l'Astronomie Chinoise* believes the compound words of three syllables to have been, originally, three distinct words, thus making twelve sign-names, each associated with a compass point. Yet another theory is that they are transliterations of Chaldean cosmological terms; alas, there is not enough space here to go into these intriguing theories in detail, but here are some pertinent facts.

There are in all twenty-eight syllables, the same as the number of the Hsiu. Only two pairs of syllables are repeated, Tun and Ta. The twenty-eight syllables are shown in a cosmological diagram below, and the meaning of each syllable has been given individually.

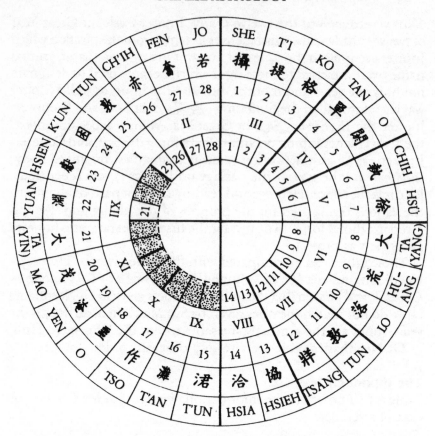

Figure 6.2 Conjectural reconstruction of the original position of the syllables of the Jupiter cycle terms. (The author's theory is that Ta [Yin] should occupy position 22, thus commanding a three-syllable name to face Ta Huang Lo; and that Tun (position 25) is similarly the commencing syllable of a two-syllable name facing Tun Tsang.)

The Meanings of the Twenty-Eight Syllables

1	She	攝 Assisting	15	T'un	涒 ? Jupiter
2	T'i	提 Lifting	16	T'an	灘 Sandbank
3	Ko	格 Limit mark	17	Tso	作 Action
4	Tan	單 Alone	18	O	噩 Startling
5	O	閼 Obstruction	19	Yen	淹 Overflow
6	Chih	執 Holding	20	Mao	茂 Luxuriant
7	Hsü	徐 Slow	21	Ta	大 Great
8	Ta	大 Great	22	Yuan	淵 Abyss
9	Huang	荒 Desolation	23	Hsien	獻 Presenting
10	Lo	落 Finality	24	K'un	困 Constraint
11	Tun	敦 Urging	25	Tun	敦 Urging
12	Tsang	牂 Dense	26	Ch'ih	赤 Crimson
13	Hsieh	協 Pulling back	27	Fen	奮 Spreading wings
14	Hsia	洽 Harmoniously	28	Jo	若 Conforming

太歲   歲星
T'ai Sui, The Wood Planet — Jupiter — The Year Star

The courses of the Sun and Moon are observed to measure the seasons, and the planet Jupiter to count the years.

Jupiter belongs to the East, and to Wood. It presides over the Spring. Its days are Chia and I (Stems 1 and 2, 甲乙). When there is a failure of justice, punishments are wrought by the Year Planet. When the Year Planet is in advance, or behind its proper place, it determines the Fate of the realm corresponding to the Hsiu in which it is found; such may not be vanquished entirely, but several prominent persons may be punished for their wrongdoings.

When the planet moves fast and overtakes the place where it should be, it is said to be 'in advance'; when it falls behind its proper place, this is called 'retardation'.

When it is in advance, the corresponding region suffers endless wars; when it is in retardation, the corresponding realm is devastated, the army leaders wiped out, the royal house collapsing in ruins. When Jupiter is in its proper place, with the other planets all gathered together in the same Hsiu, then the corresponding realm will be admired by the whole world for its stability and prudent government. (*In the first year of Han Kao Ti, 202 BC, all the planets were gathered in Hsiu 22, Ching* (井) *The Well*).

In the year She T'i Ko (攝提格), the Yin [陰, *i.e., the negative principle*] of the Year (Counter-Jupiter) moves to the left and is found in Yin (寅) (cyclical number III). The Year Star moves to the right, and is found in Ch'ou (丑) II. In the first month, together with the Hsiu 8 and 9, Tou and Niu, it rises in the morning in the East. Its name is Chien Teh (監德) the Examiner of Virtue.

Its colour is bright green.

When it is not in its proper place, but appears instead in the Hsiu 24, Liu, the Willow, the year will begin very wet, but end in drought.

The Year Star moves eastwards 12 degrees; then at the end of 100 days it stops and retrogrades through 8 degrees; at the end of 100 days it begins its journey eastwards again; in one year it travels 30 $\frac{7}{16}$ degrees; on average it travels every day by a twelfth of a degree; in 12 years it makes a complete circuit of the heavens.

It appears in the East at dawn; it sets in the West at 6pm.

The Jupiter Cycle

Table 6.2: Associated Hsiu

Month or Jupiter station	Hsiu	Hsiu, if 'correct' Hsiu is missed	Name given to alternative Hsiu, and prognostication
1	8 Tou 9 Ch'ien Niu	24 Liu	The year begins wet, followed by drought
2	10 Wu Nü 11 Hsü 12 Wei	26 Chang	Chiang Ju 降入 'Entering Downwards' Great floods

The Jupiter Cycle

Table 6.2: Associated Hsiu (*continued*)

Month or Jupiter station	Hsiu	Hsiu, if 'correct' Hsiu is missed	Name given to alternative Hsiu, and prognostication
3	13 Ying Shih 14 Tung Pi	28 Chen	Ch'ing Chang 青章 'Green Seal'. Drought, followed by floods
4	15 K'uei 16 Lou 17 Wei 18 Mao	2 K'ang	—
5	17 Wei 18 Mao 19 Pi	4 Fang	Drought, followed by floods.
6	20 Ts'ui 21 Shen	7 Chi	—
7	22 Tung Ching 23 Kuei	9 Ch'ien Niu	—
8	24 Liu 25 Chi Hsing 26 Chang	12 Wei	Ta Chang 大章 'Great Seal' Drought, but prosperity; mourning of women; epidemics
9	27 I 28 Chen	14 Tung Pi	Drought, mourning of girls
10	1 Ch'io 2 K'ang	16 Lou	—
11	3 Ti 4 Fang 5 Hsin	18 Mao	—
12	6 Wei 7 Chi	21 Shen	—

Table 6.2a: The following table shows the associated Hsiu given in other astronomical texts (See Needham, *loc. cit.*)

Month	Associated Hsiu						
	in Ssu Ma Ch'ien				Other sources		
1	8	9			12	11	10
2	10	11	12		9	8	
3	13	14			7	6	
4	15	16	17	18	5	4	3
5	17	18	19		2	1	
6	20	21			28	27	
7	22	23			26	25	24
8	24	25	26		23	22	
9	27	28			21	20	
10	1	2			19	18	17
11	3	4	5		16	15	
12	6	7			14	13	

The Jupiter Cycle

Table 6.3: Astrological Names of the Cycle

Cycle	Name		Meaning	Colour	Prognostication
1	Ch'ien Teh	監德	Examiner of Virtue	Green	—
2	Chiang Ju	降入	Entering Downwards	Large, white	—
3	Ch'ing Chang	青章	Green Seal	Green, bright	—
4	Pien Chung	跰踵	Caloused Heel	Red, lively, bright	—
5	K'ai Ming	開明	Open Brightness	Clear and bright	Cease war. No advantage for ruler, general or people.
6	Ch'ang Lieh	長列	Long File	Brilliant and clear	Favours military enterprises
7	T'ien Yin	天音	Heavenly Sound	Brilliant white	—

The Jupiter Cycle

Table 6.3: Astrological Names of the Cycle (*continued*)

Cycle	Name		Meaning	Colour	Prognostication
8	Wei Ch'ang Wang	爲長王	King Long Active	Active, with darting rays	Corresponding realm prospers. A full harvest.
9	(Ming) T'ien Hui	名天睢	(Fame) Heaven's	Strong, white	—
10	Ta Chang	大章	Great Seal	Green, bright	If the planet jumps ahead, or if the Yin appears at dawn, it is called Cheng P'ing. Correct Equality. Troops are put on the road; there is war. The corresponding realm is endowed with virtue, and can possess the Four Seas.
11	T'ien Ch'üan	天泉	Celestial Spring	Deep, strong	Rivers and lakes are abundant under this sign
12	T'ien Hao	天皓	Celestial Shine	Dark, Brilliant	—

Various Portents Shown by Jupiter

If the Year Planet is not in its proper place, but to the left or the right of it, or if it goes into retardation before it should do, and visits other constellations, then it is an inauspicious omen for the realm concerned. But the realm over which it stops for a length of time will be bestowed with great virtue.

If its rays dart*, and it shimmers, or it appears small, then large, or its colour changes frequently, it is an indication that the ruler will be afflicted.

These are the consequences when it is not in its proper place: If it moves towards the North-East, after three months there will appear a flail-shaped comet, four feet long, pointed at the end.

If it moves to the South-East, after three months there will appear a brush-shaped comet, two feet long.

*The expression 'rays' refers to a 'star-shaped' ☆ appearance, as distinct from a 'round' shape ○.

If it moves to the North-West, at the end of three months there will appear a pointed comet.

If it moves to the South-West, at the end of three months there will appear a stick-shaped comet, pointed at both ends.

The realms above which such phenomena occur cannot hope to undertake any successful enterprise, or take up arms.

On the appearance, if the planet appears to draw nearer and then enhances, the corresponding realm can undertake great earthworks.

If it appears to enhance, and then comes forward, the corresponding realm is lost.

If it is red and glitters, the region where it is found will flourish; those who take up arms against such states will not succeed. If it is red and yellow, the corresponding realm will be very fertile. If it is green and white, or ember red, the corresponding realm will be afflicted.

If the Year Planet is occulted by the Moon, then a Minister of State will be expelled.

If it is in opposition to (*Venus*), the army of the corresponding region will be destroyed.

The Year Planet is also known by the name She T'i (*as in She T'i Ko, see Table 1*). Other names are Chung Hua (重華) Splendid Flower, (*The Emperor Chuan*); Ying Hsing (應星) the Vital Planet; and Chi Hsing (紀星) the Recording Planet (*because it is used to record the cycle of twelve years in the calendar*).

The Year Planet represents the Ancestral Temple. (*Two further prognostications regarding Jupiter appear at the end of Ssu Ma Ch'ien's treatise on page 244*).

Ying Huo	THE	The Fire Planet
熒惑	PLANET MARS	火星

In order to locate the planet Mars, it is necessary to look for a steady radiance.

It is said to correspond to the South, and to the Element Fire. It presides over Summer, and the related days are Ping (丙) and Ting (丁) (Stems 3 and 4). When the rites are neglected, retribution comes from Ying Huo.

When it appears, there is war. When it disappears, soldiers can be given leave. According to the Hsiu in which it is found, so the destiny of the nation is determined.

What is the import of Ying Huo? It signifies rebellion, piracy, illness, mourning, famine, and war.

If it retrogrades for more than two Hsiu and stops for three months, there will be calamity. If it is there for five months, there will be war. If there for seven months, half the territory will be lost. If there for nine months, then the greater part will be lost.

If it appears and disappears while retrograding, the pertaining kingdom will have its sacrifices interrupted (a euphemism for being entirely destroyed).

When it stops, if calamities happen immediately, then no matter how grave the calamity, it will soon be over.

If it is late in appearance, an apparently minor calamity will turn out to be great.

When in the North, there is mourning for daughters; when in the South, mourning for sons.

If it glitters, shivers, turns, hurries ahead, falls behind, goes to the left or the right, this indicates great calamity.

When in conjunction with other planets, if their rays touch, this portends a dire result; but if they do not touch, the result is not so terrible. When this planet is followed by the other four, and all five are in the same Hsiu, the pertaining realm is capable of winning the whole empire by the correct performance of the rites.

After rising, it moves eastwards through six Hsiu, then stops. It retrogrades for a further two Hsiu, after which, at the end of sixty days, it moves eastwards through as many Hsiu as it did before it stopped. After ten more months it sets in the West.

It continues on its way unseen, and after five months rises in the East. When it is in the West it is called Fan Ming (反明) Opposing Brightness.

The man who rules men's destinies surely fears it.

When it moves to the East, it travels faster. It covers 1½° in one day.

When it moves eastwards, southwards, westwards, or northwards, and does so rapidly, soldiers gather in the places where it is found. When they engage in battle, those who follow the same direction as the planet will gain, those who move in the opposite direction will be vanquished.

When the Fire Star follows the Metal Star (Venus); the army is afflicted; when it moves away from Venus, the army stops. When it comes out of the Yin of the Metal Planet, (the North of Venus) there is division in the army; when it leaves Venus by the Yang direction (South) there is a further conflict. On its journey, if (Venus) touches it, an army will be destroyed.

When it enters T'ai Wei (太微) Hsien Yüan (軒轅) or Ying Shih (Hsiu 13) and remains there, coming into conflict with them, he who governs men's destinies must surely fear it.

Hsiu 5, Hsin, the Heart, is its Bright Hall (*Ceremonial Hall*),* Ying Huo (*Mars*) is the Ancestral Temple.

Be meticulous in observing it.

(*The following additional material on Mars is taken from passages in other sections, and has been collected under one heading here for ease of reference.*)

When the Fire Planet is found contrary to where it should be, and appears in the Hsiu Ti, Wei, or Chi (Hsiu 3, 6, and 7) then it shoots out rays, indicating battles.

When it appears in Hsiu Fang or Hsin (Hsiu 4 and 5), then kings tremble.

When the Fire Planet is found in the Northern or Southern Rivers (Pei Ho, (北河), and Nan Ho, (南河) wars begin, and the harvest does not grow.

If the Fire Planet meets the Water Planet (*Mercury*) there will be famine; if it meets with the Metal Planet, (*Venus*) then Metal melts, and there is mourning. In either case, no enterprises can be undertaken. If the military are sent out, they will be beaten.

Chen† The Regulator 塡 Planet	THE PLANET SATURN	土星 The Earth Planet

To determine the position of Chen, (塡) the Regulator Planet, observe its relation with Tou (斗), the Northern Ladle (the Great Bear).

Saturn corresponds to the Centre, and to the Element Earth. It rules the last month of Summer. Its related days are Wu and Chi (戊己) (Stems 5 and 6). It represents the Yellow Emperor. It presides over Virtue; it is the symbol of the Empress. Each year it rules a particular Hsiu.

The realm where it stays will be fortunate. When it stays where it should no longer be, that is, if having left a spot it returns to it, and remains there, the respective realm will acquire either territory, or else women.

If it is not found where it ought to be, and after having been in one place then moves eastwards or westwards, the corresponding nation will lose land or women. Such a nation can undertake no enterprise nor employ its armies successfully. Wherever it stays for a long time, the

*See above, the Eastern Palace.
†Also 鎮 The Exorcist.

corresponding realm will achieve great happiness. When it changes place, there is little happiness.

It is also called Ti Hou (地侯) the Lord of the Earth.

It regulates the year.

Each year it covers 13$\frac{5}{112}$ degrees (*the text actually says 12$\frac{5}{112}$, but this is obviously a slip of the brush*); each day it covers $\frac{1}{28}$ of a degree; in 28 years it completes a revolution of the sky. (*The degrees given here are Chinese degrees, 365.25 to the circle*).

When it is in its proper place, and all five planets are gathered in the same Hsiu, the pertaining realm can gain the empire by strength. If the rites, virtue, justice, death sentences and punishments are lacking, Saturn wavers.

If Saturn is in advance, the king is troubled. The planet Saturn belongs to the colour Yellow; its corresponding note is Kung (*Doh, in Western sol-fa*), and its pitch the Yellow Bell.

When it is not in its proper place, but ahead by two or three Hsiu it is said to be 'in advance'; then, the man who controls men's destinies will have no success, otherwise there will be floods. When it misses its proper place, and is behind by two or three Hsiu, it is said to be 'in retardation'; then the Queen will grieve, and the harvest will not grow; or else there will be celestial upheavals and earthquakes.

Tou (斗) (the principal stars of Great Bear) is the Sublime Residence; Chen (*Saturn*) is the Ancestral Temple. It is the planet of the Son of Heaven.

When the Wood Planet (Jupiter) is in conjunction with the Earth Planet (Saturn) there are interior problems (*i.e. problems within the State*) and famines. The leader will wage war unexpectedly and will be vanquished. The Water Planet (*Mercury in conjunction with Saturn*) indicates a change of policy; the Fire Planet (*Mars, in conjunction with Saturn*) indicates drought; the Metal Planet (*Venus, ditto*) reunion with those in white robes (*i.e., there will be mourning*).

If Wood is to the North, and Metal to the South (*Jupiter and Venus respectively*), it is called Pin Mou (牝牡) Female and Male; crops will ripen to maturity. If Metal (Venus) is to the North, the harvest may fail. (**Note:** *The importance of this passage is the sharp distinction between the Chinese and Western association with the planets and the sexes. Jupiter is the female planet, not Mars, and Venus is the male planet. This is a highly significant point in illustrating the independence of Chinese astrology at this period.*)

If the Earth Planet meets with the Fire Planet (Mars) there will be sorrow; it is unlucky for public dignitaries; there will be a great famine; in battle the army will be defeated; the army will be at the end of its resources; in any enterprise there will be great loss.

If the Earth Planet meets the Water Planet (Mercury), there will be prosperity, but hindrances; an army will be overthrown; the corresponding realm cannot initiate any enterprise, for if it sends out the army, they will lose home territory.

If the Earth Planet meets with the Metal Planet (Venus) there will be epidemics, civil wars, and loss of territory.

If three planets meet (*in the same Hsiu, one of the planets being Saturn*) the corresponding realm will suffer wars within and without its boundaries, and there will be bereavements; new leaders will come to power. If four planets convene, wars and bereavements will happen together; highly placed people will be afflicted; lesser men become criminals.

If five planets convene, this is called Changing Elements, I Hsing (易行). In this case, those who are virtuous will have great advantage; a new man will come to power; he will possess the Four Quarters, his descendants multiply and prosper. But those who are not virtuous will suffer mortal disaster.

(*Further comments about the Five Planets have been transferred to the end of the section on the planets.*)

From the appearance of the Regulator Planet (Saturn) pass 120 days; then it retrogrades towards the West; after moving towards the West for 20 days, it then moves back to the East. It is visible for 320 days, and then it disappears. After a further 30 days, it reappears in the East. When the Great Year (*of the Jupiter Cycle*) is in Chia Yin (甲寅)(*Year 51 in the sexagenary cycle*) the planet Chen (Saturn) can be found in Hsiu 14, Tung Pi, and 13, Ying Shih.

T'ai Peh	**THE**	The Metal
The Great White	**PLANET**	Planet
太白	**VENUS**	金星

One determines the position of the Great White by the course of the Sun. (See the astronomical note at the end of this section).

The Great White corresponds to the West and to Autumn. It keeps watch over weapons, the progress of the Moon (it was believed to cause eclipses) and comets.

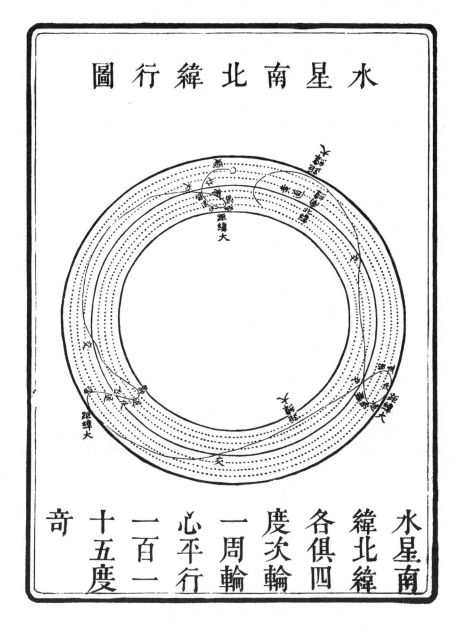

Figure 6.3 Illustration of Mercury's Path through the Ecliptic.

VENUS and MERCURY: An astronomical note.

The opening sentence of the sections on Venus and Mercury refers to a well-known astronomical phenomenon — that Venus and Mercury always appear as either morning or evening stars; either as one of the first celestial bodies to be seen in the evening, before or after sunset, or as one of the last 'stars' to rise in the early morning, before being obscured by the Sun's light.

The reason is quite simple, and it makes no difference whether one is familiar with the nature of the solar system as it is now known to be, or whether one believes the Earth to be at the centre. Diagram (a) illustrates the orbit of the Earth round the Sun, with the orbit of one of the inner planets, which might be Venus or Mercury. Diagram (b) shows how the paths of the Sun and the inner planet appear to an observer on Earth.

In the diagrams (c) and (d) it can be seen that no matter where the inner planet is stationed along its orbit, it must fall within the angle *a* to an observer on Earth. Furthermore, the planet's angular distance from the Sun — the distance it appears to be in the sky — is only half this angle, even at its maximum. It follows, therefore, that the inner planet can never be far away from the Sun as they appear in the sky; at night, when the Sun is behind the Earth, the inner planets will be there too; during the day, their light is obscured by the light of the Sun. Only on extremely rare occasions, when the angle is at its maximum and coinciding with late sunsets and early sunrises in Summer, can Venus be observed at midnight.

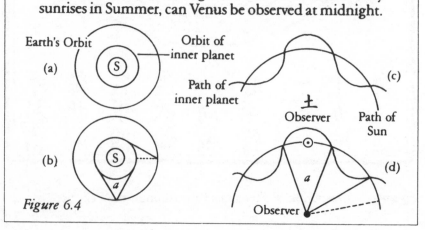

Earth's Orbit

(a)

Orbit of inner planet

Path of inner planet

(b)

(c)

Observer

Path of Sun

(d)

Observer

Figure 6.4

Its days are Keng and Hsin (庚辛) (Stems 7 and 8). It presides over killings; when someone is murdered retribution is wrought by the Great White (Venus).

When the Great White misses its normal course, the Hsiu where it is found determines the fate of the corresponding realm.

After rising, it visits eighteen Hsiu; then after 140 days it sets. After setting in the East, it remains unseen through eleven Hsiu in 130 days; after setting in the West, it is invisible through three Hsiu in sixteen days, after which it rises.

If it fails to rise or set when it should, it is said to have missed its station; if there is no uprising or destruction of the army, there is certain to be an upheaval of some kind.

The following calculations concerning the planet are of very ancient origin. In the year She T'i Ko the planet rises in the morning in the East in Ying Shih (Hsiu 13) then travels through until it reaches Chio (Hsiu 1) when it sets. Then it rises in the evening in the West in Ying Shih (Hsiu 13), then travels through to Chio (Hsiu 1) where it sets.

(To save repetitious paragraphs, the progress of the planet is set out in the following table).

T'ai Peh — Venus

Rises	in Hsiu		then sets in Hsiu	
morning	Ying Shih	13	Chio	1
evening	Ying Shih	13	Chio	1
morning	Chio	1	Pi	19
evening	Chio	1	Pi	19
morning	Pi	19	Chi	7
evening	Pi	19	Chi	7
morning	Chi	7	Liu	24
evening	Chi	7	Liu	24
morning	Liu	24	Ying Shih	13
evening	Liu	24	Ying Shih	13

Altogether, there are five risings in the East, and five in the West. The whole cycle takes 8 years and 120 days to complete. (*Another text gives 8 years 232 days*).

A complete tour of the Heavens is made in one year. (*This is because of the proximity of the planet, from a terrestrial observer's view, to the Sun, which appears to circle the sky in one year. See the astronomical note.*)

When it begins its tour, rising in the East, it travels slowly, making half a degree's progress each day; at the end of 120 days, it moves to the West by one or two Hsiu; then it moves in the opposite direction, making 1½° progress each day; at the end of 120 days, it sets.

When it is low, and close to the Sun, it is called Ming Hsing (明星) the Bright Star; this indicates change. When it is high, and away from the Sun, it is called Ta Hsiao (大囂) Great Clamour, and indicates stability.

After it has risen in the West, it moves rapidly, making about 1½° progress each day. At the end of 120 days, having reached its maximum, it moves slowly by half a degree each day. It always moves retrograde through one or two Hsiu before setting.

When it is low, and close to the Sun, it is called T'ai Peh (太白) the Great White; this indicates change. When it is high, and away from the Sun, it is called Ta Hsiang (大相) the Great Form, and indicates stability.

It rises at the hours Ch'en and Hsü (*Branches V and XI, equivalent to 8am and 8pm*).

It sets at the hours Ch'ou and Wei (*Branches II and VIII, equivalent to 2am and 2pm*).

(*These must be regarded as 'notional' times, on which the following astrological observations are based. It would be impossible to observe the setting of Venus at 2pm*).

If it fails to rise at the appointed time, or it sets too soon, there will be concealed arms, and attacks from the rear.

If it rises when it should not, or it fails to set, there is danger of war and destruction of the State.

When it rises at its proper time, the corresponding realm is prosperous.

When it is seen in the East, it presides over the East.
When it sets in the East, it presides over the North.
When it is seen in the West, it presides over the West.
When it sets in the West, it presides over the South.

If it remains in one place for a long time, the corresponding realm has the advantage over others, but if it passes over a place quickly, this is unfortunate.

When it appears in the West and retrogrades to the East, the corresponding western realm is favoured.

When it appears in the East and retrogrades to the West, the corresponding eastern realm is favoured.

On its appearance, it should not go past the meridian. If it does, this indicates a change of government.

If it is small, and pointed, wars erupt.
When it begins large, then goes small, the army is weak.
When it begins small, then goes large, the army is strong.

When it appears high, there is fortune in battle and little mishap.
When it appears low, there is little luck and great misfortune.

When the Sun is South, and the Metal Planet (Venus) further South, or else when the Sun is North, and the Metal Planet further North, this is called 'advance'. In such a case, it indicates discontent among the chiefs; it is best to advance rather than retreat.

When the Sun is South, and the Metal Planet (Venus) to the North of it, or conversely, when the Sun is North and the Metal Planet to the South of it, this is called 'retreat'. Then, the chiefs are stricken, and it is best to retreat rather than advance.

When going to war, observe the Great White, and take its movements as a guide. If the Great White moves quickly, then move quickly; if it moves slowly, then move slowly. If it shoots out rays, go into battle; if it sparkles boldly, then be bold. If it is round and still, then remain still.
If one follows the directions in which it points its rays, one will have success; otherwise, there will be misfortune.
When it appears, send the army out; when it disappears, call them back.

When it gives out red rays, there will be battle; when there are white rays, mourning. When it is dark, round, and radiant, there will be affliction in matters to do with Water.
When green, round, and radiant, there will be affliction in matters to do with Wood.
When it is yellow, round, and gives out gentle rays, then there will be fortunate events to do with Earth, and there will be a good harvest.
If, three days after its appearance, it dwindles and disappears for three days, then reappears full, this is called 'weak'. In the corresponding kingdom an army will be weakened and there will be disgrace.
If, three days after its disappearance it reappears, but small, and then after a further three days it reappears full, the corresponding region will be plunged into civil uprisings and strife, and its general taken prisoner.

Wher, it appears in the West, and misses its regular progress, a foreign country will be taken. When it appears in the East and misses its regular progress, the Middle Kingdom will be beaten.

Note these observations regarding its appearance.

When the Great White is white, it resembles the star Lang (狼) (The Wolf, 138 = Sirius).

When it is red, its appearance is like Hsin (Hsiu 5, *probably referring to Antares.*)

When it is yellow, it is like the left shoulder of Orion; when green, like the right shoulder of Orion. (*The former is Betelgeux.*)

When it is dark, it resembles the great star of K'uei (Hsiu 15).

When it is large, round, yellow, and wet, this is a good indication. When it is large, round, and red, there will be many soldiers, but no battles.

When the Great White is followed by four other planets, and all five convene in the same Hsiu, the corresponding kingdom may force the rest of the empire to comply.

If the planet only seems to do something, this is not a proper indication. The progress of a planet is a much more reliable indication than its colour; colour is a better guide than its position; actual position takes precedence over absence from its position; colour is more important than absence of colour. But above all these, the most reliable indication is its progress.

When, on its appearance, it stays low on the horizon, this is bad for the region to which it applies.

When, having risen, it moves quickly and at the end of the day has covered a third of the sky, this is bad for the kingdom to which it is opposite.

When, after having risen, it sets, or when, having set, it immediately rises, there will be a mutiny.

If it is found near the Moon, a general will become flushed with pride. If the rays of the Metal Planet (Venus) and the Wood Planet (Jupiter) meet, there will be battles in the region under them. If the rays do not meet, soldiers will be sent out to battle, but they will not engage. If the rays are mutually destroyed, the armies beneath them will also be destroyed.

If it appears in the West, and six hours later in the North, the soldiers in the North are powerful.

If it appears at the time of the evening meal, there will be weakness.

If it appears at midnight, there will be moderate weakness; if it appears at dawn, great weakness.

(*These statements are rather vague; I do not think that the passage applies to the appearance of the planet Venus, since the motions, colours and*

other aspects have been described very comprehensively already; possibly
it applies to the conjunction of Venus with Jupiter.)
This is called the dissolution of Yin in Yang.
(Again no doubt referring to the conjunction of Venus and Jupiter,
remembering that these two planets were regarding as having the Male
and Female principles respectively — not the other way round.)

When it is in the East, and at daybreak appears in the South, the soldiers
in the South are powerful. If it appears at cockcrow, this is called little
weakness; at midnight, middle weakness; at six o'clock in the evening,
great weakness. Then it is called the dissolution of Yang in Yin.

If the Great White is hidden when soldiers are sent out, they will be restless
and disquiet.

When the Great White appears South of Mao (卯 Branch IV) the South
will vanquish the North. If it appears to the North of Mao, then the North
vanquishes the South. If it appears in Mao, then the victory will go to
the East.
    When it appears to the North of Yü (酉 Cyclical number X) the North
vanquishes the South; when it appears to the South of Yü, the South
vanquishes the North; when it appears in Yü, then the victory will go
to the West.
(Here, the terms Mao and Yü refer to the division of the horizon into twelve
parts, Tzu, Branch I representing the North; Mao, IV, the East; and Yü,
X, the West.)

When it comes into contact with a single planet or star, there are minor
battles; if it comes into contact with several planets or stars, there are
major battles.
    If the celestial body which contacts The Great White is South of the
planet, the realms of the South are beaten; if the star is to the North,
the realms of the North are beaten; if it moves quickly, there is war, if
it rests, there is peace.
    When it has a white appearance with five rays, and appears in the
morning, this signifies an eclipse of the Moon. If it appears in the evening,
there will be meteors and brush-comets despatched against the
corresponding realm.
    When it appears in the East, there is virtue. In setting about any
undertaking, let the planet keep on your left when you set out, and the
result will be favourable.
    When it appears in the West, there is retribution. If setting about any
undertaking, the planet is to your right; travel with your back to it; that
would bring a favourable result. The reverse would bring misfortune.

If the brightness of the Great White is obscured, there will be loss in battle; if it is visible in broad daylight, or at midday, then it is called 'Unrivalled Brightness'; powerful kingdoms become weak; weak kingdoms powerful; the country prospers.

K'ang (Hsiu 2) is the Outer Temple; The Great White is the Ancestral Temple. The Great White is the Prime Minister.

Observe it well.

Ch'en	THE	The Water
辰	PLANET	Planet
	MERCURY	水星
	also called Mien 免	

(*Ch'en is difficult to translate; it is one of the twelve cyclical signs, representing the hours 7am to 9am, and is used to mean early morning; the term may be derived from the planet's appearance as a morning star. On the other hand, in the Chou Li the term is used to mean planets in general. The term has also been used to mean eclipse; the opening sentence of this section affords a clue as to this use of the term as well.*)

To find the position of Ch'en (Mercury) observations are made when the Sun, Moon and Earth are in alignment (Full or New Moon).

It corresponds to the North, and to the Element Water.

It is the Great Yin (太陰).

It presides over Winter, and the days Jen and Kuei (壬癸) (Stems 9 and 10).

When there are errors in judgements, retribution comes from the planet Ch'en. According to the Hsiu in which it is found, so is ordained the destiny of that State.

It determines the Four Seasons. In the second month of Spring, at the Spring Equinox, it appears in the evening at the junction of the Hsiu K'uei, Lou and Wei (Hsiu 15, 16 and 17) and the five Hsiu to the East, corresponding to the country of Ch'i.

In the second month of Summer, at the Summer Solstice, it appears in the evening next to the Hsiu Tung Ching, Kuei, and Liu (Hsiu 22, 23 and 24) and the seven Hsiu to the East of these, corresponding to the country of Ch'ou.

In the second month of Autumn, at the Autumn Equinox, it appears in the evening next to the Hsiu Chio, K'ang, Ti and Fang (Hsiu 1, 2, 3 and 4) and the four Hsiu to the East of these, corresponding to the country of Han.

In the second month of Winter, at the Winter Solstice, it appears in the morning next to the Eastern border, with the Hsiu Wei, Chi, Tou, and Ch'ien Niu (Hsiu 6, 7, 8 and 9), and travels westwards with them. It corresponds to the Middle Kingdom. The times of its appearances and disappearances are always the hours Ch'en, Hsü, Ch'ou and Wei (the Branches V, XI, II and VIII, i.e., the hours 8am, 8pm, 2am, 2pm).

Its appearance in the morning denotes an eclipse of the Sun, in the evening, a comet or a meteor.

If it fails to appear at its proper time soldiers should be kept down instead of being sent out to battle.

If it is a single period when it does not appear, this means a period of discord; if it fails to appear four times, the empire may suffer a great famine.

When it appears on time and its colour is white, this indicates drought; if yellow, the five cereals ripen; red indicates war; black, troubles by water.

When it appears in the East, large and white, there are riots outside the country's frontiers. When it stays in the East, and is red, the Middle Kingdom will be victorious.

When it is in the West and red, a foreign power will gain the advantage.

If there are no wars going on outside the kingdom, and it appears red, this is a sign that war will break out.

When it appears together with the Great White (Venus) in the East, and both are red and shoot out rays, foreign powers are vanquished and the Middle Kingdom will be victorious.

When it appears with the Great White in the West, and both are red, shooting out rays, a foreign power will be victorious. When all five planets, having been separated in the heavens, convene in the East, the Middle Kingdom has the advantage; if in the West, however, the foreign power will have the advantage.

When the four other planets accompany Ch'en (Mercury) in the same Hsiu, then the corresponding realm will gain the empire lawfully.

When Ch'en does not appear, the Great White is the Visitor; when it does appear, the Great White is the Master.

When it appears with the Great White in a Hsiu corresponding to a region where there are wars, but there is no other accompanying planet, there will be no battle.

If it appears in the East when the Great White is in the West, or appears in the West when the Great White is in the East, there is discord, but in the corresponding region, even though there are armies, there will be no battle.

If it appears at the wrong season, it will be temperate when it ought to be cold, and cold when it ought to be temperate. When it ought to appear, but does not, this is called 'attack' and great wars erupt.

When it is in conjunction with the Great White (Venus) and appears above it, the army will be defeated and the general killed; a foreign army will be victorious. If it appears beneath, the foreign power will lose territory. If Ch'en (Mercury) moves towards the Great White, and the Great White does not move away, a general will die.

If, aligned with Ch'i (旗) the Banner and appears above it, the army will be defeated, a general killed, and the foreigner the victor; if it appears below this line, the foreigner will lose territory. Consider the auspices of Ch'i (旗) to find out whether or not the army will be victorious.

When it turns on the Great White, seemingly to attack it, there will be a great battle at which the foreigner will be the victor. If Mien (免, 'cancellation' another name for Mercury) overtakes the Great White and the space between them is enough to pass a sword-blade, there will be a minor battle, and the foreigner will be victor. If Mien stops in front of the Great White, the army will be discharged; if it appears to the left of the Great White, there will be a minor battle; if it touches the Great White, there will be a battle involving several thousand men; the leader and officers will be killed.

If it appears to the right of the Great White, and is seemingly about three feet away, the army will be forced to go into battle.

If it is green, and shoots out rays, the soldiers will be afflicted.
If it is dark, and throws out rays, there will be water.
If it is red, it will be the end for soldiers exhausted by marching.

Mien has several other names: the Little Regulator; Ch'en; the Celestial Supporter; Peaceful Surround; Delicate and Brisk; the Powerful One; and the Hook.

If its colour is yellow, and appears at first to be small, then moves its position, this indicates a change of custom, not for the good.

The following are the colours as they apply to the planet Mien (Mercury)
If green and round; there will be affliction.
  white and round; mourning.
  red and round; the capital will be unquiet.
  dark and round; this is auspicious.
  red with rays; rebels will attack the frontiers.
  yellow with rays; the nation's territory will be disputed.
  white with rays; there will be weeping and wailing.

When it appears in the East, it covers four Hsiu in 48 days; then there are twenty days in which it retrogrades before disappearing into the East. When it appears on the western side, it travels through four Hsiu in 48 days; then during the next twenty days it retrogrades, disappearing into the West.

In a single period it passes the Hsiu Chio, Ying Shih, Pi, Chi, and Liu (Hsiu 1, 13, 19, 7, 24.)

When it appears betwen Fang and Hsin (Hsiu 4 and 5) there are earthquakes.

These are the colours of Ch'en:

In Spring it should be green and yellow;

In Summer red and white;

In Autumn green and white; then the harvest flourishes;

In Winter it is yellow, but does not shine.

If it is the wrong colour, the season will not prosper.

If it is not seen in Spring there will be storms and the Autumn will have no harvest.

If it is not seen in Summer there will be sixty days of drought and an eclipse of the Moon.

If it is not seen in Autumn there will be war and the following Spring the crops will not grow.

If it is not seen in Winter there will be darkness and torrents for sixty days, the townsfolk will become criminals, and in Summer nothing will grow.

Ch'i Hsing (Hsiu 25) is the Officiator; the planet Ch'en is the Ancestral Temple.

It is the planet which pertains to the Man and I tribes (of Southern China).

Remarks concerning the Five Planets

(taken from the section on Saturn)

When the Five Planets appear large, the events portended are great; when they appear small, the events are of lesser importance. If they are early, this is called 'in advance'. Being in advance signifies guests. If they appear late, this is known as retardation; this signifies the host.

There is a celestial harmony between the Five Planets and the stars in the handle of the Ladle (the Great Bear).

When planets are together in the same Hsiu, there is unanimity; when they are in opposition, there is strife. If they appear to be less than seven inches away from each other, the event is certain.

With regards to the colours of the planets:

A white ring indicates mourning and drought.

A red ring; the heart of the kingdom is unsettled, and there will be strife.

A green ring: calamity and floods.

A black ring: an epidemic.

But a yellow ring is fortunate.

Red rays coming from a planet indicates rebels attacking the frontiers.

Yellow rays: territory is disputed.

White rays: cries of woe are heard.

Green rays: war and trouble.

Black rays: inundations, soldiers on the move are frustrated.

But if the Five Planets all have the same colour, then the empire can put away its weapons, and the Hundred Tribes (the people) will be at peace and prosper.

In Spring there is wind; in Summer, heat; in the Autumn, rain, and in Winter, cold. All this is governed by the Five Planets.

Concerning the Moon 月

Note: Hsiu 4, Fang, the Room, consists of the stars β, σ, π and ϱ *scorpionis*. These stars are considered to be the four partitions in the house, so making three rooms (三間). The two central stars are the Central Chamber, and when the Moon passes through it, this is known as the Central Path. β *scorpionis*, the most northerly star of the constellation, is the Yin Star, thus the space between the Yin Star and the Central Chamber forms the Yin Chamber. 'Three feet North' of β *scorpionis* is the 'region of the Great Yin', T'ai Yin (太陰). Similarly, the space between the stars π and ϱ is the Yang Chamber (陽間), South of which is the T'ai Yang (太陽). These terms will of course be familiar to readers of the *I Ching* and other philosophical studies.

When the Moon occupies the Central Path, there is calm and peace.

When it is in the Yin room, there is plenty of water, and many events take place connected with the Yin principle. When it is three feet to the North of the Yin Star, Yin Hsing (陰星), Yin is supreme, there will be plenty of water and wars.

When it is in the Yang room, there is famine and degradation. When it is with the Yang Star, Yang Hsing (陽星), there is cruelty and imprisonment. When it is in the region of the Great Yang, there is drought and mourning.

When the Moon passes through Chio (Hsiu 1) and T'ien Men (天門) Heaven's Gate, then if it be the tenth month, waters will be released in the fourth month; if the eleventh month, the waters will be released in the fifth month, or if the twelfth month, they will be released in the sixth month.

If the Moon comes within three to five feet of the Four Supports (*the four stars of Fang, Hsiu 4*), certain Ministers of State will be put to death.

If the Moon passes by the Southern River, Nan Ho (南河) or the Northern River, Pei Ho (北河), then according to the principles of Yin and Yang explained above, so there will be drought or rains, war or mourning.

If there is an occultation by the Moon of the Year Planet (Jupiter) the corresponding country will starve and be near to ruin.

If the Moon occults the Fiery Sparkler (Mars) there will be uprisings; If it be the Exorcist (Saturn) inferiors will mutiny against their leaders; if it be the Great White (Venus) a powerful kingdom will be beaten in battle; if it be the Morning Star (Mercury) there will be troubles connected with women. If it occults Ta Chio (大角) the Great Horn (Arcturus), the preserver of destiny rnust fear it; Hsin, the Heart, (*Hsiu 5, but is undoubtedly a reference to Antares*) there will be troubles and uprisings in the interior.

If other stars are occulted, the corresponding regions will be afflicted. (*Note: I have taken this passage to refer to occultations of the stars and planets by the Moon; other authorities are of the opinion that Ssu Ma Ch'ien and his contemporaries believed that eclipses of the Moon were caused by these bodies, and read the passage accordingly. While it is true that the Grand Astrologer does frequently refer to eclipses being caused by certain bodies, I believe the reading given above makes better observational sense.*)

Regarding eclipses, their frequency is as follows: 6 × 5 months, 5 × 6 months, another 6 × 5 months, 1 × 6 months, 5 × 5 months, in all, 113 months at the end of which the cycle begins again. Such is the rule concerning eclipses of the Moon.

Compare this passage with the known facts concerning eclipses. Eclipses occur when the planes of the Earth's and Moon's orbits coincide. Eclipses of the Moon can only occur at Full Moon, and those of the Sun at New Moon. Consequently, lunar eclipses are preceded or followed - sometimes both - by solar ones at a fourteen day interval. The maximum number of eclipses in any year is three lunar or five solar.

Every solar eclipse belongs to a pattern, the Saros cycle, which recurs every years 11 days 8 hours. Its duration at each appearance increases to its maximum, and then decreases until it expires. The location of each eclipse moves a similar distance and direction with each repetition of the pattern, so that if two eclipses of a particular pattern are recorded, it is possible to pre-

dict the date and location of its next appearance. But if a cycle of eclipses commenced, say, over the Pacific, beyond the range of observation, its first appearance over China could not have been predicted by this formula.

With regard to eclipses of the Sun, these are not good omens.

On Chia and I days (甲乙 Stems 1 and 2) they concern those regions beyond the Four Seas, thus, there is no need to take any note of eclipses of the Sun or Moon on those days.

On the days Ping and Ting (丙丁 Stems 3 and 4) they concern the regions Chiang, Huai, the Sea, and the T'ai Mountain.

On the days Wu and Chi (戊己 Stems 5 and 6) they concern the Middle Kingdom, the Yellow River, and the River Chi.

On the days Keng and Hsin.(庚辛 Stems 7 and 8) they concern the region which extends to the West of the Mountain Hoa.

On the days Jen and Kuei (壬癸 Stems 9 and 10) they concern the region which extends North of the Mountain Heng.

Eclipses of the Sun concern the ruler of the country; those of the Moon concern his generals and advisers.

Concerning Various Celestial Bodies

(Note: the following are not stars, but manifestations of some kind. Whether they are meteors, novae, or whatever is not known. They are 'temporary' stars; unfortunately, without an accurate record of when or where they appeared, it is impossible to say more.)

The Star Kuo Huang (國皇) the Country's Ruler, is large and red. Its appearance is like that of the North Pole Star. The region where it appears will enlist soldiers, but even though they are powerful, they will not conquer.

The Star Chao Ming (昭明) Brightly Shining, is large and white; it has no rays; it is sometimes above, and sometimes below the region pertaining to the kingdom which it portends; such a country will enlist soldiers and there will be great changes.

The Star Wu Ts'an (五殘) the Five Fly-by-nights, appears in the East. The corresponding region is the East. It resembles the Morning Planet (Mercury) in appearance, and is about sixty feet from the Earth. It is large. *(Some commentators take this figure of 60 feet quite literally, thinking that it must be an atmospheric phenomenon. I think, however, that as in earlier passages — 'when the Moon is three to five feet away . . .' — that this is a purely subjective means of describing its apparent height in the sky.)*

The Star Tsei (賊) the Robber, appears in the South; its corresponding region is the South. It is about sixty feet from the Earth; it is large and red, and frequently darts about and sparkles.

The Star Ssu Wei (司危) the Warner, appears in the West, and its region is the West. It appears about sixty feet from the Earth, and is large and white, resembling the Great White (Venus).

The Star Yu Han (or Hsien Han) (獄漢) the Prison of the Han, appears in the North, and its region is the North. It appears about sixty feet above the Earth; it is large and red, moves frequently, and on careful inspection reveals a green centre.

Such are the stars of the Four Regions; should they appear in the region which is not proper to them, the corresponding country will be at war; to attack is not advantageous.

The Star Ssu Chen (四鎮) the Four Exorcists, appears at the four points of the compass; it is about forty feet from the Earth.

The Star Ti Wei Hsien Chuang(地維咸光) the Earth's Universal Brilliance, also appears at the four cardinal points, but is only thirty feet from the Earth. If the Moon should appear first, then the corresponding realm is troubled; those who are provoking will be lost, but the virtuous will prosper.

The Star Chou (燭) the Torch, has a form similar to the Great White. When it appears, it does not move; it shows itself, and then is extinguished. When it appears the corresponding towns are troubled.

That which is like a star but is not one, and that which is like an aura, but is not one, is called Kuei Shih (歸邪) Reverting to Evil. When Kuei Shih appears, it is certain that people will submit to the kingdom.

Stars are an emanation of Metal; their origin is Fire; when stars are numerous, the kingdom is happy, when there are few, there is discontent.
    The Milky Way is also an emanation of Metal, but its origin is Water. When the stars of the Milky Way are numerous, there is plenty of Water, but when there are few, there is drought. Such is the rule which concerns them.

T'ien Ku (天鼓) Heaven's Drum, sounds like thunder, but is not. The sound is in the Earth, and comes up through the ground. In the region corresponding to where it is found, soldiers will be sent into battle.

T'ien Kou (天狗) Heaven's Dog, is like a shooting star; it makes a noise; when it descends it stops on the ground. It is like a falling dog and a

burning fire. When seen from a distance, it is like a burst of flame; burning, it erupts in the sky. The lower half is round and resembles a field of several acres; the upper part is pointed and yellow coloured; a thousand Li from it, an army will be defeated and a general killed.
(*This reads very much like the description of a falling meteorite.*)

The Star Ke To (格澤) Reaching Choice, has the form of a brilliant star; it is yellow and white. It rises from the Earth and ascends; at its base it is wide, at the top it is pointed. When it appears, one can harvest where one has not sown. If important matters connected with the Earth are not done, there will come great harm.

The Banner of Ch'e Yü (蚩尤之旗) is like a comet, but the end is curved. When it appears, the monarch will subjugate and punish the Four Quarters.

Hsün Shih (旬始) the Week's Beginning appears at the side of the Northern Ladle (the Great Bear) and is like a pheasant. When angry, it is green and black. It has the shape of a crouching tortoise.

Wang Shih (枉矢) the Curving Arrow, is like a shooting star. It travels in a serpentine fashion, and is dark green. From a distance it appears like fur or feathers.

Ch'ang Keng (長庚) Long Age, is like a veil which covers the sky. When this appears, wars commence.

Some stars fall to earth; these are like stones. In the area between the Ho and the Chi rivers are several which have fallen from the sky. When the sky is calm, then the Resplendant Star, Ching Hsing (景星) appears. This is the star of virtue; its form is unsteady. It always appears in the region endowed with wisdom.

Haloes and Aura

I have placed the next two sections, the first on solar haloes, and the other on the phenomena known as Ch'i (氣) next to each other since although they have many points of reference it is necessary to stress the distinction between them. The solar halo is less familiar than the lunar variety, and perhaps for that reason it was regarded as more portentous. Haloes round the sun are due to its light being refracted through hexagonal crystals of ice in clouds. They are well documented in Chinese literature and for that reason alone can be taken off the list of possible meanings of the next manifestation — that of the Ch'i.

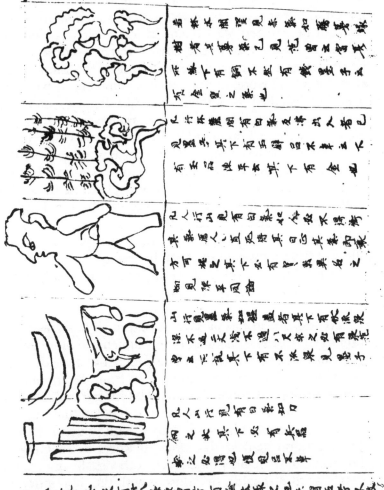

Figure 6.5 Illustration of various 'Ch'i' from a Tun Huang manuscript.

This is the most puzzling of the observations made by the Grand Astrologer, not least in view of the fact that they were regarded as important enough for the ancient Astronomical Bureau to assign twelve of its staff of twenty-six observers to keep watch on the Ch'i. These were not new to Ssu Ma Ch'ien. In 655 BC it was reported that the Duke of Lu went up to the Divine Terrace to observe the Ch'i at the equinoxes, solstices, and the beginnings of the four seasons.

But what these Ch'i were, or are, remains a mystery. A paper by Professor Hulsev listed all the known classical references, and they are described and even illustrated in a manuscript from the Dunhuang caves written a thousand years after Ssu Ma Ch'ien.

The word Ch'i (Qi) has a multitude of meanings: gas, breath, atmosphere, current, and vapour, to mention only a few. But on the other hand, it did not mean clouds or mists, because these elusive Ch'i were often compared to them. Nor did the word signify rainbows, aurora borealis, or solar haloes, because the words for these already existed. To avoid confusion, in the quoted passage which follows I have translated the term by 'aura.'

Possibly, it referred to optical illusions, mirages, or subjective interpretations of haze (as distinct from mist) or subtle changes in the light or shade.

A few years ago, I read this passage out during a talk I was giving in southern Germany. A member of the audience, whose hobby was hang-gliding, said that she immediately recognised the description as the quality of haze which can be seen from the mountains when the meteorological conditions are ideal for her aerial activities. The same conditions occur when the dreaded Fön (the German equivalent of the mistral) blows - a warm wind which is locally blamed for a general malaise, lassitude, sickness and feeling of unease. The fact that these phenomena are both visually discernible and associated with ill-health, ties closely with the description of Ch'i. Whatever the Ch'i were, they were sufficiently important for records of them to have been kept for nearly two thousand years.

Concerning Solar Haloes 暈

When two armies are set to battle, the Sun has a halo. If this is medium, the forces are equal; if it is dense, long, and broad, there will be victory; if it is thin, short, and small, there will be no victory.

When there is a double halo, this indicates a great defeat; when there is no surround, there is harmony. If it is back to back with the Sun, there is discord and division. If it stretches some distance in a straight line, there is someone who will usurp power, and it will be given to a king or lord.

A pointed halo indicates the death of a general. If it is upturned, there will be great joy. If the circle is central, this shows that the Middle Kingdom will be the victor; if the circle is outside, then outsiders will be the victors.

If it is green outside and red in the middle, this indicates separation in harmony; but if it is red outside and green in the middle, this means separation in hatred.

If the halo emanations come forward then go back, this indicates a victory for the army.

If it appears early, and leaves early, this shows advantage at first, but suffering later.

If it appears late, and goes away late, this indicates suffering at first, but advantage later.

If it arrives late and goes early, there is suffering early and late, and no advantage for the army.

If its appearance and disappearance is hasty, there will be victory but no glory.

But if it is visible for more than half a day, there will be great glory.

A white emanation with a curved form, a small point at the top and bottom, indicates great bloodshed over the region where it appears. A solar halo indicates a victory after thirty, but before sixty days. The dissolving of the halo shows the dissolving of what is unlucky; its renewal, the reappearance of fortunate things. The complete dissolving of the halo represents the power of the ruler. Make a careful note of the place where the halo is to be found, noting the Hsiu where the Sun is lodged, and adjust the time indicated by the Sun to determine the destiny of the corresponding realm.

Concerning Aura 氣

(Note: Professor Hulsevé has pointed out a significantly similar passage in the Han Shu, on which the following must have been based. Explanatory lines from the Han Shu are given in square brackets.)

[An aura is like a cloud, but is not a cloud; it is like a fog, but it is not a fog; misty, as if something were visible. When it becomes dense, five or six feet above the horizon, its origin is more than 1,500 Li]

In general, the rule for observing aura is that if one has to lift one's head in order to see them, then they are more than 300-400 Li away. If they are seen on the horizon, above the hedges, then they are more than 2,000 Li away; if one has to mount a ladder or a platform to see them, then they are 3,000 Li away (Evidence of the curvature of the Earth.)

As for aura, those which have the shape of an animal are the most important. [When an animal stays on the top of the aura, there will be victory.]

South of the Hua Mountain (East of Ch'ang An) the aura are black at the bottom, and red at the top. In the region of Sung Kao and the San Ho the aura are entirely red. North of the Heng Mountain, the aura are black at the bottom and sky-blue on top. In the region of the Po, Ch'ieh, Hai, and Tai, the aura are all black. In the region of Yangtze, the aura are always white.

The aura of forced labour is white; the aura of large-scale construction is yellow. Aura relative to transport are sometimes high, and sometimes low, continually reforming. The aura of cavalry is low and extended; the aura of infantry is crooked.

If they are low in front and high at the back, there will be sickness. [They (the infantry or cavalry) will be moving quickly.]

If they are square-shaped, and high in front, but pointed and low at the back, there is dissatisfaction. [or there is retreat]. Aura which are even proceed slowly; those which are pointed move faster than those which are square.

Those which are high in front but low at the back go to where they came from without stopping.

When there are two opposing aura, the lower one takes precedence over the upper one. Those which are pointed take precedence over those which are square.

When the aura is low, following the carriage ruts, they will leave in three or four days, and may be visible for four or five Li. When the aura is at a height of about six or seven feet, it will leave after five or six days, and remains visible for ten to twenty days. If an aura is more than ten feet high to as much as twenty feet, it will last for thirty to forty days, and be visible for fifty to sixty Li.

When sleet clouds are clear and white, the general is brave, but the soldiers cowards. When there is a kind of root growing out for some distance, there will be a battle. When they are green and white, hanging down in front, one will be victorious in battle. But if it is red in front, and rising, one will not be victorious. (The following are technical names for some of the aura.)

'Battle' aura are like standing walls.

'Spindle' aura are like spindles.

'Axle' aura are like axles, but curved, and pointed at both ends.

'Ladle' aura are like ropes, they fill half the sky, leaving the other half clear.

'Rainbow' aura are like Palace Gates.

'Hooked' aura are bent.

When such aura appear, the divination is taken from the five colours; when they are sufficiently noticeable to make people marvel at them, that is the time to take the auspices. Soldiers must not fail to take to arms against those who are in front of them.

The observations taken by the king [Wang Shuo, *a famous observer of the aura in the time of Han Wu Ti*] on the first day of the month were only made of those aura at the side of the Sun, since they were the symbol of the Emperor. For such auguries, it is the shape of the aura which is important.

Now the aura which concern the northern nomads are like herds and tents; those which concern the barbarians of the South are like boats and ships with banners.

In places where there is a great deal of water, or over battlefields where armies have been defeated, in regions where there has been destruction of kingdoms, and above places where treasure has been buried, above metal and precious objects, aura will appear and must be investigated.

By the Seas, [exhaled by the Chan (蜃) Great Clam, *a fabulous bivalve*] aura take the form of towers and terraces. On plains, aura form palaces and castles.

Concerning clouds and aura, they resemble their corresponding mountains and waterways, and the places where people congregate. That is why those who look for prosperity and decay when they visit a kingdom or a city take note whether the buildings are in order, whether the borders and hedges are well-kept, whether the doors and walls are in good shape. Then they look to the carriage-ways, the people's clothes, the state of the animals, and the produce. Where there is prosperity, this presages good fortune, where there is emptiness and decay, that is bad.

That which is like smoke, and yet not smoke, like a cloud and yet not a cloud, elegant and intricate, such is the aura of good fortune. When auspicious signs appear, there is a joyous aura. Like fog, but not fog, for hats and clothes are not made damp, when such an aura appears, the city concerned will put on armour and rush into battle.

When Heaven produces thunder and lightning, rainbows, rumblings and nocturnal glows, these are movements of the Yang aura. In Spring and Summer, it unfolds; in Autumn and Winter, it is concealed. That is why observers do not overlook anything. When the Heavens reveal the things which are suspended in it, when the Earth trembles and moves, when mountains are shaken and displaced, when watercourses spew forth and valleys are heaped up, when waters are disturbed and marshes drained and the Earth extends, such are portents.

Concerning the outer and inner walls of cities, the main gates, and the lesser gates, interior doors and shutters, living trees and dead wood, the palaces, ancestral temples, mansions and manors, the houses of greater and lesser men, the pitch of the notes produced by the crowds, the carriages and clothing, the customs of the people, what the people eat and drink, the five grains [hemp-Metal; millet-Fire; yellow millet-Earth; corn-Wood; pulse-Water] plants and trees and the places where they take root, granaries and treasuries, stables and carriage-houses, roads to the four corners of the Earth, the six kinds of animal (*horse, ox, sheep, pig, dog, fowl*),* birds and beasts, and all that they produce, fishes, tortoises, birds, and rats, and where they are to be found — all these have to be observed. That men should be terrified when they encounter such omens is obviously false.

Concerning a Variety of Matters

To know whether the harvest be good or bad, it is necessary to study the beginning of the year carefully. For this purpose, the beginning of the year is to be the day of the Winter Solstice. At that time the influences are revealed for the first time. The day after the La sacrifice, people congregate at the end of the year to celebrate the New Year; the Yang flux is manifest, and that is why it is the beginning of the year. The morning of the first day of the first month is the beginning of the year for kings (*that is to say, the beginning of the civil rather than the astronomical calendar*). The day of the beginning of Spring is the last day of the four seasons; the day which is the beginning of the four seasons is the day which one observes as the first day of the year. (*That is, disregard the Chinese civil calendar*).

During the Han dynasty, Wei Hsien combined the day of the La sacrifice with the first day of the first month in order to make prognostication by the Eight Winds.

If on that day, the wind came from the
   South-West, there would be a slight drought;
   South, a great drought;
   South-East, poor harvest and epidemics;
   East, inundations;
   North-East, a great harvest;
   North, a medium harvest;
   North-West, beans would ripen, there would be slight rain, men would be called to arms;
   West, war.

*Note the similarity to the twelve-animal cycle here.

If the wind should change direction (on that day), the more forceful wind is the one to observe; if the prognostication of one is 'small' and the other 'great' then take note of the one which indicates the greater augury. Then again, a long-lasting wind has a superior portent to a short-lasting one.

If the wind blows from dawn to breakfast-time, there will be corn; from breakfast to noon, yellow millet; from noon till dinner, millet; from dinner till supper, pulse; from supper till sunset, hemp.

If during the day there is rain, cloud, wind and sun, then there will be much reaping later.

If there is no cloud, but only wind and sun, then sow less profusely, and there will still be grain later.

If there are clouds and wind but no sun, one sows profusely for little reward.

If there is sun, but neither clouds nor wind, seed will be lost; if this happens during the time it takes to eat a meal, little loss; if during the time it takes to reap five bushels of rice, great loss. If the wind begins again, and there are clouds, sowing can begin again.

Everyone, during the season, must take note of the colour of the clouds, planting according to the portents which are revealed.

If there is rain and snow, and it is icy, the harvest will be bad.

If the day is bright, listen to the pitch of the notes produced by the throngs in the city.

   If the sound is the note Kung (C) then the harvest will be good, and the prospects good.

   If the note is Shang (D) then wars will break out.

   If the note is Chih (G) there will be drought.

   If the note is Chiao (E) the harvest will be bad.

   If the note is Yü (A), it will be damp.

Another method is to count from the first day of the first month the number of consecutive days of rain; generally there will be one Sheng (a pint measure) of food per day for each day of rain up to a maximum of seven Sheng.

Or else, count up to the twelfth day of the month; each day is the model for the corresponding month regarding dryness or humidity. This rule holds for an area up to a thousand Li round the city.

Those who take auspices for the whole empire go up to the end of the first month, noting the various Hsiu occupied by the Moon during that period; thus, regarding wind, rain, and sun, they can make a correspondence between that day and the kingdom concerned (each Hsiu

*corresponding to a particular kingdom, the weather for that day will
show the weather for the whole year.)*

Then one must also observe the progress of the T'ai Sui (the Great Year,
Counter-Jupiter). If it is in Metal, there is fertility; if in Water, ruin, if in
Wood, famine; if in Fire, drought.

If on the first Chia day of the first month (甲 Stem 1) the wind is from
the East, it is good for silkworm culture. But if it is from the West, and
there are yellow clouds, this is bad.

*(The following is virtually a scientific observation, and describes an
intriguing type of hygrometer.)*

The Winter Solstice is the shortest day. Earth and charcoal are suspended
from a balance. The charcoal becomes heavier *(by absorbing water)* when
stags lose their horns, when the stems of orchids appear, and when springs
bubble up. Such are the means of knowing when the Winter Solstice has
arrived. But more important is to study the shadow of the gnomon.

When the Year Planet (Jupiter) is found in a certain region, that is where
the five grains prosper.

Miscellaneous Observations and
Evidence for the Effectiveness of Astrology
(Extracts from the final chapter of the treatise.)

Thus spake the Lord Grand Astrologer:
From the time of man's first existence, through succeeding generations,
was there ever a time when the ruler failed to observe the motions of
the Sun or Moon? Even as anciently as the time of the Five Emperors
and the Three Dynasties were such observations made and their meanings
expounded *(that is to the time of Fu Hsi, China's first legendary ruler)*.
    In the Middle Kingdom, there are those who don the Cap and Sash
(the civilized world) and outside, there are the barbarians. Raise the head,
and contemplate the vastness of the Heavens, look round, and marvel
at the manifestations of the Earth. In the Heavens are the Five Planets;
in the Earth are the Five Elements.
    In the Heavens are Celestial Mansions; on the Earth, kingdoms and
provinces. The Three Lights (Sun, Moon and Planets) are the source of
Yin and Yang; theirs is the primaeval force on Earth. Such was recorded
by the sages of long ago.

*(There then follows a long list of historical persons who acted as Ssu
Ma Ch'ien's predecessors, as is fitting for a historical record.)*

Summarizing their observations, in the 242 years of the period of the Spring and Autumn annals (722 BC–481 BC) there were 36 eclipses and three comets; in the time of the Shang stars fell like rain, and the Son of Heaven was weakened, rulers governed by fear, the Five Kingdoms became powerful in turn and imposed their wills over the others. Afterwards the majority oppressed the minority, the great debased the small, The Ch'in, Ch'ou, Wu, Yüeh and even the barbarians imposed their wills . . .

The Kingdoms Ruled by the Twenty-Eight Hsiu

Hsiu		Kingdom	Modern equivalent
1, 2, 3	Chio; K'ang; Ti	Yen	Shantung; Chin Li
4, 5	Fang; Hsin	Yü	Ho Nan
6, 7	Wei; Chi	Yu	(Chih Li; Liao Tung)
8	Tou	Chiang; Ho	(Yangtze Kiang)
9, 10	Ch'ien Niu, Wu Nü	Yang	Kiang Su; Anhwei
11, 12	Hsü; Wei	Ch'ing	
13, 14	Ying Shih; Tung Pi	Ping	Shansi
15, 16, 17	K'uei; Lou; Wei	Hsü	Shantung; Kiang Su
18, 19	Mao, Pi	Chi	Shantung
20, 21	Ts'ui; Shen	I	Hupeh; Szechuan
22, 23	Tung Ch'ing; Yu Kuei	Yung	
24, 25, 26	Liu; Hsing; Chang	San Ho	Huang Ho
27, 28	I; Chen	Ch'ing	

The 28 Hsiu preside over the twelve provinces; the Seven Stars of the Great Bear rule over all; this knowledge is very ancient.

In the territory of Ch'in, observations are made of the Great White (Venus) and portents taken from its position with regards to the stars Lang (狼) (Sirius) and Hu (弧) the Bow.

For the territories of Wu and Ch'ou, observations are made of the Fire Planet (Mars), and portents taken from its position with regards to the

Bird Star, Niao (鳥) and Heng, the Balance (衡).

For the territories of Yen and Ch'i, observations are made of the Morning Star (Mercury) with its relation to the Hsiu Hsü and Wei, (Hsiu 11 and 12); for the territories of Sung and Cheng, observations are made of the Year Star (Jupiter) and its relation to the Hsiu Fang and Hsin (Hsiu 4 and 5); and for the territory of Chin, observations are made of the Exorcist (Saturn) and its relation to the Hsiu Shen (Hsiu 21, Orion) and the star Fa (伐, the Sword of Orion).

Ch'in absorbed the three states Chin, Yen, and Tai; all that extended South of the Yellow River and the Hua Mountain became the Middle Kingdom; the Middle Kingdom lies between the Four Seas. That which is to the South-West is Yang; and that which is Yang corresponds to the Sun, the Year Star (Jupiter), the Fire Star (Mars), the Regulator Star (Saturn) and the portents taken from the South of Star Chieh (街). The Hsiu Pi (Hsiu 19) presides.

Those who live to the North-West, the Ho, the Mi, the Yüeh Chih and those people who wear padded felt clothing and draw bows live in the Yin region. Corresponding to Yin are the Moon, the Great White (Venus) and the Morning Star (Mercury) and auspices are taken North of the star Chieh (街); Mao, the Pleiades (Hsiu 18) presides.

Regarding mountains and watercourses in the North East of the Middle Kingdom, their body and head lies in the P'o and Chieh, which is why those people dress in warlike clothing.

Returning to the auspices taken from the Great White, it presides over the Middle Kingdom, and when the Ho and Mi make their raids and pillages, such are portended by the appearance of the Morning Star (Mercury). The planet Mercury appearing and disappearing indicates malecontents and upheaval. It presides over the barbarians Ti and I; these two planets play the roles of Host and Guest.

The Fire Planet (Mars) operates conversely; outside the kingdom, it controls wars; internally it controls governments; for this reason it is said 'Even when there is a wise Son of Heaven, one must not fail to note where the Fire Planet is found.' During the time when kings gained power by turns, the records of auspicious and extraordinary phenomena failed to be kept.

In the time of Ch'in Shih Huang, in the fifteenth year (232 BC) there were four appearances of comets; the longest lasting was seen for forty-eight days and was so large that it covered nearly all the sky.

Then the Ch'in, by virtue of arms, annihilated the six kingdoms, and under the Emperor's hands the Middle Kingdom was united for the first time, the barbarians repulsed to the four corners of the Earth, and the enemy dead lay scattered like the hemp stalks.

When Hsiang Yu came to the aid of Chiu Lo (in 207 BC) a Twisting Arrow travelled westwards; to the East of the Mountains a pact was made between the lords of the lands, while in the West the people of Ch'in were exterminated and the citizens of Hsien Yang put to the sword.

Then when the Han triumphed, the Five Planets appeared altogether in conjunction in the Hsiu Tung Ching (Hsiu 22).

When the city of P'ing Ch'eng was encircled by troops, a lunar halo appeared when the Moon was in the Hsiu Shen and Pi (Hsiu 21 and 19). When the Lu family revolted, there was a solar eclipse which made the day as dark as night.

When there were seven kingdoms, including the Wu and the Ch'ou, rising up in revolt, a great comet, several chains long, and T'ien Kou, Heaven's Dog (天河) crossed the zone which corresponds to the country of the Liang. Then war burst out, corpses were piled up, and blood ran in torrents.

In the reigns of Yuan Kuang and Yuan Shou (元光 and 元狩 134-129 BC, and 122-117 BC) the Banner of Ch'e Yü (蚩尤之旗) appeared twice, so great that it filled half the sky. After that, armies were sent out from the capital four times; the tribes I and Ti were massacred for decades, and attacks against the Ho became ever more violent.

When the kingdom of the Yüeh perished (111 BC) the Fire Planet (Mars) was to be found in the Northern Ladle (*the principal stars of the Great Bear; this is astronomically impossible, because the zodiac, the mean path of the planets, does not touch this constellation*).

When the kingdom of Ch'ao Hsien was destroyed (in 108 BC) there was a comet in Ho Chîai (河戍), the River Guardian.

When our forces subjugated the Ta Yüan (in 102 BC) a comet obscured Chao Yao, the Bringer of Conflict (*a different constellation from Chao Yao* (earlier) *in the Central Palace*).

Such are the kinds of things which are manifested in the Heavens. As for other phenomena, these are beyond count; but there was never a celestial portent which did not presage an event on Earth. Since the Han, there have been many celebrated calculators of destiny; among these have been T'ang Tou (*he was the teacher of Ssu Ma T'an, Ssu Ma Ch'ien's father*) who took observations by the stars; there was Wang Shuo, who knew all about aura; and Wei Hsien, who knew how to forecast about harvests. (*Wang Shuo is mentioned in the section on the observation of aura, page 227. Wei Hsien on page 228.*)

In former times, with regards to the motions of the planets as expounded in the annals of the Chan and Shih, only the Fire Star

(Mars) was known to move backwards (retrograde). Later, auspices were taken not only when retrograde motion was observed in the place occupied by Mars, but also when other planets were observed to have retrograde motion, and when the Sun or Moon occulted or eclipsed.

I have studied the historical writings and examined all the references to retrograde motion. In the last hundred years (i.e., prior to 90 BC) all five planets have at some time retrograded. When they have done so, they have always changed colour. Whether the Sun or Moon becomes veiled or eclipsed, or whether they travel North or South, is determined by astronomical laws. Now the Purple (Central) Palace, Fang and Hsin (Hsiu 4 and 5), Ch'üan (權) and Heng (衡), Hsien Ch'ih (咸池), and the Hsiu Hsü and Wei (Hsiu 11 and 12) serve to catalogue the stars.

These are the seats and residences of the Five Governors of the Heavens which rule with unalterable law. Their sizes and distances are always constant.

The planets of Water, Fire, Metal, Wood, and the Regulator Planet are the Assistants of Heaven. They are the links in the chain between Heaven and Earth. They appear and disappear at fixed times; their route and their progress, their advance and retreat are all regulated.

If the Sun changes, one must strive to achieve Virtue. If the Moon alters, one must reduce punishments; if the planets vary, one must form alliances.

Every time there is a change in Heaven, it is a portent for the Earth and the princes of State Those who are virtuous will prosper, but those who are weak and wicked will fail.

When he who is of the first rank strives to achieve virtue, those beneath him will govern better; those who serve them will assist better, and those of the lowest rank will be as they should be.

Changes in fixed stars only happen on rare occasions.

These are the auspices which are taken from the most notable celestial bodies:

Regarding haloes and darkenings of the Sun and Moon, clouds and winds, and aura which are not of celestial origin, when they appear, there is great movement.

When the Green Emperor manifests his power T'ien Men (天門), the Celestial Gate opens. When the Red Emperor manifests his power T'ien Lao (天牢), the Celestial Prison empties; when the Yellow Emperor manifests his power T'ien Shih (天矢), the Celestial Arrow flies.

An unceasing North West wind on the days Keng and Hsin (Stems 7 and 8) which appears three times in Autumn means a minor amnesty; if it appears five times, a great amnesty.

When the White Emperor manifests his power on the 20th and 21st days of the First Month there will be a lunar halo of circular shape, which means in one year there will be a major amnesty; this is said to be the Great Yang.

One authority says: When the White Emperor manifests his power, Hsiu Pi and Mao (Hsiu 18 and 19) are surrounded; if they are so surrounded for three nights the influence is complete, if less than three nights, or the circle is not complete, the influence is not complete.

Another authority says: If a halo is produced on a Ch'en (辰 *Branch V; this usually refers to months and hours, but the next part of the sentence suggests that one interpolates 'day' here. This is another example of the origin of Fate Calculation having its roots in Han dynasty practice*) one must not go out for ten (days).

When the Black Emperor wishes to manifest his power, the Celestial Barrier, T'ien Chuan (天關) is shaken.

When Heaven exerts its power for Virtue, the Son of Heaven begins a new year; when it does not exert its virtue, wind and rain break stones.

The Three Eminences and the Three Balances form the Celestial Court. When a strange star visits the Celestial Court, this is a singular event.

If from ancient times to the present day the auspices of the Heavens are diligently observed, recorded, and their ordinances kept, then the work of the Governors of the Heavens will be complete.

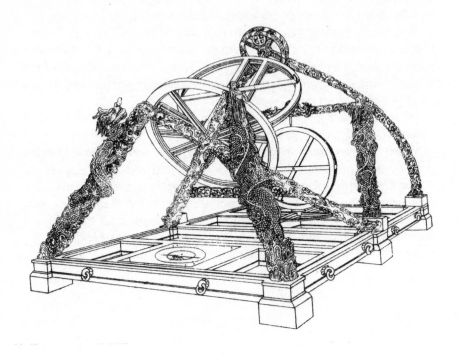

Glossary of Chinese Terms for Planetary Motion
Used by Ssu Ma Ch'ien

Direct motion	順	Shun
Retrograde motion	逆	Ni
Advancing	進	Chin
Retarding	退	T'ui
Change of motion	返	Fan
Retreat (retrograde motion followed by direct motion)	縮	So
Acceleration	贏	Ying
Residing (arrest of motion)	居	Chü
Detained (arrest of motion)	留	Liu
Lodging (detained for a length of time)	宿	Hsiu
Maintaining (oscillation, without leaving the degree)	守	Shou
Rapid motion (an apparent 5 inches to a foot each day)	速行	Su Hsing
Slow motion (one to two inches each day)	遲行	Ch'ih Hsing
One degree per day	疾	Chi

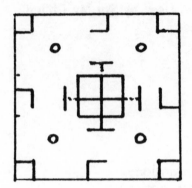

Representation of a divining board from a Wu Liang tomb, Han
Dynasty, *circa* A.D. 147.

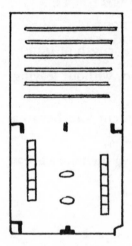

Diagram of the markings on the Liu Po board, made in glazed pottery,
associated with two pottery figures from a Han Dynasty tomb. The original can
be seen in the British Museum.

7.

DIVINATION PLATES
AND FENG SHUI

The Divination Plate found in Chinese horoscopes and almanacs has a long and complex history, and is the result of a gradual amalgamation of several divination methods, astrological, geomantic, and numerological. It is easiest to deal with its antecedents in order of simplicity rather than chronologically, especially since all three systems claim that their moulds were cast at the dawn of time. To begin with, therefore, here are a few remarks on Magic Square Divination.

(i) Lucky Colours and Directions

Magic Squares, in which names of colours were written, feature prominently in the Tun Huang almanacs, and they are still to be found in almanacs of the present day. There is a system of divination known as 'Nine House Divination' which is related to the system of Magic Squares. Magic Square divination is of great antiquity, and legend has it that the numbers were found inscribed on the back of a tortoise. The Nine Chambers of the Emperor's Palace, each appropriate to certain seasons and colours, is described in the *Li Chi* (Book of Rites).

The colours of the Magic Squares not only determined lucky and unlucky directions, but they were also shown on such everyday objects as rulers, set-squares, and other measuring instruments. The proportions, sizes, and relationships of the various parts of a house were determined by the matching colours, and these are described in an early carpenter's manual, the *Lu Pan Ching*, or *Canon of Lu Pan*.

Lu Pan is the patron deity of carpenters and house-builders, and all manner of inventions, such as the saw-horse, block and tackle, and other useful implements, are credited to him. The historical figure Kung-shu Tze, known as Lu Pan, was born in 506 BC, and is mentioned in Mencius. The mystical craft of master-builders which adopted Lu Pan as their patron appears to have been founded in the time of the Yung Lo Emperor (reigned 1403–1425), who posthumously awarded Lu Pan the title of Grand Master, Sustainer of the Empire.

The name Lu Pan should not be confused with the Feng Shui instrument, the Lo P'an.

There are six colours, and three white squares, in the Magic Square. These are Pai (白), White, or blank; Tzu (紫) purple; Ch'ih (赤) red; Huang (黄) yellow; Pi (碧) turquoise; Lü (綠) green; and He (黑) black.

One Magic Square was arranged to portend the year's events, and another the months.

Since each colour was allocated to a particular number, the Magic Squares may be given as numbers, or more strikingly by using colours only. In the calendar fragment from Tun Huang, dated Jen Wu (9-VII) the following series of Magic Squares used colours only.

紫 Purple	黄 Yellow	赤 Red
白 White	白 White	碧 Turquoise
綠 Green	白 White	黑 Black

The Year Square

赤 Red	碧 Turquoise	黄 Yellow
白 White	白 White	白 White
黑 Black	綠 Green	紫 Purple

First Month

白 White	黑 Black	綠 Green
黄 Yellow	赤 Red	紫 Purple
白 White	碧 Turquoise	白 White

Second Month

黄 Yellow	白 White	碧 Turquoise
綠 Green	白 White	白 White
紫 Purple	黑 Black	赤 Red

Third Month 'Having 30 days'

Examples of Magic Colour Squares from a calendar fragment from Tun Huang, dated Jen Wu (壬午), i.e., AD 982.

Note: The manuscripts are known to date from the middle of the tenth century; Jen Wu is the 19th cyclical number, hence from Table C on page 74, Jen Wu must be six years after the 'Rat' year in the *second* column, hence 922 or 982, and the latter date the more likely.

The numbers appropriate to each colour are:

1. (White)	4. Green	7. Red
2. Black	5. Yellow	8. (White)
3. Turquoise	6. (White)	9. Purple

Applying this code to the Magic Colour Squares from Tun Huang, we have the following results:

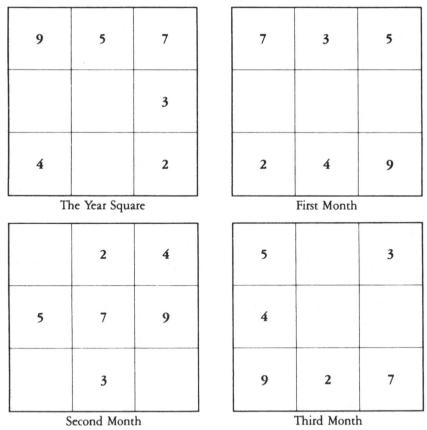

The Year Square

First Month

Second Month

Third Month

At first sight, it does not appear that these could be magic squares at all, since each line, vertically, horizontally, and diagonally cannot add up to the same total. Clearly, in the first square, 9 + 5 + 7 is not the same as 7 + 3 + 2. But the solution lies in the fact that each line adds up either to a certain figure, or that figure plus a multiple of nine! With this clue in mind, the magic squares can be solved, and numerical values given to the 'blank' squares.*

9	5	7
(8)	(1)	3
4	(6)	2

The Year Square

7	3	5
(6)	(8)	(1)
2	4	9

First Month

(6)	2	4
5	7	9
(1)	3	(8)

Second Month

5	(1)	3
4	(6)	(8)
9	2	7

Third Month

The Nine House System of Magic Squares and Colours

The basis of the Nine House system of Magic Square divination is the simple Magic Square which has the number 5 at the centre. It is this series of numbers which links the nine digits to the Eight Directions, the Eight Trigrams, and the Centre.

If each number of the Lo Shu is made the central figure of eight other squares placed at each of the directions, the series of Nine

*For further remarks on Magic Squares, see Walters (1) pages 49ff, and Walters (2) pages 201ff).

Houses is generated, of which the fifth (central) house is the Lo Shu itself.

The complete sequence of Nine Houses is therefore:

	SOUTH-EAST				SOUTH				SOUTH-WEST	
3	8	1		8	4	6		1	6	8
2	**4**	6		7	**9**	2		9	**2**	4
7	9	5		3	5	1		5	7	3

2	7	9		4	9	2		6	2	4
1	**3**	5		3	5	7		5	7	9
6	8	4		8	1	6		1	3	8

EAST (left of middle row) · WEST (right of middle row)

7	3	5		9	5	7		5	1	3
6	**8**	1		8	**1**	3		4	**6**	8
2	4	9		4	6	2		9	2	7

| | NORTH-EAST | | | | NORTH | | | | NORTH-WEST | |

Divination by the Nine House System

It is apparent that a number of methods exist for the calculation of the central number of the Magic Squares. In Chu and Sherrill (2) tables of the number for each year are given, but it is not made clear on which date the year actually begins. In the *Wan Nien Li* (Hong Kong) the 'years' are based on ten consecutive months, intercalary months included. The following rules produce results which tally with the Tun Huang manuscripts, having been calculated empirically. They are valid only for the years 1900-1999, since it is in fact a 'short-cut' method. It assumes that the date in question is later than the Chinese New Year; if dates are before the Chinese New Year, take the previous year as being applicable. In essence, the procedure is:

Find the number of the present year.

Find the number of the year of birth.

Find the position of the number of the year of birth in the Magic
  Square for the present year.
Use the position (direction) of the number to determine the course
  of events (as described in the section on Pentology, page 25).

To find the number for the year. For years beginning 19-, add the
last two digits and subtract from 10; (if the answer is 0 or 10, call
this 1. The final figure is the Year Number.
To find the number for the year of birth. Males follow the same
procedure. Females, who are 'Yin' use a different rule. Take the last
two figures of the date of birth, divide by 9, and note the remainder.
If the remainder is 0, call this 9.
Divination. Find the position of the number of the year of birth
in the Magic Square for the present year, and refer to the tables of
auspices on page 47ff.

(ii) The Mongolian 'Black Dog of Heaven' (Tangri qara noqai)

The Mongolian Black Dog of Heaven is described as a creature with
the head of a dog, body of a man, haunches of a pig, wings and
talons of a bird, and the tail of a snake. It was regarded as the reckoner
of hours, days, months and years, and regulated the lives of men.
The size of three continents, the Black Dog revolved round Mount
Sumeru (in Chinese, K'un Lun) which is usually identified with the
Pamirs, the mountain range North of Pakistan, and which could
be regarded as the central mountains of Asia, although there are
others which might also fit the description. The Mongolian
jobsiyermek means to make a respectful procession round a thing
or object, and this word is used to describe the Black Dog's rotation
of the heavens. In this respect there are many factors which at once
suggest similarities between the Black Dog and the Northern Ladle
or Pei Tou, the marker of the seasons and the T'ai Sui (Counter-
Jupiter) which regulates the years and is connected with the twelve-
animal cycle.

   The season of the year determines the orientation of the Black
Dog of Heaven, and as a consequence, favourable or unfavourable
directions for undertaking particular enterprises. During the spring
season the Head faces the East, the Mouth the South-East, the Tail
points to the West, the Back to the North, and the Belly to the South.
This suggests that there are eight compass directions, although as
will be seen from the circular and square diagrams of the Black Dog
of Heaven, twelve compass points are actually used.

   Certain directions are regarded as being favourable in particular
years, numbered according to the animal cycle, and given, in the

following table, with their corresponding Chinese Branch in Roman numerals. One interesting peculiarity is that the directions are not evenly distributed.

In Rat, Dragon and Monkey years (Branches I, V, IX) North-East is favourable.

In Ox, Snake and Cock years (Branches II, VI, X) North-West is favourable.

In Tiger, Horse and Dog years (Branches III, VII, XI) South is favourable.

In Rabbit, Sheep and Hog years (Branches IV, VIII, XII) East is favourable.

The directions which favour certain enterprises according to the four seasons can be ascertained from the following directions which pertain to the Spring, and rotating the schema with the Head pointing to the East in Spring, to the South in Summer, the West in Autumn, and to the North in Winter.

When the Head is in the East (as in Spring) the Mouth faces South-East, the Tail faces West, the Back is in the North, and the Belly in the South. Fortunate directions are as follows:

The Head or the Belly is fortunate for receiving a daughter-in-law;
The Mouth is favourable for sacrificing to the Earth or to Water;
The Back favours military expeditions, the construction of a house,
    or taking a corpse in procession. (These directions tally to a great
    extent with the observances in the ancient books of rites.)

Unfortunate directions:

The Head is unfortunate for the construction of a house;
The Mouth is unfortunate for embarking on military expeditions;
The Back is unfortunate for receiving a daughter-in-law;
The Belly is unfortunate for carrying a corpse in procession.

(iii) The Diviner's Plate

In an earlier chapter, reference was made to the significance of the seven main stars of the Great Bear (the Northern Ladle), acting as a cosmic clock. The rotation of the heavens once a year together with their diurnal rotation meant that it was necessary to have some kind of map which could be adjusted to match the time of the day with that of the year. With such an instrument, nowadays familiar to

amateur astronomers as a planisphere, it is possible to find the time
of day if the season is known, as well as the times of sunset and sunrise.
The earliest simple planispheres consisted of a circular 'Heaven Plate'
rotating on a square base, or 'Earth Plate'. Examples of these cosmic
boards, called Shih (式) 'a model' have been excavated from the
early Han dynasty onwards, having originally been placed there,
presumably, so that the soul of the deceased could find its way to
Paradise. In the earliest forms of the Shih, the upper Heaven Plate
was marked with the stars of the Northern Ladle, the twenty-eight
Hsiu, and had peg holes for the twelve months of the year. (See
Figure 7.2, 3.) In the course of time these instruments became more
and more elaborate, although their astronomical function was not
improved one whit. In an example from the Sui dynasty (see
Figure 7.4, 5) the Heaven Plate was marked additionally with cyclical
signs, and the names of twelve 'Monthly Spirits' of which more anon.
The base plate was also inscribed with the twenty-eight mansions,
cyclical signs, and the names of the thirty-six mystical animals,
described on page 67. The four diagonals were inscribed with the
compass points, names and symbols of the associated trigrams, and
technical divination terms. Other excavated examples of the Shih
show the gradual evolution of the simple Han planisphere into the
elaborate instrument of the Sui dynasty. (Further details of these
other instruments are given in Loewe, and Kalinowsky, see
bibliography.)

It is reasonable to suppose on the basis of circumstantial rather
than actual documentary evidence, that early astronomers, having
adjusted the Heaven Plate and the Earth Plate to the time of day
and the month of the year, placed pieces representing the five planets,
the Sun, and the Moon, on to the board to calculate their positions.
Certainly it has already been shown that the game of Liu Po had
its origin in an astrological board, and that this precursor of the
planisphere gave rise to such games as diverse as Mah Jongg and Chess,
while board games from Ludo to Monopoly actually had their origins
in the Earth Plate; the similarity between the Sui dynasty Earth Plate,
and the game of Ludo can be seen at once. (For an account of the
development of these games see Walters (1), pages 23ff.)

Despite the increasing complexity of the design of the Shih through
the centuries of its evolution, its truly astronomical function ceased
once the Month marker had been adjusted to correspond with the
Hour marker. But the Shih did generate whole schools of divination,
more importantly Fate Calculation and Feng Shui, which although
not astrological in structure, are nevertheless akin.

Figure 7.1 The Lo P'an, the Geomantic compass of Feng Shui, is an apparatus used for calculating the directions of influential currents. Although this is a relatively modern instrument, its ancestors were the diviner's boards of Han times (see page 66). The Horniman Museum, Forest Hill, has three such instruments, one of which is illustrated *above*, but there is no shortage of illustrative material regarding these instruments — see the examples given in *Science and Civilisation in China*, Vol. IV, Pl. CXIX-CXXI.

Unfortunately, these sources tend to give the impression that these Dial Plates are complete instruments, when in fact they are only the top halves. The Lo P'an should actually rest in a square 'terrestial plate' which has a bowl-shaped recess, in which the Lo P'an may be turned to line up with the magnetic North. A red thread cursor is then drawn over the compass needle in the Lo P'an to read the directions of the various currents. Without the base plate, the Lo P'an is as functionally incomplete as a clock with no face.

·The instrument used by Feng Shui geomancers is the Lo P'an (羅盤), 'Reticulated Plate'. There are enough examples of this instrument for it to be familiar, and it may be recognized at once as the Heaven Plate of a Shih of more than usually complex design, but it must be emphasized that this Heaven Plate is in fact only half the complete instrument. The underside of the Lo P'an Heaven Plate usually curves inwards, enabling it to fit and rotate in a receiving trough hollowed into the base, or Earth Plate. Where the Lo P'an is the Heaven Plate, the 'Dial Plate' found on the first and last pages of Chinese almanacs actually represents the Earth Plate. Remarks on the Dial plate, and some of its technical terminology will be met with later, but before going on to that branch of the art, it may be of interest to see how the Divining Board was used in the Sui dynasty, that is to say, at the half-way stage between genuine planetary astrology and its offspring, Fate Calculation and Feng Shui.

Table of the Twelve Monthly Spirits

Key letter	Branch		Monthly Spirit		
A	子	I	Shen Hou	神後	After the Spirit
B	丑	II	Ta Chi	大吉	Great Fortune
C	寅	III	Kung Ts'ao	功曹	Merit Official
D	卯	IV	T'ai Chung	太衝	Great Thoroughfare
E	辰	V	Tien Kang	天罡	The four stars which form the square of the Great Bear
F	巳	VI	T'ai I	太一	Great Monad
G	午	VII	Sheng Hsien	勝先	Equal to the Best
H	未	VIII	Hsiao Chi	小吉	Little Fortune
J	申	IX	Ch'uan Sung	傳送	Sending
K	酉	X	Ts'ung Kuei	從魁	Following 'Kuei'
L	戌	XI	Kuei	魁	The Literary Star
M	亥	XII	Cheng Ming	徵明	Clearly Shining

Names of the Guardians of the Five Seasons are given in the section on the *Yüeh Ling*, page 189.

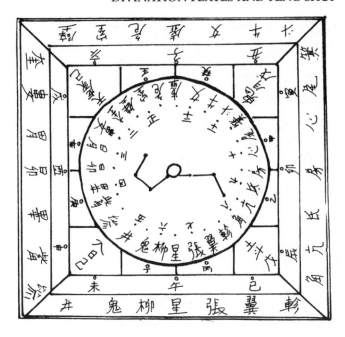

Figure 7.2 Early Han Diviner's Instrument.

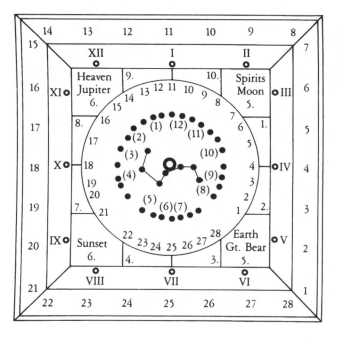

1 - 28 Hsiu
I-XII Branch
1.-10. Stem
(1)-(12) Chinese nu
     representing
     months of t
     year

Figure 7.3 Key to Early Han Diviner's Instrument.

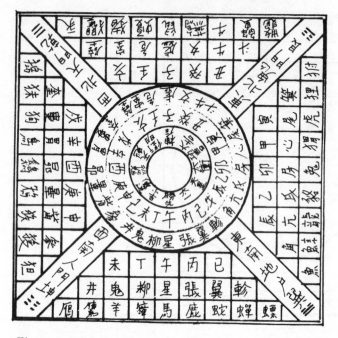

Figure 7.4 Divination Plate Sui Dynasty (581-618). For a description, see Kalinowsky.

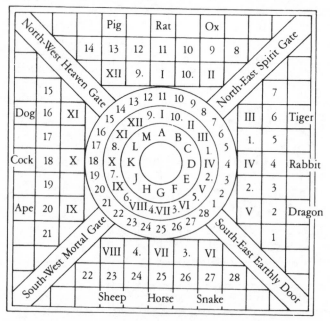

I-XII Branch
1.-10. Stem
A - M Monthly
        Spirit
1 - 28 Hsiu

Figure 7.5 Key to Sui Dynasty Divination Plate. (For details of the remaining animals in outer ring, see page 67.)

Method of Using the Diviner's Plate

The process of divination which uses the Diviner's Plate is extremely involved, and dare one suggest, tedious. Since its eventual result is far removed from astrological procedure, only its elementary details are given here, for reasons which will become apparent. The example

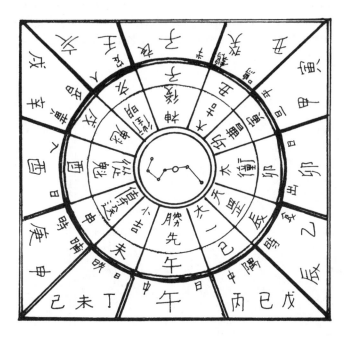

Figure 7.6 Diviner's Plate starting position.

here follows Kalinowsky (see bibliography) and is drawn from the *Yellow Emperor's Book of the Golden Casket and Jade Beam*, Tao Tsang, Schipper (284). The month, hour, and cyclical signs for the day are noted. In this example, the Monthly Spirit is Shen Hou, 'After the Spirit' (Key Ⓐ) the Hour, Ping Tan 'Nearly Dawn' (Key Ⓒ) and the cyclical number of the day Jen Shen (9-IX). For reasons which need not detain us, in this system the first month, Branch I, does not correspond to the first month of the civil calendar.

The Heaven Plate is rotated so that the Monthly Spirit is in line with the Hour.

Now, it is necessary to make Four Examinations. The accompanying diagrams are clearer than any explanation can be.

First, find the *day Stem* on the Earth Plate, and note the

corresponding Branch on the Heaven Plate. Find this Branch on the Earth Plate, and note the corresponding Monthly Spirit.

Repeat the process with the *day Branch*. Find the day Branch on the Earth Plate, note the corresponding Branch on the Heaven Plate; find this Branch on the Earth Plate, and note the corresponding Monthly Spirit.

From the pairs of signs given by the Four Examinations, one is chosen in which the respective elements are in the Mutually Destructive order (see the remarks on Pentology, page 41).

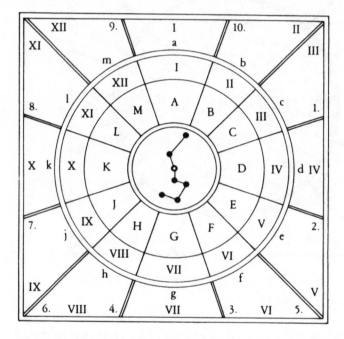

I-XII Branch
1.-10. Stem
a - m Hour name
A - M   Monthly
           Spirit

Figure 7.7 Diviner's Plate key to starting position.

Having selected the dominant Monthly Spirit, Three Translations are made, in a similar process to the Four Examinations, by which a final Monthly Spirit eventually results. The diviner now looks at his handbook of questions and answers, and finds the answer to the question most near to that posed by the inquirer, on such subjects, say, as marriage, travel, sickness, and so on.

In fact, a moment's thought will show that there are only twelve possible answers once the Shih has been adjusted, and that the rest of the procedure is mutually cancelling; it would be far quicker, but

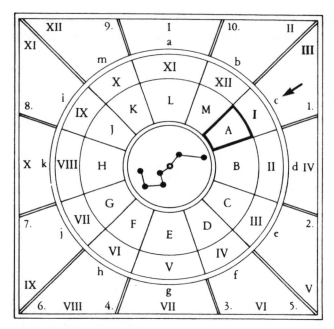

STAGE 2

Figure 7.8a The
Central Plate is
rotated so that the
Monthly Spirit
co-incides with
the Hour Marker.

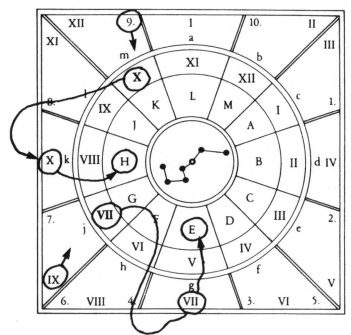

STAGE 3

Figure 7.8b The
Stem of the Day is
noted; the branch
opposite found again
on earth plate, and
the Monthly Spirit
opposite noted.

The same then applies to the Branch of the Day: the Branch opposite is
noted, observance of this taken again on the Earth plate, and the Monthly
Spirit opposite noted.

probably less impressive, for the relevant Monthly Spirit to be read off from the divining board immediately the Hour and Month were lined up together.

(iv) Dial Plates

It has already been remarked that if there is one aspect of Chinese astrology which was its most distinguishing feature, it is its emphasis on direction.

The Eight Directions are an integral part of every branch of Chinese Divination, from the Eight Diagrams of the *I Ching* to that peculiarly Chinese art which calculates the best position for a house or tomb, and is known to the Chinese as Feng Shui, but usually referred to as 'geomancy'.

Every Chinese almanac, even those as ancient as the ones from Tun Huang, carry octagonal, square or circular charts whose function is the same, whatever the shape. The Dial Plate, related to the map of the heavens, the face of the clock, the diviner's board, the Lo P'an of the geomancer, the compass box of the navigator, and the games of the Chinese gambler, expound the significantly lucky and unlucky directions for the hour, day, month, season and year. At this point we need to look at the Chinese compass itself, now examining the smaller divisions of the 'box'. The Chinese divide this into twenty-four divisions, or directions, and relate these to the hours of the day (the 'fore' and 'aft' double-hours), the twenty-four solar periods, and the twelve years of the Jupiter Cycle.

The Compass Plate is an obvious descendent of the Diviner's Plate. Twelve of the points are marked by the twelve Branches: these are placed at their appropriate points on the clock-face, thus Tzu, Branch I, representing midnight, is placed at the North, and the other eleven Branches are distributed accordingly.

The four 'corners' corresponding to North-West, South-West, South-East and North-East are marked either by the four corresponding trigrams or their Chinese names:

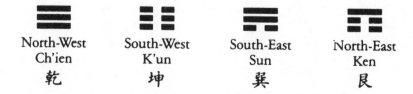

North-West	South-West	South-East	North-East
Ch'ien	K'un	Sun	Ken
乾	坤	巽	艮

The remaining points are occupied by eight of the Ten Stems, Chia

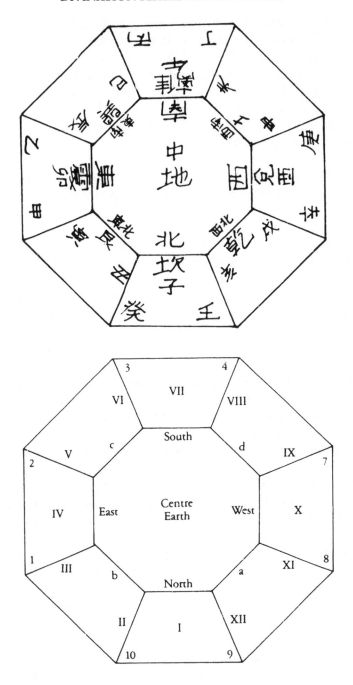

Figure 7.9 **The Chinese Compass Plate**
Roman Numerals represent the Twelve Branches; ordinary figures the Ten
Stems. The letters a, b, c, d, represent four of the Eight Trigrams.

and I (甲乙) Stems 1 and 2, pertaining to Wood and the East, are placed in the positions each side of East; Ping and Ting (丙丁) Stems 3 and 4, pertaining to Fire and the South, are accordingly placed either side of South; Keng and Hsin (庚辛) Stems 7 and 8, pertaining to Metal and the West, are placed each side of West, and Jen and Kuei (壬癸) pertaining to Water and the North, are placed each side of North. Wu and Chi, which pertain to Earth and the Centre, are omitted from the scheme.

It may be found helpful to study the accompanying diagrams of the compass positions in conjunction with the above paragraphs.

Description of the Dial Plate

Apart from the Dial Plate for the year, found on the first or second pages, many Chinese almanacs have at least twelve other Dial Plates, either one for each month of the year, and sometimes one for each of the twelve years of the animal cycle. The former type appear in personally drafted horoscopes, the second kind in popular almanacs of a general horoscope nature. They can be distinguished immediately by noting what lies at the centre of the Dial Plate. If it is a mundane Dial Plate, the centre relates to the other numbers of the Magic Square, and their corresponding colours, in one of the rings of the Dial Plate. The other type of Dial Plate depicts either the cyclical animal, or the Chinese character for the animal, at the centre.

In the central area of the Dial Plate are the four characters for the Four Directions, usually with North at the bottom. The innermost circle bears the Chinese characters for the Eight Trigrams, described earlier; the next circle, if there is no Magic Square in the centre of the figure, will carry the appropriate numbers and colours of the pertinent Magic Square. The next circle carries the twenty-four compass points described above.

Thus the inner circle of eight characters, and the third circle of twenty-four characters remains the same, whatever the year. The intermediary circle (the Magic Numbers and their colours) and the next, outer, circle vary from year to year. The outermost compartments usually contain six characters each, giving aspects for the twenty-four directions. These are for the most part astronomical and astrological terms, including actual names of stars, concepts such as Counter-Jupiter, or the Moon's nodes, stellar deities and other terms formed by analogy.

For example, a real star in Ursa Minoris is known as Yin Teh, meaning Hidden Virtue. But since there is a *Yin* virtue, by analogy, there must also be a *Yang* virtue to complement it. By extension, every planet was to have its 'virtue' and, as a complement, its opposite 'curse'.

The Imperial Manual of Astrology lists well over two hundred and fifty of these Dial Plate Terms, but happily, most almanacs confine themselves to the use of about two dozen of its own preferences, the efficacy of which distinguishes one almanac from its rival publications.

The diagrams here give the Dial Plate Terms for the six consecutive years 1982-1987, from which it is possible to analyse the movements and significance of the stellar influences.

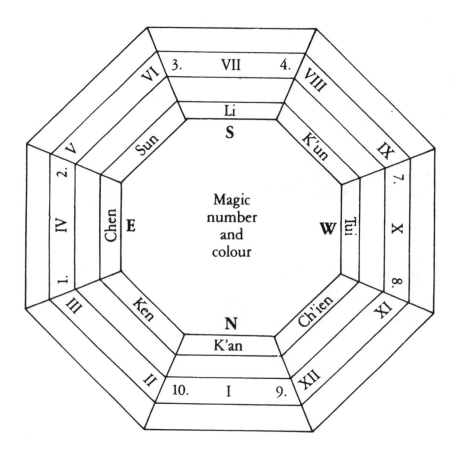

Figure 7.10 **The Basic Dial Plate**
The functions shown in the diagram are fixed. The inner blank circle is occupied by the numbers and colours of the year magic square. The outer circle is occupied by Dial Plate Terms.

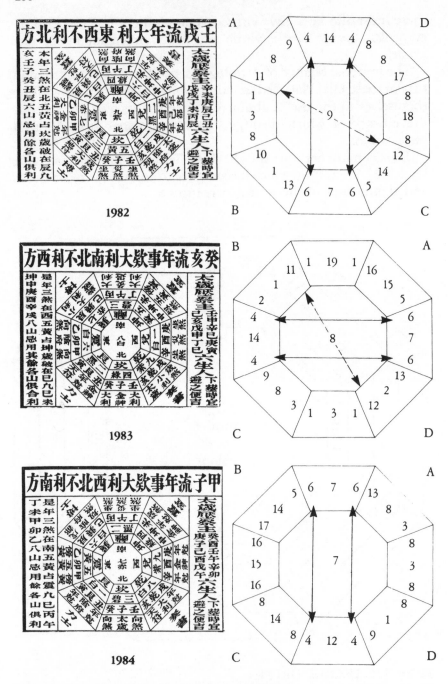

Figure 7.11 **Dial plates for the years 1982-1987**
Arrows indicate the T'ai Sui (Counter-Jupiter), the Year Opposer, and the Year Curse. The central numeral is the Magic Square year number.

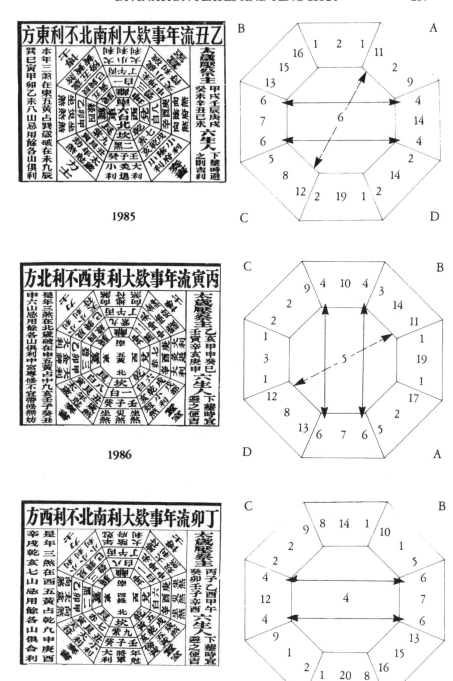

1985

1986

1987

Key to Dial Plate Terms

1.	大利	Ta Li	Great Advantage	
2.	小利	Hsiao Li	Small Advantage	
3.	金神	Chin Shen	Metal Spirit	
4.	向煞	Hsiang Sha	Facing Curse	
5.	劫煞	Chieh Sha	Robber Curse	
6.	坐煞	Tso Sha	Place Curse	
7.	災煞	Tsai Sha	Calamity Curse	
8.	年尅	Nien K'e	Year Subduer	
9.	天符	T'ien Fu	Heaven's Amulet	
10.	地符	Ti Fu	Earth's Amulet	
11.	歲破	Sui P'o	Year Breaker	
12.	太歲	T'ai Sui	Great Year (Counter-Jupiter)	
13.	歲煞	Sui Sha	Year Curse	
14.	陰符	Yin Fu	'Yin' Amulet	(Likely to be
	陰府	Yin Fu	'Yin' Treasure-house	the same term)
15.	五黃	Wu Huang	Five Yellow	
16.	傍黃	P'ang Huang	Near Yellow	
17.	戊都	Wu Tu	'Wu' section	
18.	己都	Chi Tu	'Chi' section	
19.	灸退	Ch'iu T'ui	Moxa cautery	
20.	將軍	Chiang Chün	Take the enemy ('check' in chess)	
A.	蠶室	Ts'an Shih	The House of the Silkworms	
B.	博士	Po Shih	The Learned Scholar	
C.	力士	Li Shih	The Warrior Scholar	
D.	奏書	Tsou Shu	The Memorial to the Throne	

Remarks on the Dial Plate Terms
The above list represents only those Dial Plate Terms taken from

one almanac over six consecutive years; some appear regularly, others very infrequently (such as, for example 20, Chiang Chün). A selection from different almanacs would very much broaden the scope of this list, since, as has already been mentioned, each publication has its own preferred Terms which distinguish it from rival editions.

The Feng Shui technical term for the twenty-four Dial Plate positions is Shan (山), meaning 'mountain'. I will hazard an opinion that in fact the term is a misconstruction of some other character such as Chu (出) 'to go out' and signifies a direction of movement rather than a static direction, like the difference between 'West' and 'westward' where the first word signifies a position, and the second the direction in which one must travel in order to get there.

Below the Dial Plate there is usually a table indicating the greater or lesser fortunes of each Shan. Thus beneath the Dial Plate for 1982 (not shown in the illustration) the three Shan which are occupied by the Three Curses are marked 'No Advantage'.

The Shan which corresponds with the cyclical sign of the year, if not overtaken by higher terms, will be advantageous. The same will be true of those positions which are in harmony with the places occupied by the cyclical signs of the Branch and Stem. The harmonious places are those which form 60° angles, echoing the techniques of Fate Calculation and Western astrology. If such places are counteracted by malefic influences, there may nevertheless be some small advantage. The Branch of the year is always occupied by the T'ai Sui, which leaves a possible five places which might be marked 'Great Advantage'.

To the left and right of the Dial Plates are columns indicating the positions and influences of the principal Shan. The bad news is always given first in the left-hand column, that is, the place of the Three Curses. Then the position of the Five Yellow Earth is given. This must occupy the sector corresponding to the position of 5 in the Magic Square of the Year. In 1982, there was no Five Yellow Earth because this place was occupied by the Three Curses. In 1983, when 8 was the central number, it occupied the South-West position, as one would expect from the Lo Shu diagram (see above, page 47). By the same rule, it occupied the East in 1984, the South-East in 1985, and the North-West in 1987. It did not appear in 1986 because in that year Five Yellow was the central figure of the Magic Square of the Year.

Interpreting the Dial Plate Terms
1, 2.   Great Advantage, Small Advantage. One would expect

Shan housing the cyclical signs for the year to be advantageous; thus, in 1983 the Stem and Branch is 10 and XII; since no malevolent influences occupy position 10 the Shan is fortunate, and thus marked. The Branch, however, always marks the position of the T'ai Sui. The advantageous months for that particular Shan are therefore listed as the 2nd, 3rd, 5th and 6th, 10th, 11th and 12th, and there are no disadvantageous ones.

3.   Metal Spirit. This is regarded as being the influence of the Metal Planet, Venus. For some reason, only Venus is especially regarded as having a prime position on the Dial Plate, though it is important to remember that 'Metal' has many other meanings, as well as being the name of one of the planetary elements. It is the equivalent of the Seventh Curse in Fate Calculation, but its ominous-sounding name must not be taken as indicating a malefic portent. In Fate Calculation the presence of the Seventh Curse is needed to balance the evil influence of the Matching Official. On the Dial Plate, the presence of the Metal Spirit may balance out other unfortunate aspects. The Metal Spirit is found in the following vacant spaces:

In years with the Stem 1 and 2   at Shan VII, VIII, IX, X

3 and 4,	V, VI
5 and 6,	III, IV, V, VI, I, II
7 and 8,	III, IV, XI, XII
9 and 10	X, I, II

4, 6.   Facing Curse, and Place Curse. These two Terms are found as opposite pairs situated at either side of two opposite cardinal points. The Place Curse is regarded as extremely unfortunate, being the Seat (or Place) of the Three Curses. Directly opposite, however, is the Facing Curse, which is also directly opposite in nature, and consequently a fortunate Shan. A glance at the examples of Dial Plates will show how these four Terms are usually disposed.

5, 7,   The Three Curses: The Robber Curse, the Calamity Curse, 13.   and the Year Curse. These are regarded as extremely malevolent aspects, the last, the Year Curse, being the most dreaded of all; it therefore needs to be avoided at all costs, or has to be well fortified by opposing influences. They are all regarded as being an excess of Yin forces, and might therefore be assuaged if there are counteracting Yang forces in evidence. The Robber Curse brings misfortune through robbery and assault; the Calamity Curse through natural catastrophes such as fire and flood. They may only occupy the following Shan:

(5) Robber Curse: XII, IX, VI, III
(7) Calamity Curse: I, X, VII, IV
(13) Year Curse: II, XI, VIII, V

Each Term moves to its next position, anti-clockwise, in the following year.

6. See 4.

7. See 5.

8. The Year Subduer. This is the subduer of evil influences, and is therefore fortunate. Although the term is of classical usage, its employment as one of the Dial Plate Terms seems to be of very recent date. It appears in the Dial Plate in default of other Terms.

9, 10. Heaven's Amulet and Earth's Amulet. These are fortunate Terms; Heaven's Amulet moves backwards by six Shan each year; the Earth's Amulet precedes it, but will however lose its place to one of the more important Terms.

11. The Year Breaker. This is a very unfortunate aspect; unless it is overtaken by a more important Term it is always placed opposite the T'ai Sui. No digging or earthworks should be undertaken in the direction of this Term.

12. T'ai Sui (Counter-Jupiter). The most important of all the Terms, and one of the most ancient indigenous Chinese astrological concepts. It is used as an anchor for many of the calculations of the other terms. It occupies the Shan of the year Branch. Each year it has a particular name.

13. Year Curse. See above, under 5.

14. Yin Amulet or Treasure House. In older almanacs, the character Fu, meaning 'amulet', is the same as that for the Heaven's and Earth's Amulets; in modern almanacs the character is changed to mean 'treasure house' although the

pronunciation is the same. This Term is a beneficial one; it is the counterpart to the Calamity Curse, in the same way that the Facing Curse (No. 4) is the counter-agent to No. 6, Place Curse. Consequently, the Yin Amulet will usually be found situated between the two Facing Curse Terms. It may, however, also appear at any of the Eight Directions, which it does when displaced by some other Term having priority.

15, 16,   Five Yellow, and its neighbour Near (or next to) Yellow are
17, 18.   the symbols of the Earth element. In this they share the same quality as Wu Tu and Chi Tu. All four of these Terms would not normally be accorded places in the Shan because they relate to the element Earth, i.e. Centre. The change of element in the cyclical characters of the Year Stem and Branch means that the balance of the elements can always be assessed for each of the directions, with the exception of the Earth element; since the Year Branch and Stem will regularly include characters which relate to the Earth element, these have been introduced, through the medium of the two Yellows, and the two Earth-Stem 'departments' Wu and Chi, to redress the balance.

Their influence will accordingly be good or bad, depending on which Branch or Stem they become associated with.

19.   Moxa cautery. This Term refers to the exorcism of disease by burning moxa powder; the meaning of the Term itself is taken to mean the ridding of evil influences, but is more usually understood to mean the most propitious direction for the practice of moxybustion and acupuncture.

20.   Take the Enemy. This term occupies any position left vacant. It is considered unlucky.

Planetary Terms

Although rarely found on Dial Plates of recent times, the Planetary Terms are of considerable interest since they are sometimes encountered in Chinese horoscopes.

Each planet has its own Term, although as we have seen, only the Metal Planet Term appears regularly on the Dial Plate. Just as the astronomical planets have their periods of revolution and orbit, so

the influences of the Planetary Terms wax and wane in accordance
with their cycles of activity. Each Term has two such cycles, one of
which will be recognized by the astronomically-minded reader as
the period of the planet's orbit.

The Wood Planet, Jupiter, governs Birth and Death
(but actually Birth and Growth; being of the element Wood, it is associated
with the Spring, and therefore new growth).
Its Lesser Cycle is 12 years, its Greater Cycle 83 years.
The Spirit is called Tzu Ch'i (紫氣) Purple Aura.
It governs everything that is precious and pleasurable.

The Fire Planet, Mars, governs Growth and Development.
Its Lesser Cycle is 2 years, its Greater Cycle 79 years.
Lo Hou (the Moon's Ascending node) is the Evil Aura of Mars. It
is always opposite Chi Tu*, the Evil Aura of Saturn.
It produces conflagration and brigandage.

The Earth Planet, Saturn, governs the Growth of Virtue.
Its Lesser Cycle is 9 years, its Greater Cycle 29 years.
Chi Tu* (the Moon's Descending node) is the Evil aura of Saturn.
It penetrates all the directions, and is the creator of widows and orphans.

The Metal Planet, Venus, governs the Harvest.
Its Lesser Cycle is 1 year, its Greater Cycle 8 years.
(See above, note 3.)

The Water Planet, Mercury, governs Divination.
Its Lesser Cycle is 1 year, its Greater Cycle 65 years.
Yueh Pen (月孛) the Lunar Comet (or halo?) is the Evil Aura of
Mercury.
It is extremely unlucky, turning fortune aspects into unfortunate ones.

The Four Celestial Gates
In addition to the Terms found in the Dial Plate itself, octagonal
Dial Plates often have four characters marked in the outside corners,
at the inter-cardinal points. These progress anti-clockwise, taking
twelve years to make a revolution, but since they are confined to the
four corners, remain in the same position for three years at a time,

*There are two Chinese terms which transliterate as Chi Tu: 己都 Dial
Plate Term 18, and 計都, the Moon's descending node.

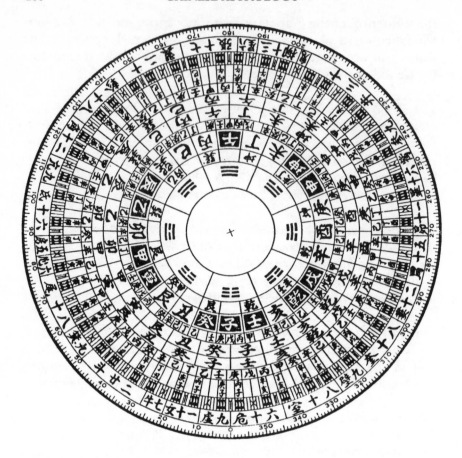

Figure 7.12 'San Ho' Lo P'an

thus representing the Four Seasons of the Great Year. In this they follow the Sui Hsing (歲星) or Year Planet, i.e. true Jupiter.

These four pairs of characters are regarded as the Guardians of the Celestial Gates, of which there are four, disposed at the inter-cardinal points in this way: North-East is the Gate for Ghosts, and opposite is the Gate for Men; North-West is the Gate to Heaven, and opposite is the Gate to Earth. It will be seen that in the Dial Plates shown, the disposition of the Four Guardians has moved one place between 1982 and 1983, thus marking the end of one three-year period, and thereafter remains the same. The following are the relationships between the Gates and the Guardians, and their portents.

(a) The House of the Silkworms. Some commentators believe that this is a euphemism for 'prison'. It is unlucky, augurs badly for the development of silkworms, and is a threat of imprisonment. Element: Wood.

(b) The Learned Scholar. Liu Po, the Game of the Six Learned Scholars, was a game played in Han times; the Liu Po board is related to the Diviner's Board, and ultimately the Lo P'an. It produces wise counsel to the government. It is generally fortunate, apart from anything to do with digging, earthworks, or burial. Element: Fire.

(c) The Warrior Scholar. The Emperor's bodyguard. It governs punishments and retribution. Element: Metal.

(d) The Memorial to the Throne. Generally very fortunate. Governs administration. Element: Water.

The Lo P'an

The Lo P'an is the instrument that unites astrology, divination by the heavens, with Feng Shui, or, for want of a better term, geomancy, divination by the contours of the earth.

Although any detailed account of Feng Shui is by definition beyond the scope of this book, its essential instrument, the Lo P'an, is worthy of mention because of its obvious relationship to the Dial Plates used by astrologers of old, and also because of a remarkable feature revealed in different models of Lo P'an.

First of all, until this century, scholars had believed that the discipline of Feng Shui was introduced in the ninth century AD by the philosopher Yang Yung-sung. This was despite the existence of a Feng Shui manual called 'The Yellow Emperor's Classic of Dwellings' reputedly written by a certain Wang Wei in the fifth century. Obviously, once a book has been repeatedly copied, it is difficult to assess when it was originally composed, and without any contemporary evidence, there was no means of dating the 'Yellow Emperor' classic. The book was reprinted in its entirety in the *K'ang Hsi Encyclopaedia* (discussed more fully in a later chapter), and includes diagrams similar in appearance to the Dial Plates described above.

But then came a discovery, astonishing in its implications for the history of Feng Shui. In recent years, archaeological excavation of tombs known to be of the Anterior Han dynasty (*c.* second century BC) has uncovered remarkable astrological instruments which match the diagrams in the 'Yellow Emperor' classic in virtually every detail. This shows that the 'Yellow Emperor' classic, far from being written later than the fifth century, must have been based on oral, if not written, traditions which were even then several centuries old. Thus the Dial Plates printed in almanacs today continue a practice that was ancient when Buddhism was introduced into China.

The Lo P'an is primarily a compass, the eight points of the compass being subdivided into an increasingly greater number of divisions, depending on the size of the instrument. The simplest instruments show only the Eight Trigrams, which mark the four cardinal points and the points in between, and subdivide these into the twenty-four points of the Chinese compass. For further remarks on the geomantic features of the Lo P'an, the reader is directed to another work by the present author[1].

From the astrological viewpoint, the most interesting feature of the Lo P'an is its outermost rim. On all but the smallest examples of Lo P'an, this outer rim is divided into 365 or 366 divisions, being the number of Chinese degrees in a circle, but here accurately representing the divisions of the heavens marked by the course of a sun in a true solar year. Inside the rim of degree divisions is a band marking the twenty-eight constellations, either graphically with little patterns illustrating the constellation patterns themselves, or else in Chinese characters. If the Lo P'an is sufficiently large, the equatorial extent of each constellation is also given. (See Chapter 4, The Twenty-Eight Lunar Mansions.)

The purpose of these divisions is clear. The vagaries of the Chinese calendar mean that it is quite unreliable for the purposes of astronomical observation. If, for example, an observation of the position of a star was taken on the first day of the first month in two successive years, it could appear, because of the floating calendar, that the star had moved by as many as thirty degrees: in Western terms, a whole zodiacal sign. This is not the case, however, with the Western calendar, which is a fairly true approximation of the true astronomical year. But without the Western calendar, it was necessary for Chinese astronomers to use a true solar calendar, which could only be determined by practical observation. This could be ascertained by observing the position of the Full Moon, which is always opposite the Sun. The outer divisions of the Lo P'an therefore inform the Feng Shui master what particular stellar influences are appropriate for each direction of the compass on different days of the year, so that Heaven and Earth may be in concord.

Mention has already been made of the fact that there are various sizes of Lo P'an to be seen. They may be anything from 10cm across, to two or three times that size. An intriguing feature of the Lo P'an is that although superficially they may seem to differ only in their

[1] Walters, D. *Chinese Geomancy*. Element Books, Shaftesbury (1989).

Figure 7.13 Astrologer casting a horoscope.

size, and the number and complexity of the rings, close inspection reveals subtle differences of detail. In fact, modern Feng Shui scholars identify two classes of Lo P'an, regardless of the size: the San Ho (Three Harmonies) and the San Yuan (Three Primes). There are in fact more.

The essential difference in the various types of Lo P'an lies in the alignment of the First Point of the compass (that is, the midpoint of Tzu, the First Branch) with the degrees of the celestial equator at the edge of the disc.

In the Divination Plate from the Han dynasty, Tzu is aligned with the midpoint of the eleventh lunar mansion, Hsu, 102° from the Dragon's Horn. In the San Yuan Lo P'an, Tzu is aligned with the fourth degree of Nu, the tenth mansion; in the San Ho, the alignment is with the commencement of Wei, the twelfth mansion. These deviations suggest that the various types of Lo P'an are preservations of models which were made for specific periods, and represented the constellation which would have been observable due north on a specific date. The precession of the equinoxes, which shifts the positions of the heavens by one degree every 72 years, would account for the differences, suggesting that the examples of Lo P'an represent observation of the heavens taken at different times over a 2,000 year period.

8.

CHINESE HOROSCOPES FROM THE EIGHTH TO THE TWENTIETH CENTURIES

While astrology, as a means of counsel for the State has a long and well documented history in China, personal horoscopes arrived comparatively late, almost certainly after the arrival of Buddhism. One of the first books to deal with personal horoscopic astrology was the *Mo Teng Chieh Ching* by Chu Lü Yen [摩登伽經 ; 竺衝炎] the title being a transliteration of the *Matangi Sutra*. This enigmatic work has been ascribed to the period of the Three Kingdoms (about the third century) contemporaneously with the *Kuan Lu Tzu*, a lost book on Fate Calculation. It would seem that the *Matangi Sutra*, however, is later than the *Kuan Lu Tzu*, and probably an eighth century translation from the Sanskrit. Curiously, the *Matangi Sutra* makes no mention of the Mithraic seven-day week, but the *Mo Teng Chieh Ching* does.

During the T'ang period, the *Hsiu Yao Ching*, the 'Classic of the Hsiu and Planets', was widely circulated. This was a translation of the 'Discourses of the Boddhisatva Manjusri and other Sages regarding Auspicious Times and Days, the Good and Evil Hsiu, and the Planets'. Unlike the *Matangi Sutra* the original text includes remarks on the seven-day planetary week. The sutra was translated in about 759 by the monk Pu K'ung (不空) and is included in the Tripitaka (N 1356; TW 1299*). Another work on the Hsiu and planets was written about 710 by the venerated monk I Hsing (一行), whose name is seldom far from a discussion on Chinese Fate Calculation. His work is also to be found in Tripitaka, TW 1304. It includes an example of a Western style horoscope, to which has been added such details as the Hsiu and the seven-day week.

*These numbers refer to the two indexes of the Chinese translations of the Tripitaka: Nanjio's *Catalogue of Chinese Translations of the Tripitaka* and Takakusu and Watanabe's *Tables du Taisho Tssaikyo*.

The Western zodiac has also been cited as appearing in an even earlier work, the *Ta Chi Ching* (大集經), but while this is possible, one must, in the absence of manuscript evidence, remember that nearly all early Chinese texts are copies of copies. Without corroborative evidence is it is difficult to know what items are genuinely historic, and what are tacit additions by later copyists.

Of great interest is the *Ch'i Yao Jang Tsai Chueh* (七曜攘災決) or 'Formulae for Avoiding Calamities According to the Seven Luminaries' since this work actually gives the planetary positions for AD 794, together with notes on the Hsiu, the associations between the planets and the five elements, and the names of the days of the week with the 'Seven Luminaries' and their correspondence with the stars of the Great Bear. Whatever period this dates from, it must have been commenced at least prior to the year 794 for the work to have been of any use at all. There may of course have been later additions, but what is of particular interest is the inclusion of the names of the Five Elements and the correspondence between the planets and the stars of the Great Bear, which shows that the work may be of indigenous Chinese authorship, and not a translation of a Western work.

Under the auspices of the great Ch'ien Lung, Emperor of the Ch'ing dynasty who received Lord Macartney when Britain unsuccessfully tried to establish an Embassy in China, the most important works of astrology were gathered together in a vast work called the *Ch'in Ting Hsieh Chih Pien Fang Shu* (欽定協紀辨方書) 'The Book of Harmonizing Dividers and Distinguishing Directions' — the dividers being the calendrical cycles, and the movements of the planets. In thirty-six volumes, published in 1742, it embraces all the divinatory aspects of Chinese philosophy at no little length. The subjects covered include the Lo Shu and the Ho T'u (The Lo River Diagram and the Ho River Picture: both systems of Magic Squares); the Eight Trigrams, the divisions of the calendar, the twenty-eight Hsiu, the cyclical animals, the twelve musical notes, the Five Kinds of Rat and the Five Kinds of Tiger (not a zoological treatise, but a means of distinguishing the cyclical years by the Five Elements); the order of the compass points and matters relating to Feng Shui, with a description of the Lo P'an in its different forms, the Changes and Revolutions of the Grave Dragon, the Correct Arrangement of the Centre Needle, the Destruction of Disagreeable Mountains, and many other matters too arcane to describe here.

It was intended to be the standard work of reference for members of the Imperial Board of Astrology to produce the annual almanac, which was distributed throughout the Empire.

Fate Calculation

Suan Ming (算命) could be accurately translated as 'fortune-telling' in the old sense of the word 'tell' — meaning to reckon or calculate (as in 'bank teller'). However, the expression has such a specific meaning that it is now translated by the term 'Fate Calculation'. This is a method of looking into future events by means of a complex system of numerology which is peculiarly Chinese, having no parallel in any other culture. A by-product of astrology, its calculations are based directly on the calendar rather than the astronomical events on which the calendar is based. The reasons for its creation stem from the fact that Grand Astrology was reserved for the Imperial Court, and there was a demand for a Lesser Astrology which could be used to determine the destinies of the common people. Although the use of tables of planetary positions was forbidden on pain of death, it seemed to some astrologers that so regular and ordered were the motions of the Heavens that it was no longer necessary to observe them. In this, of course, the Fate Calculators differed from the Heaven Watchers, who discovered and recorded such events as comets, novae — and the mysterious Ch'i. In fact, the criteria of Fate Calculation were entirely numerical. The Stem and Branch of the year is a notional figure, independent of the calendar, and the same is true of the Stem and Branch of the day. But the Branch of the hour is tenuously related to an astronomical event — the length of the day, itself determined by the position of the Earth relative to the Sun. Similarly, the Branch for the month is determined by the progress of the Earth round the Sun, the Branch changing at (nearly) every New Moon. Cheng Hsüan (鄭玄) AD 127-200, in his commentaries to the *Shih Ching* (Book of Poetry) speaks of lucky and unlucky years, seasons, months, days, stars, and lunar phases. Thus, the foundation for the discipline were known in Han times, but it was not until the T'ang that it became the exact system which it has remained to this day. Its regularization is generally ascribed to Li Hsü Chung, although his book on the subject is regarded as an expansion of an older, lost work. The complex history of the subject is dealt with by Chao Wei Pang in an exhaustive study published in English in Peking in 1946. (As this is now difficult to obtain, a bibliography will be found in the appendix to the present volume.)

To disregard Fate Calculation completely on the grounds that it is not based on astronomical data would make the understanding of Chinese horoscopes impossible. Since the T'ang, Fate Calculation and Chinese astrology have been inextricably linked, and many of the terms used in astrology are incomprehensible without an understanding of the basic principles of Fate Calculation. But it must be stressed again, that virtually all of what passes for Chinese astrology, both in and out of China, is in fact Fate Calculation. Popular Chinese astrology, which treats solely of the twelve 'zodiac' signs is merely one aspect of Fate Calculation where the Branch of the Year has been replaced by an animal figure, and, in more detailed horoscopes, the Stem of the Year with the relevant element.

Chinese Almanacs

Chinese almanacs are as old as the invention of printing. From the single-sheet calendar-almanacs of the ninth century, to the bound volumes of today, the central core of information is common to all of them. Essentially, almanacs list the days of the year by month, and day, and by cyclical sign. To this, even the earliest known almanacs add the 'notional Hsiu' of the twenty-eight day cycle. During the last dynasty, a memorial was addressed to the Emperor regarding the desirability of excluding various items of superfluous information such as 'clothes-cutting days' and the twenty-eight notional Hsiu, but a counter-memorial argued that such information ought to be retained; the 'clothes-cutting' days had religious significance, while the twenty-eight Hsiu (which always coincided with the Western week) 'enabled people from distant lands, who named the days of the week after the Seven Regulators, to tally with the reckoning by Stems and Branches'.

Although the publication of a pirate edition of the Imperial Almanac was an offence punishable by death, this did not deter printers from issuing unofficial almanacs, and over the years a long list of private almanacs became available, originating from different parts of China. Today there is still a wide variety to choose from, published in Hong Kong, Taiwan, Macao, Viet Nam, Korea, Japan, Indonesia, and other parts of South-East Asia. At least one Hong Kong publisher issues several versions of the same almanac, while some of this information (pertaining to the year following the year of issue) turns up in yet another publisher's almanac a year later as the current issue!

Although the essential information in the almanacs remains the same, there are major differences in the ancillary articles used to fill the covers. They are a curious combination of reference work, book of religious observation, popular horoscope, and calendar; and are, in effect, like a combination of Year Book, Diary, and manual of divination. The smaller almanacs may confine themselves to being a list of tables with prognostications (rather like Raphael's or Old

Moore's). The larger ones include tales from the classics (such as the examples of the 'Twenty-Four Kinds of Filial Piety'), and the astonishing 'Thousand Character Classic'* much used as a school primer by Chinese schoolchildren, while one of the more essential features is (for those who may have wondered how the Chinese manage to send telegrams) a telegraphic code which lists every Chinese character by number.

The days referred to globally as 'clothes-cutting days' include the days for going on journeys, visiting the Emperor, entering office, betrothal, receiving friends, marrying, moving house, taking a bath, shaving the head, writing wills, carrying on a trade, collecting money, sweeping a room, buying cattle, burying the dead, opening drains, cutting down trees, wearing fine clothes, placing corner-stones, planting beans, buying stock, digging ditches, demolishing houses, entering school, taking medicine secretly, repairing roads, acupuncture, moxybustion, and raising the timbers for a new house. This last had to be done at the hour shown, and not always at an hour convenient for the builders, especially if they had to be summonsed from their beds in the middle of the night. It was well known that one had to be very careful in dealing with workmen since they could if they so wished, curse the house by using malign proportions in the measurements, or erecting a doorpost at an inauspicious hour. The householder did not therefore haggle too much over the wages. But the more wily client would have his own set of spells and talismans handy, and woe betide the sorceror-builder who attempted to curse the timbers of the house he was building.

Although the almanacs compiled and published by the Astrological Division of the Board of Rites included all necessary calendrical information and the times of sunrise and sunset, they did not always include information concerning the movements of the planets. This is in astonishing contrast to the almanac produced at Tun Huang in 794, which included a planetary ephemeris, evidence indeed, if it were needed, of the decline in interest in planetary astrology in China. Such astrological information as is there is confined to the influences of the Stellar Divinities, and Dial Plate Terms. No meteorological predictions are included apart from the twenty-four solar terms, and 'Diverse Information of Value to

*This extraordinary work, as its title suggests, contains exactly one thousand characters, not one of which is repeated. It is attributed to Chou Hsing Ssu, of the third century; legend says that it was composed in a single night, but that the effort turned the author's hair white.

Navigators' a list of favourable winds calculated according to the birthdays of particular divinities. Usually, the daily information also includes verses from the *Hsia Hsiao Cheng* and the *Yueh Ling*, such as 'Hibernating insects begin to move' and 'fish swim up to the ice'.

Sung Dynasty Calendar Almanacs in the British Library

The British Library possesses a number of handwritten and printed calendar almanacs which date from the Sung dynasty. These tenth century almanacs are very similar in many respects to present day almanacs published in Hong Kong, Macao, and Taiwan, and it is astonishing that the traditional format of the almanac can be traced back for at least a thousand years.

The Sung almanacs were found in a sealed-off chamber in the 'Caves of the Thousand Buddhas' an ancient monastery sited in the remote vastnesses of Western China, between the deserts of the North, and the almost inaccessible mountains of Tibet in the South. The cave temples, constructed by the followers of Lo Tsun who began the excavations in about AD 366, were dug out of cliffs of gravel conglomerate. The crumbly nature of the material limited the size of the caves, though eventually a 'facetted' method of construction enabled the caves to be made somewhat larger. Adjoining one of the major temple constructions was a small shrine which had been excavated to house the venerated remains of the monk Wang Yuan Lu who had been the temple's incumbent at the time of the expulsion of the Tibetans from Tun Huang. By a curious accident of Fate, the shrine was to become the most famous of all the caves. At some point, the wooden image of Wang was removed to an upper chamber, and the room used to store a vast collection of ephemera, which were to become renowned as one of the most remarkable hoards of literature ever recovered, and certainly equal in importance to that of the more famous Dead Sea Scrolls. It was formerly believed that the manuscripts were hidden pending an attack by invaders, but more recent opinion is that the manuscripts were stored in the shrine during a re-painting of the temple. Whatever the reason, once the manuscripts were sealed up, they were forgotten about, but perfectly preserved there for nearly a thousand years. It was only in 1909 that Aurel Stein, having heard rumours of the discovery of the manuscripts, visited Tun Huang with the object of purchasing as many of them as he could, to be followed after by an increasing succession of expeditionary archaeologists, headed by Professor Paul Pelliot, of the Bibliotheque Nationale, Paris, until eventually the Chinese authorities were alerted to the possible value of the manuscripts and halted any further removal by foreign scholars.

The almanacs which were among these archives are in varying stages of completeness, only two or three of those in the Stein collection in the British Museum being anything near intact. Oddly enough, many of these incomplete fragments are every bit as intriguing as the complete documents. For example, there is a sketch for a complete scroll, with the ruled framework for the calendar and horoscope sections carefully outlined. In a bold hand, the title announces 'Fully annotated Calendar, astronomically accurate, for the year Mou Yin (戊寅), the third year of the reign of T'ai P'ing Hsing Kuo (大平興國)' (reigned 976-984, which dates the calendar AD 978-979). The scroll commences with a chart of the Nine Directions, showing the Five Colours and Eight Diagrams, followed by a beautifully executed drawing of the Year God surrounded by the Twelve Cyclical animals and the Four Guardians.* Alas! heavy squiggles drawn through several columns of the text tell a sad story. The calculations were wrong! It is hard not to sympathize with the poor monk who had suddenly realized that the painstakingly drawn up chart, on its costly paper, and the so-skillfully delineated icons, which would have bestowed so much spiritual merit on the monk, were all wasted. All the suppressed frustration comes to life, a thousand years later, as one looks at those thick lines of ink daubed through those woeful characters. Possibly because of the elegance of the drawing, or perhaps religious reasons held the icons to be sacred, the calendar was not scrapped, but carefully put to one side, for it to reveal its secret a thousand years later.

The earliest calendar in the British Library's collection is actually a printed one; but the fact that it is not handwritten does not in any way detract from its being an exquisite piece of craftsmanship; the miniature characters and finely-lined diagrams have been executed with wonderful precision. This calendar, pasted over an earlier manuscript text can be dated from a year list which ends Ting Yu (丁酉) (the 34th in the cycle of 60) equated with the fourth year of the reign of Ch'ien Fu (乾符), (reigned AD 874-879). From the table on page 338ff it can be seen that Ting Yu years are AD 817, AD 877, and AD 937, of which only AD 877 corresponds to the reign of Ch'ien Fu. Further corroboration of this date lies in the fact that the second moon of the calendar is repeated (an intercalary month), which would happen in AD 877, but not the other Ting Yu years.

*See page 65.

Another calendar is represented by only the smallest fragment which barely includes the title column. This reads 'Chien-Nan (province) Sze Chuan (Country of the Four Rivers) Ch'eng Tu Fu (city) Fan-Sheng Family Almanac'. Even this little scrap is enough to reveal that well-placed families not only had their horoscopes and calendars drawn up for them, but printed copies were made for distribution among important members of the family. Family horoscopes would have included information, not only about lucky and unlucky days, and auspicious or inauspicious directions, but also indications for the fortunes and calamities that awaited the sons, daughters, and parents of the family. The Tun Huang monastery had links with the whole of South-East China — it lay on the 'silk roads' — and the city of Ch'eng Tu lies some seven hundred miles to the South-East, across what is some of the most desolate and depressing terrain in the world. Was this scrap part of an almanac printed to order by the monks? Or was it perhaps brought there by a young member of the family who had joined the monastery? Perhaps a search of the archives may eventually uncover a written list of monks which includes the family name Fan-Sheng among them.

A Calendar Fragment from the Tun Huang Monastery
Stein 1473

The following description of a fragment of a calendar from the Tun Huang monastery will show how very little different are Chinese almanacs of today.

The date is clear from the title column which gives the reign year, and the cyclical characters for that year, being the seventh year of the T'ai Ping Emperor, Hsing Kuo. After the title column, a list of the months indicates whether they are 'Great' (having thirty days) or 'Small' (having only twenty-nine).

There follows a Magic Colour Square for the year, and Magic Colour Squares for each month; the fragment stops just after the diagram for the fifth month. Daily columns, containing six characters give the day of the month, followed by Jih (day), the cyclical characters for the day, the element of the day, and the character from the Chien Ch'ü system of lucky and unlucky days (see page 349).

A calendar of about AD 960 is interesting in that it throws light on the worship of stellar and other deities, principally the stars of the Plough, and the twelve spirits believed to reside in the cyclical 'branches', curiously apotheosizing the abstract qualities of numerical relationships.

Calendar Fragment from Tun Huang AD 982

Number	四	三	二	一	壬	大	正
'Day'	日	日	日	日	寅	建	月
Stem	丙	乙	甲	癸	赤	碧	黄
Branch	申	未	午	巳	白	白	白
Element	木	金	金	火			
Chien Ch'ü Symbol	厄	破	執	定	黑	綠	紫
Date:	4th	3rd	2nd	1st	Red	Green	Yellow
Cyclical number	33	32	31	30			
Element	Wood	Metal	Metal	Water	White	White	White
Huai Nan Tzu Symbol	8	7	6	5	Black	Blue	Purple

Of the other calendars in the collection, one of the most complete is a scroll dated for the year Ping Ch'en (丙辰), the third year of the reign of Hsien Teh (顯德) (reigned AD 954-960), so dating the calendar at AD 956. This scroll is usually on display in the British Museum's galleries. Like other calendars, this one shows each seventh day marked in red with the character Mi (家) so denoting Sundays.

Horoscopes from the *I Shu Tien*

The vast Imperial Encyclopaedia published under the aegis of the Emperor K'ang Hsi includes several volumes on the subject of divination, compiled from a number of older sources. Volume 584 of the section on arts and professions, the *I Shu Tien*, contains chapters attributed to Chang Kuo of the T'ang dynasty (*ca* AD 800). A later section, Cheng Shih Hsing An (鄭氏星案) 'The Treatise on Astrology by Cheng the Sage' was written about 1350, although it is based on older sources. Significantly, there is no mention of the 'animal cycle' names in this work.

The section contains examples of forty sample horoscopes ranging from 1312 to 1376, and hence they must have been compiled at about this period. The general description of the horoscopes is given below, together with a detailed analysis of one of them, No. 37. Readers who would like to analyse another for themselves will find one illustrated on page 353, Volume II of Needham's *Science and Civilisation in China*. Because of the extreme fragility of the encyclopaedia in the British Library (the only known complete copy outside China), the horoscope reproduced here is not taken directly from the original edition, but a later reprint. (Inspection of the illustration in *Science and Civilisation* shows that this is also the case with regards to that work.) However, all the notes and comments which follow are actually based on the original edition, and no remark concerning errors or discrepancies in the horoscopes has been made without first checking the original in the British Library.

Before describing the horoscopes themselves, a word may be said about the remarkable work from which they are taken. The Imperial Encyclopaedia was commenced in the mid-eighteenth century during the reign of the Emperor K'ang Hsi (reigned 1662-1723), and was intended to embrace all human knowledge. The total number of books in the finished work was over ten thousand, forty volumes of which listed the table of contents alone. Printed from type cast in copper, it was the biggest typesetting feat ever undertaken, and arguably the greatest achievement of its kind for all time. Despite the enormous size of the undertaking, scarcely a hundred copies were printed; indeed one estimate suggested that only thirty copies were completed. Worse, as it was printed, the valuable copper type began to disappear, undoubtedly pilfered, until it was eventually decided to melt down the whole fount for coinage. Only three copies are known to exist outside China, and only one of these, in the British Library, is complete and original. This is the copy which the present author has been privileged to examine.

General Format of the Horoscopes

(The reader will no doubt find it convenient to refer to the illustration and the accompanying Key A on page 283ff.)

All the horoscopes in the *I Shu Tien* have the same format, with a dodecagonal 'spider's web' chart in the centre. This is an important point, because despite the fact that these horoscopes have much that is of Indian origin, they do not use the Indian 'square' grid, which can be seen in later Ch'ing horoscopes.

Along the top edge are three headings. In the central block A, the slightly larger type reads 'The Fate of (such and such a person)' depending on whether the native of the horoscope is destined to become rich, famous, or lead a mediocre life. Not all are men's horoscopes; some state 'Woman's horoscope' (R) above the 'spider's web' chart. Careful inspection of the charts reveals subtle differences in terminology for ladies' horoscopes.

The top right-hand corner contains the fortunate signs (D), and the top-left hand corner the unfortunate ones (E). Below the title appear the Eight Characters, sometimes called the 'Four Pillars'. These are discussed more fully in respect of the dating of these and other horoscopes. It is always a useful exercise to check that these are consistent; for example, an even Stem cannot be paired with an odd Branch, *et v.v.* In some of the re-editions of the work, several such errors occur. A further check is to see whether the Stem of the Hour and Month agree according to the rules of Fate Calculation, which again is not always the case. Errors in the Four Pillars lead one to suspect the accuracy of other aspects of the horoscope. Distributed round the main frame are forty little boxes (F). These contain planetary and pseudo-planetary aspects. They range from terms used in Fate Calculation to Dial Plate Terms, and show favourable or other influences and planetary influences for different circumstances. In default of better terminology, these boxes will be referred to as 'the 42 Boxes'.

Now to the spider's web itself, this being the dominant feature of the horoscope. At the centre are a few Chinese characters written bold (G). These read 'Fate', followed by the name of one of the lunar mansions, and then the number of degrees by which the horoscope is aligned; it states, therefore, the horoscope's 'ascendant'.

Moving outwards from the centre, the first circle (H) gives the Twelve Branches; these serve to number the twelve sectors of the horoscope, and their positions are invariable. Tzu (子) Branch I, always appears at the bottom, and so represents the Northern part of the celestial sphere. The second circle (J) contains the planetary and pseudo-planetary positions, defined by the lunar mansion, and the number of degrees. By 'pseudo-planets' is meant real or imaginary phenomena such as the lunar nodes, the Aura, and the 'Comet'.

Houses

The third narrow band (K) lists the twelve spheres of influence, or 'houses' as they are usually known to Western astrologers. A list of these is given on page 301. At first glance they may appear to be identical with the Western houses, but they do not correspond exactly. Nor does every Chinese astrologer agree to the order or even the direction in which they appear. Huard-Durand remarks that in Viet Nam the houses run in a clockwise direction but according to Chu-Sherrill (2) they run anti-clockwise in Fate Calculation horoscopes. Other manuals suggest that the direction of the houses is clockwise for men, anti-clockwise for women. In the *I Shu Tien* however, all the horoscopes, for men and women, run in a clockwise direction.

The next band (L) shows a grid of three bands divided into tenths; these are meant to represent divisions of the circle. By being placed in this unusual fashion, it is clear to the Chinese reader that these are divisions of the circle into 360° (Western) instead of the 365¼° (Chinese degrees). The marks in this grid give the positions of the planets and other astrological data, but there are frequently errors in the engraving, as can be found by reference to the text itself.

Outside the degree-division band is a band (M) which denotes the positions of the twenty-eight lunar mansions. The penultimate ring (N) contains the cyclical signs which harmonize with those to be found in the Four Pillars. Finally, the outer ring (P) (Q) contains two separate series of characters. On the right-hand side of each outer segment is the name of one of the Twelve Life Cycle Palaces. These must not be confused with the Twelve Houses. The Life Cycle Palaces are the stages in a person's life, from conception to burial.

The other characters in band (P) (Q) are yet more Dial Plate Terms, described in greater detail in the section following the Ch'ing horoscope.

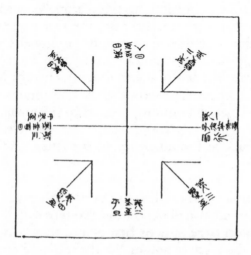

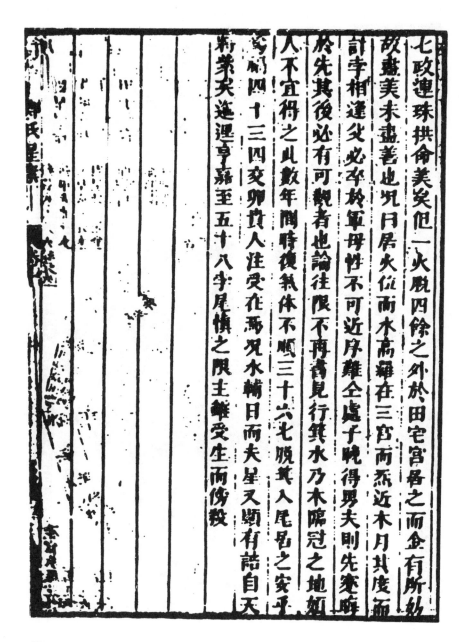

Figure 8.1

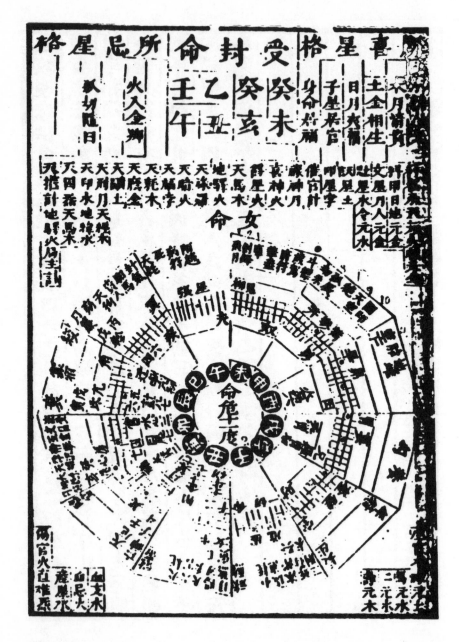

Figure 8.1

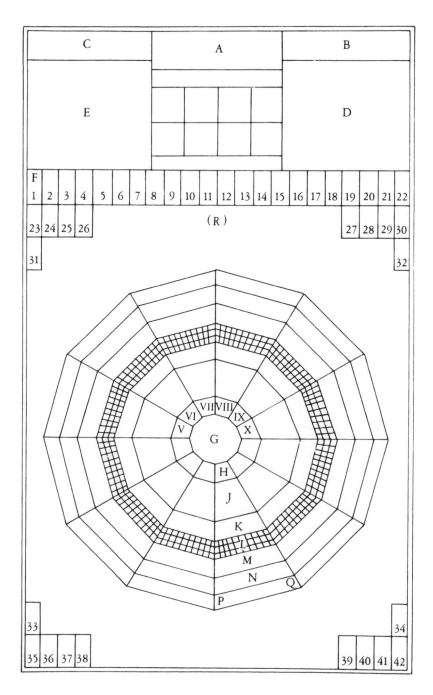

Figure 8.2 General Key to Horoscopes.

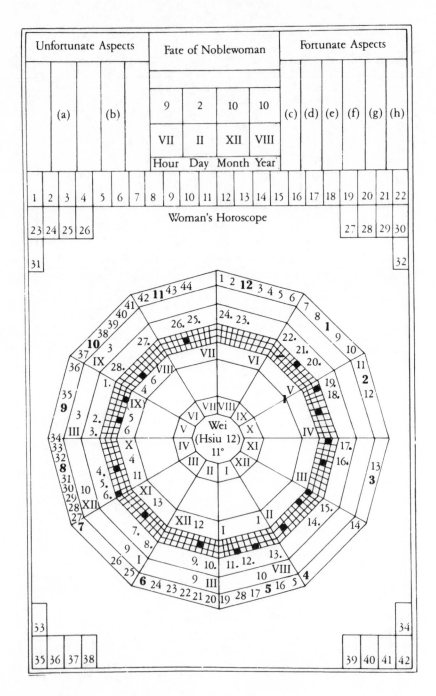

Figure 8.3 Key to Horoscope A.

KEY to Horoscopes in the I Shu Tien

A	Name (or type) of horoscope.
B	'Fortunate aspects'.
C	'Unfortunate aspects'.
D	The principal fortunate aspects.
E	The principal unfortunate aspects.
F (1-42)	The '42 Boxes' (listed in Table 8.1).
G	The mid-heaven.
H	The Twelve Branches, orienting the horoscope. These are invariable. North is at the bottom.
J	Positions of the planets and other celestial phenomena.
K	The twelve 'houses' (listed in Table 8.2).
L	Division of the horoscope into degrees, with planetary positions.
M	The 28 lunar mansions.
N	Harmonizing cyclical signs.
P	The Twelve Life Cycle Palaces (see Table 8.3).
Q	Dial Plate and other terms. Further details of these are given at the end of the description of the Ch'ing horoscope.
R	(If present) 'Woman's horoscope'.

The 42 Boxes

The responses shown in the right-hand column are those pertaining to the horoscope illustrated on page 283, and analysed below. The Chinese characters refer to the five elements, which here of course refer to the five planets, the Sun, Moon, ascending node, descending node, Aura, and Comet. These are:

Shui　水　Water planet, Mercury

Chin　金　Metal planet, Venus

Huo　火　Fire planet, Mars

Mu　木　Wood planet, Jupiter

T'u　土　Earth planet, Saturn

Yüeh　月　Moon

Jih　日　Sun

Lo　羅　Moon's ascending node, the evil aura of Mars

Chi　計　Moon's descending node, the evil aura of Saturn

Ch'i   炁   Aura; the evil aura of the Metal planet, Venus

P'ei   孛   Comet; strictly 脖 'lunar halo', the evil aura of Mercury, the Water planet

Table 8.1

Box			Response
1. T'ien Chüan	天權	Celestial Balance	計
2. T'ien Ch'in	天囚	Celestial Prison	炁
3. T'ien Yin	天印	Celestial Seal	水
4. T'ien Hsing	天刑	Celestial Retribution	月
5. T'ien Szu Kuei	天嗣貴	Celestial Hereditary Honour	土
6. T'ien Yin	天廕	Celestial Haven	金
7. T'ien Hao	天耗	Celestial Wasting	木
8. T'ien Fu	天福	Celestial Prosperity	孛
9. T'ien An	天暗	Celestial Obscurity	火
10. T'ien Lu	天祿	Celestial Favour	羅
11. Ti I	地驛	Terrestial Posthorse	火
12. T'ien Ma	天馬	Celestial Horse	木
13. Chüeh Hsing	爵星	Promotion Star	火
14. Hsi Shen	喜神	Joyous Spirit	火
15. Lu Shen	祿神	Favourable Spirit	月
16. Ts'ui Kuan	催官	Urgency Official	計
17. Yin Hsing	印星	Seal Star	孛
18. T'ien Kuan Hsing	天官星	Celestial Official Star	土
19. K'uei Hsing	魁星	Literary Star	水
20. Wen Hsing	文星	Literature Star	月
21. K'o Chia	科甲	Class Chief — 1st Degree	日

Box *Response*

No.				
22. K'o Ming	科名	Classification — 2nd Degree	水
23. Ti I (same as 11)	地驛	Terrestial Posthorse	火
24. T'ien Ma (same as 12)	天馬	Celestial Horse	木
25. Ti Wei	地緯	Terrestrial Latitude	水
26. T'ien Ching	天經	Celestial Scripture	木
27. Ch'ih Yüan	今元	Present Chief	水
28. Jen Yüan	人元	Human Chief	金
29. Ti Yüan	地元	Earth Chief	金
30. T'ien Yüan	天元	Heaven Chief	火
31. Chü Chu	局主	Position Master	羅
32. Chih Yüan	職元	Official Chief	金
33. Shang Kuan	傷官	Sickness Official	火
34. Sheng Kuan	生官	Life Official	木
35. Chih Nan	直難	Upright Rebukes	炁
36. Ch'an Hsing	產星	Inheritance Star	水
37. Hsüeh Chi	血忌	Blood Avoidance	火
38. Hsüeh Chih	血支	Blood Descendants	水
39. Shou Yüan	壽元	Longevity Chief	木
40. Jen Yüan	仁元	Virtue Chief	水
41. Ma Yüan	馬元	Horse Chief	水
42. Lu Yüan	祿元	Favourable Chief	土

Table 8.2: **The Twelve Houses**

House	Name	Meaning	Equivalent in Fate Calculation*	Fc .ivalent in Western Astrology
I	Ming 命	Destiny	Destiny	Personality
II	Ts'ai 財	Wealth	Parents	Wealth
III	Hsiung 兄	Brothers (and sisters)	Ancestral benefits	Brothers and sisters
IV	T'ien 田	Real estate	Real estate	Inheritance
V	Nan 男	Sons, Males	Emoluments	Offspring
VI	Nü 奴	Servants	Servants	Servants
VII	Ch'i 妻 Fu 夫	Marriage Husband	Travel	Marriage
VIII	Chi 疾	Sickness	Sickness	Death
IX	Ch'ien 遷	Removal	Wealth	Long journeys
X	Kuan 官	Official position	Children	Honour
XI	Fu 福	Happiness	Women; marriage	Aspirations
XII	Hsiang 相	Appearance	Brothers and sisters	Secret enemies

*Sources: (a) Huard and Durand (b) Chu and Sherrill (2). (c) Wan Nien Li, etc.

Table 8.3: **The Twelve Life Cycle Palaces**

Of the twelve Life Cycle Palaces of Feng Shui, ten of them are identifiable as of astrological origin. Only 'Conception' and 'Burial' are missing from astrological horoscopes.

1.	受氣	Shou Ch'i	Receiving Breath
2.	胎	T'ai	Womb
3.	養	Yang	Nourishment
4.	生長	Sheng	Life [length of]
5.	沐浴	Mu Yu	Cleansing
6.	冠帶	Kuan Tai	Cap and Sash
7.	臨官	Lin Kuan	Attainment of Office
8.	旺	Wang	Prosperity
9.	衰	Shuai	Decaying
10.	病	Ping	Sickening
11.	死	Ssu	Death
12.	葬	Tsang	Burial

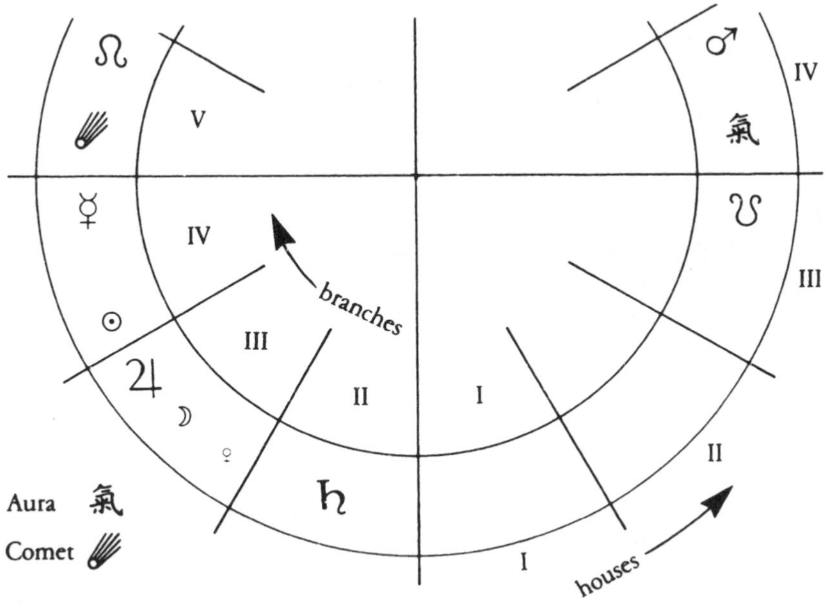

Figure 8.4 The horoscope in Western terms.

Horoscope 37 Analysed in Greater Detail

Having established the general outline of the horoscopes in the *I Shu Tien*, it is now possible to take a look at one of the horoscopes in greater detail. The example on page 284 is No. 37 in the series, but not the 37th chronologically, which can be seen from the tables of astronomical data in Appendix II. Key B should be used in conjunction with the General Key, on page 285, which uses the same code-letter scheme.

A   'Fate of a Noblewoman':
Under the title are the Four Pillars. A check with the rules of Fate Calculation on page 80ff will confirm that these are in order.

B-E Unlucky and lucky aspects:
    (a) 'Sun stands alone'
    (b) 'Mars enters domain of Venus'
    (c) 'The Body Fate is fortunate' ·
    (d) 'The Children Star is in the Official Palace'
    (e) 'Sun and Moon are fortunate'
    (f) 'Saturn and Venus show Self Life' (i.e. longevity)
    (g) 'Jupiter and Moon show great honours'
    (h) 'Mercury supports the Bright Light' (that is, Mercury and the Sun are in close conjunction)

F   42 Boxes:
These are given, for ease of reference, in the table on page 288.

G   Mid-heaven:
Wei (Hsiu 12) 'Roof' (or 'Danger') 11°.

H   The Twelve Branches:
As stated above, the position of these is invariable. They represent the divisions of the celestial equator and are used to align the mid-heaven.

J   Planetary and pseudo-planetary positions:
The major planetary positions are given in the astronomical tables in Appendix II. The following pseudo-planetary positions also appear:
Aura 17-1°; Lo Hou 17, number of degrees not given; Chi Tu 2-7°; Comet 2-1° (as in the astronomical tables, the first figure refers to the lunar mansion in which the phenomenon appears).

K   Twelve Houses:
     Here the Roman numerals represent the Twelve Houses of
     Indian astrology, adopted by the Chinese, and fully described
     above. Note that because this is a female's horoscope, the
     alternative character 'Fu' appears at the VII position. Character
     IX is a variant form. The other characters which appear are
     Chinese numerals, not always written conventionally. They refer
     to significant ages in the person's life. Beginning at the Branch
     I position, it reads:

     Destiny (Fate) first year; Appearance twentieth year; happiness
     thirtieth year; official position forty/forty-first year; wealth
     five/six (fiftieth-sixtieth years?); sickness six/four (sixty-fourth
     year).

L   Grid:
     Small circles are meant to represent the position of the heavenly
     bodies at the time of birth. These are not rotated according
     to the ascendant, but are aligned with the position of the Twelve
     Branches (see above).

M   28 Hsiu:
     These follow the usual order, i.e, counter-clockwise. Chio, Hsiu
     1, represents the mid-heaven.

N   Harmonizing signs:
     Harmonizing Branches and Stems are given in the appropriate
     places; this is of course related more to Fate Calculation rather
     than to astrology. The eagle-eyed will notice that at the ten
     o'clock position (戊) Stem 5 appears in place of (戌) Branch
     XI, a not uncommon misprint which does not, however, appear
     in the original edition.

P   The Palaces:
     Bold figures in the key represent the astrological palaces, Nos
     2-11 of the Twelve Palaces of Fate Calculation, together with
     two others, 12, 'Treasure House' (i.e., a euphemism for burial)
     and 1, 'Cut Off'. The figures in lighter type refer to terms which
     are dealt with in the notes to the next horoscope.

The Date of the Horoscope

Usually, Chinese dates can be calculated from the cyclical sign for
the year, and the reign-year. In the case of the horoscopes in the *I
Shu Tien*, no reign-year is given, and it is of great importance to
be able to put the horoscopes in historical perspective. Without the

reign-year, other methods have to be tried in order to establish the date.

The first step is to note the cyclical sign for the year, given in the Four Pillars. Since every sixtieth year after AD 4 (including 1924 and 1984) has the cyclical sign 1, it follows that the cyclical sign for the year in this horoscope, 10-VIII, or sexagenary number 20, indicates the year to be a date with the formula $23 + 60x$. Working backwards from the publication of the *I Shu Tien* gives the series 1703, 1643, 1583 . . .

The other data contained in the Four Pillars reveal that the month is Branch XII and that the day cyclical number is 2-II, or sexagenary number 2. Calendrical rules indicate that Branch XII refers to the Tenth Month. Because of the close proximity of the Sun and Moon in the horoscope, the Chinese date would mean the beginning of the month, as all Chinese months begin with the New Moon. Such years as 1583, for example, are therefore ruled out because in that year, although the day with the sexagenary number 2 fell in the tenth month, it was the 17th of the month, when the moon would have been full. Although this limited the number of possibilities, it did not actually focus on a particular date, and a friend, Raymond Mercier of Southampton University Department of Mathematics ingeniously suggested that the positions of the slow-moving planets Saturn and Jupiter could narrow the field, without having to take into account all the permutations of planetary positions in the horoscopes. This was a most welcome suggestion, for at that stage, it must be realised, it was not actually appreciated that these were real horoscopes, and not merely invented models to demonstrate some philosophical point.

My friend's suggestion proved to be the answer; a close conjunction of the planets Saturn and Jupiter in horoscope No. 6, a 2-II year, determined the date of that horoscope to be 27 May 1325. The fact that nearly all the planetary positions in the other horoscopes tallied with this and related dates not only verified the date, but also established the fact that these were real horoscopes drawn up for real people. Furthermore, the general level of accuracy led to the discovery of errors and discrepancies in the astronomical data, one of the most interesting conclusions being an obvious deviation in the calculation of the intercalary months at that time. A full analysis of the planetary positions of the 40 horoscopes in the *I Shu Tien* is given here.

An Analysis of Horoscopes in the I Shu Tien

Horoscope No.	Date	Sun	Moon	Jupiter	Mars	Saturn	Venus	Mercury
32	49 11 57	8-12 286°	7-05 268°	18-01 53°	no data	8-12 286°	8-16 290°	7-03 263°
	1312 Dec 27	284°	270°	51°	258°	282°	286°	269°
12	57 6 4	24-11 137°	13-17 353°	8-02 276°	2-07 219°	15-05 16°	22-10 100°	26-10 158°
	1320 Jul 25	130°	0°	273°	207°	18°	95°	152°
22	60 5 38	22-13 93°	1-00 200°	16-03 30°	22-14 104°	18-05 57°	18-02 54°	21-03 84°
	1323 Jun 14	90°	200°	24°	100°	54°	52°	91°
3	1 12 11	9-01 301°	28-27 200°	18-06 58°	15-06 17°	19-07 70°	7-00 263°	8-11 285°
	1325 Jan 7	295°	190°	55°	10°	67°	264°	293°
6	2 4 31	19-04 67°	4-01 236°	21-00 81°	22-13 103°	21-00 81°	17-08 46°	17-14 52°
	1325 May 27	73°	243°	77°	101°	77°	40°	51°
5	4 8 17	27-08 174°	11-06 326°	26-10 158°	27-18 184°	22-28 118°	28-18 200°	26-14 162°
	1327 Aug 31	165°	331°	146°	170°	113°	192°	152°
21	4 8 30	28-01 184°	25-03 144°	(26-13 161°)	28-07 190°	22-29 119°	2-02 214°	28-00 183°
				see Mercury				(26-13 161°)
	1327 Sep 13	178°	147°	150°	182°	114°	210°	177°

Horoscope No.	Date	Sun	Moon	Jupiter	Mars	Saturn	Venus	Mercury
27	7 6 45 1330 Jul 14	23-02 124° 119°	22-02 92° 95°	2-05 217° 213°	18-10 62° 57°	26-08 156° 143°	22-29 119° 117°	22-20 110° 107°
15	8 5 10 1331 Jun 4	21-03 86° 81°	19-03 66° 62°	6-03ʳ 248° 247°	27-03 169° 154°	27-04 170° 152°	17-03 41° 48°	17-04 42° 61°
19	8 6 51 1331 Jul 15	23-01 123° 120°	3-15 236° 240°	5-05 245° 244°	27-00 166° 168°	27-13 179° 156°	19-04 67° 73°	23-01 123° 125°
11	9 2 50 1332 Mar 10	14-03 5° 358°	1-06 206° 146°	8-12 286° 284°	13-09 355° 344°	27-11 177° 166°	14-06 8° 1°	15-11 22° 0°
35	9 8 9 1332 Sep 25	28-04 187° 190°	5-03 243° 250°	8-07 281° 279°	24-01 127° 122°	28-00 183° 176°	4-03 238° 238°	27-13 179° 179° *1
4	9 9 29 1332 Oct 15	2-02 214° 211°	26-04 152° 150°	8-09 283° 281°	24-11 137° 132°	28-03 186° 178°	6-08 253° 257°	1-09 209° 212°
2	13 1 50 1336 Feb 18	13-00 346° 337°	16-02 29° 43°	16-13 40° 32°	14-04 6° 0°	3-03 221° 219°	13-07 353° 349°	11-06 326° 324°
7	15 3 51 1338 Apr 9	16-05 32° 27°	6-06 251° 264°	22-13 103° 98°	18-01 53° 50°	5-03 243° 241°	14-06 8° 1°	17-10 48° 46°
39	17 7 22 1340 Aug 27	27-04 170° 162°	1-03 203° 210°	27-17 183° 173°	26-16 164° 154°	6-15 260° 258°	2-00 212° 205°	26-09 157° 143° *2

Horoscope No.	Date	Sun		Moon		Jupiter		Mars		Saturn		Venus		Mercury		
16	18 1 23 1341 Feb 24	13-06	352° 341°	19-15	78° 83°	1-02	202° 196°	8-02	276° 273°	8-00	274° 274°	9-02	302° 296°	13-14	0° 0°	*3
28	19 6 51 1342 Jul 17	24-03	129° 122°	8-20	294° 285°	2-03	215° 217°	26-02	150° 140°	8.08	282° 282°	24-00	126° 120°	22-17	107° 103°	
25	20 4 7 1343 May 29	19-15	78° 75°	24-07	133° 129°	6-08	253° 255°	15-01	12° 357°	7-03	266° 298°	21-06	87° 78°	21-06	87° 91°	*4
37	20 10 2 1343 Nov 20	6-07	252° 246°	7-07	270° 270°	7-02	265° 264°	18-06	58° 54°	9-00	300° 295°	8-17	291° 295°	5-03	243° 246°	*5
30	21 5 39 1344 Jun 24	22-13	103° 101°	6-03	248° 260°	8-15	289° 287°	26-00	148° 140°	10-06	314° 308°	19-02	65° 62°	21-06	87° 85°	
17	21 6 8 1344 Jul 23	24-08	134° 128°	8-02	276° 260°	8-11	285° 285°	27-04	170° 152°	10-05	313° 307°	22-08	98° 91°	24-12	138° 136°	
9	23 2 53 1346 Feb 28	13-11	357° 348°	19-04	67° 70°	13-05	351° 341°	22-07	97° 93°	12-06	336° 326°	11-03	323° 313°	15-03	14° 349°	
33	24 10 3 1347 Oct 31	3-08	229° 225°	27-18	184° 180°	16-11	38° 34°	25-00	141° 131°	13-03	349° 340°	no data	197°	6-04	249° 248°	*6
34	24 11 54 1347 Dec 21	8-06	280° 282°	24-04	130° 135°	16-08	35° 30°	26-07	155° 145°	13-15	1° 341°	6-16	261° 263°	7-01	264° 262°	

Horoscope No.	Date	Sun	Moon	Jupiter	Mars	Saturn	Venus	Mercury
23	25 8 23 1348 Sep 15	28-04 187° 180°	19-09 72° 89°	19-14 77° 76°	3-06 227° 217°	14-02 4° 356°	3-06 227° 229°	28-14 197° 197°
18	25 9 42 1348 Oct 4	1-04 204° 199°	17-00 38° 340°	22-00 90° 75°	26-14 162° 231°	13-16 359° 354°	5-04 244° 245°	3-05 226° 222°
13	26 8 39 1349 Jul 28	28-15 198° 162°	14-06 8° 341°	22-20 110° 103°	24-11 137° 113°	15-05 16° 10°	28-16 199° 156°	2-05 217° 180° *7
1	27 2 37 1350 Mar 23	15-07 18° 10°	27-11 177° 180°	22-13 103° 100°	27-00 166° 161°	15-11 22° 14°	18-00 52° 51°	15-08 19° 353°
29	27 8 43 1350 Sep 25	(28-14 197°) see Moon 190°	22-29 119° (28-14 197°) 126°	25-02 143° 134°	5-01 241° 238°	'Niu' 16-02ʳ 29° 23°	26-07 153° 142°	28-16 199° 196°
10	29 2 50 1352 Mar 25	15-05 16° 13°	22-13 103° 128°	27-07 173° 163°	2-02 214° 209°	17-05 43° 39°	12-03 333° 335°	17-01 39° 32° *8
36	30 7 3 1353 Jul 31	*25-02 143° 135°	*25-03 144° 146°	1-01 201° 196°	24-01 127° 119°	19-05 68° 66°	28-01 184° 180°	26-03 151° 149° *9

*Hence, should be 1st day of Chinese month.

Horoscope No.	Date	Sun	Moon	Jupiter	Mars	Saturn	Venus	Mercury
26	30 10 51 1353 Nov 16	5-04 244° 243°	24-04 130° 130°	2-07 219° 218°	28-12 195° 188°	19-03 66° 64°	1-05 205° 195°	6-10 255° 258°

Horoscope No.	Date	Sun	Moon	Jupiter	Mars	Saturn	Venus	Mercury
40	31 11 31	8-06 280°	12-14 344°	6-05 250°	13-04 350°	21-00 81°	11-03 323°	8-00 274°
	1354 Dec 21	278°	350°	250°	342°	77°	317°	265° *10
38	34 8 6	(28-00 183°) see Moon	26-06 154°	11-03 323°	2-05 217°	23-01 123°	1-07 207°	24-10 136°
	1357 Sep 11	177°	(28-00 183°) 135°	324°	325°	121°	173°	195°
24	34 9 26	1-01 201°	17-13 51°	11-03 323°	3-06 227°	23-01 123°	28-10 193°	24-07 133°
	1357 Oct 1	195°	34°	323°	181°	123°	198°	179°
20	40 7 6	26-07 155°	27-05 171°	26-14 162°	28-11 194°	28-13 196°	22-18 108°	26-14 162°
	1363 Aug 11	146°	164°	152°	185°	187°	192°	161°
14	41 11 7	7-00 263°	15-11 22°	1-05 205°	27-01 167°	2-04 216°	6-09 254°	8-12 286°
	1364 Dec 4	261°	1°	200°	156°	210°	261°	277°
8	53 14	11-09 329°	22-13 103°	28-03 186°	19-15 78°	12-08 338°	13-13 359°	10-10 318°
	1376 Feb 2	323°	100°	179°	65°	330°	339°	321°
31	53 6 34	(22-20 110°) see Moon	8-02 276°	27-08 174°	26-06 154°	13-04 350°	19-12 75°	21-09 90°
	1376 Jul 1	108°	(22-20 110°) 280°	173°	144°	341°	72°	88°

Notes

The first figure, 'horoscope number' gives the place of the horoscope among the forty in the *I Shu Tien*, which are arranged, not in chronological order, but in order of details pertaining to the text. This is followed by the Chinese date given in the 'Four Pillars' of the horoscope, i.e., the cyclical number for the year, the lunar month (obtained by subtracting 2 from the Branch) and the cyclical number for the day.

Solar, lunar, and planetary longitudes are first given as they appear in the horoscope, that is, the lunar mansion (Hsiu) and the number of Chinese degrees. The second figure gives the approximate longitude expressed in Western degrees. This has been calculated on the basis that each Hsiu consists of a whole number of Chinese degrees, beginning at Chio = 0°. After converting these into Western degrees by a constant factor of 0.986 (no allowance has been made for differences between ecliptic and equator, as the figures are only approximations) 200 was added in order to align the 0° meridian with Western longitudes.

The second line of figures give the longitudes of sun, moon and planets for the equivalent Western date. In le Père Hoang's sino-western calendar, several discrepancies are noted in the numbering of the months. These are listed below.

*1   Hoang: 9th month.
*2   Hoang: 8th month.
*3   Hoang: 2nd month.
*4   Hoang: 5th month.
*5   Hoang: 11th month.
*6   Hoang: 9th month.
*7   I am doubtful about this date. There was an intercalary seventh month in 1349, but the cyclical sign refers to the first of a pair of months. The astronomical data suggest that there is an error in the date.
*8   Hoang: 3rd month.
*9   Note the close conjunction of the Sun and Moon, resulting in a New Moon; this is confirmed in Hoang as being the 1st day of the 7th month.
*10   Hoang: 12th month.

Explanation of the Horoscope

Facing the horoscope chart are notes which draw attention to the main details on the chart, and give some sketchy prognostications.

Diagram C gives the position of the planets in conventional astrological terms, and it may be found useful to refer to this diagram in conjunction with the horoscope itself.

In the first column of explanatory text (that is, the right-hand column; the text written from right to left) the isolated position of Mars (the Fire planet) is noted, together with the fact that the other four planets are bunched together on the opposite side of the chart. The second column remarks that the Sun is opposed to Mars and in close conjunction with Mercury. The proximity of the Wood planet (Jupiter) to the Moon is noted. The horoscope notes also suggest that it would be preferable for the Evil Aura of Saturn, Chi Tu (the Moon's descending node) to be interchanged with the Comet, the Evil Aura of Mercury, which actually meets it.

The interpretation of the horoscope suggests that the mother came from a military family, and that the family is now separated; sons would be gained later in life. The fourth column promises that posterity will be enshrined in a book (that at least was to come true).

The position of the Wood planet (Jupiter) in the Basket (Hsiu 7) warns against men under the influence of Saturn, or 'earthy' types. Aspects are bad for the ages 36-37, until malefic influences take Jupiter out of the Basket into the Tail, when there will be contentment.

The best time for happiness (column six) is the age 43-44. Honour is shown by Branch IV. Mercury, the Water planet, being close to the Sun indicates a high position for the husband, which is also close to the Sun. The Purple Aura, the benign influence of Jupiter, shows riches will arrive at about the age of 58, as does the presence of the Comet in the Tail constellation, having moved there from its position in the Neck constellation in the natal chart.

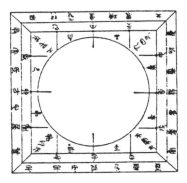

Horoscopes of the Ch'ing Dynasty

There is a gap of several centuries between the horoscopes of the
I Shu Tien and the following examples, but as will soon be seen,
the style of the Chinese horoscope remained virtually unaltered
during this period up to the nineteenth century, when a significant
number of changes overtook the traditional Chinese method of
setting out a horoscope. The British Library Department of Oriental
Manuscripts has two Ch'ing horoscopes in its collection. The first

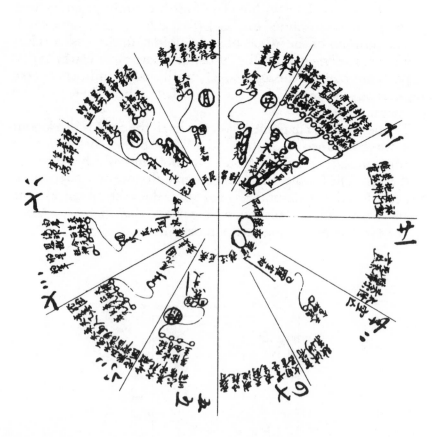

Figure 8.5

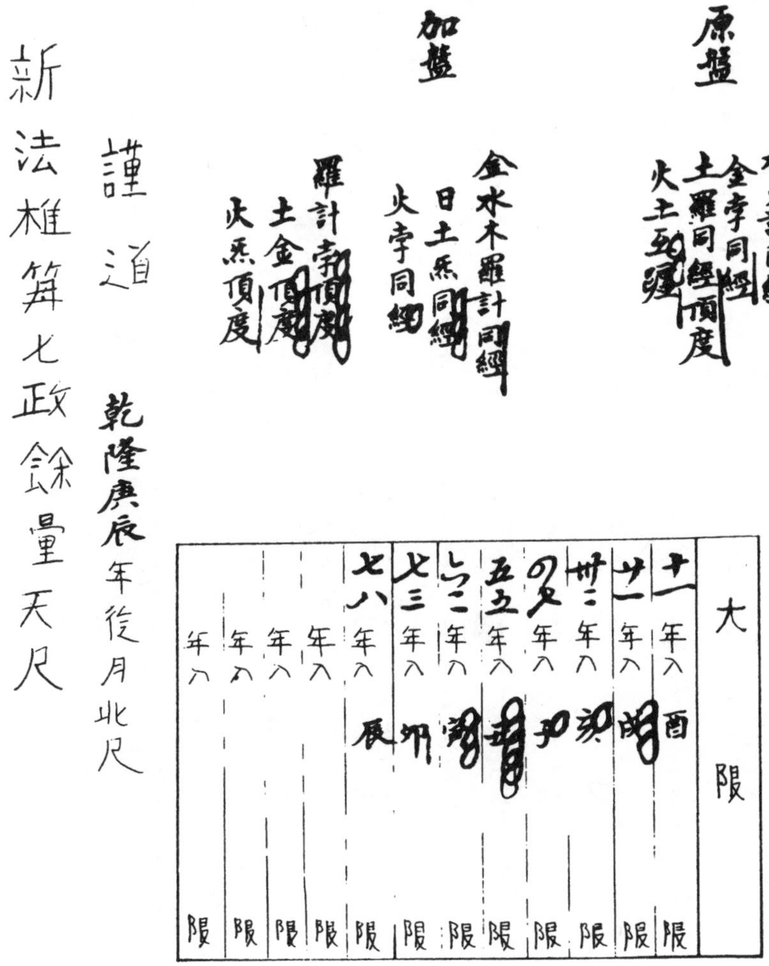

加盤　　　原盤

原盤：
水火計同經
金孛同經
土羅同經頂度
火土到躔

加盤：
金水木羅計同經
日土炁同經
火孛同經
羅計帝頂度
土金頂度
火炁頂度

謹道　乾隆庚辰年後月北尺

新法推算七政餘量天尺

大限

大限										
十一年入酉	廿一年入明	廿二年入戌	卅二年入卯	五五年入午	七三年入丑	七八年入辰	年入	年入	年入	年入
限	限	限	限	限	限	限	限	限	限	限

Figure 8.6

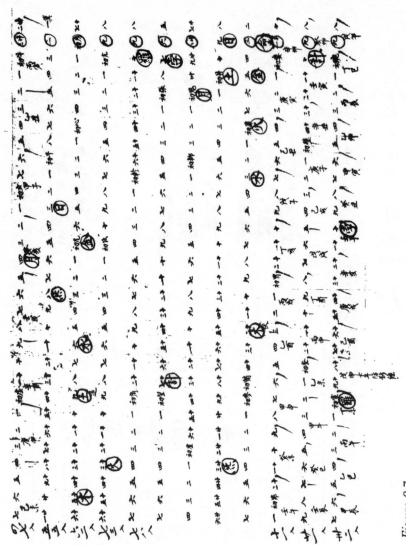

Figure 8.7

of these OR 13037 is written in black and red ink on a red printed form, the printed ink being sadly so faded that it is virtually impossible to distinguish even under ultraviolet light. The accompanying illustrations of this horoscope have been able to reproduce only the handwritten parts of the horoscope; where important to the sense, frame lines and other details have been added to the photograph. These are only a rough approximation of the original, which in some cases had to be interpolated from an examination of the impression marks left by the engraver's plate.

The second horoscope, being more recent, has fared somewhat better, partly on account of the process by which it was reproduced. In this horoscope, OR 11174, the form and other details have been printed hectographically in violet ink, the main details written in black, and attention drawn to details in red ink. Since planetary positions are also printed in violet, the astrologer must have had the forms printed up to order at intervals. The calligraphy is of high quality when printed, and obviously the draughtsman — perhaps the astrologer himself — took more pains over the hectograph originals. The hectograph process may be familiar to some readers. Now virtually extinct, the antiquated procedure involved writing an original in a special ink — the aniline dye used for the process was discovered in the mid-nineteenth century — and this original was pressed on to a bed of seaweed jelly. Frequently employed by choirmasters for producing sets of choral music, the process was nevertheless good enough for a dozen or so legible copies to be produced.

Horoscope OR 13037 — Wu Fu Ch'üan Tu

The title page does not give the reign year, but this can be found quite easily from the Chinese date. The cyclical sign for the year is Hsin Wei, 8-VIII, sexagenary number 8, thus indicating the years 1811, 1871, etc. The Chinese date is 5th Month 4th Day; from the Four Pillars the cyclical sign for the day is seen to be 8-VI, sexagenary number 18, which actually fell on the Fifth Month Fourth Day in 1811. This corresponds with the Western date 24 June, 1811. The second page has a circular format horoscope chart, similar but not identical to the format of the *I Shu Tien* horoscopes. The '42 Boxes' are absent, although the aspects which pertain to them are disposed around the horoscope. The chart does not show the Four Pillars, which are already given on the title page, together with the Chinese date. This circular chart will be described in greater detail shortly. The next page of the horoscope document, the *recto* of the next folded sheet, and facing the horoscope chart, contains a list of important planetary aspects, and are the equivalent of the 'fortunate' and 'unfortunate' divisions of the *I Shu Tien* horoscope.

The following double-page (2 *verso* and 3 *recto*) is a kind of ephemeris from which the astrologer has computed the most significant years in the querent's life. At the right-hand side of the table were printed the Twelve Branches, now almost completely faded, representing the twelve divisions of the heavens. Each row is divided into thirty compartments, so that each compartment represents one celestial degree. These are marked by Hsiu and degree numbers. For example, the seventh row down begins with Branch Wu (VII) and the first four compartments are numbered in Chinese figures

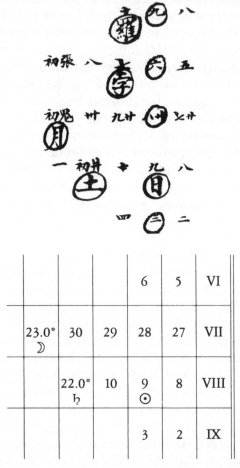

				6	5	VI
23.0° ☽	30	29	28	27	VII
	22.0° ♄	10	9 ☉	8	VIII
			3	2	IX

Figure 8.8 A fragment of the Ephemeris from Horoscope MS OR 13037 (See Text).

27, 28, 29, 30. The next compartment reads Kuei 0° and this can clearly be seen to be followed by the Chinese numerals 1, 2, 3. The exceptionally large number of degrees which precedes Kuei indicates that these are the latter degrees of the lunar mansion Ching, the very wide division of the equator Hsiu 22. This can be seen, not in the row above, but in the row below, one division to the right of Chio 0°, thus showing that the Hsiu divisions run from the bottom of the table to the top. The Moon (月) can be seen sited at Chio 0°, and Saturn (土) at Ching 0°.

At the extreme left of the table can be seen the significant ages in the querent's life; these figures can also be seen written round the circular horoscope chart. This table is therefore a tabulated form of the circular horoscope chart, but is more particularly related to actual astronomical observation. The next page of the horoscope is a blank, for the simple reason that the paper is a single sheet, not folded, and therefore with no available writing surface. After the table there are a further three pages of horoscope text, explaining the planetary positions and interpreting them.

A Description of the Horoscope Chart

At this stage we turn to look in greater detail at the horoscope chart itself, compare this with the chart in the horoscopes of the *I Shu Tien*, and examine more closely some of the technical terms.

At the centre of the chart the twelve Branches were originally printed in red, in identical positions to those in the *I Shu Tien* horoscopes. These Branches have now completely disappeared. The innermost visible circle consists of twelve pairs of characters which are the equivalent of the twelve houses, Band K of the *I Shu Tien* diagrams. Although their names are slightly different, the order is identical. 'Fate' the first house, appears in the Branch V sector, at the two o'clock position.

The next band gives planetary and pseudoplanetary positions in Hsiu and degrees, corresponding with Band J in the earlier horoscope. Thus, these two bands have a reversed position which in no way affects their significance. In these planetary aspects, a specific reference is made to Saturn and Mars being in retardation (this term is discussed by Ssu Ma Ch'ien in his treatise, q.v.). Also, the astrologer has drawn attention to the position of the Sun (at the one o'clock position) as well as the Comet, the Aura of Mercury, and the planet Mercury itself. The complete list of planetary positions is:

Planet	Hsiu and degree	Longitude equivalent
Sun	21-09°	90°
Jupiter	19-12°	75°
Mercury	19-03°	66°
Venus	18-05°	57°
Lo Hou	13-00°	336°
Aura	8-08°	282°
Saturn	6-09° R	254°
Mars	3-13° R	234°
Chi Tu	26-17°	165°
Comet	25-07°	147°
Moon	23-00°	122°

It will be found instructive to compare this table with the fragment on page 306, where the Moon, for example, will be seen to be at its appointed place: Kuei 0°. The other bodies shown in this fragment are the Sun and Saturn.

The four characters which stand on their own, circled, represent the positions of the Four Pillars on the horoscope chart. These are the Year (at the one o'clock position); the Month (at the eleven o'clock position); the Day (ten o'clock) and the Hour (at the seven o'clock position, opposite the Year).

The outer two bands consist of Dial Plate Terms. The innermost of these contains terms related to Fate Calculation, such as Fate Degree (命度), Body Ruler (身主), and Food Spirit (食神). Others can be found among the '42 Boxes'; examples of these are Virtue Chief (仁元), Celestial Seal (天印), and Literature Star (文星). The terms in the outer band are discussed in more detail below.

Somewhat confusingly, the Life Cycle Palaces are also to be found among the terms in the outer band (as in the *I Shu Tien* horoscopes) but here run in a reverse order. As in the other key, Life Cycle Palaces are designated here in bold figures.

Notes on the Dial Plate Terms
Some, but by no means all, of the Dial Plate Terms are common to both horoscopes. In the Imperial Manual of Astrology, the Dial Plate Terms are divided into several grades, the higher grades taking precedence and displacing subordinate ones which may take the same position.

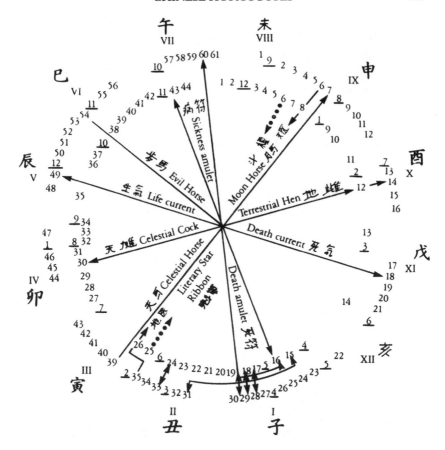

Figure 8.9 Chart showing a comparison between Dial Plate Terms in two Horoscopes.
Outer band: Dial Plate Terms in OR 13037
Inner band: Dial Plate Terms in I Shu Tien 37

In the following notes, the numbers refer to the position of the Dial Plate Terms in the chart; an oblique stroke after the reference number indicates a Dial Plate Term from the Yuan dynasty horoscope, and an oblique stroke before the reference number refers to a term in the Ch'ing dynasty horoscope.

3/1   Hua Kai 華蓋   Flowery Cover
        Though it appears in both horoscopes, it is not one of those listed in the principal four grades of Dial Plate Terms.

8/, /5 Ku Ch'en, Ku Shen 弧辰神   Orphan Planet,
                                                        Orphan Spirit

These are not identical terms, although they occupy identical positions in both horoscopes (see Hua Kai, Flowery Cover). Ku always appears opposite the position of the 11th lunar mansion, Void, and was regarded as an extremely unfortunate current.

7/10   Chieh Sha 刦殺   Robber Curse
         This is the 'Robber' of Fate Calculation.

12/14   Ti Tz'u 地雌   Terrestial Hen
         According to the Ming scholar, Ch'en Jen Hsi, in his commentary to the *T'ai Hsüan Ching*, the Terrestrial Hen represents the planet Venus. In the earlier horoscope the Terrestrial Hen is to be found opposite 30/, T'ien Hsiung, (天雄) the Celestial Cock, but this term is absent from the Ch'ing horoscope.

The following terms are grouped closely together in both horoscopes, but note that they are arranged in contrary order to each other.

15/31   San Hsing 三刑   Three Punishments

16/30   Ssu Fu 死符   Death Amulet
         This guarded against accident or murder, and is directly opposite 43/60 (疾符) Chi Fu, the Sickness Amulet.

17/28   Hsien Ch'ih 咸池   Many Lakes
         This is the name of a circumpolar constellation. It was listed by Ssu Ma Ch'ien in his treatise, and further remarks on its significance may be found there.

18/29   Hsiao Hao 小耗   Lesser Destroyer

24/33   Ta Hao 大耗   Greater Destroyer
         These terms form an axis; the earlier horoscope also has two further terms, Terrestial Destroyer 28/, and Celestial Destroyer 42/, forming another axis which cuts the major axis at right angles to it.

25/19   K'uei T'ai 魁帶   Literary Star Ribbon
         This appears directly opposite 6/, the Great Bear Pointer. The Literary Star is one of the seven stars forming the 'Ladle' of the Great Bear constellation.

33/24   Wen Ch'ang 文昌   Literary Brilliance
Another of the stars which indicate literary prowess.

38/56   T'ien Kou 天狗   Celestial Dog
Although 'Celestial Dog' is the literal translation of T'ien
Kou, the phrase also means Kingfisher, but it is more
probably a dog-like creature, since the mythology is likely
to be related to the Mongolian 'Black Dog of Heaven' (see
page 260).

/8   Yueh Ma 月馬   Moon Horse

/39   T'ien Ma 天馬   Celestial Horse

40/   Jih Ma 馹馬   Post Horse
The Post Horse, shown in the earlier horoscope, is the 'Post
Horse' of Fate Calculation; its absence from the second
horoscope is in accordance with the rules described by Chao
Wei Pang (1) (see Bibliography).

The Celestial Horse, one might expect, would be opposite
the Terrestrial Horse, but here, instead, it is opposite the
Moon Horse. These form an axis at right angles to which
can be found the Evil Horse, /54.

Table for Calculating the First Grade of Heavenly Stem Dial Plate Terms

The following table gives the method of calculating the
'responses' to seven of the Dial Plate Terms found among
the '42 Boxes' in the horoscopes of the *I Shu Tien*. The table
and accompanying notes are self-explanatory.

The figures in brackets refer to the position in the list of
the '42 Boxes' on page 299

A	Hsi Shen	Joyous Spirit	(14)
B	Lu Shen	Favourable Spirit	(15)
C	Ts'ui Kuan	Urgency Official	(16)
D	Yin Hsing	Seal Star	(17)
E	Kuan Hsing	Official Star	(18)
F	K'uei Hsing	Literary Star	(19)
G	Wen Hsing	Literature Star	(20)

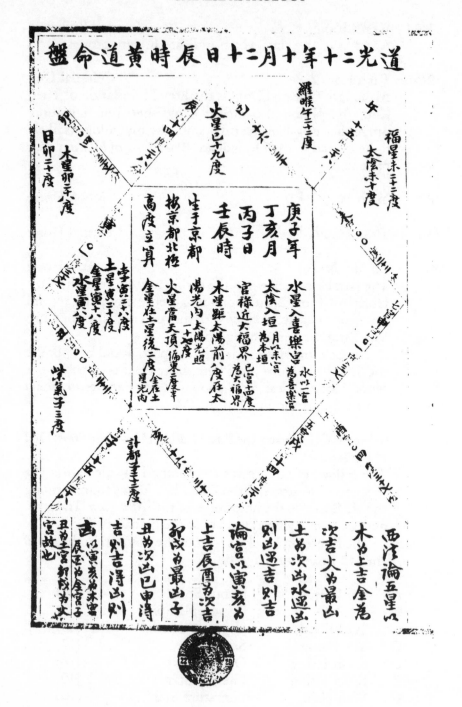

Figure 8.10

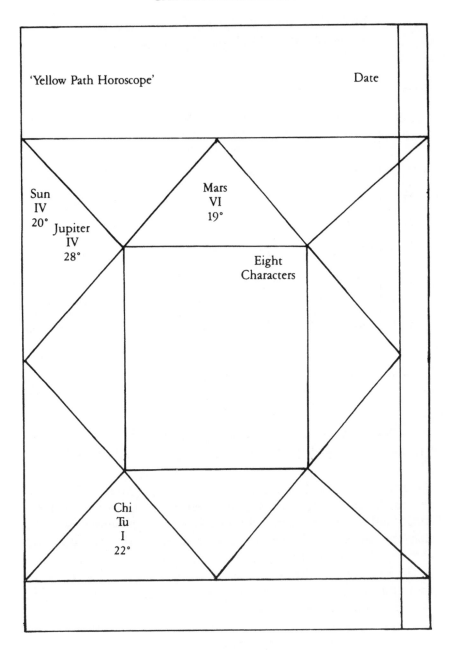

'Yellow Path Horoscope'

Date

Sun
IV
20°
Jupiter
IV
28°

Mars
VI
19°

Eight
Characters

Chi
Tu
I
22°

Figure 8.11 Horoscope of the Ch'ing period; Key to points mentioned in the text.

Table Used for Calculating the First Grade of Heavenly Stem Dial Plate Terms (Examples)

Dial Plate
Term:

Stem	A 喜神	B 祿神	C 催官	D 印星	E 官星	F 魁星	G 文星
甲 1	Lo Hou	Jupiter	Venus	Jupiter	Aura	Moon	Lo Hou
乙 2	Chi Tu	Mercury	Mercury	Sun	Mercury	Sun	Chi Tu
丙 3	Aura	Chi Tu	Sun	Mars	Lo Hou	Lo Hou	Venus
丁 4	Mercury	Lo Hou	Lo Hou	Sun	Chi Tu	Chi Tu	Mars
戊 5	Moon	Saturn	Jupiter	Saturn	Comet	Mars	Venus
己 6	Saturn	Mars	Aura	Lo Hou	Mars	Venus	Aura
庚 7	Venus	Venus	Comet	Venus	Venus	Mercury	Jupiter
辛 8	Jupiter	Aura	Saturn	Chi Tu	Jupiter	Comet	Saturn
壬 9	Comet	Sun	Moon	Mercury	Moon	Aura	Sun
癸 10	Mars	Moon	Chi Tu	Comet	Saturn	Mars	Moon

Horoscope OR 11174 — Chih Ming Shu Han Hsüeh

The horoscope of Chih Ming 'Knowing Fate' is a lengthy document of some two dozen pages, sewn into a paper cover with a label. The document is dated T'ao Ch'ing 20th Year, 10th Month, 20th Day; i.e., 13 November, 1840. It is remarkable in having a square format, Indian fashion, like the old-fashioned Western-style horoscope, rather than the Chinese spider-web or circular model. In the top right-hand corner of the central oblong the Eight Characters are displayed, which to the initiated might appear as twelve characters since the words 'year, month, day, hour' are also added. A check with a concordant calendar confirms the correctness of the cyclical characters: Keng Tzu (7-I) for the year, Ping Tzu (3-I) for the day. Beneath the Eight Characters are listed the major aspects of the planets; other planetary positions and aspects are noted along the lines of the diagram (see Key). For example, directly above the Eight Characters is the position of Mars, the Fire Planet. In the triangle at the bottom of the diagram, directly under the edge of the left-hand side of the oblong, is the position of Chi Tu, the descending lunar node. The whole column reads 'Chi Tu Tzu 22°' meaning the cyclical Branch I; this indicating the first segment of the horoscope. The significance of this will be pointed out in a moment. Meanwhile, the curious reader may like to examine the vertical columns of text in the triangles, looking for the elemental signs which are the names of the ecliptic, and the Chinese numerals which give the degrees. But in addition to the five planets (Wood, Water, and so on) note the additional presence of the imaginary planets such as the T'ai Yin, Counter-Jupiter. In other words, this is a Western horoscope inhabited by Chinese planets and stellar deities, or 'Dial Plate Terms.'

But there is an even more curious feature.

After several pages of interpretation appears a table; this has twelve divisions from top to bottom, and thirty divisions across; it might at first glance be taken for a year's forecast showing the twelve months divided into days. In the right-hand column are the names of the twelve divisions: White Sheep, Metal Ox, Yin-Yang, Square Creature, Lion, Twin Maids, Celestial Beam, Celestial Tree-weevil, Man-Horse, Sharpened Deerskin, Precious Vase, and Twin Fish. Shorn of their exotic names they can be seen to be none other than the Western signs of the Zodiac.

These twelve zodiacal names are given the Chinese equivalent Branch; Aries, note, is Branch XI, Taurus X, Gemini IX, the sequence proceeding regularly in this way. Thus, the zodiacal signs are not so much divisions of the ecliptic as exotic titles for the twelve houses. The chart is followed by ten more pages, in a rapidly deteriorating hand, of text pertinent to the interpretation of the chart, which is no doubt why the horoscope is catalogued in the British Library as a treatise on astrology rather than as a horoscope. Following this text there are two more charts, prominently sketched across the double page, for the dates Kuang Hsü Eighth Year, 10th Month, 3rd Day, and Kuang Hsü Ninth Year, 10th Month, 14th Day. It might be supposed, since these two dates are the years 1882 and 1883 respectively, that they represent the horoscopes of the querent's children. However, translated into Western dates, the two horoscopes are both for the 13th of November, the same Western date as the original horoscope. From this it can be assumed that this horoscope — the entire horoscope, that is — *was first of all drawn up according to a Western date (November 13th)* and then translated into Chinese terms, as if the customer had asked for a horoscope reading for his birthdate, with two years' readings, according to the Western calendar.

The square format of this horoscope, and the use of the Western zodiac, are further proofs of the fact that here is a Chinese astrologer who has expanded his sights by adopting Western calendrical and astrological methods. This horoscope therefore represents a significant step in the decline of indigenous Chinese astrological method.

The next horoscope, which is devoid entirely of planetary terms, shows how Chinese divination was to strike out firmly in the direction of Fate Calculation, and abandon the old astrological method completely.

A Late Ch'ing Horoscope

The fourth example of a Chinese horoscope is taken from Doré's *Recherches et Superstitions* volume IV, where somewhat surprisingly it is given the briefest of captions without any explanatory notes, or other information. The following paragraphs will go some way to rectifying that omission, even though it be more than half a century overdue!

It is an example of a horoscope based entirely on Fate Calculation methods, and is therefore not a true astrological horoscope at all. However, its inclusion here is of vital importance, since it serves to highlight the differences between true Chinese astrology, and the related art of Fate Calculation.

The original was written on a printed form, prettily decorated in green with a bamboo pattern. Coloured ink serves to punctuate the text and highlight aspects of the horoscope regarded by the diviner as noteworthy.

The following notes are numbered according to the leaves of the document, from right to left, Chinese fashion. The running script in the top margin, described later, reviews and interprets the factors given in the main body of the document.

1. **Title page:** Shao-Tzu horoscope. (Shao-Tzu is a place in Fukien).

2. **Date and Cyclical Characters**
    The date is not given in Western years, but from the cyclical signs given in the right-hand column, indicating the year, it can be seen to be the 18th year of the sexagenary cycle; 8-VI (see the table on page 318).

    The right-hand column of the leaf gives the date in the Chinese style: 'Fifth Month, 18th Day' and by consulting a Chinese calendar this can be shown to be the cyclical sign Chi Mao, 14th June in the year 1881.

    What is particularly interesting is that above the frame of the

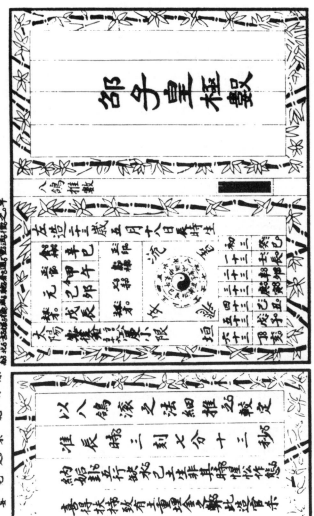

Figure 8.12

horoscope the first (right-hand) column states 'This year Kuei Mao' which is cyclical sign 40; hence the horoscope was calculated in 1903.

戊	己	甲	辛	5	6	1	8
辰	卯	午	巳	V	IV	VII	VI

3. **Analysis of the Chart**
The first two columns refer to the 8 characters, and expand the data by giving the hour, minute, and second of birth: VIth hour, 3rd quarter, 7th minute, 13th second. The other two columns of text note that of the five elements, Water is lacking, and that there is an excess of Earth.

4. **Brief interpretation**
The man is not of great intellect [*because Water, associated with Mind, is lacking, and Earth preponderates*] but his fortune is very successful. He is ambitious, coarse, with a loud voice, and he is hot-tempered. He has a sound business acumen. At the age of 24 he will be in his prime (*and for the following ten years; see next.*)

5. **Decennial Fate Cycle**
A summary of the fortunate years.

Top Margin — above leaf 2.
The stellar deities and lucky directions pertaining to each month of the current year (1903).

Above leaf 3 et ff.
This person was born in a different province to the one in which he resides now. He is of humble parents, nevertheless he will make his own fortune. The ages 24-34 have the most fortunate influences. His relatives treated him badly, but they died whilst he was still a child. He is reckless and takes insufficient care of himself, but he has been stopped on the brink of a disaster. At the age of 24 he becomes more mature. He is advised to sell things from the South — later he will twice be promoted to official position, then settle down to enjoy his fortune. He will become well-known, and have many descendants. Eleven years of fortune are ahead.

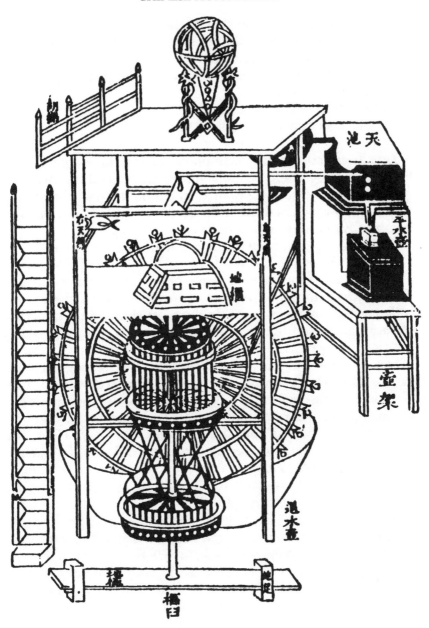

The Mechanical Clock of Su Sang, built in 1092. This extraordinary astronomical machine was regulated by water pouring through a series of reservoirs, ultimately turning an elaborate system of wheels, gears and levers. These were connected to a series of model figures which indicated the time, day, and season. At the top, a kind of orrery revealed the movements of the heavens, even during the daytime.

The mother dies first, then his father. He will not attend his father's funeral; he could not support his parents himself.

At 16 he was delinquent.

He will marry at 25, have two sons, two daughters, 3 grandsons and granddaughters.

At 49 he will grow a beard.

His ancestors graves will be spoiled.

A Late Twentieth-Century Computer-written Horoscope

Perhaps nothing would be more appropriate to end this historical survey of Chinese horoscopes than an examination of a computer-written horoscope obtained in the Summer of 1988 from a market booth in Kaohsiung, southern Taiwan.

The horoscope has been calculated according to a system of Fate Calculation known as Tzu Wei [紫 微] or Purple Crepe Myrtle. This star is said to be the incarnation of the reigning emperor. The origin of the name is obscure, but a plausible reason is given below.

Tzu Wei astrology is probably the most widely known method of Fate Calculation there is, and tables for reckoning the various positions of the stellar deities can be found in almost every Chinese 'Thousand Year Calendar'. Nevertheless, Tzu Wei astrology has many variant methods, not only in the number of stellar deities which are considered, but even in the rules for establishing their positions. At least three such methods have been described by western commentators (Sherrill and Chu in *An Anthology of I Ching*; the present author in *The Chinese Astrology Workbook*; Kwok in *Authentic Chinese Horoscopes*) while the number of Chinese textbooks presently available in Hong Kong and Taiwan reveals a seemingly endless diversity of detail.

Tzu Wei, the name of the principal 'star' or stellar deity of the system, is regarded as the imperial star, and is also the patron deity of masons, who sometimes invoke it before commencing a new building. There is, however, a further interesting point about the name, for the syllables 'Tzu' and 'Wei' are also homonyms for the first and eighth branches: Tzu 子 and Wei 未. In the Pai Hua system, 子 and 未 are significant starting points in the calculation of the positions of certain stellar deities, but unfortunately, even if the coincidence is not accidental, it does not reveal whether the name Tzu Wei was applied to the system because of the significance of the names of these two branches, or whether these two branches acquired their specific role because their names suggested their importance.

```
|破天諫七紫|力胎 天鈴左火文|喬養    天地|小長  句劫天右文|
|碎殤存殺微|士  哭羊輔星昌|龍    侯空|耗生  中廉壽弼曲|
|    4 0 3|     -2  4-2|          |          2|
|劫小    天|忌大  封天|天龍  指白      |
|煞耗    官|煞耗  誥虛|煞德  背虎      |
| 0 20 32 44| 9 21 33 45|10 22 34 46|11 23 35 47|
| 56 68 80 92|57 69 81 93|58 70 82 94|59 71 83 95|
|   55-- 64 癸|  65-- 74 甲|  75-- 84 乙|  85-- 94 丙|
|  朋友宮 巳|  遷移宮 午|  疾厄宮 未|(身)財帛宮 申|
|官晷  龍天陀天天|                乾|將沐  天天破擎|
|府    池月羅梁機|                造|軍浴  喜越軍羊|
|        4 4 1|                |          -2 0 1|
|        權|子 身 令    丙|        忌|
|華宮      散|年 主 主    子|病天          |
|蓋符      鸞|斗 : :    年|池德          |
| 7 19 31 43|君 火 貪    |12 24 36 48|
| 55 67 79 91|: 星 狼   三|60 72 84 96|
|   45-- 54 壬|黃    月|   95--104 丁|
|  官祿宮 辰|        |  子女宮 酉|
|伏死  紅天地天|        八|喜冠  台真間陰殷|
|兵    鸞姚劫相|        日|昌帶  輔宿閽煞神|
|        -2|      辰|              |
|息害          |土  陽 時|月吊          |
|神索          |    建|煞客          |
| 6 18 30 42|五    生| 1 13 25 37|
| 54 66 78 90|局  男| 49 61 73 85|
|   35-- 44 辛|        |   105--114 戊|
|  田宅宮 卯|        |  夫妻宮 戌|
|大病  天天鈴巨太|病衰  八三天貪武|喜帝  哈天天太天|飛臨  天天天|
|耗    巫馬星門陽|符    座台空狼曲|神旺  雷福才陰同|廉官  刑魁府|
|      4 4 3|      4 4|      4 3|      2|
|            |            |      祿|
|歲喪    天孤擧明|將歲      |恩病  亡病|
|驛門    貴辰鞍氣|星建      |光神  神符|
| 5 17 29 41| 4 16 28 40| 3 15 27 39| 2 14 26 38|
| 53 65 77 89|52 64 76 88|51 63 75 87|50 62 74 86|
|   25-- 34 庚|  15-- 24 辛|  5-- 14 庚|  115--124 己|
|  福德宮 寅|  父母宮 丑|  命 宮 子|  兄弟宮 亥|
```

Fig. 8.13 Tzu Wei Computer Horoscope.

The names of many of the other stars are old names for the stars
and star-groups of the Purple Palace, (that is, the region around the
Pole Star, associated with the Imperial family) especially those of
the Great Bear. Indeed, many Chinese text-books on Tzu Wei
astrology refer to the Great Bear (Tou, 斗) in their titles. The names
of two particular stellar deities, the T'ai Yang (Great Yang) and T'ai
Yin (Great Yin), are thought by some writers to refer to the Sun
and Moon, but this is unlikely. As Ssu Ma Ch'ien reveals (in the note
'Concerning the Moon' on page 000) these terms are also used to
refer to certain stars, and even to areas of the sky. Similarly, the 'Fire
Star' should not be considered to be Mars, but Antares (the
determining star of Hsiu 5). In the Pai Hua version of Tzu Wei
astrology the fourteen principal stars of the system are not fixed stars,
but 'flying stars' or meteors which, of course, have no permanence
and astronomically speaking cannot therefore be identified.

The creation of Tzu Wei astrology has been attributed to the Taoist
philosopher Ch'en T'uan [陳 搏], of the early Sung dynasty (died
c. 990), although the actual authorship is probably unknown. The
'Pai Hua' [白 話] system, (summarized in *The Chinese Astrology
Workbook*) is the least complex and consequently in all probability
the earliest existing method. The method is expounded in the *Tao
Tsang* (the Taoist Canon) Vol. 1,114, section 1474. Shu and Cherrill
refer to a system using 63 stars, and a simplified system using only
14, but add, curiously, that there is only one book on Tzu Wei
astrology in Chinese. The method outlined by Kwok, using 36 stars,
is clearly derived from the same source as the computerized horoscope
from Taiwan, although the latter has considerably greater detail,
showing, *inter alia*, the twelve 'Life Cycle Palaces'. The horoscope
is analysed briefly below. Further details of Tzu Wei astrology can
be found in *The Chinese Astrology Workbook* which deals with the
practicalities of drawing up Chinese horoscopes.

Description of the Tzu Wei Horoscope
Tzu Wei horoscopes are traditionally constructed on a rectangular
frame-shaped grid, divided into twelve smaller rectangles. To identify
these twelve divisions, they are numbered according to the twelve
branches, beginning with the second rectangle from the right at the
bottom of the frame, and continuing clockwise round the frame.
In the keyed diagram, the twelve branches are shown as roman
numerals. As is the case in Ring H in the horoscopes from the *I Shu
Tien*, the position of these twelve branches is invariable. Various factors
such as the date of birth for the person whose horoscope is being

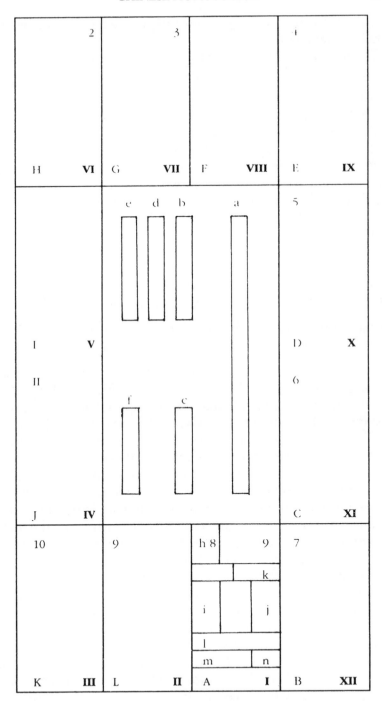

Fig. 8.14 Key to the Tzu Wei Computer Horoscope.

constructed will be written in the centre of the frame, together with other relevant factors.

The following notes refer to the keyed diagram, which should be compared with the horoscope itself.

Central Box:

(a) Male destiny: 3-I year, 3rd Month, 8th Day, 5th double-hour birth date.

(b) Fate Ruler: Greedy Wolf. (*The Greedy Wolf star, however, is not in the Fate Palace in this horoscope, but adjacent to it. See below.*)

(c) Yang Male. (i.e. male born in a *yang* year.)

(d) *Body Ruler:* Fire Star.

(e) I (1st branch) *year, tou chün:* 3rd branch

(f) Earth 5 *type.*

Outer divisions:

In general, the composition of the twelve boxes follows the same pattern as that of the first division, as follows:

Roman numerals I-XII: the twelve branches, always in these same positions, serving to identify the twelve divisions of the horoscope.

Capital letters A-L: the names of the twelve aspects of fate (in Western astrology, 'houses'). These commence with the Fate Palace (conveniently and coincidentally in this horoscope situated in the first division) and run anti-clockwise. They may be compared with the lists in Table 8.2, which (in reverse order) they closely resemble, thus: Fate; Brothers; Marriage; Children; Wealth; Sickness; Travel; Friends; Official position; Real estate; Luck and fortune; Parents.

(g) Names of stellar deities. In this horoscope, the five pairs of characters in top right-hand corner of the first division read: T'ien T'ung 'All Heaven'; T'ai Yin 'The Great Recessive' (see the remark above); T'ien Ts'ai 'Celestial Talents'; T'ien Fu 'Heaven's Fortune'; Ha Lui 'Thunderous Laughter'.

(h) The characters in the top left-hand corner of the divisions refer to various aspects shown by the positions of particular stellar deities; in this instance, Hsi Shen, 'Joyous Spirit'.

The right-hand characters (identified in the key by the numerals 2-11) refer to the twelve Life Cycle Palaces, as distinct from the twelve 'houses' (A-L). They are almost identical to the list given earlier, except that as in *I Shu Tien* horoscope (see note P, the Palaces) the first palace, Shou Ch'i 'Receiving Breath' is replaced by Chüeh, 'Cut Off' and the name of the last palace, Tsang, 'Burial', is replaced by a euphemism.

(i) The two pairs of characters refer to further astrological terms, in this case Sui Yün 'Establishing the Year' and Chiang Hsing 'The General Star'.

(j) (Not always used). Further stellar deities and astrological terms may appear in the right space. In this instance, the characters read Lu En Kuang 'Prosperity, Grace, and Honour'.

(k) The numbers in this area are a kind of 'points' system for good fortune; the greater the benefits shown by the stellar deities, the greater the number of points shown.

(l) The numbers which run consecutively clockwise round the chart represent yearly ages in the person's life, showing what aspect of destiny comes to bear in a twelve-year cycle.

(m) The lower pair of numbers represent the ages of the ten-yearly periods in the decennial fate cycle. Thus, in this horoscope, the formative ten-yearly cycle began at the age of 5.

(n) The character is one of the ten Stems, a factor in the calculation of the decennial fate cycle, referred to above. In this horoscope, the sequence begins in division III with Stem 7. As there are only ten Stems to be apportioned to the twelve divisions, two of them will inevitably be repeated, viz., the first two Stems which began the sequence, in this case, Stems 7 and 8.

A lengthy interpretation of the horoscope follows the chart, explaining the horoscope house by house. By far the longest section is that explaining the first house, Fate, while only a few cursory lines are given to the House of Brothers, and less than a line of text to the House of Land and Property, although fairly lengthy sections are given to the Houses of Parents, Children, Travel, and Official position.

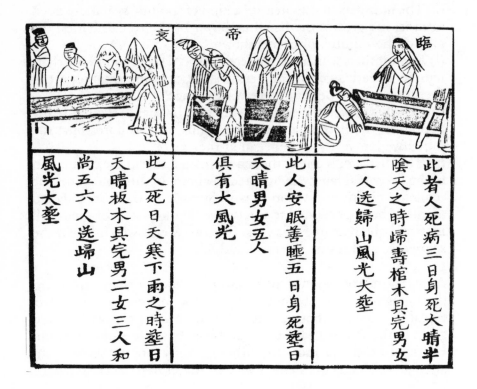

A typical page from the traditional astrological text 'San Shi Xiang' – 'Three Worlds' on which the posthumous horoscopes described in Jin Ping Mei were based

APPENDICES

Tables

and

Additional Text

The Hundred K'o
(and their equivalent time in hours, minutes and seconds)

K'o	H M S	K'o	H M S	K'o	H M S	K'o	H M S	K'o	H M S
1	23.00.00	21	03.48.00	41	08.36.00	61	13.24.00	81	18.12.00
2	23.14.24	22	04.02.24	42	08.50.24	62	13.38.24	82	18.26.24
3	23.28.48	23	04.16.48	43	09.04.48	63	13.52.48	83	18.40.48
4	23.43.12	24	04.31.12	44	09.19.12	64	14.07.12	84	18.55.12
5	23.57.36	25	04.45.36	45	09.33.36	65	14.21.36	85	19.09.36
6	00.12.00	26	05.00.00	46	09.48.00	66	14.36.00	86	19.24.00
7	00.26.24	27	05.14.24	47	10.02.24	67	14.50.24	87	19.38.24
8	00.40.48	28	05.28.48	48	10.16.48	68	15.04.48	88	19.52.48
9	00.55.12	29	05.43.12	49	10.31.12	69	15.19.12	89	20.07.12
10	01.09.36	30	05.57.36	50	10.45.36	70	15.33.36	90	20.21.36
11	01.24.00	31	06.12.00	51	11.00.00	71	15.48.00	91	20.36.00
12	01.38.24	32	06.26.24	52	11.14.24	72	16.02.24	92	20.50.24
13	01.52.48	33	06.40.48	53	11.28.48	73	16.16.48	93	21.04.48
14	02.07.12	34	06.55.12	54	11.43.12	74	16.31.12	94	21.19.12
15	02.21.36	35	07.09.36	55	11.57.36	75	16.45.36	95	21.33.36
16	02.36.00	36	07.24.00	56	12.12.00	76	17.00.00	96	21.48.00
17	02.50.24	37	07.38.24	57	12.26.24	77	17.14.24	97	22.02.24
18	03.04.48	38	07.52.48	58	12.40.48	78	17.28.48	98	22.16.48
19	03.19.12	39	08.07.12	59	12.55.12	79	17.43.12	99	22.31.12
20	03.33.36	40	08.21.36	60	13.09.36	80	17.57.36	100	22.45.36

Dates of the Twenty-Four Ch'i for the Years AD 1900 to 2000*

Ch'i	23	24	1	2	3	4	5	6	7	8	9	10	11	12	13	14	15	16	17	18	19	20	21	22
Year: 19--	Jan		Feb		Mar (EQUINOX)		Apr		May		Jun (SOLSTICE)		Jul		Aug		Sep (EQUINOX)		Oct		Nov		Dec (SOLSTICE)	
00	6	20	4	19	6	21	5	20	6	21	6	22	7	23	8	23	8	23	9	24	8	23	7	22
01	6	21	4	19	6	21	5	21	6	22	6	22	8	23	8	24	8	24	9	24	8	23	8	22
02	6	21	5	19	6	21	6	21	6	22	7	22	8	24	8	24	8	24	9	24	8	23	8	23
03	6	21	5	20	7	22	6	21	7	22	7	22	8	24	9	24	9	24	9	24	8	23	8	23
04	7	21	5	20	6	21	5	20	6	21	6	22	7	23	8	23	8	23	9	24	8	23	7	22
05	6	21	4	19	6	21	5	21	6	22	6	22	8	23	8	24	8	24	9	24	8	23	8	22
06	6	21	5	19	6	21	6	21	6	22	6	22	8	24	8	24	8	24	9	24	8	23	8	23
07	6	21	5	20	7	22	6	21	7	22	7	22	8	24	9	24	9	24	9	24	8	23	8	23
08	7	21	5	20	6	21	5	20	6	21	6	22	7	23	8	23	8	23	9	24	8	23	7	22
09	6	21	4	19	6	21	5	21	6	22	6	22	8	23	8	24	8	24	9	24	8	23	8	22
10	6	21	5	19	6	21	6	21	6	22	6	22	8	24	8	24	8	24	9	24	8	23	8	23
11	6	21	5	20	7	22	6	21	7	22	7	22	8	24	9	24	9	24	9	24	8	23	8	23
12	7	21	5	20	6	21	5	20	6	21	6	22	7	23	8	23	8	23	9	24	8	23	7	22
13	6	20	4	19	6	21	5	21	6	22	6	22	8	23	8	24	8	24	9	24	8	23	8	22
14	6	21	4	19	6	21	5	21	6	22	6	22	8	24	8	24	8	24	9	24	8	23	8	23
15	6	21	5	20	6	22	6	21	6	22	7	22	8	24	8	24	9	24	9	24	8	23	8	23
16	6	21	5	20	6	21	5	20	6	21	6	22	7	23	8	23	8	23	8	24	8	22	7	22
17	6	20	4	19	6	21	5	21	6	21	6	22	8	23	8	24	8	23	9	24	8	23	7	22
18	6	21	4	19	6	21	5	21	6	22	6	22	8	24	8	24	8	24	9	24	8	23	8	22
19	6	21	5	20	6	22	6	21	6	22	7	22	8	24	8	24	9	24	9	24	8	23	8	23
20	6	21	5	20	6	21	5	20	6	21	6	22	7	23	8	23	8	23	8	24	8	22	7	22
21	6	20	4	19	6	21	5	20	6	21	6	22	8	23	8	24	8	23	9	24	8	23	7	22
22	6	21	4	19	6	21	5	21	6	22	6	22	8	24	8	24	8	24	9	24	8	23	8	22
23	6	21	5	19	6	21	6	21	6	22	7	22	8	24	8	24	9	24	9	24	8	23	8	23
24	6	21	5	20	6	21	5	20	6	21	6	22	7	23	8	23	8	23	8	24	8	22	7	22
25	6	20	4	19	6	21	5	20	6	21	6	22	8	23	8	24	8	23	9	24	8	23	7	22
26	6	21	4	19	6	21	5	21	6	22	6	22	8	23	8	24	8	24	9	24	8	23	8	22
27	6	21	5	19	6	21	6	21	6	22	7	22	8	24	8	24	8	24	9	24	8	23	8	23

*The first (single digit) figure for each month is the date of the Chieh, or Monthly Festival.

Ch'i	23	24	1	2	3	4	5	6	7	8	9	10	11	12	13	14	15	16	17	18	19	20	21	22
Year: 19--	Jan		Feb		Mar (EQUINOX)		Apr		May		Jun (SOLSTICE)		Jul		Aug		Sep (EQUINOX)		Oct		Nov		Dec (SOLSTICE)	
28	6	21	5	20	6	21	5	20	6	21	6	21	7	23	8	23	8	23	8	23	7	22	7	22
29	6	20	4	19	6	21	5	20	6	21	6	22	7	23	8	23	8	23	9	24	8	23	7	22
30	6	21	4	19	6	21	5	21	6	22	6	22	8	23	8	24	8	24	9	24	8	23	8	22
31	6	21	5	20	6	21	6	21	6	22	7	22	8	24	8	24	8	24	9	24	8	23	8	23
32	6	21	5	20	6	21	5	20	6	21	6	21	7	23	8	23	8	23	8	23	7	22	7	22
33	6	20	4	19	6	21	5	20	6	21	6	22	7	23	8	23	8	23	9	24	8	23	7	22
34	6	21	4	19	6	21	5	21	6	22	6	22	8	23	8	24	8	24	9	24	8	23	8	22
35	6	21	5	19	6	21	6	21	6	22	6	22	8	24	8	24	8	24	9	24	8	23	8	23
36	6	21	5	20	6	21	5	20	6	21	6	21	7	23	8	23	8	23	8	23	7	22	7	22
37	6	20	4	19	6	21	5	20	6	21	6	22	7	23	8	23	8	23	9	24	8	23	7	22
38	6	21	4	19	6	21	5	21	6	22	6	22	8	23	8	24	8	24	9	24	8	23	8	22
39	6	21	5	19	6	21	6	21	6	22	6	22	8	24	8	24	8	24	9	24	8	23	8	23
40	6	21	5	20	6	21	5	20	6	21	6	21	7	23	8	23	8	23	8	23	7	22	7	22
41	6	20	4	19	6	21	5	20	6	21	6	22	7	23	8	23	8	23	9	24	8	23	7	22
42	6	21	4	19	6	21	5	21	6	22	6	22	8	23	8	24	8	24	9	24	8	23	8	22
43	6	21	5	19	6	21	6	21	6	22	6	22	8	24	8	24	8	24	9	24	8	23	8	23
44	6	21	5	20	6	21	5	20	5	21	6	21	7	23	8	23	8	23	8	23	7	22	7	22
45	6	20	4	19	6	21	5	20	6	21	6	22	7	23	8	23	8	23	8	24	8	22	7	22
46	6	20	4	19	6	21	5	21	6	22	6	22	8	23	8	24	8	23	9	24	8	23	8	22
47	6	21	4	19	6	21	5	21	6	22	6	22	8	24	8	24	8	24	9	24	8	23	8	23
48	6	21	5	20	5	21	5	20	5	21	6	21	7	23	7	23	8	23	8	23	7	22	7	22
49	5	20	4	19	6	21	5	20	6	21	6	22	7	23	8	23	8	23	8	24	8	22	7	22
50	6	20	4	19	6	21	5	20	6	21	6	22	8	23	8	24	8	23	9	24	8	23	8	22
51	6	21	4	19	6	21	5	21	6	22	6	22	8	24	8	24	8	24	9	24	8	23	8	23
52	6	21	5	20	5	21	5	20	5	21	6	21	7	23	7	23	8	23	8	23	7	22	7	22
53	5	20	4	19	6	21	5	20	6	21	6	22	7	23	8	23	8	23	8	24	8	22	7	22
54	6	20	4	19	6	21	5	20	6	21	6	22	8	23	8	24	8	23	9	24	8	23	7	22
55	6	21	4	19	6	21	5	21	6	22	6	22	8	23	8	24	8	24	9	24	8	23	8	22
56	6	21	5	20	5	20	5	20	5	21	6	21	7	23	7	23	8	23	8	23	7	22	7	22
57	5	20	4	19	6	21	5	20	6	21	6	22	7	23	8	23	8	23	8	24	8	22	7	22
58	6	20	4	19	6	21	5	20	6	21	6	22	7	23	8	23	8	23	9	24	8	23	7	22
59	6	21	4	19	6	21	5	21	6	22	6	22	8	23	8	24	8	24	9	24	8	23	8	22
60	6·	21	5	19	5	20	5	20	5	21	6	21	7	23	7	23	7	23	8	23	7	22	7	22
61	5	20	4	19	6	21	5	20	6	21	6	21	7	23	8	23	8	23	8	23	7	22	7	22
62	6	20	4	19	6	21	5	20	6	21	6	22	7	23	8	23	8	23	9	24	8	23	7	22
63	6	21	4	19	6	21	5	21	6	22	6	22	8	23	8	24	8	24	9	24	8	23	8	22
64	6	21	5	19	5	20	5	20	5	21	6	21	7	23	7	23	7	23	8	23	7	22	7	22

Ch'i	23	24	1	2	3	4	5	6	7	8	9	10	11	12	13	14	15	16	17	18	19	20	21	22
Year: 19--	Jan		Feb		Mar (EQUINOX)		Apr		May		Jun (SOLSTICE)		Jul		Aug		Sep (EQUINOX)		Oct		Nov		Dec (SOLSTICE)	
65	5	20	4	19	6	21	5	20	6	21	6	21	7	23	8	23	8	23	8	23	7	22	7	22
66	6	20	4	19	6	21	5	20	6	21	6	22	7	23	8	23	8	23	9	24	8	23	7	22
67	6	21	4	19	6	21	5	21	6	22	6	22	8	23	8	24	8	24	9	24	8	23	8	22
68	6	21	5	19	5	20	5	20	5	21	5	21	7	23	7	23	7	23	8	23	7	22	7	22
69	5	20	4	19	6	21	5	20	6	21	6	21	7	23	8	23	8	23	8	23	7	22	7	22
70	6	20	4	19	6	21	5	20	6	21	6	22	7	23	8	23	8	23	9	24	8	23	7	22
71	6	21	4	19	6	21	5	21	6	22	6	22	8	23	8	24	8	24	9	24	8	23	8	22
72	6	21	5	19	5	20	5	20	5	21	5	21	7	23	7	23	7	23	8	23	7	22	7	22
73	5	20	4	19	6	21	5	20	5	21	6	21	7	23	8	23	8	23	8	23	7	22	7	22
74	6	20	4	19	6	21	5	20	6	21	6	22	7	23	8	23	8	23	9	24	8	23	7	22
75	6	21	4	19	6	21	5	21	6	22	6	22	8	23	8	24	8	23	9	24	8	23	8	22
76	6	21	5	19	5	20	4	20	5	21	5	21	7	23	7	23	7	23	8	23	7	22	7	22
77	5	20	4	19	6	21	5	20	5	21	6	21	7	23	7	23	8	23	8	23	7	22	7	22
78	6	20	4	19	6	21	5	20	6	21	6	22	7	23	8	23	8	23	8	24	8	23	7	22
79	6	21	4	19	6	21	5	21	6	21	6	22	8	23	8	24	8	23	9	24	8	23	8	22
80	6	21	5	19	5	20	4	20	5	21	5	21	7	23	7	23	7	23	8	23	7	22	7	22
81	5	20	4	19	6	21	5	20	5	21	6	21	7	23	7	23	8	23	8	23	7	22	7	22
82	6	20	4	19	6	21	5	20	6	21	6	22	7	23	8	23	8	23	8	24	8	22	7	22
83	6	20	4	19	6	21	5	20	6	21	6	22	8	23	8	24	8	23	9	24	8	23	8	22
84	6	21	4	19	5	20	4	20	5	21	5	21	7	22	7	23	7	23	8	23	7	22	7	22
85	5	20	4	19	5	21	5	20	5	21	6	21	7	23	7	23	8	23	8	23	7	22	7	22
86	5	20	4	19	6	21	5	20	6	21	6	22	7	23	8	23	8	23	8	24	8	22	7	22
87	6	20	4	19	6	21	5	20	6	21	6	22	7	23	8	24	8	23	9	24	8	23	7	22
88	6	21	4	19	5	20	4	20	5	21	5	21	7	22	7	23	7	23	8	23	7	22	7	21
89	5	20	4	19	5	20	5	20	5	21	6	21	7	23	7	23	7	23	8	23	7	22	7	22
90	5	20	4	19	6	21	5	20	6	21	6	21	7	23	8	23	8	23	8	24	8	22	7	22
91	6	20	4	19	6	21	5	20	6	21	6	22	7	23	8	23	8	23	9	24	8	23	7	22
92	6	21	4	19	5	20	4	20	5	21	5	21	7	22	7	23	7	23	8	23	7	22	7	21
93	5	20	4	18	5	20	5	20	5	21	6	21	7	23	7	23	7	23	8	23	7	22	7	22
94	5	20	4	19	6	21	5	20	6	21	6	21	7	23	8	23	8	23	8	23	7	22	7	22
95	6	20	4	19	6	21	5	20	6	21	6	22	7	23	8	23	8	23	9	24	8	23	7	22
96	6	21	4	19	5	20	4	20	5	21	5	21	7	22	7	23	7	23	8	23	7	22	7	21
97	5	20	4	18	5	20	5	20	5	21	5	21	7	23	7	23	7	23	8	23	7	22	7	22
98	5	20	4	19	6	21	5	20	6	21	6	21	7	23	8	23	8	23	8	23	7	22	7	22
99	6	20	4	19	6	21	5	20	6	21	6	22	7	23	8	23	8	23	9	24	8	23	7	22
2000	6	21	4	19	5	20	4	20	5	21	5	21	7	22	7	23	7	23	8	23	7	22	7	21
2001	5	20																						

The 24 Qi [氣]

with their approximate dates

Feb 4	Feb 19	Mar 6	Mar 21	Apr 5	Apr 20
III ☿1	♓	IV ☿2	♈	V ☿3	♉
Spring Begins	Rain Water	Wakening Insects	Spring Equinox	Clear and Bright	Corn Rain
li chun	*yu shui*	*jing shi*	*chun fen*	*qing ming*	*gu yu*
立春	雨水	驚蟄	春分	請命	穀雨
May 6	May 21	Jun 7	Jun 21	Jul 8	Jul 22
VI ☿4	♊	VII ☿5	♋	VIII ☿6	♌
Summer Begins	Little Fullness	Corn Ripens	Summer Solstice	Little Heat	Great Heat
li xia	*xiao man*	*mang zhong*	*xia zhi*	*xiao shu*	*da shu*
立夏	小滿	芒種	夏至	小暑	大暑
Aug 8	Aug 23	Sep 8	Sep 23	Oct 9	Oct 23
IX ☿7	♍	X ☿8	♎	XI ☿9	♏
Autumn Begins	End of Heat	White Dew	Autumn Equinox	Cold Dew	Frost Descends
li qiu	*chu shu*	*bai lu*	*qiu fen*	*han lu*	*shuang jiang*
立秋	處署	白露	秋分	寒露	霜降
Nov 8	Nov 22	Dec 7	Dec 22	Jan 6	Jan 20
XII ☿10	♐	I ☿11	♑	II ☿12	♒
Winter Begins	Little Snow	Great Snow	Winter Solstice	Little Cold	Great Cold
li dong	*xiao xue*	*Da xue*	*Dong zhi*	*xiao han*	*da han*
立冬	小雪	大雪	冬至	小寒	大寒

I   II   *etc*   Branch of Month;   ☿1 ☿2 *etc*   Solar month , *jie* 節

Table of Bright and Dark Years

The following table shows which years are 'blind' and which years are doubly auspicious by having Li Ch'un (usually occurring on the 4th of February) at the beginning as well as the end of the year.

Years in which the Li Ch'un, according to calendar tables, falls on New Year's day need special consideration, since the actual timing of the Li Ch'un is crucial to knowing whether the year is blind. If the Li Ch'un, say, occurs at noon GMT, then for all places east of the Greenwich meridian, the year will have already begun, and the coming year will include the Li Ch'un. Conversely, for the western hemisphere (i.e., all places west of Greenwich) the year will be blind. The actual moments of the Li Ch'un in these critical years are:

```
1905   19hr49
1924   09hr50
1943   00hr41
1992   21hr54
```

Table of Bright and Dark Years

Key

- □   Bright years; the year commences before the Li Ch'un
- ■   Blind years: the Li Ch'un occurs before the New Year
- ◇   Doubly-bright years, beginning before the Li Ch'un and ending after the next
- ◆   Doubly-blind years with no Li Ch'un either at the beginning or end of the year
- ☆   A 'critical' year, commencing on the date of the Li Ch'un itself

Bright and Dark Years

Year			Year			Year		
1901	■		1931	■		1961	■	
1902	■	♦	1932	■	♦	1962	■	♦
1903	□	◇	1933	□	◇	1963	□	◇
1904	■		1934	■	♦	1964	■	♦
1905	☆		1935	□		1965	□	
1906	□	◇	1936	□	◇	1966	□	◇
1907	■	♦	1937	■	♦	1967	■	♦
1908	□		1938	□	◇	1968	□	◇
1909	□	◇	1939	■		1969	■	
1910	■	♦	1940	■	♦	1970	■	♦
1911	□	◇	1941	□	◇	1971	□	◇
1912	■		1942	■		1972	■	♦
1913	■	♦	1943	☆		1973	□	
1914	□	◇	1944	□	◇	1974	□	◇
1915	■	♦	1945	■	♦	1975	■	♦
1916	□		1946	□		1976	□	◇
1917	□	◇	1947	□	◇	1977	■	
1918	■	♦	1948	■	♦	1978	■	♦
1919	□	◇	1949	□	◇	1979	□	◇
1920	■		1950	■		1980	■	
1921	■	♦	1951	■	♦	1981	■	♦
1922	□	◇	1952	□	◇	1982	□	◇
1923	■		1953	■	♦	1983	■	♦
1924	☆		1954	□		1984	□	◇
1925	□	◇	1955	□	◇	1985	■	
1926	■	♦	1956	■	♦	1986	■	♦
1927	□		1957	□	◇	1987	□	◇
1928	□	◇	1958	■		1988	■	
1929	■	♦	1959	■	♦	1989	■	♦
1930	□	◇	1960	□	◇	1990	□	◇
1991	■		2001	□	◇	2011	□	
1992	☆		2002	■	♦	2012	□	◇
1993	□	◇	2003	□		2013	■	♦
1994	■	♦	2004	□	◇	2014	□	◇
1995	□	◇	2005	■	♦	2015	■	
1996	■		2006	□	◇	2016	■	♦
1997	■	♦	2007	■		2017	□	◇
1998	□	◇	2008	■	♦	2018	■	
1999	■		2009	□	◇	2019	■	♦
2000	■	♦	2010	■	♦	2020	□	◇

Stem and Branch Combinations

Table A: To find the sexagenary Number from the Stem and Branch

	Stem:	1 Chia 甲	2 Yi 乙	3 Ping 丙	4 Ting 丁	5 Wu 戊	6 Chi 己	7 Keng 庚	8 Hsin 辛	9 Jen 壬	10 Kuei 癸
子	I Tzu	1	—	13	—	25	—	37	—	49	
丑	II Ch'ou	—	2	—	14	—	26	—	38	—	50
寅	III Yin	51	—	3	—	15	—	27	—	39	—
卯	IV Mao	—	52	—	4	—	16	—	28	—	40
辰	V Ch'en	41	—	53	—	5	—	17	—	29	—
巳	VI Ssu	—	42	—	54	—	6	—	18	—	30
午	VII Wu	31	—	43	—	55	—	7	—	19	—
未	VIII Wei	—	32	—	44	—	56	—	8	—	20
申	IX Shen	21	—	33	—	45	—	57	—	9	—
酉	X Yu	—	22	—	34	—	46	—	58	—	10
戌	XI Shu	11	—	23	—	35	—	47	—	59	—
亥	XII Hai	—	12	—	24	—	26	—	48	—	60

Table B: To find the Stem and Branch from the sexagenary Number

1	1—I	16	6—IV	31	1—VII	46	6—X
2	2—II	17	7—V	32	2—VIII	47	7—XI
3	3—III	18	8—VI	33	3—IX	48	8—XII
4	4—IV	19	9—VII	34	4—X	49	9—I
5	5—V	20	10—VIII	35	5—XI	50	10—II
6	6—VI	21	1—IX	36	6—XII	51	1—III
7	7—VII	22	2—X	37	7—I	52	2—IV
8	8—VIII	23	3—XI	38	8—II	53	3—V
9	9—IX	24	4—XII	39	9—III	54	4—VI
10	10—X	25	5—I	40	10—IV	55	5—VII
11	1—XI	26	6—II	41	1—V	56	6—VIII
12	2—XII	27	7—III	42	2—VI	57	7—IX
13	3—I	28	8—IV	43	3—VII	58	8—X
14	4—II	29	9—V	44	4—VIII	59	9—XI
15	5—III	30	10—VI	45	5—IX	60	10—XII

Table C: The Cyclical Numbers and Stem and
Branch for the 'Century' Years

100	37 庚子 7—I	600	57 庚申 7—IX	1100	17 庚辰 7—V	1600	37 庚子 7—I
200	17 庚辰 7—V	700	37 庚子 7—I	1200	57 庚申 7—IX	1700	17 庚辰 7—V
300	57 庚申 7—IX	800	17 庚辰 7—V	1300	37 庚子 7—I	1800	57 庚申 7—IX
400	37 庚子 7—I	900	57 庚申 7—IX	1400	17 庚辰 7—V	1900	37 庚子 7—I
500	17 庚辰 7—V	1000	37 庚子 7—I	1500	57 庚申 7—IX	2000	17 庚辰 7—V

Table D: Tzu (子) or 'The Five Rat' Years, AD 4 to 2032

1 甲子	13 丙子	25 戊子	37 庚子	49 壬子
Wood	Fire	Earth	Metal	Water
4	16	28	40	52
64	76	88	100	112
124	136	148	160	172
184	196	208	220	232
244	256	268	280	292
304	316	328	340	352
364	376	388	400	412
424	436	448	460	472
484	496	508	520	532
544	556	568	580	592
604	616	628	640	652
664	676	688	700	712
724	736	748	760	772
784	796	808	820	832
844	856	868	880	892
904	916	928	940	952
964	976	988	1000	1012
1024	1036	1048	1060	1072
1084	1096	1108	1120	1132
1144	1156	1168	1180	1192
1204	1216	1228	1240	1252
1264	1276	1288	1300	1312
1324	1336	1348	1360	1372
1384	1396	1408	1420	1432
1444	1456	1468	1480	1492
1504	1516	1528	1540	1552
1564	1576	1588	1600	1612
1624	1636	1648	1660	1672
1684	1696	1708	1720	1732
1744	1756	1768	1780	1792
1804	1816	1828	1840	1852
1864	1876	1888	1900	1912
1924	1936	1948	1960	1972
1984	1996	2008	2020	2032

公元二○○一年　歲次辛巳

西曆二○○一年　太歲姓鄭名祖　肖蛇

小月六	大月五	小月四閏	大月四	小月三	大月二	大月正	別月
未乙	午甲		巳癸	辰壬	卯辛	寅庚	支干
白六	赤七		白八	紫九	白一	黑二	星九

節氣

- 六月（未乙）：大暑 初三 3時5分（寅時）；立秋 十八 19時34分（戌時）
- 五月（午甲）：夏至 初一 16時12分（申時）；小暑 十七 9時52分（巳時）
- 閏四月：芒種 十四 23時19分（夜子時）
- 四月（巳癸）：立夏 十三 19時7分；小滿 廿九 8時6分（辰時）
- 三月（辰壬）：清明 十二 1時33分（丑時）；穀雨 廿七 8時43分（辰時）
- 二月（卯辛）：驚蟄 十一 20時30分（戌時）；春分 廿六 21時24分（亥時）
- 正月（寅庚）：立春 十二 2時20分（丑時）；雨水 廿六 22時11分（亥時）

六月 國曆/干支	五月 國曆/干支	閏四月 國曆/干支	四月 國曆/干支	三月 國曆/干支	二月 國曆/干支	正月 國曆/干支	農曆
7 21 酉乙	6 21 卯乙	5 23 戌丙	4 23 辰丙	3 25 亥丁	2 23 巳丁	1 24 亥丁	初一
7 22 戌丙	6 22 辰丙	5 24 亥丁	4 24 巳丁	3 26 子戊	2 24 午戊	1 25 子戊	初二
7 23 亥丁	6 23 巳丁	5 25 子戊	4 25 午戊	3 27 丑己	2 25 未己	1 26 丑己	初三
7 24 子戊	6 24 午戊	5 26 丑己	4 26 未己	3 28 寅庚	2 26 申庚	1 27 寅庚	初四
7 25 丑己	6 25 未己	5 27 寅庚	4 27 申庚	3 29 卯辛	2 27 酉辛	1 28 卯辛	初五
7 26 寅庚	6 26 申庚	5 28 卯辛	4 28 酉辛	3 30 辰壬	2 28 戌壬	1 29 辰壬	初六
7 27 卯辛	6 27 酉辛	5 29 辰壬	4 29 戌壬	3 31 巳癸	3 1 亥癸	1 30 巳癸	初七
7 28 辰壬	6 28 戌壬	5 30 巳癸	4 30 亥癸	4 1 午甲	3 2 子甲	1 31 午甲	初八
7 29 巳癸	6 29 亥癸	5 31 午甲	5 1 子甲	4 2 未乙	3 3 丑乙	2 1 未乙	初九
7 30 午甲	6 30 子甲	6 1 未乙	5 2 丑乙	4 3 申丙	3 4 寅丙	2 2 申丙	初十
7 31 未乙	7 1 丑乙	6 2 申丙	5 3 寅丙	4 4 酉丁	3 5 卯丁	2 3 酉丁	十一
8 1 申丙	7 2 寅丙	6 3 酉丁	5 4 卯丁	4 5 戌戊	3 6 辰戊	2 4 戌戊	十二
8 2 酉丁	7 3 卯丁	6 4 戌戊	5 5 辰戊	4 6 亥己	3 7 巳己	2 5 亥己	十三
8 3 戌戊	7 4 辰戊	6 5 亥己	5 6 巳己	4 7 子庚	3 8 午庚	2 6 子庚	十四
8 4 亥己	7 5 巳己	6 6 子庚	5 7 午庚	4 8 丑辛	3 9 未辛	2 7 丑辛	十五
8 5 子庚	7 6 午庚	6 7 丑辛	5 8 未辛	4 9 寅壬	3 10 申壬	2 8 寅壬	十六
8 6 丑辛	7 7 未辛	6 8 寅壬	5 9 申壬	4 10 卯癸	3 11 酉癸	2 9 卯癸	十七
8 7 寅壬	7 8 申壬	6 9 卯癸	5 10 酉癸	4 11 辰甲	3 12 戌甲	2 10 辰甲	十八
8 8 卯癸	7 9 酉癸	6 10 辰甲	5 11 戌甲	4 12 巳乙	3 13 亥乙	2 11 巳乙	十九
8 9 辰甲	7 10 戌甲	6 11 巳乙	5 12 亥乙	4 13 午丙	3 14 子丙	2 12 午丙	二十
8 10 巳乙	7 11 亥乙	6 12 午丙	5 13 子丙	4 14 未丁	3 15 丑丁	2 13 未丁	廿一
8 11 午丙	7 12 子丙	6 13 未丁	5 14 丑丁	4 15 申戊	3 16 寅戊	2 14 申戊	廿二
8 12 未丁	7 13 丑丁	6 14 申戊	5 15 寅戊	4 16 酉己	3 17 卯己	2 15 酉己	廿三
8 13 申戊	7 14 寅戊	6 15 酉己	5 16 卯己	4 17 戌庚	3 18 辰庚	2 16 戌庚	廿四
8 14 酉己	7 15 卯己	6 16 戌庚	5 17 辰庚	4 18 亥辛	3 19 巳辛	2 17 亥辛	廿五
8 15 戌庚	7 16 辰庚	6 17 亥辛	5 18 巳辛	4 19 子壬	3 20 午壬	2 18 子壬	廿六
8 16 亥辛	7 17 巳辛	6 18 子壬	5 19 午壬	4 20 丑癸	3 21 未癸	2 19 丑癸	廿七
8 17 子壬	7 18 午壬	6 19 丑癸	5 20 未癸	4 21 寅甲	3 22 申甲	2 20 寅甲	廿八
8 18 丑癸	7 19 未癸	6 20 寅甲	5 21 申甲	4 22 卯乙	3 23 酉乙	2 21 卯乙	廿九
	7 20 申甲		5 22 酉乙		3 24 戌丙	2 22 辰丙	三十

Page from a Chinese Calendar – the first semester of 2001

HOW TO
READ A
CHINESE
CALENDAR

Casting or interpreting a Chinese horoscope demands knowledge of the Chinese calendar. It is possible to convert the western date to the Chinese system using formulae, but this only solves half of the problem. It is far easier, eventually, to become familiar with the Chinese 'Ten Thousand Year Calendar' or Wan Nian Li. These not only give the correspondences between the western and Chinese calendars, but also provide additional factors for horoscopic and fengshui computation.

The calendar pages are essentially two tables in one.

The main, or lower, part of the table shows the corresponding western and Chinese months and dates, while the upper part gives monthly information, including the dates and times when the 24 qi change.

Traditional calendars would be read from right to left, but similar publications from mainland China may be set according to western fashion.

f 曆	e 國	d 支	c 干	b 曆	農	a	Farmer's Calendar, Stem and Branch [of Day], Western Calendar
1	24	亥	丁	一	初		一初 = 01 = 1st [day of Chinese Month]
1	25	子	戊	二	初		1 = January
1	26	丑	己	三	初		26 = 26th (of January)
1	27	寅	庚	四	初	歲	
1	28	卯	辛	五	初	次	Calendar Assistant (= AD)
1	29	辰	壬	六	初		
1	30	巳	癸	七	初	二	2
1	31	午	甲	八	初	0	0
2	1	未	乙	九	初	0	0
2	2	申	丙	十	初	一	1
2	3	酉	丁	一	十	年	year
2	4	戌	戊	二	十		立春 Li Chun, Beginning of Spring,
2	5	亥	己	三	十	辛	is 4th February = 12th of Chinese Month
2	6	子	庚	四	十	巳	8 - VI [Stem and Branch of the Year]
2	7	丑	辛	五	十		

Lower part of the table

The first column, *a*, gives the year date written vertically in Chinese numerals. Generally speaking, the numerals are Chinese or western script as appropriate to the calendar.

Below the year appears the stem and branch for the year.

Column *b* gives the date within the Chinese month - the character 初 having no more significance than the 0 in the western date 04.05.06. *Note that the first day of the Chinese month will always be the New Moon.* The Full Moon therefore occurs on the 15th.

Columns *c* and *d* give the stem and branch of the day. The stem is always spoken of first, and in traditional calendars the stem and branch are written from right to left.

Columns *e* and *f* give the date and month according to the western calendar.

The Upper Table

The upper part of the table is more complex.

The top row gives the number of the Chinese month (first month, second month, etc) followed by the character for large 大 or 小 small. This refers to the number of days in the month, either 29 or 30, which can easily be verified by looking at the foot of the column to see whether the last day of the Chinese month is the 29th or 30th.

The second row shows the stem and branch for each month. As before, the stem is on the right.

The third row gives the Luo Shu number for the month (in Chinese numerals), together with its appropriate colour. Each Luo Shu number always has the same colour. For example, numbers 1, 6 and 8 (一 六 八) are always marked 'white' (白).

The 24 Qi

The fourth row, using Chinese numerals, gives the date of the Chinese month on which the Qi, the 24 solar half-months begins.

Below this the column divides. The right hand side shows two characters which form the name of one of the 24 seasons. Below it are two characters which give the Branch of the Chinese Double-Hour when the Qi changes.

For greater accuracy, the left hand column gives the time, in hours and minutes according to the western 24-hour clock, and following the convention mentioned earlier, the time is given in western numerals.

大	月	正		別	月		Long or short month (*30 or 29 days*)
寅		庚		支	干		Stem and branch [*of the month*]
黑		二		星	九		Nine Stars and Colours [*for fengshui*]
六	廿	二	十		節		節氣 (jie: Solar month; qi: fortnight) [*Date of CHINESE month when the season changes*]
							Actual time when jie *or* qi *changes:*
22	雨	2	立				*Chinese clocktime*
时	水	时	春				立春 Li Chun Spring Begins
11	亥	20	丑				丑時 2nd Chinese hour;
分	时	分	时	氣			*Western clock time* 2 hrs 20 minutes

In this example, the Chinese numerals 二十 signify that the Qi changes on the 12th day of the (Chinese) month, equivalent to February 4th.

The right hand half-column reveals that the Qi in question is the Li Chun, beginning of Spring, and commences at the 丑 hour, equivalent to the time between 1am and 3am.

The left hand column gives the time more specifically as 2 hrs 20 minutes.

To Find the Stem for the Hour from the Day-Stem

Hour-Branch	I 子	II 丑	III 寅	IV 卯	V 辰	VI 巳	VII 午	VIII 未	IX 申	X 酉	XI 戌	XII 亥
Day-Stem	Hour-Stem and Cyclical Number											
甲 1 or 6 己	1 1	2 2	3 3	4 4	5 5	6 6	7 7	8 8	9 9	10 10	1 11	2 12
乙 2 or 7 庚	3 13	4 14	5 15	6 16	7 17	8 18	9 19	10 20	1 21	2 22	3 23	4 24
丙 3 or 8 辛	5 25	6 26	7 27	8 28	9 29	10 30	1 31	2 32	3 33	4 34	5 35	6 36
丁 4 or 9 壬	7 37	8 38	9 39	10 40	1 41	2 42	3 43	4 44	5 45	6 46	7 47	8 48
戊 5 or 10 癸	9 49	10 50	1 51	2 52	3 53	4 54	5 55	6 56	7 57	8 58	9 59	10 60

To Find the Stem for the Month from the Year-Stem

Month:	I	II	III	IV	V	VI	VII	VIII	IX	X	XI	XII
Month-Branch	III 寅	IV 卯	V 辰	VI 巳	VII 午	VIII 未	IX 申	X 酉	XI 戌	XII 亥	I 子	II 丑
Year-Stem	Month-Stem and Cyclical Number											
甲 1 or 6 己	3 3	4 4	5 5	6 6	7 7	8 8	9 9	10 10	1 11	2 12	3 13	4 14
乙 2 or 7 庚	5 15	6 16	7 17	8 18	9 19	10 20	1 21	2 22	3 23	4 24	5 25	6 26
丙 3 or 8 辛	7 27	8 28	9 29	10 30	1 31	2 32	3 33	4 34	5 35	6 36	7 37	8 38
丁 4 or 9 壬	9 39	10 40	1 41	2 42	3 43	4 44	5 45	6 46	7 47	8 48	9 49	10 50
戊 5 or 10 癸	1 51	2 52	3 53	4 54	5 55	6 56	7 57	8 58	9 59	10 60	1 1	2 2

From the factors given above, it is now possible to calculate the Four Pillars, two natural and two artificial. The two natural pillars are the Stem and Branch for the day and the year, and the two artificial are the Stem and Branch for the hour and month, obtained by reference to the tables above.

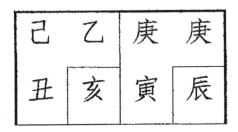

Calculating the Hsiu from a Zodiacal Position

The astrological Hsiu in which the Moon or a planet is situated can be found from the zodiacal position given in a Western ephemeris, and converted by the following four factors. Firstly, the zodiacal position in degrees is converted into the equatorial position by a formula which takes into account the angle ε between the planes of the equator and the ecliptic; this position is converted into Chinese degrees, and the position of the unequal Hsiu found by consulting the Hsiu equatorial extension figures.

The angle ε is of greater or lesser importance depending on the field of study. It changes slowly decade by decade, and while this need not concern anyone using astronomical tables for the current years, it is a significant factor for historical researchers (perhaps, say, for defining the position of eclipses recorded in the Han Shu in the first century of our era), which if the value of ε were not taken into account, would render the results wildly inaccurate.

However, for present-day astrological purposes, the following table should suffice. It takes ε to be 23½° and shows the correspondence between zodiacal position and the Hsiu, the former in Western, the latter in Chinese degrees. Interpolations can be made for figures in between those which are given, all of which have been rounded to the nearest degree.

Conversion Table
Western Zodiac to Equatorial Hsiu

Ecliptic degree	Zodiacal degree	Hsiu degree	Equatorial degree	Ecliptic degree	Zodiacal degree	Hsiu degree	Equatorial degree
0	Aries	11	159	90	Cancer	6	250
3	3	14	162	93	3	*22	253
4	4	*14	164	95	5	2	255
5	5	1	165	97	7	4	257
7	7	3	167	100	10	6	259
10	10	6	170	103	13	9	262
13	13	*15	173	105	15	12	265
15	15	2	175	107	17	14	267
17	17	5	178	110	20	16	269
20	20	8	181	113	23	19	272
23	23	11	184	115	25	21	274
25	25	13	186	117	27	23	276
27	27	*16	189	120	Leo	25	278
30	Taurus	3	192	123	3	28	281
33	3	7	196	125	5	30	283
35	5	9	198	127	7	32	285
37	7	*17	201	128	8	*23	286
40	10	3	204	130	10	2	288
43	13	6	207	132	12	*24	290
45	15	8	209	133	13	1	291
47	17	10	211	135	15	3	293
50	20	13	214	137	17	5	295
51	21	*18	215	140	21	7	297
53	23	2	217	143	23	10	300
55	25	3	218	145	25	13	303
57	27	5	220	147	27	*25	305
60	Gemini	8	223	150	Virgo	3	308
63	3	*19	226	153	3	6	311
65	5	2	228	154	4	*26	312
67	7	4	230	155	5	2	314
70	10	6	232	157	7	5	317
73	13	9	235	160	10	7	319
75	15	11	237	163	13	10	322
77	17	13	239	165	15	12	324
80	20	15	241	167	17	15	327
82	22	*20	242	170	20	*27	330
83	23	1	243	173	23	3	333
84	24	*21	244	175	25	6	336
85	25	2	246	177	27	9	339
87	27	3	247				

Conversion Table
Western Zodiac to Equatorial Hsiu

Ecliptic degree	Zodiacal degree	Hsiu degree	Equatorial degree	Ecliptic degree	Zodiacal degree	Hsiu degree	Equatorial degree
180	Libra	12	342	270	Capri.	4	68
183	3	15	345	273	3	7	71
185	5	*28	348	275	5	10	74
187	7	2	350	277	7	*8	75
190	10	5	353	280	10	2	77
193	13	8	356	283	13	5	80
195	15	10	358	285	15	7	82
197	17	13	361	287	17	9	84
200	20	16	364	290	20	11	86
201	21	*1	0	293	23	14	89
203	23	2	2	295	25	16	91
205	25	4	4	297	27	18	93
207	27	7	7	300	Aquar.	20	95
210	Scorpio	10	10	303	3	23	98
212	2	*2	12	305	5	25	100
213	3	1	13	306	6	*9	101
215	5	3	15	307	7	1	102
217	7	6	18	310	10	3	104
220	10	*3	21	313	13	7	108
223	13	3	24	314	14	*10	109
225	15	5	26	315	15	2	111
227	17	7	28	317	17	4	113
230	20	9	31	320	20	6	115
233	23	12	34	323	23	9	118
235	25	13	35	325	25	*11	121
236	26	*4	36	327	27	2	123
237	27	1	37	330	Pisces	5	126
240	Sagit.	*5	41	333	3	8	129
243	3	3	44	334	4	*12	131
245	5	*6	46	335	5	1	132
247	7	2	48	337	7	4	135
250	10	4	50	340	10	6	137
253	13	7	53	343	13	9	140
255	15	9	55	345	15	11	142
257	17	11	57	347	17	14	145
260	20	13	59	350	20	*13	148
263	23	15	62	353	23	3	151
265	25	*7	64	355	25	5	153
267	17	1	65	357	27	9	157

Lunar and Solar Correspondences

As an example of the use of the foregoing table, here is a table of 'solar' correspondences throughout the year.

Western Zodiac	Hsiu			
Aries	– 13,	14,	15,	16 –
Taurus	– 16,	17,	18,	19 –
Gemini	–19,	20,	21 –	
Cancer	– 21,	22 –		
Leo	– 22,	23,	24,	25 –
Virgo	– 25,	26,	27 –	
Libra	– 27,	28 –		
Scorpio	– 28,	2,	3,	4 –
Sagittarius	– 4,	5,	6,	7 –
Capricorn	– 7,	8 –		
Aquarius	– 8,	9,	10,	11 –
Pisces	– 11,	12,	13 –	

The following are approximate solar dates:

30 December, Hsiu 8, Tou, Dipper
26 January, Hsiu 9, Niu, Ox
3 February, Hsiu 10, Nü, Maiden
14 February, Hsiu 11, Hsü, Void
24 February, Hsiu 12, Wei, Roof
11 March, Hsiu 13, Shih, House
26 March, Hsiu 14, Pi, Wall
14 April, Hsiu 15, K'uei, Astride
18 April, Hsiu 16, Lou, Mound
28 April, Hsiu 17, Wei, Stomach
12 May, Hsiu 18, Mao, Pleiades
25 May, Hsiu 19, Pi, Net
13 June, Hsiu 20, Tsui, Beak
15 June, Hsiu 21, Shen, Orion

26 June, Hsiu 22, Ching, The Well
1 August, Hsiu 23, Kuei, Ghosts
5 August, Hsiu 24, Liu, Willow
20 August, Hsiu 25, Hsing, Star
28 August, Hsiu 26, Chang, Bow
13 Sept., Hsiu 27, I, Wings
29 Sept., Hsiu 28, Chen, Carriage
15 October, Hsiu 1, Chio, Horn
26 October, Hsiu 2, K'ang, Neck
3 November, Hsiu 3, Ti, Base
19 November, Hsiu 4, Fang, Room
23 November, Hsiu 5, Hsin, Heart
28 November, Hsiu 6, Wei, Tail
18 December, Hsiu 7, Chi, Basket

Tables to Calculate the Notional Hsiu
For Any Date, 1901 to 2000

The following tables will enable the 'notional Hsiu' as given in Chinese almanacs to be calculated for any date from 1901 to 2000. From the first table, the figure for the year of the date in question is noted. To this is added the figure for the month, given in Table II, and the date of the day of the month, without conversion. If the date occurred in a leap year on or after 1 March, a further 1 is added to account for leap years. If the total is greater than 28, 28 is subtracted successively until 28 or less remains. This is the number of the notional Hsiu for the date.

Example   What is the notional Hsiu for 28 April, 1944?
            The figure for 1944 is   3
            The figure for April is   5
            The date of the month is   28
            1944 was a leap year; add   1
                                        _____
            Total   37
            Substract 28   − 28
                                        _____
            Answer   9

Therefore, the notional Hsiu for 28 April, 1944 is Hsiu 9, Niu, the Ox.

As a check on one's calculations, it is worth recalling that the notional Hsiu always fall on certain days of the week.

1,	8,	15,	22,	Thursday
2,	9,	16,	23,	Friday
3,	10,	17,	24,	Saturday
4,	11,	18,	25,	Sunday
5,	12,	19,	26,	Monday
6,	13,	20,	27,	Tuesday
7,	14,	21,	28,	Wednesday

Table I:
Year Number

1901	6	1921	3	1941	28	1961	25	1981	22
1902	7	1922	4	1942	1	1962	26	1982	23
1903	8	1923	5	1943	2	1963	27	1983	24
1904	9	1924	6	1944	3	1964	28	1984	25
1905	11	1925	8	1945	5	1965	2	1985	27
1906	12	1926	9	1946	6	1966	3	1986	28
1907	13	1927	10	1947	7	1967	4	1987	1
1908	14	1928	11	1948	8	1968	5	1988	2
1909	16	1929	13	1949	10	1969	7	1989	4
1910	17	1930	14	1950	11	1970	8	1990	5
1911	18	1931	15	1951	12	1971	9	1991	6
1912	19	1932	16	1952	13	1972	10	1992	7
1913	21	1933	18	1953	15	1973	12	1993	9
1914	22	1934	19	1954	16	1974	13	1994	10
1915	23	1935	20	1955	17	1975	14	1995	11
1916	24	1936	21	1956	18	1976	15	1996	12
1917	26	1937	23	1957	20	1977	17	1997	14
1918	27	1938	24	1958	21	1978	18	1998	15
1919	28	1939	25	1959	22	1979	19	1999	16
1920	1	1940	26	1960	23	1980	20	2000	17

Table II:
Month Number

January	27	May	7	September	18
February	2	June	10	October	20
March	2	July	12	November	23
April	5	August	15	December	25

Addendum:
Table of Year Numbers for Calculating the notional hsiu for dates post 2000

2001	2002	2003	2004	2005	2006	2007	2008	2009	2010
19	20	21	22	24	25	26	27	1	2

2011	2012	2013	2014	2015	2016	2017	2018	2019	2020
3	4	6	7	8	9	11	12	13	14

2021	2022	2023	2024	2025	2026	2027	2028	2029	2030
16	17	18	19	21	22	23	24	26	27

Table to Calculate the Mid-Heaven House

Chinese Month	I	II	III	IV	V	VI	VII	VIII	IX	X	XI	XII
Month Branch	III	IV	V	VI	VII	VIII	IX	X	XI	XII	I	II
Chinese hour												
I	II	I	XII	XI	X	IX	VIII	VII	VI	V	IV	III
II	I	XII	XI	X	IX	VIII	VII	VI	V	IV	III	II
III	XII	XI	X	IX	VIII	VII	VI	V	IV	III	II	I
IV	XI	X	IX	VIII	VII	VI	V	IV	III	II	I	XII
V	X	IX	VIII	VII	VI	V	IV	III	II	I	XII	XI
VI	IX	VIII	VII	VI	V	IV	III	II	I	XII	XI	X
VII	VIII	VII	VI	V	IV	III	II	I	XII	XI	X	IX
VIII	VII	VI	V	IV	III	II	I	XII	XI	X	IX	VIII
IX	VI	V	IV	III	II	I	XII	XI	X	IX	VIII	VII
X	V	IV	III	II	I	XII	XI	X	IX	VIII	VII	VI
XI	IV	III	II	I	XII	XI	X	IX	VIII	VII	VI	V
XII	III	II	I	XII	XI	X	IX	VIII	VII	VI	V	IV

Celestial Divisions and Lunar Mansions

I	II	III	IV	V	VI	VII	VIII	IX	X	XI	XII
12 11 10	9 8	7 6	5 4 3	2 1	28 27	26 25 24	23 22	21 20	19 18 17	16 15	14 13

COMBINATIONS OF THE SIXTY STEMS-AND-BRANCHES AND THEIR CONTAINED ELEMENTS

1	1	I	Gold from the sea	*Rat on the Roof*
2	2	II	Gold from the sea	*Sea Ox*
3	3	III	Fiery Furnace	*Tiger in the Forest*
4	4	IV	Fiery Furnace	*Rabbit dreaming of the Moon*
5	5	V	Forest Wood	*Dragon of Pure Virtue*
6	6	VI	Forest wood	*Snake of Happiness*
7	7	VII	Ditch Earth	*Palace Horse*
8	8	VIII	Ditch Earth	*Lucky Sheep*
9	9	IX	Sharp Sword	*Elegant Monkey*
10	10	X	Sharp Sword	*Barnyard Rooster*
11	1	XI	Volcano Fire	*Guard Dog*
12	2	XII	Volcano Fire	*Travelling Pig*
13	3	I	Channeled Water	*Field Rat*
14	4	II	Channeled Water	*Lake Buffalo*
15	5	III	Ramparts Earth	*Tiger climbs the Mountain*
16	6	IV	Ramparts Earth	*Rabbit of Woods and Mountains*
17	7	V	Cast metal	*Dragon of Patience*
18	8	VI	Cast metal	*Hibernating Snake*
19	9	VII	Pliant Wood	*War Horse*
20	10	VIII	Pliant Wood	*Sheep in a flock*
21	1	IX	Rains and Springs	*Tree Monkey*
22	2	X	Rains and Springs	*Cock crowing at Noon*
23	3	XI	Rooftop Slates	*Sleeping Dog*
24	4	XII	Rooftop Slates	*Pig traversing a Mountain*
25	5	I	Lightning Fire	*Granary Rat*
26	6	II	Lightning Fire	*Ox in the Byre*
27	7	III	Hardwood	*Tiger leaves the Mountain*
28	8	IV	Hardwood	*Rabbit in the Burrow*
29	9	V	Flowing Water	*Rain Dragon*
30	10	VI	Flowing Water	*Snake in the Grass*

31	1	VII	Excavated Metal	*Horse in the Clouds*
32	2	VIII	Excavated Metal	*The Serious Sheep*
33	3	IX	Foothill Fire	*Mountain Monkey*
34	4	X	Foothill Fire	*Solitary Rooster*
35	5	XI	Scrubland twigs	*Mountain Dog*
36	6	XII	Scrubland twigs	*Monastic Pig*
37	7	I	Earthen Walls	*Rat on the Crossbeam*
38	8	II	Earthen Walls	*Ox on the Road*
39	9	III	Bronze Mirror	*Tiger crossing the forest*
40	10	IV	Bronze Mirror	*Rabbit leaving the forest*
41	1	V	Lamplight	*Dragon in the Whirlpool*
42	2	VI	Lamplight	*Snake leaving a hole*
43	3	VII	The River Han (The Milky Way)	*Travelling Horse*
44	4	VIII	The River Han (The Milky Way)	*Lost Sheep*
45	5	IX	Roadworks Earth	*The Independent Monkey*
46	6	X	Roadworks Earth	*Cock pecking for food*
47	7	XI	Brooch pins	*Temple Dog*
48	8	XII	Brooch pins	*Farmer Pig*
49	9	I	Mulberry wood	*Rat on the Mountain*
50	10	II	Mulberry wood	*Ox by the Gate*
51	1	III	Fresh stream water	*Tiger standing firm*
52	2	IV	Fresh stream water	*The Enlightened Rabbit*
53	3	V	Sand and clay	*Dragon in the Sky*
54	4	VI	Sand and clay	*Snake in the Pool*
55	5	VII	Heavenly Fire	*Horse in the Stable*
56	6	VIII	Heavenly Fire	*Sheep in Pasture*
57	7	IX	Pomegranate wood	*Monkey eating fruit*
58	8	X	Pomegranate wood	*Caged Rooster*
59	9	XI	Sea water	*Watch Dog*
60	10	XII	Sea water	*Pig in the Forest*

THE LUOPAN

The instrument used by fengshui practitioners is the luopan or reticulated plate, (羅 盤), commonly known as a fengshui compass. In the original edition of 'Chinese' Astrology' I remarked that there are enough examples of this instrument to be seen for it to be familiar - by which I meant that they were displayed in one or two museums in the country. Now it seems that every shop in China sells them at a knock down price to tourists.

Perhaps a few myths about the luopan can be dispelled, a few scientific facts aired, and possibly a conjecture or two put forward.

To begin with, the luopan was originally a scientific instrument, used for astronomical observation, the purpose of which was twofold - one to keep the calendar in synchronisation with the seasons, and secondly, as an instrument for divination. Being ultimately derived from the diviner's board or shi (式) which had the twenty-eight lunar mansions inscribed on both the Earth (base) plate and the Heaven (upper) plate, it follows that a luopan cannot be properly so called unless it has these divisions marked on it.

The circumference of the Chinese astronomical luopan was divided into 365.25 degrees, so that each day represented one day of the solar year; modern 'fengshui' luopans which divide the rim into 360 Euclidean degrees are therefore missing the original purpose of the instrument.

This is an opportune moment to scotch a couple of fallacies which have crept into text-books. Chinese museums, particularly those concerned with the history of science and technology frequently display a model of a diviner's plate with a metallic spoon-shaped object in the centre, which is claimed to be a replica of the world's first magnetic compass. The spoon, made of magnetic material, when left to rotate freely comes to rest with its handle pointing to the south. The device is pure conjecture; it never existed. The concept is based on a misreading of the description of the Diviner's *Shi*, which had at its centre a disc with a depiction of the seven stars of the Great Bear. This constellation is known in America as the Dipper, and in China as the Ladle. It is merely the representation of those stars revolving through the night, with the tail of the Bear always pointing to the North Star, which is the 'spoon' in the centre. Another fallacy, concerning the apparent discovery of magnetic deviation, is dealt with in the description of the luopan today.

A luopan without a base plate has no function; without it, and its guide threads, the luopan is virtually impractical, and has no other function than as an oriental curiosity.

Function of the Luopan

The original purpose of the luopan was to correlate the solar and lunar calendars. The Sun was known to move round the heavens, in the same way that the Moon does. This had often been recorded at times of total eclipse, when the position of the Sun could be seen against a background of stars. But this would be the only time. Where, for the rest of the time, was the Sun?

The Sun is always in the opposite part of the sky to the Moon when the Moon is full. Thus, by seeing in which part of the sky the Full Moon was, it was sufficient to find the position of the Full Moon in the divisions of the outer disc of the luopan, and then see which division lay directly opposite. This would then give the position of the Sun in the 365-day year, in other words, the solar date.

Other divisions of the luopan gave the 24 seasons, which matched the solar dates, and the 24 divisions of the compass.

Eventually, with the continued appropriation of the luopan for purely geomantic purposes, the original function of the luopan became ignored, and ultimately forgotten altogether.

But the luopan is essentially an instrument for investigating both the celestial and chthonic manifestations, which is why it combines purely a geographical function - direction finding - with an essentially astronomical one.

The Luopan Today

Luopans on sale today consist of a flat disc rotating in a depression in a base plate. Unless the workmanship is very fine, either the plate sticks when it revolved because it is not perfectly circular, or else it is too small, rotating too freely, which can cause the exterior divisions to be misread by a significant number of degrees.

There is now an endless variety of circular luopan-like instruments on the market. Some are cheap, mass-produced pieces of nonsense that are little more than toys, whose usefulness would be tested in trying to find one's way out of a lift. Functional instruments may be about ten centimetres across, showing little more than the eight principal compass directions, the eight trigrams, and the twenty-four sub-divisions of the compass.

In the past ten years, the sudden rush of interest in fengshui has led to the marketing of two kinds of luopan, one called the Three Principals (San Yuan 三元) and the other the Three Harmonies, (San He 三合). The San Yuan has one ring of 24 directions, the San He three, which leads to the dispelling of yet another scientific myth about the Chinese compass.

Time and again, Chinese text-books on the history of science state that the presence of the three direction rings on the Chinese compass reveals that magnetic deviation was known to the ancient Chinese. It does no such thing. The San He compass first shows the twenty-four directions in their standard position, with the north/south line aligned with the compass needle. A second ring of the 24 directions is aligned 7.5 degrees to the left, and a third 7.5 degrees to the right. The reason for this is entirely practical.

In some fengshui calculations, there are initially only eight basic divisions to be considered, representing either the eight trigrams or their corresponding luo shu numbers. In the second stage of the calculation, the smaller divisions of the 24-directions have to be observed. But when a reading is taken of a position which is close to the edge of one of the principal trigram divisions, it is difficult to make a correspondence between the position, and the three smaller compartments of the 24 division ring which are now no longer aligned centrally with that position.

However, by having three rings, the principal central ring can be used when the observation lies to the centre of the division, and the off-set rings used when the observation is closer to either edge of the principal division. The names for the three rings are the 'true needle' for the one which is aligned centrally; the 'seam needle' for the one displaced 7.5 degrees clockwise and the 'middle needle' for the one displaced 7.5 degrees anti-clockwise. The incongruous name is due to its being placed between the true and seam rings.

Other rings

This description of the luopan, though necessary, has already strayed beyond the confines of Chinese astrology, so it must suffice to add that other rings on the Chinese compass may include *Luo Shu* numbers, *Yi Jing* trigrams and hexagrams, names of stars, and many other additions entirely at the fancy of the particular practitioner or teacher. Note that the word *luo* (洛) in *luo shu* is not the same word as the *luo* (羅) as the *luo* in luopan. The former is the name of the River Luo on which the actual capital of China, Luoyang, still stands; the later means a net.

It is important to remember, however, that the original function of the luopan was as an astronomical and calendrical instrument, and it is this fact which leads to other problems. It is not sufficient to say that to be functional, the outer ring of the luopan must show the twenty-eight mansions and the divisions of the solar year. I recently examined five luopans, all of which showed the twenty-eight mansions, and all of which were different.

Not only was the position of the twenty-eight mansions different, only one of the luopans showed the year divided into 365.25 days, the others preferring a day of 360 days - one for each degree of the western draughtsman's protractor. Of these four, two showed the lunar mansions progressing in a clockwise direction, the others in reverse order.

The reason for the discrepancy in position of the twenty-eight lunar mansions is due to the movement of the heavens. Two thousand years ago, the mid-points of the four Great Constellations, Dragon, Bird, Tiger and Tortoise marked the four compass directions. The diviner's plate showed Xu, Mansion 11, at the North point and the Bird Star at the South point. As the heavens change their position these fixed points are no longer true by about one degree every century. Consequently, genuine luopans which have been made for actual computation will show the lunar mansions in their true positions.

ECLIPSES

Eclipses recorded in the Chinese Classics

The oldest known references to eclipses in China are to be found on Oracle bones of the semi-legendary bronze age Shang dynasty.

They often record the Stem and Branch of the Day and sometimes the month as well, but the year is not given. Most of the inscriptions follow a standard formula, giving the stem and branch followed by the expression *ri you shi zhi* [日 有 食 之] 'The Sun was eaten' (or Moon, in the case of a lunar eclipse).

From the Shu Jing

Many eclipses have been recorded in the Chinese classics, from the *Shu Jing (Shu Ching)* (Book of History) onwards. The Records of the Xia (Hsia) dynasty present a remarkable passage which states that Xi and He (Hsi and Ho), hereditary holders of the office of Court Astronomers, had failed to predict an eclipse, and thus the special rituals required to dispel the malign forces were not organised. The ruler Zhong Kang, at the start of his reign in BC 2159 put the Prince of Yin in charge of the armed forces, and ordered him to punish the astronomers, not so much for having failed in their duties, but more for the fact that they led such dissipated lives and cared little for their responsibilities or the consequences of the eclipse.

The Shu Jing (The Records of the Xia, Book IV) takes up the tale.

'*Now here are Xi and He; depraved and stupefied by wine. They have deserted their posts, and have allowed the regulations of Heaven to crumble. On the first day of the last month of autumn, there was a near total eclipse in the constellation Fang* (the 4th lunar mansion, central point of the Dragon Quarter corresponding to 45 degrees past the first point of the Celestial Equator, or one eighth division of the sky). *Yet though the blind musicians beat the drums, and all the people rushed about, the families of Xi and He behaved like deaf mutes and did nothing. The old edicts declare: When they anticipate the time of an event, or when they are behind the time, let them be put to death without mercy.*'

Theoretically, this is one of the first passages in Chinese history for which possible to calculate a precise date.

Zhong-Kang was the title of the fourth of the seventeen reigns in the records of the Xia dynasty. He acceded in BC 2159 and reigned 13 years, limiting the date of the eclipse to sometime between 2159 and 2146 BC.

Bearing in mind that (a) it was a partial eclipse visible in China;

(b) it occurred in the constellation Fang; and (c) it happened on the first day of the last month of Autumn, that is, at the time of the New Moon following the Autumn Equinox) attempts have been made to compute the actual date. One suggestion is 22 October, 2137BC. Sadly modern scholarship prefers to dismiss the account as a mere legend.

What became of the families of Xi and He is not recorded.

A later account of an eclipse and attendant ceremony is given in the *Zuo Chuan*, the Additonal Commentaries on the Spring and Autumn Annals, a work whose compilation is ascribed to the editorial hand of Confucius. In the Annals of Duke Chuang, 25th Year, there is a record of an eclipse occurring on the the the Day Xin Wei (Stem 8 Branch VIII) of the Sixth Month, when drums were beaten and sacrifices made to the Earth God. The Zuo Chuan states:

'When an eclipse occurred, the Emperor fasted, and had the drums beaten before the altar of the Earth God, while the princes of the States presented offerings before their altars and had the drums beaten in their own courts.'

Ceremonies similar to those described in the Shu Jing were still performed in China as late as the nineteenth century.

From the Yi Jing

There are several references to eclipses in the Yi Jing (Book of Changes), though the obscure language has sometimes eluded translators and commentators. One reference has already been mentioned (see the section on the Lunar Mansions, no. 2, the Dragon's Neck). Other references occur in the texts of Hexagram 36, *Ming Yi*, Brightness Diminished.

Several lines may be interpreted as references to eclipses and the Lunar Mansion in which they occurred. Thus, Line 1 may refer to an eclipse in the 27th Mansion, Wings; in Line 4 to Lunar Mansion 5, the Heart; and in Line 5 to Lunar Mansion 7, the Basket.

The final line may be read as a reference to an eclipse which did not occur, with the astronomer being reprimanded by the King for a false calculation.

Hexagram 55, with its reference to stars being visible at noon, is another obvious eclipse reference.

However, for the most part, these remarks regarding eclipses and their portents only hint at astronomical observation.

From the Shi Jing

The Shi Jing (Shih Ching) Poetry Classic is a collection of folk-

songs, poems and ballads, 305 altogether, reputedly assembled by
Confucius. It comprises poems and lyrics from 11th to 6th centuries
BC. Many refer to historical events, and several have astronomical
references, drawing on their mythology and symbolism for effect,
and there are also clear references to the practice of fengshui,
though not identified as such.

The Minor Festal Ode IV includes a reference to an eclipse on
the day Xin-Mao (Stem 8 Branch IV) , the first day of the Tenth
Month in the reign of King Yu, who reigned 781-770BC. The
poem also refers to the preceding lunar eclipse.

The day stem-and-branch is significant; xin also means 'bitter'
and the branch mao is associated with the Pleiades, bringer of rain
and tears.

'In the tenth month was the changing;
On the day xin-mao, bitterness and sorrow,
The Sun was eclipsed, The worst of omens for the future.
So the Moon was eclipsed before,
This time the Sun's turn has come....'

From the Chun Qiu

The Spring and Autumn Annals, Chun Qiu, are a catalogue of
historical events compiled by Confucius. The annals are first
divided into reigns, then into years, and next into seasons, (from
which the work derives its name) even when no event worthy of
note occurred. Altogether 37 solar (but no lunar) eclipses are
recorded, three of them total. Frequently, the eclipse record is
followed by an observation of some event which might have been
attributed to the influence of the celestial manifestation.

Sometimes the day of the month is given: as eclipses can only
occur at the New Moon, by which the Chinese months are defined,
it is apparent that there were occasional error in calendrical
computation, which could be rectified by observation of the
eclipses. This is the case with the first record, for 14th February
720BC.

'In the 3rd year of the King, in Springtime,
In the 2nd month, on the day Ji-Si (Stem 6 Branch VI)
The Sun was eclipsed.
In the 3rd month, on the day Geng-Xu (Stem 7 Branch XI)
The Heaven-appointed King died.'

*(A commentary added later states that the King Ping actually died on
the day Jen-Xu, twelve days previously.)*

	Chun Qiu	Month	Stem	Branch	Date (BC)	Notes
1	I iii 1	2	己	巳	14 Feb 721	
2	II iii 4	7	壬	辰	9 July 709	Total
3	II xvii 8	10	-	-	? 695	no date
4	III xviii 1	3	-	-	? 676	no date
5	III xxv 3	6	辛	未	20 May 669	
6	III xxvi 5	12	癸	亥	3 Nov 668	
7	III xxx 5	9	庚	午	22 Aug 664	
8	V v 8	9	戊	申	12 Aug 655	
9	V xii 1	3	庚	午	29 Mar 648	
10	V xv 5	5	-	-		no date
11	VI i 2	1	癸	亥	26Jan 626	
12	VI xv 5	6	辛	丑	20Apr 612	
13	VII viii 8	7	甲	子	12 Sep 601	Total
14	VII x 3	4	丙	辰	26 Feb 599	
15	VII xvii 4	6	癸	卯	5 Oct 592	
16	VIII xvi 4	6	丙	寅	1 May 575	
17	VIII xvii 11	12	丁	巳	17 Oct 574	
18	IX xiv 2	2	乙	未	8 Jan 559	
19	IX xv 5	8	丁	巳	23 May 558	
20	IX xx 8	10	丙	申	25 Aug 553	
21	IX xxi 5	9	庚	戌	13 Aug 552	
22	IX xxi 6	10	庚	申	12 Sep 552	?doubtful
23	IX xxiii 1	2	癸	酉	30 Dec 551	
24	IX xxiv 4	7	甲	子	12 June 549	Total
25	IX xxiv 7	8	癸	巳	11 July 549	?doubtful
26	IX xxvii 6	12	乙	亥	7 Oct 546	?doubtful
27	X vii iv	4	甲	申	11 Mar 535	
28	X xv 4	6	丁	巳	10 Apr 527	
29	X xvii 2	6	甲	戌	14 Aug 525	
30	X xxi 4	7	壬	戌	3 June 521	
31	X xxii 10	12	癸	酉	18 Nov 520	
32	X xxiv 3	5	乙	未	1 Apr 518	
33	X xxxi 7	12	辛	亥	7 Nov 511	
34	XI v 1	3	辛	亥	10 Feb 505	
35	XI xii 8	11	丙	寅	15 Sep 498	
36	XI xv 10	8	庚	丑	15 July 495	
37	XII xiv 5	5	庚	辰	467 Post-Confucius	

Additional Remarks on the Eclipses

2. The total eclipse seemed to have been a favourable omen, since it was followed by a treaty, marriage, and alliances. The text adds *'It was a good year.'*

3. The stem and branch is not given. The eclipse occurred during the final months of the rule of Duke Huan, the most celebrated of the great chiefs of the time. The scandals which followed the eclipse brought his reign to a close. The Duke Huan and his wife Jiang travelled to see the Marquis of Zi, his brother-in-law. There, the wife had relations with the Marquis, her brother, who used his half-brother, Pang-Sang, to get the Duke drunk, and then had him murdered him in his coach. Later, Pang-Sang was lynched and murdered by the rabble. Duke Huan was succeeded by his 13-year old son, who reigned for 32 years.

4. The text adds *'In the Autumn, there were* yi' - a mysterious creature that spat sand at people, causing pain.

5. The text adds: *'Drums were beaten, and sacrifices made to the Earth God. In the Autumn, there were great floods. Drums were beaten, and sacrifices made to the Earth God at the Gates.'*

6. Again the eclipse seemed to be a good omen, as the following year was exceptional for the number of royal marriages.

7. The text adds *'Drums were beaten, and sacrifices made to the Earth God.'*

8. The text adds *'In Winter, the men from Qin seized the Duke of Yu.'* Note the date of the eclipse -1st day of 9th month. The Commentary to the Chun Qiu then adds this remarkable passge:
   In the 8th month, the Marquis of Qin laid siege to Shang-yang. He asked the astrologer Yen whether he would succeed. Yen replied: 'The children have a song which says,
   "When the Ping-day has begun,
   The Dragon's Tail will hide the Sun.
   The flags and banners onward go
   The army marches on to Guo,
   The Shun-star twinkles in the night,
   But Heaven's Key is not so bright.
   The Fire Star shines up in the sky,
   The Duke of Guo must flee or die"

According to this,' continued the Astrologer, 'You will succeed at the meeting of the 9th and 10th months. In the morning of *bing-zi* (stem 3, branch I) the Sun will be in Wei, and the Moon in Ce (策). Shun-he will be exactly in the South. This is sure to be the time.'
In Winter, at the 12th Moon, first day, a bing-zi day, the Marquis of Qin extinguished Guo, and the Duke Zhou fled the capital.'
The passage calls for some explanation. The Sun and Moon would have to be in the same part of the sky for there to be an eclipse. Long Wei (龍尾) the Tail of the Dragon, is the 6th Lunar Mansion. Ce (策) means divining sticks. Or should this be Ji (箕) the 7th Lunar mansion? This would signify that the eclipse took place at the cusp between Wei and Ji.

9. The text adds, *In the summer of that year, the people of Huang withheld paying tribute to Cuo, believing that it was too far away for them to take it by force. But they were mistaken, and an army from Cuo sacked Huang.*

10. The text adds, *In Autumn in the 7th month an army from Ce and an army from Cao invaded Luo. In the 8th month, there was a plague of locusts.*

11. The text adds, *The Heaven-appointed King sent Shu-fu (renowned as a historian and face-reader) to be present at the burial of the Duke of He. In Summer, in the fourth month, day Ding-Si (stem 4- branch VI) Duke He was buried.*

12. The text adds, *'Drums were beaten, and sacrifices made to the Earth God.'*

13. As this was a total eclipse, it is worth noting whether the events of the year were favourable or otherwise.
In Summer, in the sixth month, on the day xin-si (8-VI), there was a great sacrifice in the Temple. Zhong Sui died.
On jen-wu (9-VII) day, the rite was repeated, but without music
On Wu-zi (5-I) day, the Lady Ying died.
Armies invaded Qin.
An army from Cuo sacked Shu-liao.
In Autumn in the seventh month, the Sun was eclipsed totally.
In Winter, in the tenth month, on the day chi-chou (6-II), arrangements had been made for the burial of Lady Ying. Because of rain, it was postponed until the next day geng-yin (7-III) at noon.

14. The text adds, *On the chi-si (6-VI) day the Marquis of Zi died.*

    In the autumn there were floods and famine.

15. The eclipse was sufficiently ominous for the ruler to consult with the Yi Jing before embarking on a battle at the end of the month.

19. The text should read sixth month intercalary.

    Water (水) and Fire (火) would happen on a bing-zi (3-I) or jen-wu (9-VII) day, since the elements associated with these stems and branches represent Fire and Water.

20. The calculated date does not match the text.

22. The eclipse was followed by a year of upheaval, deaths, and uprisings.

23. The total eclipse was followed by great floods; the second (partial) eclipse by great famine.

24. There is a suggestion that the date is impossible. If the calendar was out of step with the seasons, it would also account for the fact that the Chun Qiu records that there was no ice during the following winter.

25. The Zuo Chuan provides the following instructive commentary, which not only gives some insight into the way that prognostications were taken from eclipses, but also refers to the passage from the Shi Jing (Poetry Classic) quoted earlier.

    The Marquis of Chin asked Si Wan-bi what the eclipse portended and was told,
    'The states of Lu and Wei will both feel its evil effect, Wei greater, and Lu lesser.'
    'Why should that be?' asked the Marquis.
    'Because the eclipse went from Wei to Lu. There will be calamity in the former, and Lu will feel it too.'
    He asked, 'What does it mean in the Ode: *The Sun was eclipsed, Worst of omens for the future*'?
    Si Wan-bi replied, 'It shows the effect of bad government. When a state is not governed properly, it brings reproof from the calamity of Sun and Moon. Three things are important: election of the right people to office, consideration for the people, and proper observance of what is appropriate for the season.'

26. From the additional Commentary, on the day *yi-chou (2-II)* , Shou, the King's eldest son, died.
   In Autumn, in the eighth month, on the day *wu-yin (5-III)* Queen Mu died.

27. The Commentary describes a discussion about the appropriate rituals to be performed when an eclipse occurs. When the eclipse occurred, the Priest and the Grand Historian asked for offerings of silk.
   Chao-zi replied, 'When an eclipse happens, the Son of Heaven does not have his table fully spread, and commands the drum to be beaten at the altar of the Earth God. Princes of the states present offerings of silk at the altar and cause the drums to be beaten in their courts.'
   Ping-zi said 'No, it is only at the first month, before the evil effects are known, that it is the rule. At other times there is no such rule.'
   More intiguing is the fact that the eclipse was followed by the appearance of a comet in the part of the sky called Da Chen
   (大辰). This was another name for Da Huo (Great Fire) one of the twelve divisions of the sky which some three thousand years later became the Twelve Animals of the Chinese Zodiac. It comprises the lunar mansions Fang, Xin, and Wei, the Room, Heart, and Tail of the Dragon. It was regarded as an omen of fire.
   The additional commentary adds an interesting reference to the calendar: the star Huo appeared in the 3rd month of the Xia dynasty, the 4th of the Shang, and the 5th of the Zhou (at the time of the Annals) due to the astronomical phenomenon of the precession of the equinoxes.
   The commentator, Zi Shen, reasoned that the calamity, for which the Chinese character (災) is a composite of the characters for Water(水) and Fire (火) would happen on a bing-zi (3-I) or jen-wu (9-VII) day, since the elements associated with these stems and branches represent Fire and Water.

28. From the additional Commentary:
   The Duke asked Zi Shen 'What is the significance of the eclipse?'
   He replied, 'At the solstices and equinoxes the eclipse does not indicate calamity. The Sun and Moon, in their

travels, are in the same path at the equinoxes, and pass each other at the solstices. At other times, there is disaster, the yang cannot overcome the yin, and hence there is always disaster from water.'

Zi Shen's opinions on the meaning of eclipses was to be put to the test again six years later (see the note to No. 30).

29. The year following the eclipse was beset by disasters, including an earthquake.

30. The main text relates that in Autumn, in the eighth month, there was a great sacrifice for rain. But the additional Commentary tells us more. After the eclipse, the astronomer Zi Shen said there would be floods, but Chiao Zi said it signified drought! Chiao's explanation was that because the Sun had passed the equinox, the yang influence had not yet predominated, but when it did, it would be calamitous. His prediction turned out to be correct.

31. The additional Commentary states that because of the eclipse, the historian Mi predicted that six years hence, in the same month, the armies of Wu would attack the state of Ying. But it would not be a successful enterprise. The reasoning was that the day would be a *geng-chen (7-V)* day. The Sun and Moon would be in the Eighth Lunar Mansion Wei of Da-Xin, *(see the remarks on Eclipse 27)* but the day of the change in the Sun was geng-wu (7-VII). Fire overcomes Metal, so Wu could not succeed.

37. Confucius concluded his Spring and Autumn Annals with the Spring of the Fourteenth Year of Duke Ai, recording nothing more than the discovery of a Lin, the Unicorn which had the power to discern good from evil. He took this as an appropriate point to conclude his chronicle.

The annals for that year were completed by another hand, which also recorded that the appearance of a comet that winter was followed by famine.

References to Comets in the Chun Qiu

	Chun Qui	Month	Date (BC)	Notes
1	VI xiv 5	7	613	in the Great Bear
2	X xvii 5	Winter	525	in Ta-chen
3	XII xiii 10	11	468	in the East
4	XII xiv 15	Winter	467	

Specific dates are not given for comets, which may have been visible for several days or even weeks.

Illustration from the novel Jin Ping Mei

The Horoscopes in Jin Ping Mei 金瓶梅

The book *Jin Ping Mei* 金瓶梅 is regarded as one of the classic Chinese works of fiction – the others being *Romance of the Three Kingdoms, Outlaws of the Marsh,* and *Journey to the West.* The title is a composite of the names of the three main ladies in the tale, Jin Lian (Golden Lotus), Ping Er (Precious Vase), and Chun Mei (Spring Plum-blossom). Professor Henri Cordier, writing towards the close of the nineteenth century, extolled it for its descriptions of 'all the human situations that can arise in life.' Its hundred chapters are an account of the rise and fall of a merchant family, as engrossing as any modern television serial. My Chinese friends were amused by my interest in it, declaring that it was a book 'to show how a man can keep a lady happy.' Certainly, it has no shortage of salacious passages, but for me its chief interest lies in its depictions of various ways of fortune-telling, the preparation of magical spells, and methods of casting horoscopes.

Its authorship is not known precisely, but the style suggests that the author came from the Shandong province, and lived at the close of the sixteenth century. The story, however, deals with life in the times of the Song Dynasty, during the reign of the emperor Hui Cong (1106-1126). A legend says that the reputed author, Wang Shi-cheng, who died in 1593, wrote the manuscript in poisoned ink, in order to bring the death of the Prime Minister who would slowly absorb the toxin as he turned the lethal pages – so anticipating by several centuries the plot of Umberto Eco's *'The Name of the Rose.'*

Apart from various accounts of meetings with diviners, monks, priests and charlatans, several horoscopes are described at length. Remarkably, the cyclical signs for the years quoted in the descriptions of horoscopes are compatible not only with the period in which the novel was written, but also with its historical setting, although occasionally the chronology is confusing. The supposed date of the first horoscope, a jia-chen year, (the 17th in the cycle of sixty) is equivalent to 1124, which agrees with the reign of Hui Cong (1101-1126).

The astrologer's explanations of the horoscopes are so precise, using technical astrological terminology, that it might appear that these are actual horoscopes of real people. But there are occasional puzzles which lead to the conclusion that the horoscopes may have been deliberately contrived with impossible data out of respect for living persons who might have identical combinations of stems and branches in their own horoscopes.

The Horoscope of *Jin Lian*
(Chapter 12)

Jin Lian (Golden Lotus), the lady of the book's title, has her fortune told by a blind astrologer, who calculates her horoscope on his fingers using the Zi Ping (Tzu P'ing) method of Fate Calculation.

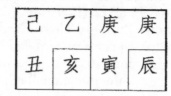

The Eight Characters as given (see above) cannot be correct, because the stems for the hour and the month are not possible: the stem for the first month, in a Chen (Branch V or Dragon) year, should be Wu (戊), not Geng (庚). Similarly, the stem for the

Chou hour, on a Yi (小) day, should be Ding (丁). However, for a Ji (己) day, at the Chou hour, the stem would in fact be Yi (乙). Perhaps the two stems have been reversed (See the Table for Calculating Stems and Branches in the Appendix).

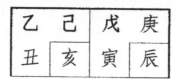

'The 8th of the month is the Spring Day; we must reckon your fate as from the First month'

Jin Lian was born in the first month (寅) of the Chinese calendar. The 8th of that month is said to have been the Li Chun.

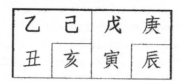

'...This Year is the Jia Chen... a sign of coming calamity.'

Jin Lian was born in the 17th year of the 60-year cycle, and the year of the narrative was the 41st. This would make her about 24.

Stem of current year	甲	庚	Stem of Jin Lian's birth year
Branch of current year	辰	辰	Branch of Jin Lian's birth year
Year of Cycle	41	17	Year of Cycle

The 41st year of the cycle is equivalent to 1124AD.

'The eight characters are clear, but the Husband-and-Wife star is never favourable, nor is the matter of children.

Yi-wood (stem 2) grows in the first month which is favourable for health to an extent.

Geng-metal (stem 7) appears twice (see remarks above) and the Sheep's Shoulder-blade star is very strong.

The husband-and-wife star is a problem. You will outlive two husbands.'

In the novel, Jin Lian has already had her first husband murdered!

'The Water of Gui is in Hai as well as Chou'

This is reference to the fact that stem 10, Gui, belongs to the Water element, as does the twelfth branch Hai.

Thus a superabundance of water rushes out of a single Ji Earth. The stars Guan and Sha are reversed. When the Sha star is dominant, it brings a man eminence. But for women, it indicates that they attract men, and will be a threat to their husbands.'

(2) The Horoscope of Ximen Qing

(Chapter 29)

Ximen Qing is the main character in the novel, the husband of Jin Lian. His horoscope is compiled by the Venerable Wu, whose knowledge of the mantic arts also includes the Liu Ren (Liu Jen) described earlier.

Ximen Qing tells the Venerable Wu that his animal is the Tiger, his age 29, and that he was born at noon on the 28th of the 7th month.

| 丙 | 壬 | 辛 | 戊 |
| 午 | 午 | 酉 | 寅 |

Here, the stems and branches are technically correct, and follow the chronology of the tale. Born in the year of the Tiger, 1098AD, Ximen would have been 26 (27 by Chinese reckoning) when Jin

Lian's horoscope was cast, which was in a Dragon year. Thus two years have elapsed since then. The date would be 1126AD.

The Venerable Wu then proceeds to explain how he calculates the Fate Cycle, taken from Ximen Qing's month of birth, following the Ziping method.

'The 23rd of the 7th Month is Bai Lu '.

White Dew, the first day of the solar month, is September 8th in the present calendar.

'Therefore we reckon your Fate from the eighth month. Your fortune starts in your seventh year, xin-you (8-X) at seventeen it becomes ren-xu (9-XI), at 27 to gui-hai (10-X), at 37 to jia-zi (1-I), at 47 to yi-chou (2-II).

Wealth and riches increase, and you will attain an official position. Then your luck will change. But there is too much Earth in your horoscope: you were born at the end of the 7th month, giving too much vitality.

Your day of birth, ren-wu (9-VII); gui (stem 10) Water interposes between Zi and Chou (branches I and II), balancing the Fire and Water elements.

The birth hour bing-wu (3-VII) harmonises with xin (8-Metal), so you will become prosperous and reach a high position.

When happy, you are like the Spring breeze, when angry, like thunder and lightning.

You will enjoy wealth, women, and honours, and leave two sons.

This year Ding and Ren join together; this signifies both officials and ghosts, so either you will be elevated to a high position, or leave the earth itself.

You are moving to gui-hai (10-XII) and we see Earth in Wu (stem 5) and Water in Gui (stem 10) mingling - a sign of fruition and growth.

The Red Feng-bird appears, indicating a son. The Life Official is on a post-horse, moving towards shen (branch IX) indicating the seventh month. These events will come to pass very soon.

Regarding the future, alas, there is too much Water. After you have reached the peak at jia-zi (1-I); the ren-wu (9-VII) fate is washed away. Before your 36th year, you will suffer haemorrhages and sickness'

The horoscope follows the Ziping method precisely: what makes it so fascinating is in the reasoning of its interpretation. Naturally, this being a novel, all the predictions eventually come to pass as foretold.

The Venerable Wu continued his consultation by asking Ximen Qing to walk, in order to study his gait, and then examined his face and hands. Ximen Qing also asked the Venerable Wu to delineate the fortunes of his five ladies, but for these persons the sage restricted his observations to physiognomy.

(3) The Lady Fortune-teller
(Chapter 46)

Some months later, Ximen's ladies call on the services of an itinerant fortune-teller. Although the ladies give their dates and times of birth, the old woman does not calculate a detailed horoscope, but recites their fortunes at length after studying some cards.

The first lady gives her year of birth as the Dragon, though the old lady is unable to discern without asking whether she is 30 or 42. As we shall see in a moment, her uncertainty is curiously significant.

Following the previous chronology, this would place the incident six years later than the first horoscope; the year would be a Dog or Rooster year, 1129 or 1130.

The old lady tells their fortunes from a combination of spinning dial, like a roulette wheel, and fortune cards bearing pictures, a kind of Chinese tarot, but she also uses the astronomical terms for the 'Contained Sounds' , the names of the sixty combinations of stems-and-branches, (see the table in the Appendix pages 350 and 351.) Her pronouncements reveal an interesting creativity, as she expands the mere names of the stem-and-branch combinations into something substantially more informative and with greater relevance for her clients.

To the first lady, she says that Wu and Ji (stems 5 and 6) represent a great forest (see the table), showing someone who is devout, charitable, and careful to follow her religious practices.

The second lady, who gives her age as 34, is told that her birth year was jia-zi (1-I). This would be impossible; the jia-zi year preceeding 1130 was 1084, which would make her 46. She would be 34 if she were born in a jia-xu (1-XI) year, but that would make nonsense of the old fortune teller's remarks, *'Jia-zi, together with yi-chou (2-II) produce gold from the sea,'* which is in agreement with the table on page 350. Yet whether her subsequent pronouncements are based on the sixty characters or on the fortune-telling cards is not clear. But she makes no reference to any birthday or time factors other than the stem-and-branch of the years.

The third lady says she is a Sheep, born at noon on the 15th day of the 1st month. The old lady tells her that this would be a xin-wei (8-VIII) year, corresponding to 1091, again making the lady twelve years older than she claimed. But as we saw with the first of the three ladies, the fortune-teller was either not so good at telling

people's ages, or perhaps more likely, was not so easily fooled when
ladies were coy about their real ages! As before, the year names given
by the old fortune-teller tally with the table on pages 350 and 351.

*'Xin-wei and geng-wu produce Earth by the Ditch. She has a high
position and will inherit. She is virtuous and does not hanker after worldly
possessions, though she will have these in plenty. She will be troubled by
little people who do not care for her. '*

(4) The Horoscope of Guan Ge
(Chapter 59)

Between 3pm and 5pm, on the 23rd of the 8th month, Guan Ge,
the baby son of Ximen Qing passed away.

In accordance with custom, an astrologer, Master Xu, was
summoned to cast a horoscope for the child.

His details were that he was born at the Monkey hour on the
23rd day of the 6th month in a bing-shen (3-IX) year, equivalent
to 1116 – which again throws the chronology of the story into
confusion.

The horoscope, however, is of great interest since it is an
example of a posthumous horoscope. The Eight characters are:

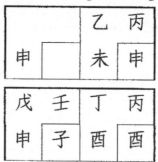

Master Xu interpreted the posthumous horoscope by reading
from a book of spells which he had brought with him.

*'The ren-zi day and ding-you month show that he has another life before
him...*

*The only mourners allowed must be relatives, and no-one born under
the sign of the Snake, Dragon, Rat or Hare must be present.'*

After some alarming details of his character in a previous life,
the sage concludes by adding,

*'He will be born again into another family called Wang. He will be a
military officer and live to the age of 68.'*

There is a similar description of Master Xu's reading out a
posthumous horoscope from an astrological manual , with details of

the past and future lives, in a later chapter of the novel. Again, the reading specifies who should and who should not be present as mourners.

(5) The Natal and Fatal Horoscopes of Li Ping-er
(Chapter 61)
When Li Ping-er, the second lady of the book's title, fell gravely ill, Ximen Qing hastened to the temple of where the Venerable Wu usually resided. The monk not being there, it was suggested that he employ the services of another astrologer of high reputation, Master Huang. The Eight characters of Li Ping-er, born at noon on the fifteenth of the first month, were given as:

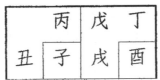

The stems and branches are feasible, and suggest the year 1091AD.

The astrologer calculates the ten-year periods as beginning at the ages of 4, 14, 24 and so on, as in the case of Xi-men Qing. The current year is given as *ding-you* (4-X), corresponding to 1117AD.

The prognostication is not encouraging. Master Huang declares that her life is ruled by Jidu (Chi-Tu), the Moon's descending node, regarded as the evil emanation of Saturn, the Earth Star.

The following chapter records the death of Li Ping-er.

Her posthumous horoscope records the characters for the day of her passing as:

The combination of stem and branch for the month is not correct for the year.

Master Huang declares that no-one should be present at the burial who was born in the Dragon, Tiger, Rooster or Snake years.

Although her passing was at midnight, Master Huang declared that the sign for her birth hour was *chou* (branch II, 1am-3 am), although this neatly side-steps the problem of the actual day on which she died.

The Horoscope of Lady Diana Spencer, Princess of Wales

To close this chapter of historical and fictional horoscopes, following the style of the foregoing examples, here is an instructive example from a period closer to our own time - that of the late Princess of Wales. Firstly, therefore, her Eight Characters, based on her date and time of her birth, July 1st, 1961, at the Rabbit hour.

At first glance, her marriage to Prince Charles should have been a match, for his year sign is the Rat and hers the Ox, which are a matching pair. Yet her Eight characters contain the Horse as the Month Branch, which is in opposition to the Rat, while her Ox is opposite the Sheep day in her Eight characters, signifying marriage problems. The stems 1 and 2 signify *'gold from the sea'* a sign of wealth and riches obtained through inheritance or marriage rather than personal industriousness.

Her Life Cycle ten-year phases begin at the age of two. When she was two years old the influencing signs were 2-VIII; between twelve and thirty-one the signs were 3-IX, and 4-X, Fire and Metal. This was the most popular and powerful time in her life. She married in the year of the Rooster, which is in harmony with the Ox.

In the period beginning at 32 years of age, the signs change to 5-XI, both Earth. This element was too dominant. Her marriage broke down, leading to divorce in1992, the year of the Monkey, directly opposite the Tiger - *'One Ox can fight two Tigers'* - and her untimely death in a tunnel beneath the ground, in 1997 - was in another Ox, or Earth, year.

CONVERSION TABLE OF CHINESE PHONETICS

In the first edition of Chinese Astrology, Chinese terms were transcribed according to the system most familiar to English readers at the time, that known as the Wade-Giles system.

But authors writing in French, German and other languages used transcription systems which better suited their own orthography, so that one of the most familiar of Chinese philosophical terms might be transcribed as Ch'i (Wade-Giles), Chi, Tsi, Tschi, or even Ki. To rectify such a confusing situation, about the middle of the twentieth century the Chinese government introduced the standardised romanisation known as pinyin. This is now gradually superseding the older forms of transcription, having been adopted by the majority of modern authors, both Western and Chinese, writing about China and its culture. The Conversion Table of Chinese Phonetics will prove useful to those readers familiar with only one of the two main transcription systems.

Unfortunately however, the table cannot accommodate the many variants to be found in works written by authors more familiar with Cantonese or dialect pronunciation, and whose writings include otherwise familiar terms presented in an unorthodox transcription. The Supplementary Table briefly lists a few expressions taken from the writings of other authors who have used variant romanisation.

One significant innovation in Chinese literature has been the introduction of simplified Chinese characters. These are used almost universally in mainland China, and to a lesser extent beyond its present frontiers. By reducing the number of strokes needed to construct a character the writing of Chinese is made much easier, although many of the new simplified characters are not instantly recognisable to readers only familiar with the traditional forms.

A few of the commoner simplified characters are shown in the Supplementary Table.

Wade-Giles	pinyin	Wade-Giles	pinyin	Wade-Giles	pinyin
a	a	chiu	jiu	fa	fa
ai	ai	ch'iu	qiu	fan	fan
an	an	chiung	jiong	fang	fang
ang	ang	ch'iung	qiong	fei	fei
ao	ao	cho	zhuo	fên	fen
cha	zha	ch'o	chuo	fêng	feng
ch'a	cha	chou	zhou	fo	fo
chai	zhai	ch'ou	chou	fou	fou
ch'ai	chai	chu	zhu	fu	fu
chan	zhan	ch'u	chu	ha	ha
ch'an	chan	chü	ju	hai	hai
chang	zhang	ch'ü	qu	han	han
ch'ang	chang	chua	zhua	hang	hang
chao	zhao	ch'ua	chua	hao	hao
ch'ao	chao	chuai	zhuai	hê	he
che	zhe	ch'uai	chuai	hei	hei
ch'ê	che	chuan	zhuan	hên	hen
chei	zhei	chüan	juan	hêng	heng
chen	zhen	ch'uan	chuan	ho	he
ch'ên	chen	ch'üan	quan	hou	hou
cheng	zheng	chuang	zhuang	hu	hu
ch'êng	cheng	ch'uang	chuang	hua	hua
chi	ji	chüeh	jue	huai	huai
ch'i	qi	ch'üeh	que	huan	huan
chia	jia	chui	zhui	huang	huang
ch'ia	qia	ch'ui	chui	hui	hui
ch'ian	qian	chun	zhun	hun	hun
chiang	jiang	ch'un	chun	hung	hong
ch'iang	qiang	chün	jun	huo	huo
chiao	jiao	ch'ün	qun	hsi	xi
ch'iao	qiao	chung	zhong	hsia	xia
chieh	jie	ch'ung	chong	hsien	xian
ch'ieh	qie	chüo	jue	hsiang	xiang
chien	jian	ch'üo	que	hsiao	xiao
chih	zhi	ê	e	hsieh	xie
ch'ih	chi	eh	ê	hsin	xin
chin	jin	ei	ei	hsing	xing
ch'in	qin	ên	en	hsiung	xiong
ching	jing	êng	eng	hsiu	xiu
ch'ing	qing	êrh	er	hsü	xu

Wade-Giles	pinyin	Wade-Giles	pinyin	Wade-Giles	pinyin
hsüan	xuan	k'u	ku	lüo	lüe
hsüeh	xue	kua	gua	lun	lun
hsüo	xue	k'ua	kua	lung	long
hsün	xun	kuai	guai	luo	luo
jan	ran	k'uai	kuai	lüo	lüe
jang	rang	kuan	guan	ma	ma
jao	rao	k'uan	kuan	mai	mai
jê	re	kuang	guang	man	man
jên	ren	k'uang	kuang	mang	mang
jêng	reng	kuei	gui	mao	mao
jih	ri	k'uei	kui	me	me
jo	ruo	kun	gun	men	men
jou	rou	k'un	kun	mêng	meng
ju	ru	kung	gong	mi	mi
juan	ruan	k'ung	kong	mian	mian
jui	rui	kuo	guo	miao	miao
jun	run	k'uo	kuo	mieh	mie
jung	rong	la	la	min	min
ka	ga	lai	lai	ming	ming
k'a	ka	lan	lan	miu	miu
kai	gai	lang	lang	mo	mo
k'ai	kai	lao	lao	mou	mou
kan	gan	lê	le	mu	mu
k'an	kan	lei	lei	na	na
kang	gang	lêng	leng	nai	nai
k'ang	kang	li	li	nan	nan
kao	gao	lia	lia	nang	nang
k'ao	kao	lien	lian	nao	nao
kê	ge	liang	liang	nê	ne
k'ê	ke	liao	liao	nei	nei
kei	gei	lieh	lie	nên	nen
k'ei	kei	lin	lin	neng	neng
kên	gen	ling	ling	ni	ni
k'ên	ken	lio	lüe	niang	niang
kêng	geng	liu	liu	niao	niao
ko	ge	lo	le	nieh	nie
k'o	ke	lou	lou	nien	nian
kou	gou	lu	lu	nin	nin
k'ou	kou	lü	lü	ning	ning
ku	gu	lüeh	lüe	nio	nüe

Wade-Giles	pinyin	Wade-Giles	pinyin	Wade-Giles	pinyin
niu	niu	p'o	po	ta	da
no	nuo	pou	bou	t'a	ta
nou	nou	p'ou	pou	tai	dai
nu	nu	pu	bu	t'ai	tai
nü	nü	p'u	pu	tan	dan
nuan	nuan	sa	sa	t'an	tan
nüeh	nüe	sai	sai	tang	dang
nung	nong	san	san	t'ang	tang
nüo	nüe	sang	sang	tao	dao
o	o	sao	sao	t'ao	tao
ou	ou	sê	se	tê	de
pa	ba	sên	sen	t'ê	te
p'a	pa	sêng	seng	teng	deng
pai	bai	sha	sha	t'eng	teng
p'ai	pai	shai	shai	ti	di
pan	ban	shan	shan	t'i	ti
p'an	pan	shang	shang	tien	dian
pang	bang	shao	shao	t'ien	tian
p'ang	pang	shê	she	tiao	diao
pao	bao	shei	shei	t'iao	tiao
p'ao	pao	shên	shen	tieh	dieh
pei	bei	shêng	sheng	t'ieh	tieh
p'ei	pei	shih	shi	ting	ding
pên	ben	sho	shuo	t'ing	ting
p'en	pen	shou	shou	to	duo
pêng	beng	shu	shu	t'o	tuo
p'eng	peng	shua	shua	tou	dou
pi	bi	shuai	shuai	t'ou	tou
p'i	pi	shuan	shuan	tu	du
pien	bian	shuang	shuang	t'u	tu
p'ien	pian	shui	shui	tuan	duan
piao	biao	shun	shun	t'uan	tuan
p'iao	piao	so	suo	tui	dui
pieh	bie	sou	sou	t'ui	tui
p'ieh	pie	ssu	si	tun	dun
pin	bin	su	si	t'un	tun
p'in	pin	suan	suan	tung	dong
ping	bing	sui	sui	t'ung	tong
p'ing	ping	sun	sun	tsa	za
po	bo	sung	song	ts'a	ca

Wade-Giles	pinyin	Wade-Giles	pinyin	Wade-Giles	pinyin
tsai	zai	ts'ong	cong	wêng	weng
ts'ai	cai	tsou	zou	wo	wo
tsan	zan	ts'ou	cou	wu	wu
ts'an	can	tsu	zu	ya	ya
tsang	zang	ts'u	cu	yan	yen
ts'ang	cang	ts'ü	ci	yang	yang
tsao	zao	tsuan	zuan	yao	yao
ts'ao	cao	ts'uan	cuan	yeh	ye
tsê	ze	tsui	zui	yi (or I)	yi
ts'ê	ce	ts'ui	cui	yin	yin
tsei	zei	tsun	zun	ying	ying
ts'ên	cen	ts'un	cun	yo	yo
tsêng	zeng	tzu	zi	yu	you
ts'êng	ceng	wa	wa	yü	yu
tsi	zi	wai	wai	yüeh	yue
ts'i	ci	wan	wan	yüen	yuan
tso	zuo	wang	wang	yün	yun
ts'o	cuo	wei	wei	yung	yong
tsong	zong	wên	wen		

Examples of Some Commoner Simplified Characters

	East	Book	Classic	Qi	Yin	Yang	Door	Wind	Calendar	Look	Dragon	Tortoise
Wade-Giles	t'ung	shu	ching	ch'i	yin	yang	mên	fêng	li	chien	lung	kuei
Traditional form	東	書	經	氣	陰	陽	門	風	曆	見	龍	龜
Simplified form	东	书	经	气	阴	阳	门	风	历	见	龙	龟
pinyin	dong	shu	jing	qi	yin	yang	men	feng	li	jian	long	gui

Table of Some Unconventional Romanisations of Chinese Terms used in Astrology and Fengshui

Unconventional spelling	Chinese Character			*pinyin*
Paqua	八卦		Eight Trigrams	ba gua
Doey	兌	*Trigram name*		dui
Dzan	震	*Trigram name*		zhen
Gan	艮	*Trigram name*		gen
Kam	坎	*Trigram name*		kan
Kin	乾	*Trigram name*		qian
Kwan	坤	*Trigram name*		kun
Lei	離	*Trigram name*		li
Soen	巽	*Trigram name*		xun
Ba Chop	八宅		Eight Houses	ba zhai
Jut Ming	絕命	*Location name*	Cutting Fate	jue ming
Luk Saa	六煞	*Location name*	Six Curses	liu sha
Ng Quai	五鬼	*Location name*	Five Ghosts	wu gui
Sang Chi	生氣	*Location name*	Generating Breath	sheng qi
Tin Yi	天乙	*Location name*	Celestial Unity	tian yi
[Tin Yi]	[天醫]	*Location name*	[Celestial Healer]	tian yi
War Hoi	禍害	*Location name*	Accidents and Mishaps	huo hai
Yim Lin	年延	*Location name*	Lengthened Years	nian yen
Fei Sin	飛星		Meteors (Flying Stars)	fei xing
Goy Moon	巨門	*Star name*	Chief's Entrance	ju men
Jau Bat	右弼	*Star name*	Right assistant	you bi
Luk Tsyn	祿存	*Star name*	Fortune preserved	lu cun
Man Kuk	文曲	*Star name*	Literary songs	wen qu
Mou Kuk	武曲	*Star name*	Military songs	wu qu
Por Kwan	破軍	*Star name*	Destruction of the army	po jun
Tang lung	貪狼	*Star name*	Greedy wolf	tan lang
Za Fu	左輔	*Star name*	Left supporter	zuo fu

BIBLIOGRAPHY

I — Books and Articles in Western Languages

(Anon.) *New Archaeological finds in China*. Foreign Languages Press, Peking (1973).

Aubier, Catherine, (1) *Zodiaque Chinoise*. (In 12 vols, one for each Chinese animal year). 1982. English edition (1984).

____, (2) *Astrologie Chinoise*. M.A. Editions, Paris.

Bailly, J.S. (1) *Traité de l'Astronomie Indienne et Orientale*. Debure, Paris (1787).

____, (2) *Histoire de l'Astronomie Ancienne*. Paris (1781).

Bawden, C.R. *Astrologie und Divination bei den Mongolien*. Die schriftlichen Quellen (1958).

Bentley, John. *Hindu Astronomy*. London (1825).

Bernier, F. *Voyage to the East Indies* (vol 2, p. 114). Dass (SPCK), Calcutta (1909).

Berry, A. *A Short History of Astronomy*. Murray (1898).

Bezold, C. 'Sze Ma Ts'ien und die Babylonische Astrologie'. *Ostasiatische Zeitschrift*, 1919, 8 (1942).

Bielenstein, H. (1) 'An interpretation of portents in the Ts'ien Han Shu'. *Bulletin of the Museum of Far Eastern Antiquities*, No. 22 (1950).

____, (2) 'The Restoration of the Han Dynasty'. *BMFEA*, No. 26 (1954).

Biot, E. (trs) *Le Tcheou Li ou Rites des Tcheou*. Imprimerie Nationale, Paris (1851).

Bodde, Derk. 'The Chinese Cosmic Magic known as "Watching the Ethers"'. *Studia Sercia Bernhard Karlgren Dedicata*. Copenhagen, Munksgaard (1959).

Boutell's Heraldry. See: Scott-Giles, C. W.

Brennand, W. *Hindu Astronomy*. Straker, London (1896).

Bulling, A. 'The Guide of Souls picture in the Western Han tomb in Ma Wang Tui near Ch'ang Sha'. *Oriental Art*, XX 2, 1974, 158-73.

Burgess, E. *Surya Siddhanta*. Calcutta (1860).

Burkhardt, V.R. *Chinese Creeds and Customs*. South China Morning Post, Hong Kong. Volume 1, 1963. Volume 2, 1955. Volume 3, 1958. Abridged in one volume, 1982.

Carus, Paul. Chinese Occultism. *Monist*, vol xv, vol xviii.

——, (2) *Chinese Thought*. Open Court, Illinois (1907). Reprinted as *Chinese Astrology* (1974).

Chao Wei Pang. Fate Calculation. *Folk Lore Studies* (now Asian Folk Lore Studies). Peiping 1946 — 5, 279.

——, (2) The Fu Chi (= Chinese Planchette, or sand-writing). *Folk Lore Studies*, Peiping, 1942 — 1, 9.

Chatley, H. (1) Huai Nan Tzu. Translation of chapter 3 'T'ien Wen'. MS, East Asian History of Science Library, Cambridge. Has valuable additional MS notes by Joseph Needham.

——, (2) Chinese Natural Philosophy. *Journal of the Royal Society of Arts*, 1911, 59, 557.

——, (3) Ancient Chinese Astronomy. *Asiatic Review*, 1938, Jan.

——, (4) The date of the Hsia Hsiao Cheng. *Journal of the Royal Asiatic Society*, 1938, 523.

——, (5) The riddle of the Yao Tien. *ibid* p. 530.

——, (6) The Heavenly Cover. *Observatory*, 1938, 61, 10.

——, (7) The Cycles of Cathay. *Journal of the Royal Asiatic Society*, North China Branch, 1934, 65, 36.

——, (8) Notes on planetary conjunctions, etc. *ibid* p. 187.

Chavannes, Eduard. *Les Memoires Historiques de Se-Ma Ts'ien* (particularly volume III). Ernest Leroux, Paris (1898).

Chiba, Reiko. *Japanese Fortune Calendar*. Charles Tuttle Co., Tokyo (1965).

China — Facts and Figures, Rare Plants and Animals. Foreign Languages Press, Beijing (1982).

China Review — Hong Kong.

    I   — p. 237, Chinese Almanacs
    II   — p. 164, Charms and Spells
    III   — p. 269, 275, 331, 337, Folklore in China
    IV   — p. 58, Anglo-Chinese Calendar
              p. 1, 67, 69, 139, 145, 213, 279, 282, 364, Folklore in China
    V   — p. 41, 268, Folklore in China
    VI   — p. 213, Imperial Encyclopaedia

VII   — p. 134, Consulting the Oracle
VIII   — p. 320, Duodenary Cycles
IX   — p. 120, Chaldean Geomancy
X   — p. 223, 326, 432, Errors in the Chinese Calendar
XIII   — p. 431, Kirghiz Duodenary Cycle
         p. 357, Calendar signs
XIV   — p. 223, Chronology
         p. 49, 90, 166, 297, 345, 358, Astrology
XV   — p. 53, 126, Astrology
         P. 249, Calendar
         p. 376, Corean prophecy
XVI   — p. 56, 257, 337, 370, Star Names
         p. 95, Persian and Chinese Calendar
         p. 121, 369, Elements
XVII   — p. 302, Astrology
         p. 32, Lo Shu
         p. 49, Elements
XVIII — p. 379, Calendar
         p. 54, Chess
XXI   — p. 58, Astrology
         p. 54, 56, 57, Star Names
XXIII — p. 361, Chronology

Chu K'o Chen. The Origin of the 28 Lunar Mansions. *VIII International Conference on the History of Science*, Florence (1956). See also: Coching Chu.

Chu, W.K. and Sherrill, W.A. (1) *The Astrology of I Ching*, RKP (1976).

_____, (2) *An Anthology of I Ching*. RKP (1977). (Despite its title, this work contains a considerable amount of astrology-related material.)

Cleaves, Francis Woodman. *Manual of Mongolian Astrology*. Harvard University Press, Cambridge, Mass. (1969).

Coching Chu. Origin of the 28 Lunar Mansions. *Popular Astronomy*, 1947 — 55, 62. Also see: Chu K'o Chen.

Couling, Samuel. *Encyclopaedia Sinica*. Kelly and Walsh, Shanghai (1917). Reprinted, Ch'eng Wen (1973).

Couvreur, S. (1) *Li Ki, ou, Memoires sur les Bienseances et les Ceremonies*. (Texte Chinois avec une double translation en francais et en latin.) Imprimerie de la Mission Catholique, Ho Kien Fou (1899).

Culin, S. (1) Chess and Playing Cards.

_____, (2) Chinese Games with Dice and Dominoes. *Annual Reports of the US National Museum*, 1896 — 671, 1893 — 491.

Cullen, C. 'Some further points on the Shih'. *Early China*, 6. Berkeley (1981).

Cumont, Franz. *Astrology and Religion among the Greeks and Romans*. (trs J.B. Baker) Putnam (1912).

David-Neel, Alexandra. *With Mystics and Magicians in Tibet* (1931). Also Penguin (1936).

Delahaye, H. 'Recherches recentes sur le theme de l'ascension celeste'. *Bulletin de L'ecole francaise d'extreme orient*. Paris (1983).

Demieville, P. (editor). *Mélanges posthumes sur les religions et l'histoire de la Chine*, vol III, Civilisations du Sud. Paris (1950). Musée Guimet, Bibliothèques de Diffusion No. 59.

DeWoskin, Kenneth J. *Doctors, Diviners and Magicians of Ancient China*. Columbia University Press, New York (1983).

Doolittle, Justus. *Vocabulary and Handbook of the Chinese Language*. Foochow (1872).

Doré, H. *Récherches sur les Superstitions en Chine*. In 15 vols, profusely illustrated. T'u Se Wei Press, Shanghai.

(Earlier volumes, translated by M. Kennelly, S.J., were also published under the title Researches into Chinese Superstitions. Vols IV and V are the most relevant to the present subject. Pagination of French and English editions differs.)

Vol 1. Birth, marriage and death customs.

Vol 2. Talismans, exorcisms, and charms.

Vol 3. Divination methods.

Vol 4. Seasonal festivals.

Vol 5. Horoscopes and talismans.

Vols 6-9. Theology: gods.

Vols 10-11. Spirits.

Vol 12. Stellar deities.

Vols 13-14. Popular Confucianism.

Vol 15. Popular Buddhism.

Douglas, Robert K. *The Calendar of the Hea (Hsia)*. London, Trubner and Co (1882).

Dubs, Homer H. The Beginnings of Chinese Astronomy. *Journal of the American Oriental Society*. Volume 78, 4. New Haven, Connecticut (1958).

Duffett-Smith, Peter. *Practical Astronomy with your Calculator*. Cambridge University Press (1979).

Dulling, G.K. *Introduction to the Turkmen Language*. Central Asian Research Centre (1960).

Eberhard, W. The Political function of Astrology and Astronomy in Han China. Fairbank: *Chinese Thought and Institutions*. University of Chicago Press (1957)

___, (2) Lexicon chinesischer Symbole. Eugen Diederichs Verlag, Köln (1983).

Edkins, J. Star Names among the Ancient Chinese. See *China Review*.

Eitel, E.J. *Feng Shui*. Trubner and Co. (1873). Also, Pentacle Books, Bristol; Cockaygne (1973).

van Esbroeck, G. (1) Commentaires Etymographiques sur les Jades astronomiques. *Mélanges Chinoises et Bouddhiques*, 1951 — 9, 161.

___, (2) Les Sept Etoiles Directrices. *ibid* p. 171.

Fairbank, John K. (Ed). See Eberhard, W.

Forke, A. *World Conception of the Chinese*. Probsthain, London (1925).

Freeman, K. *Pre-Socratic Philosophers*. Blackwell, Oxford (1946).

Frigara, X., and Li, H. *Tradition Astrologique Chinoise*. Dangles.

Fritsche, H. *On Chronology and Construction of the Calendar with Special Regard to the Chinese Computation of Time Compared with the European*. Lithographed, St. Petersburg (1886).

Gascoigne, Bamber. *Treasures and Dynasties of China*. Jonathan Cape (1973).

Geddes, Sheila. *Astrology*. Macdonald Guidelines. Macdonald Educational (1976).

Giles, Lionel. (1) *Alphabetical Index to the Chinese Encyclopaedia*. British Museum (1911), reprinted Ch'eng Wen (1970).

___, (2) *Descriptive Catalogue of Chinese MSS* from Tun Huang in the British Museum. British Museum, London (1957).

Gingerich, O. See Stahlman.

de Groot, J.J.M. Dissecting Written Characters. *T'oung Pao*. 1890 I.

___, (2) *The Religious System of China*. Brill, Leiden (1872). In six vols.

vol. 1   Funeral Rites
vol. 2   Graves and Tombs
vol. 3   Feng Shui
vol. 4   Nature Spirits
vol. 5   Demonology and Sorcery
vol. 6   Wu (shamanism).

Grünwedel, A. *Mythologie du Buddhisme en Tibet et en Mongolie*.

Harper, D. 'The Han Cosmic Board'. *Early China*. 4, 6. Berkeley, (1979, 1981).

Hartner, W. Pseudoplanetary Nodes. *Ars Islamica*, 1938, 5, 113.

Hauer, E. *Handworterbuch der Mandchusprache* (1952).

Hawkes, David. *Songs of the South*. Beacon Paperbacks (1962).

Heissig, W. *Mongolische Handscriften*, Blockdrücke, Landkartes. *Verzeichnis der orientalische Handscriften in Deutschland* (1961).

Hoang (Huang), P. le P. (1) Catalogue des eclipses . . . dans les documents chinoises. *Varietes sinologiques* 56.

———, (2) Concordance des chronologies neomeniques chinoise et européene. *Varietes sinologiques* 29. Shanghai (1910); Taichung (1968).

Ho Peng Yoke. *Astronomical Chapters of the Chin Shu*. Mouton et Cie., Paris (1966).

———, (2) Modern Scholarship on the History of Chinese Astronomy. *Occasional paper 16*, Faculty of Asian Studies, Australian National University, Canberra (1977).

Hopkins, L.C. Archives of an oracle. *Journal of the Royal Asiatic Society*, 1915, 49.

Hou Ching Lang. Récherches sur la peinture du portrait en Chine au début de la dynastie Han, 206-141 avant J.C. *Arts Asiatiques*, XXXVI (1981).

Huard P. and Durand, M. Caractèristiques Macro-Microcosmiques de la culture spirituelle Vietnamienne. *Connaissance du Viet-Nam*. Imprimerie Nationale, Hanoi (1954).

Hulsewe, A.F.P. Watching the Vapours, an Ancient Chinese Method of Prognostication. *Zeitschrift fur Kultur und Geschichte Ost- und Sudostasiens*. 125 (1979).

Institute of the History of National Sciences, Chinese Academy of Sciences. (Compilers.) *Ancient China's Technology and Science*. China Knowledge Series. Foreign Languages Press, Beijing (1983). (This volume is highly recommended as an alternative shorter version of the great Needham work.)

Kalinowsky, M. 'Les instruments astro-calendriques des Han et la methode Liu Jen'. *Bulletin de l'ecole francaise d'extreme orient*. Paris (1983).

Karlgren, B. (1) Trs. Shu King. Book of Documents. *Bulletin of the Museum of Far Eastern Antiquities*, Stockholm 1950, 22, 1.

———, (2) Grammata Serica Recensa *BMFEA* Stockholm (1972).

Kaufman, Walter. *Musical References in the Chinese Classics*. Detroit Monographs in Musicology (1976).

Kennedy, E.S. (1) The Astrological Doctrine of Transit. *Journal of the American Oriental Society*, vol 78, 4. New Haven, Conn. (1958).

———, (2) *The Planetary Equatorium of Jamshid Ghiyath al-Din-al-Kashi*. Princeton.

Kermadec, J.M. H. de. *The Way to Chinese Astrology*. Trs. N. Derek

Poulsen. Allen and Unwin (1983).

Klepesta, J. and Rükl, A. *Constellations*. Paul Hamlyn (1969).

Kliene, Charles. *An Anglo-Chinese Calendar for 250 years*. Man Yu Tong. Hong Kong (1906).

Kotewall, R. and Smith, N.L. *Penguin Book of Chinese Verse*. Penguin (1962).

Kwok Man Ho. *Authentic Chinese Horoscopes*. (Series of twelve titles, although identical save for the opening chapter to each volume.) Arrow Books, London (1987).

Lai, T.C. *Selected Chinese Sayings*. University Book Store, Hong Kong (1960).

Laufer, B. *Jade*. Perkins, Westwood, Hawley. South Pasadena (1946).

———, (2) *A Study in Chinese Archaeology and Religion*. Field Museum of Natural History Publication 154.

Lawrence, Anthony. *The Love of China*. Octopus (1979).

Le Blanc, Charles. *Huai Nan Tzu – Philosophical synthesis in Huai Nan Tzu*. HKUP (1985).

Legeza, Laszlo. *Tao Magic — The Secret Language of Diagrams and Calligraphy*. Thames and Hudson, London (1975).

Legge, James. *The Four Books*. English-Chinese edition. Culture Book Co. n.d.

———, (2) Li Ki. *Sacred Books of the East* (Max Muller, ed.) vol. 27.

Li Xueqin. *The Wonder of Chinese Bronzes*. Foreign Languages Press, Beijing (1980).

Loewe, Michael. *Ways to Paradise*. George Allen and Unwin.

Loewe, Michael, and Blacker, Carmen (editors). *Divination and Oracles*. George Allen and Unwin, London (1981).

McNeill Wm and Sedlar, Jean. *Readings in World History, vol 5, Classical China*. Oxford University Press (1970).

Maloney, Terry. *Astronomy*. Macdonald Guidelines, Macdonald Educational (1977).

Maspero, Henri. L'astronomie Chinoise avant les Han. *T'oung Pao*, vol xxvi. Leide (1929).

———, (2) *Le Taoisme et les religions chinoises*. Editions Gallimard (1971). Also see: Demieville, P.

Major, J.S. 'Astrology in the Huai Nan Tzu and some related texts'. *Bulletin for the study of Chinese Religions* (1980).

Mayers, William Frederick. *Chinese Readers' Manual*. American Presbyterian Mission Press, Shanghai. Trubner, London (1874).

Medhurst, W.H. *Shoo Ching*. (Appendix A). Shanghai (1846).

Metropolitan Museum of Art. *Treasures from the Bronze Age of China*. Ballantine Books (1980).

Michel, H. (1) Les Jades Astronomiques Chinois. *Communication de l'Acadamie Marine*, Brussels.

———, (2) Chinese Astronomical Jades. *Popular Astronomy*, 1950, 58, 222.

———, (3) Astronomical Jades. *Oriental Art.* 1950, 2, 156.

———, (4) Les Tubes Optiques avant le telescope. *Ciel et Terre*, 1954, 70, 3.

Mills, H.R. *Versatile Astrolabe and Planisphere.* Stanley Thorne, Cheltenham (1980).

Mitton, J. and S. *Star Atlas.* Crown Publishers, New York (1979).

Morgan, Carole. (1) *Le Tableau du Boeuf de printemps.* Institut des Hautes Etudes Chinoises (1980).

———, (2) See Soymie, Michel.

Morrison, R. *A Dictionary of the Chinese Language.* (1815, 1819).

Needham, Joseph. *Heavenly Clockwork.* Cambridge (1960).

———, (2) Time and Eastern Man. *Journal of Royal Anthrop. Inst.* (1965).

Needham, Joseph, and Wang Ling. *Science and Civilisation in China.* In Particular, volumes 2 (Chinese Natural Philosophy, etc.) and 3 (mathematics and astronomy), and parts of volume 4, tome I, physics. Cambridge University Press (1962) continuing.

Ngo Van Xuyet. Divination, Magie, et Politique dans la Chine ancienne. Bibliotheque de L'Ecole des Hautes Etudes, *Sciences Religeuses*, vol. lxxviii. Presses universitaires de France (1976).

Nicolson, Iain. *Astronomy — A Dictionary of Space and the Universe.* Arrow (1977).

Palmer, M. (ed. and trs.) with Mak Hin Chung, Kwok Man Ho, and Angela Smith. *T'ung Shu — The Ancient Chinese Almanac.* Rider and Co. (1986).

———, (2) *Three Lives.* Century, London (1987).

Parker, A.P. The Chinese Almanac. *Chinese Recorder*, vol. xix. Foochow.

Pattie, T.S. *Astrology.* British Library (1980).

Pelliot, Paul. Le Plus Ancien exemple du cycle des douze animaux chez les Turcs. *T'oung Pao* XXVI Leide (1929).

Pirazzoli-T'Serstevens. *Living Architecture — Chinese.* Macdonald, London (1971).

Playfair, G.L. and Hill, S. *The Cycles of Heaven.* Souvenir (1978).

'Raphael'. *Key and Guide to Astrology.* A complete system of genethliacal astrology. W. Foulsham and Co. Ltd. (1905).

———, (2) *Mundane Astrology.* W. Foulsham. n.d.

Reeves, John. *List of Stars.* MS, British Museum, OR 8133.

A manuscript notebook in which the Chinese star-names are indexed, with comprehensive pencil-notes and diagrams of the constellations in more than one hand. This is likely to be the manuscript for (2).

———, (2) Star lists in Morrison's *Dictionary of the Chinese Language*, part II.

Rey, H.A. *A New Way to See the Stars*. Paul Hamlyn (1966).

Rigby, P. and Bean, H. *Chinese Astrologics*. South China Morning Post, Hong Kong. n.d. (*ca.* 1982).

Ronan, C.A. *The Practical Astronomer*. Pan Books (1981).

Rufus, W.C. Astronomy in Korea. *Journal of the Royal Asiatic Society*, Korean Branch. 1936, 26, 1.

de Saussure, Leopold. Prolégomènes d'Astronomie primitive comparée. *Archives des Sciences physiques et naturelles*. 1907 4° ser. 23, 112-537.

———, (2) Le texte astronomique du Yao Tien. *T'oung Pao*, series II, vol 8, pp. 301-389. Leide (1907).

———, (3) Les Origines de l'astronomie chinoise. Maisonneuve Frères. (Reproduction of a series of articles in *T'oung Pao*, including (2).

Schafer, Edward H. (1) *Ancient China*. Time-Life International. Nederland B.V. (1968).

———, (2) *Pacing the Void — T'ang Approaches to the Stars*. University of California Press (1977).

Schjoth, F. *Chinese Currency*. University of Oslo (1929). Reprinted by Andrew Publishing Co. (1976).

Schlagintweit, Emil. *Buddhism in Tibet*. London (1868).

Schlegel, Gustave. *Uranographie Chinoise*. Vols 1, 2 and maps. La Haye, Leide (1875).

Scott-Giles, C.W. *Boutell's Heraldry*. Frederick Warne and Co., London (1950).

Serruys, Paul, Les Ceremonies du Mariage. *Connaissances de Viet Nam*. Hanoi (1954).

Sesti, G.M. et al. *Phenomenon Book of Calendars*. Phenomenon Publications (1973).

Severini, A. (trs). *Astrologia Giapponese. (Atsume Gusa)*. Georg, Geneva (1874).

Seymour-Smith, Martin. *The New Astrologer*. Sidgwick and Jackson (1981).
Highly comprehensive, with an ephemeris.

Sherrill, W.A. See Chu, W.K.

Shigeru Nakayama. (1) Characteristics of Chinese Astrology. *I.S.I.S.*, 57, 1966.

———, (2) History of Japanese Astronomy: Chinese Background and

Western Impact. *Harvard Yenching Institute*, 1969, vol. xviii.

Shih Sheng-Han. (1) 'Fan Sheng-Chih Shu' An Agricultural Book of China. Science Press, Peking (1982).

———, (2) 'Ch'i Min Yao Shu' An Agricultural Encyclopaedia of the 6th Century. Science Press, Peking (1982).

Shirkogorov, S.M. Shamanism. *Journal Royal Asiatic Society*, North China Branch, 1923, 54, 246.

Sivin, N. Cosmos and Computation in Early Chinese Mathematical Astronomy. *T'oung Pao*, lvi — 3, 1969.

Skinner, Stephen. *Living Earth Manual of Feng Shui*. Routledge Kegan Paul (1982).

Smith, D.H. *Chinese Religions*. Weidenfeld and Nicolson (1968).

Soymie, Michel (Editor). *Nouvelles contributions aux etudes de Touen-Houang*. Geneve, Libriarie Droz (1981). (Includes an article by Carole Morgan on prognosticatory diagrams.)

Stahlman, Wm, and Gingerich, Owen. *Solar and Planetary Longitudes 2500 BC to AD 2000*. University of Wisconsin (1964).

Steens, Eulalie. *L'Astrologie chinoise*. Editions du Rocher. Monaco (1985).

Stein, Aurel. Manuscripts and printed documents from Tun Huang:

———, (1) Twenty-five aurae, 13 star maps, and illustration of the God of Lightning. Stein 3326.

———, (2) Military Divination by Aurae. Stein 2669.

———, (3) Astrological notes. Stein 930.

———, (4) Astrological notes on the Southern constellations. Stein 5777.

———, (5) Short notes on four of the elements. Stein 6167.

———, (6) Good and Evil revealed by the Hammer, the 17th Mansion. Stein 4282.

The above documents ought perhaps more properly to be listed in the Chinese Bibliography, but are included here for ease of reference. Further notes about these manuscripts may be found in the Giles Catalogue, q.v.

Sun, Ruth Q. *Asian Animal Zodiac*. Charles Tuttle Co., Tokyo (1974).

Teboul, Michel. Sur quelques particularités de l'Uranographie polaire chinoise. *T'oung Pao*, Vol LXXI. Brill Leiden (1985).

Teichman, Eric. *Journey to Turkistan*. Hodder and Stoughton (1937).

Thompson, R.C. *Reports of the Magicians and Astrologers of Nineveh and Babylon*. Luzac, London (1900).

Tong Juo-shiang. *Horoscope Chinois: Ba Zi*. Tong, Paris (1987).

Tuckerman, Bryant. *Planetary, lunar and solar positions*. Vol 1. 601 BC-AD 1. Vol. 2 AD 2-AD 1649. Philadelphia (1964). (Memoirs of the American Philosophical Society.)

Ueta, J. Shih Shen's Catalogue of Stars. *Memoirs of the College of Science*, Kyoto Imperial University, 13 (1930).

Waddell, L. Austine. *Lamaism, the Buddhism of Tibet*. W. Heffer and Sons (1934).

Wales, H. G. Quaritch. *Divination in Thailand*. Curzon Press, London (1983).

Walters, Derek. (1) *Your Future Revealed by the Mah Jongg*. Aquarian Press (1982). Reprinted as *Fortune Telling by Mah Jongg* (1987).

_____, (2) *The T'ai Hsüan Ching*. Aquarian Press (1983).

_____, (3) Review of Kermadec, J.M.H. de. *Times Literary Supplement*, 6.4.84.

_____, (4) Review of DeWoskin, K.J. *Journal of the Royal Asiatic Society*. Vol. 2 (1984).

_____, (5) *Ming Shu: The Art and Practice of Chinese Astrology*. Pagoda, London (1987).

_____, (6) Review of Palmer et al. *Journal of the Royal Asiatic Society*, Vol 2 (1986).

_____, (7) *Cast Your Own Chinese Horoscope*. (Series of twelve miniature handbooks.) Pagoda, London (1988).

_____, (8) *The Chinese Astrology Workbook*. Aquarian Press, London (1988).

_____, (9) *Chinese Geomancy*. (A commentary on the Feng Shui chapters of de Groot's Religious System of China.) Element Books, Shaftesbury (1989).

_____, (10) *Chinese Mythology*. Aquarian Press, London (1992).

Watson, Burton. *Records of the Grand Historian of China*. Columbia University Press, 2 vols (1961).

Watson, William. *Cultural Frontiers in Ancient East Asia*. Edinburgh (1971).

Watts, A.W. *The Way of Zen*. Pantheon (1957). Also, Mentor (1959).

Weber, Harald. *Das chinesische Horoskop*. Schikowski, Berlin (1978).

Wheatley, Paul. *The Pivot of the Four Quarters*. A preliminary enquiry into the origins and character of the ancient Chinese city. Edinburgh University Press (1971).

White, S. *L'Astrologie Chinoise*. Tchou.

Whitney, W.D. (1) On the Lunar Zodiac of India, Arabia and China. Art. No. 13, *Oriental and Linguistic Studies*, 2nd Series, p. 341. Scribner, New York (1874). Also: Riverside, Cambridge (1874).

_____, (2) On the Views of Biot and Weber respecting the relations of the Hindu and Chinese systems of asterisms. *Journal of the American Oriental Society*, 1864, 8, 1, 94.

Whitney, W.D. and Lanman, C.R. (Trs). *Atharvaveda Samhita.* (Lists the 28 naqshatra) 2 vols. Harvard University Press, Cambridge, Mass. (1905). Harvard Oriental Series, 7, 8.

Wilson, Colin. *Starseekers.* Hodder and Stoughton (1980).

Wylie, Alexander. *Chinese Researches.* (op psth).

_____, (1) On the knowledge of a weekly Sabbath in China.

_____, (2) The Mongol astronomical instruments in Peking.

_____, (3) Eclipses recorded in Chinese works.

_____, (4) List of fixed stars.

Shanghai (1897).

Wylie, Alexander. Mongol Astronomical Instruments in Peking. *Vol. II, 3rd session du congres international des orientalistes.*

Zinner, E. Gerbert und das Sehrohr. *Berichte d. naturforsch.* Gesellschaft Bamberg, 1952, 33, 39.

II — Books and Articles in Chinese

For a note about the Chinese Classics, see the Introduction, page 21. Manuscripts from Tun Huang are listed in Bibliography I under 'Stein', and calendars in Bibliography III in chronological order.

As the authors of many of the Chinese works are unknown, these are listed by title, in alphabetical order of their usual transliteration. For this reason, the title is given first, followed by the author when known.

Ch'en Tzu Hsing Ts'ang Shu. 陳子性藏書
Master Ch'en's Storehouse of Wisdom. In 8 Chüan (1684).

Divination by directions and cyclical signs. Has 60 model octagon diagrams for each of the sexagenary cyclical numbers.

Cheng Shih Hsing An. 鄭氏星室
The Star Records of Cheng the Sage (732).

Chiao Shih I Lin. 焦氏易林
Chiao Kan. Han work, edited by Mao Shih in 1808.
The Grove of Chiao the Sage.

Ch'in Ting Hsieh Chi Pien Fang Shu. 欽定協紀辨方書
Wang Yün Lu (Editor) (1739).
The Imperial Manual of Astrology.

Chung Kuo Ku Tien Wen Hsüeh Pan Hua Hsüan Chi.
中國古典文學版畫選集
People's Publishing House, Beijing (1981).
Selected Printed Block Illustrations from Chinese Classics.

Chung Kuo Suan Ming Fa. 中國算命法
Ta Chung Publishers, Hong Kong. n.d. (*ca* 1978).
Rules of Chinese Fate Calculation.

Fen Yeh Ch'i Shu. 分野奇書
MS. British Library OR 6194 (*ca* 1850).

A treatise on the 28 Hsiu, with diagrams of the constellations, and
prognostications for various degrees of the lunar mansions.

Ho Lo Ching Yün. 河洛精
Chiang Yung (*ca* 1750).
Star Diagrams of the Ho and Lo.

See also: Shu Hsüeh; T'ui Pu Fa Chieh.

Hsing Ching. 星經甘公石申
Kan Kung and Shih Shen.
The Star Classic (*ca* 600).
Tao Tsang (284), reprinted Shanghai (1936).

The reprint is bound with Schall von Bell's treatise in Chinese; the Hsing
Chia 星家 by Tsou Huai; and Mattei Ricci on the 28 lunar mansions.

Hsing P'ing Hui Hai. 星平會海
Shui Chung Lung (*ca* 1750).
On Astrology, in six volumes.

Hsing P'ing Yao Chüeh. 星平要訣
On Astrology (1820).

Hsing Tsung. 星宗
Chang Kuo (*ca* 732). 張果
The Assembly of Stars.

Ku Ch'in T'u Shu Chi Ch'eng. 古今圖書集成
Section I Heavenly Bodies.
        II Calendar

    III Astronomical Instruments
    IV Unusual Phenomena
   XVII Astrology
  XVIII Deities
    XX Plants
Peking (1726). See also: Bibliography I — Giles, 1.

Lü Shih Ch'un Ch'iu 呂氏春秋
(Ssu Pu Ts'ung Kan reprint) (*ca* 239 BC).
The Spring and Autumn of Lü the Sage.

Ming Yün Ta Kuan. 命運大觀
Huang Yao Teh Chin Ying.
Hong Kong Wen Yin Publishing Co. n.d. (*ca* 1970).
The Wheel of Fate Thoroughly Examined.

P'ing Chu Yüan Hai. 評註淵海子平大全
Tzu P'ing (attrib.) (1828).
Work on Divination and Fate Calculation.

San Ming T'ung Hui Chuan. 三命通會卷
Encyclopaedia of Fate Calculation. Ch'ing.

San Shih Hsiang Fa. 三世相法
Yen Ch'in. 演禽
Three Worlds Physiognomy Rules.
Wu Chow Publishing Co. Taipei. (n.d. *ca* 1970).

Book of Divination based on the twenty-eight cyclical animals. The Taipei
copy is a reprint of a much older work.

San Ts'ai I Kuan T'u. 三才一貫圖
Early twentieth century.

A large linen-backed chart encompassing all the tenets of Chinese
philosophy and divination methods on a single sheet, 58×38.

Shih Chi. 史記
The Historical Record. First century BC. 司馬遷
Ssu Ma Ch'ien. See: Watson, Burton, Chavannes, Edouard.

Shu Hsüeh. 數學
Chiang Yung (*Ca* 1750). 江永
The Study of Mathematics (of Astrology).

T'ien Wen Ta Ch'eng Chi Yao. 天文大成輯要
Huang Ting (1653). 黃鼎
Treatise on Astrology and Astronomy.

Chuan 21 has illustrations of Ch'i (aurae).

T'ien Wen T'u. 天文圖
Huang Shang (1195). 黃棠
(Stone rubbing of a) Planisphere.

Tso Chuan. 左傳
Tso Ch'iu (attrib.) (*ca* 430-250 BC).
Master Tso Ch'iu's commentaries on the Ch'un Ch'iu (722-453 BC).

T'ui Pu Fa Chieh. 推歲法解江永
Chiang Yung (*ca* 1750).
Analysis of Celestial Motions.

T'u Shu Chi Ch'eng.
See Ku Chin T'u Shu Chi Ch'eng; also, Giles, L., in Bibliography I.

Wen Wu. 文物
'Literature'. Chinese Periodical.
Articles in 1958 — 7; 1974 — 7; 1977 — 1; 1978 — 2; 1978 — 8.

Wu Hsing T'ai I. 五行太一
Hsiao Chi (*ca* 600). 蕭吉
The Five Elements and the Great Unity.

Yü Chao Ting Chen Ching. 王照定真經
Kuo P'o (attrib.) (*ca* 300).
Jade Shiners Manual.

Yüeh Ling.
See: Lü Shih Chün Ch'iu.

III — Almanacs, Calendars, and Horoscopes
in Chronological Order

Calendar 59 BC
British Museum/British Library OR8211/25-35.

Although incomplete, the information regarding the lengths of the months and other details on these bamboo slips is enough to enable the whole calendar to be reconstructed.

Stein P6
Calendar for the year Ting Yu, 4th Year of Ch'ien Fu (877).
Also in Bulletin S.O.S. ix pl VII, p. 1033.

Stein P10
Family Calendar of Fan Shang of Ch'eng Tu Fu (882).

Stein 95
Fully annotated calendar of the 3rd Year Hsien Teh (956).

Stein 2404
(Title missing) . . . prepared by Head of Military Escort.

The calendar details show it to be AD 960.

Stein 612
Fully annotated calendar of the 3rd Year of T'ai P'ing Hsing Kuo (978).

Stein 6886
Ditto. 6th Year of T'ai P'ing Hsing Kuo (981).

Stein 1473
Ditto. 7th Year of T'ai P'ing Hsing Kuo (982).

Stein 276
Fragment.

Shows the day, cyclical character, element, seasonal phenomena, practical advice, the notional Hsiu, related parts of the body and combinations of colours.

Stein 2620
Fragment. 大唐鄰隨曆
'Ta T'ang Lin Sui Li' at end. Undateable. Some diagrams.

Chi Ch'i Pien Lan T'ung Shu. 集七政要覽通書
All Celestial Bodies Handy Almanac (1691). BM 15298b45.

Yü Ting Wan Nien Li. 御定萬年曆
Ch'ien Lung, 17th Year.

Gives the Year Cycle according to the Emperor's Reign and sexagenary figure; states whether each month is long or short (29 or 30 days); gives the Stem, and the Branch is smaller type for the 1st, 11th and 21st days of the month (1752-1880).

Jih Yung Chi Fu T'ung Shu. 日用集福通書
Daily Use All Happiness Almanac (1757), BM 15298a32.

Hsin Wei. 辛未
Fragment for the Year Hsin Wei.

Examined by a purchaser in 1770, so likely to be 1766 rather than 1706. The second page clearly indicates a Lo P'an, with a compass needle in the centre; the only almanac seen by the author which shows a Dial Plate with this feature.

Chü Chia Pi Yung Pai Pien. 居家必用一百篇
Family Management Compendium (1780).

(T'ung Shu).
Fragment, beginning 6th Month.

Calendar, Taoist Charms, Virtuous Tales. Eighteenth century.

Hsin Tseng Hsiang Chi Pei Tao T'ung Shu. 新增象吉備要通書
Chin Ch'ang Shu Publishers (ca 1800).
Newly Extended Almanac of Lucky Days.

Jen Shou Ch'ang Ch'un. 人壽長春
Extensive Virtue Palace Handy Family Almanac (1808). SOAS c41 k6.

Wu Fu Ch'üan T'u. 五福全圖
Five Happinesses Nativity.
Horoscope for year Hsin Wei; 5th Month, 4th Day (1811).

Pai Chung Ching. 百中經
The Classic of the Hundred Centres (1813).

Handbook on divination with a 100 year almanac. On the Eight
Characters, with much information on the subsidiary parts of popular
almanacs.

Ta Chüan T'ung Shu. 大全通書
Almanac (1814). SOAS c41 t2.

Tan Chu Tang Ta Tzu Ch'i Cheng. 丹桂堂大字七政
Cinnamon Hall Large Type Ephemeris (1816). SOAS c41 t7.

Tsou Chi Pien Lan. 訊吉便覽
Choosing Lucky Days (1820). SOAS c41 t6.

Fu Lan Tang Ta Tzu Ch'i Cheng. 福賢堂大字七政
Happiness Hall Large Type Ephemeris (1820). SOAS c41 t8.

Cheng Pai Pien Ta Ch'uan. 正百篇大全
Chief Hundred Complete Almanac (1821). SOAS c41 t7.

Jih Chiao. 日脚
Daily Basis (Almanac) (1820). SOAS c41 t7.

Ta Tzu. 大字
Large Type (Almanac) (1820). SOAS c41 t8.

Ch'ung Tao Tang. 崇道堂
Venerable Way Palace (Almanac) (1820).

Ta Ch'uan. 大全
Thorough (Almanac) (1820).

Pien Min. 便民
Handy Popular (Almanac) (1844).

Kuang Wen Tang. 光文堂
Excellent Language Hall (Almanac) (1844). SOAS c41 t7.

T'ai P'ing T'ien Kuo Yü P'i Chun. 太平天國御批准

Ch'ang Tsao Kuei Hao San Nien Hsin Li Pan. 昌癸好三年新曆

Hsing T'ien Shang Tzu Hao Yin Ying Ti. 行天下子好寅榮
Calendar of the 3rd Year of the Heavenly Kingdom of the Heavenly
Peace Dynasty, incorporating the New Celestial Signs, and
Promulgated by Imperial Edict (1853).

This extraordinary calendar is a particularly interesting historical document.
It was issued by the rebel Emperor Hung Hsiu Ch'üan (洪秀全) who
believed himself divine. Born in 1813, he became involved in a kind of
Christian Mysticism. He was proclaimed Emperor in Nanking in 1851,
but though the rebels took several provinces from the Manchu, they were
unable to form a strong government themselves. The dynasty collapsed
in 1865, after some twenty million people had been killed in battle or
executed. The calendar is a curiosity not only in that it perpetuates the
memory of that abortive rebellion, but also in that it was designed as
a calendar reform. The calendar begins with the Inauguration of Spring
(立春) which is the key to unravelling this calendar. In 1853, this occurred
on the 4th of February, which by the established Chinese calendar was
the 27th day of the twelfth Moon. Thereafter the months were designed
to relate to the Solar Periods; thus the first month of the T'ai P'ing Calendar
had the unusual (for the Chinese) number of 31 days. The normal
reckoning methods by Cyclical Characters and notional Hsiu were retained,
although curiously, four of the Branches were altered to (好榮底閒),
being the new cyclical signs for Branches II, IV, V, and XII, respectively.
The assumption must be that these were the cyclical signs in the nativity
of either Hung Hsiu Ch'üan, or the establishment of the new dynasty,
and their substitution of the 'Heavenly Branches' in the calendar of the
'Heavenly Peace' dynasty of the 'heavenly Kingdom' was therefore to
avoid a taboo.

Hsien Feng Pa Nien Hsin T'ung Shu. 咸豐八年新通書
Hsien Feng Eighth Year Almanac (1858).

A modern style almanac with engravings of the spirits of the Hsiu (1858).

Chih Ming Shu Han Hsüeh. 矢命術漢學
Nativity for 1876.
British Library OR 11174.

Though the title suggests that this is a treatise on astrology, it is in fact
a Fate Calculation nativity, with the Eight Characters clearly defined.

Yung Ch'ing T'ang. 永經堂
Wing King Tong Co. Ltd. Hong Kong (1957).

The traditional format almanac, still published annually. See 1982, 1983.

T'ien Ti Li. 天體曆
Wu Shih Ch'ing. Hong Kong (1962).

Ch'ung Kuo Li Han Ch'i Nien. 中國曆漢紀年
Calendar of the Han Dynasty. Taiwan (1978).

Hsin Pien Wan Nien Li. 新編萬年曆
Newly Arranged Ten Thousand Year Calendar, 1840-2000. Beijing (1979).

Yung Ch'ing T'ang. 永經堂
Wing King Tong Co. Ltd. Hong Kong (1982, 1983).

Chung Kuo Min Li. 中國民曆
Chinese People's Almanac.
Nan Kwok Publishing Co. (1983).

Kuei Hai Nien Li. 癸亥年曆
Chia Chia Pi Pei. Hong Kong (1983).
Almanac for the year Kuei Hai (1983).
Also, years 1984 ff.

Chung Kuo Li Shih Chi Nien Piao. 中國曆史紀年表
Chinese historical Calendar Charts, Chou to Present.
Peking (1978).

Chung Kuo Li Shih Chi Nien Piao. 中國歷史紀年表
Chinese historical Calendar Charts, 841 BC-Present.
Shanghai (1980).

Ch'ing Tai Chung Hsi Li Piao. 清代中西曆表
Chinese People's Publishing House (1980).
Manchu (Ch'ing) Dynasty Chinese-Western Calendar Charts.

Wan Nien Li. 萬年曆
Ch'en Hsiang Book Publishers (n.d.) Hong Kong.
'Ten Thousand' Year Calendar (1905-1983).
(Includes tables for Magic Square Divination.)

Wan Nien Li. 萬年曆
Hsin Ch'i-Yeh T'u-Shu Chu-Pan-Shë (n.d.) Macau.
'Ten Thousand' Year Calendar (1882-2031).
(Includes tables and instructions for Fate Calculation.)

Also see: Bibliography I, Kliene, Charles.

BIBLIOGRAPHICAL APPENDIX

A brief survey of some important books on Fate Calculation, in reverse historical order.

1. 三命通會　　　　　　　　　　萬民英
   San Ming T'ung Huei, in 12 chüan. Wan Min Yang.
   This book has been popular since the Ming Dynasty as the authoritative work on the subject.

2. 淵海子平　　　　　　　　　　徐大升
   Yüan Hai Tzu P'ing. Attributed to Hsü Ta Sheng.
   This is probably the most popular book on Fate Calculation which is presently available. Supposedly based on the *Yüan Yüan*, it might well be the *San Ming Yüan Yüan* enlarged and edited by Ming commentators. Note the title, which uses the name 'Tzu P'ing'; a practice derived from the writer of one of the lost books on Fate Calculation, Hsü Tzu P'ing, who lived in the first half of the tenth century AD. He passed his methods on to Ch'ung Hsü Tzu, through him to Tao Hung, and ultimately to one of the more famous Fate Calculators, Hsü Ta Sheng.

3. 子平三命淵源註
   Tzu P'ing San Ming Yüan Yüan Chu, in 1 chüan.
   This book is credited to Hsü Tzu P'ing (see note above). Further commentaries were added in the Yüan Dynasty. This is probably the *San Ming Yüan Yüan* mentioned above.

4. 定真論
   Ting Chin Lun.
   The San Ming T'ung Huei (note 1 above) attributes this work to the scholar Hsü Ta Sheng.

5. 玉照定真經

   Yü Chao Ting Chin Ching.

   This is a work of the Sung dynasty, and still in existence. It is quoted by Yüan commentators, which gives a clue to its antiquity.

6. 珞琭子三命消息賦

   Lao Lu Tzu San Ming Hsiao Hsi Fu.

   This is the work to which Hsü Tzu P'ing added his commentaries. It was apparently popular in the Sung dynasty, and achieved prominence between AD 1120 and 1130.

7. 命書   李虛中

   Ming Shu; by Li Hsü Chung.

   This is the oldest book on Fate Calculation still in existence. Although in all probability this book is by Li Hsü Chung, copies still in existence claim that Li Hsü Chung is merely the editor, and that the book was originally by Kuei Ku Tzu; the latter was a renowned ancient sage, and modern scholarship discounts the possibility of the book being that ancient. This 'antique' claim seems to have been a fairly recent invention, since the book is mentioned in Sung dynasty library catalogues and bibliographies, where there is no hint that the authorship might be any other than Li Hsü Chung's.

   In any case, it is more important that the author was indeed Li Hsü Chung, because this would indicate that the Ming Shu was a collection of the teachings of the most famous Fate Calculator of the T'ang dynasty, I Hsing (一行), whose own books are now lost. Unfortunately, present editions of the Ming Shu are heterogenous compilations of early and late commentaries, and it is extremely difficult to sift the original writing of Li Hsü Chung from the additions of later copyists and editors.

INDEX

'Account of the Travels of
Emperor Mu' 54
Acupuncture 264
Alfard (star) 122, 143
Almanacs, Chinese 274ff
    Sung Dynasty 276
Altair (star) 99, 100ff
Anatolia 63
Animal cycles
    comparison, table 67
    twelve 50
    thirty-six 66
    twenty-eight 66, 126
Animals, twelve, possible origin 160
Antares (star) 87, 94, 96, 143, 149
Aquarian age 56
Aristotlean science 40
Arcturus (star) 145, 187
    Aspirin 121
Armillary sphere 6
Astrologer, Grand 224
Astrology
    Evidence for 230ff
    Imperial Board of 272
    Tzu Wei 320
Aura *see* Ch'i

Betelgeux (star) 149
Bible 19
Big Dipper (constellation) *see*
    Northern Ladle
Bird omens 17, 25
Boat inspection 167
Book of Documents 60
Branches, Twelve 58ff
Bright and Dark Years, Table of 334

Builders, Chinese 275
Bulling, Anneliese 62
Bureau of Astronomy 224

Calendar
    Chinese, how to read 352
    printed, earliest 277
    western 268
    T'ai P'ing 369
Cardinal points, Five 28ff
Cat, absence from zodiac 69
Cave of the Thousand Buddhas 276
Celestial Equator 10, 14, 193
Celestial Pole 35
Chan, mythological mollusc 227
Chemical workers 32
Chen (technical term) 46, 150, 214
Cheng Hsi Ch'eng, Astrologer 23
Cheng Hsuan (scholar) 273
Ch'eng Tu city 278
Chess 246
Ch'i (aura or vapour) 8, 120, 176, 182,
    193, 222, 225ff
Ch'i (technical term) 52ff
    (solar terms) Table of 330
Chiao Zi, Astrologer 363
Chien, calendrical month 130
    Table of 330
Ch'ien Chu divination system 55, 129
Ch'ien Han Shu (History of the Earlier
    Han) 180
Ch'ien Lung Emperor 272
Ch'ih, mythological animal 127
Chih Lin, mythological animal 89
Ch'in Yu mythological creature 127
Ch'in dynasty 39

Chin Shu (History of the Chin dynasty) 64, 175, 181, 193
Chinese Month see Month, Chinese
Ching (Chinese classics) 22
Ching Ming (festival) 54
Ch'i Yao Jang Tsai Chueh (book) 273
Chou Li, Rites of the Chou Dynasty 150
Chou Tzu (book) 39
Chou Yen (philosopher) 37
Chuan, Emperor 185
Ch'un Chiu 60
Circular horoscope format 305
Clam, mythological creature 227
Clear and Bright (festival) see Ching Ming
Clerical workers 32
Clock, Mechanical 319
'Clothes-cutting days' 274, 275
Colours 78
Comet 220, 232, 365
    in horoscope 307
Compass, Chinese 255
Concerts see Music
Condiments, five 92
Confucius 364
Contained Elements 350, 351, 371
Counter-Jupiter 193, 230, 244, 258, 263
Couper, Heather 9
Crop sowing, dates for 179
Crow in the Sun 24
Cycle, Metonic see Metonic
Cycle, Saros see Saros
Cycle, sixty year 50
Cyclical signs for the Day, Table to find 339, 341-2

Decennial Fate Cycle 318, 325
Deities presiding over years 65
Dial Plates, in almanacs 254ff
    Terms 275, 281
    Terms, table of 260
    Terms, interpretation of 261ff
    see also Divination plate
Dipper, constellation see Northern Ladle
Directions, Eight 28, 46ff, 254
    lucky 239
    Table of 47
'directionology' 16, 26ff
Divination plate 66, 245, 246ff, 352ff
Divining boards 49, 62, 238
Dodecagonal format see 'spider's web'

Dog, Black, Mongolian 244ff
Double-hours 58ff
Dragon bones 18
Dynasties, rise and fall of 39

Earth, element see Element, five
Earth Planet (Saturn) see Saturn
Earth Plate see Divining Boards, Divination Plate
Earth's tilt 176
Easter 54
Eclipses 150, 180, 214, 219, 231, 344ff
Ecliptic 10, 14
    plane of 344
Eco, Umberto 367
Eight Characters see Four Pillars
Eight Directions see Directions, Eight
Eight Trigrams see Trigrams, Eight
Eight Winds 178
Electrical workers 32, 36
Elements, five 18, 25ff, 37ff
    attributes 78
    contained, 350, 371
    order of the 40ff
    personality types 36ff
Elements, four 40
Elements, six (Mongolia) 37
Elixir of Life 176
Emblems, Twelve 140
Ephemeris 275, 306
Epoch, defined 50
Equator, celestial 137
Equatorial extension, defined 84
Equinox 54, 145, 167, 364
Erh Ya, dictionary 56

Fan Sheng Chih, book of 178
Farmers 32, 35
Face Reading 361, 370
Fate Calculation 23, 30, 176, 248, 273ff, 281, 308, 311, 316ff
Female labour, inspection of 169
Feng Shui 11, 27, 248, 267
Fire see Elements, five
Fire Planet see Mars
Fire Star see Antares, Mars
Five elements see Elements, five
Five Palaces see Palaces, five
Fixed Stars, portents of 185
Flute, when to play 102

Format of horoscopes *see*
    'spider's web'; Indian grid; circular
Four Palaces 85
Four Pillars 281

Geese 150
God of Wealth 107
Grand Astrologer 224
Great Bear (constellation) *see* Northern
    Ladle
Great Cold, solar term 55
Great Year (of twelve years) 50, 61ff, 194ff
    names of the twelve years 194
Guardian (newspaper) 32

Haloes, solar 222, 224ff
Han Shu (history of the Han) 344
Han Yu, poet 82
Harvest 228
Hare in the Moon 24
Heaven Plate 49; *see also*
    Divining Boards, Divination Plates
'Heavenly Clockwork'
    (Needham) 58
Hectograph 305
Herodotus 121
Historical Record 23
Horniman Museum 247
Horoscope, dating of 294ff, 305, 316
Hou Han Shu (History of the Later Han)
    180
Hours, Chinese 58
Houses, in horoscope
    Table 290
    six, personality types 66
    mid-heaven, Table to
        calculate 350
    twelve 281ff
Hsia Hsiao Cheng, document 141, 276
Hsiho, legend of 142, 356
Hsing Ching, Book of Stars 98, 175
Hsing Tsung 'Company of Stars' 23
Hsiu (lunar mansions) 49, 66, 81ff, 161,
    306
    associated with Jupiter Cycle,
    Table 198ff
    notional, defined 82
    notional, Tables to calculate 348
    oldest list of 177
    and related kingdoms 231

summary table 128
table of 161
to calculate from western zodiac
    position 344ff
to find corresponding to western
    zodiac 345
Hsiu Yao Ching (book) 273
Hsiung Nu (Huns) 181
Huai Nan Tzu (Book of the Prince of
    Huai Nan) 23, 30ff, 55, 60, 75ff,
    84, 129, 142, 175ff, 180, 182
Hung Lieh Chuan (Vast and Eminent
    Chronicle) 176
Hung Hsiu Ch'uan, rebel
    Emperor 369
Huns 181
Hyades (constellation) 114
Hygrometer 230

I Ching 16, 22, 26, 46, 47, 56, 64ff, 92,
    121, 254, 357
I Hsing (monk) 273
Imperial almanac 274
Imperial Astrologer 186
Imperial Encyclopaedia 11, 23
Indian grid horoscope format 280, 312ff,
    315
Indian Summer 57
Intercalary months 55
I Shu Tien (astrological manual) 279ff
    Analysis of planetary data in 295ff

Jade ornaments in sacrifice 167
Jen Hsi (scholar) 310
Jin Ping Mei (novel) 366ff
jobsiyermek (Mongolian
    procession) 244
Jupiter (planet) 16, 192ff, 265
    Cycle 195ff
    portents 201
    stations 193ff

K'ang Hsi encyclopaedia 267, 279ff
Kan Teh (astronomer) 23, 132, 175
King Lear 15
Kirghiz 63
K'o, division of time 58
    Tables 329
Korea, animal zodiac 64
Kuan Tzu (Book of Master Kuan) 75, 76,
    271

Kung Kung, legendary rebel 176
Kung-shu Tze see Lu Pan
K'un Lun (mountain) 244
Kurdish animal cycle 63

Ladle (Chinese constellation) see
     Northern Ladle
Li Chi, Book of Rites 159, 160, 239
Li Chun, Inauguration of Spring 54, 130,
     368
     Table of 334, 341
Life Cycle Palaces see Palaces, Life Cycle
Li Ki see Li Chi
Li Ling, General 181
Liu An, Prince of Huai Nan 175, 180
Liu Po (game) 238, 267
Liu P'an (divining board) 247ff, 266,
     267ff
Lo P'an (Luopan) 247ff, 352ff
Lo Tsun (monk) 276
Ludo (game) 246
Lu Pan (patron of carpenters) 239
Lunar calendar 149
Lunar mansions see Hsiu
Lunation 51
Luopan, see Lo P'an
Lu Shih Ch'un Chiu (Annals of Master
     Lu) 39, 159

Macartney, Lord 273
Magic Squares 78, 239ff
     Colours of 240
Ma Hsu (historian) 180
Management and administration 34
Manchu Calendars 129
Manchuria 64
Manjusri 273
Mars 202, 231, 265
     orbit, diagram of 333
Masons and carpenters 320
Matangi sutra 273
Meal, sacrificial 160
Mencius 239
Mercier, Raymond 9
Mercury, path of, illustration 207
Mercury (planet) 208, 214, 265, 307
Metal see Elements, five
Metal planet see Venus
Metallurgy, avoidance of 75
Meteors 220
Metonic cycle 55

Mid-heaven 350
Miners 32, 35
Ming Shu see Fate Calculation
Mithraic influence 82
Mithraic week 273
Mongolian animal cycle 63
Mongolian divination 244
Mongolian elements see Elements, six
Mongol Tatars 181
Monopoly (game) 246
'Monthly Instructions' 159ff
     text of 163ff
Monthly Spirits 246, 248ff
Months, Chinese 51, 55ff, 130
     literary names for 56ff
Months, intercalary see Intercalary
Moods 79
Moon 218
     'Concerning the' 322
     diameter of 51
     Full 268
     New 273
     nodes 139, 265, 287
Moxybustion 264
Musical assemblies 109
Musical concerts 124, 168, 173
Music inspection 165, 167, 168, 169,
     171, 173
Musical notes 78
     divination by 229

Navigators, information for 275
Nebula 116, 117ff
Nine Chambers (of Emperors's palace)
     164, 239
Nine Houses (Magic Squares)
     divination 242ff
Nine Regions 177
Nodes see Moon's nodes
Nonary calendar 55
Northern Ladle (constellation) 45, 49,
     98, 149, 186, 204, 244, 245ff

Occultations of stars 219
Occupations 32
Oedipus 15
Oracle bones 19, 60
Organ of body 79
Orion (constellation) 115ff
Ox-boy and Weaving Maiden 19ff,
     100ff, 192

'Pacing the Void' Schafer 81
Palace, Purple 322
Palaces, five 44, 85, 185ff
Palaces, Life Cycle 282, 308, 322
    Table 291
Palaces, Nine 48
Path, Red see Equator, Celestial
    Yellow see Ecliptic
'Pearl Geared Jade Rail' see Armillary
    Sphere
Pegasus, Square of 106
Pelliot, Paul 63, 276
Personality, types 66, 70ff
    compatibility 71
    see also Animal-, Element-
Pheasant 64
Phoenix 89
Physiognomy see Face Reading
Pillars, Four 79
    Planetary Terms in divination plates
    264
Planets, five 44, 192
    motion of, terms for 237
    'remarks concerning the' 217
    see also Jupiter, Mars, Mercury,
    Venus, Saturn
Planisphere 66
Pleiades (constellation) 62, 112, 143, 149
Plough (constellation) see Northern Ladle
Poetry Classic see Shih Ching
Pole star 49
Post Horse (in Fate Calculation) 311
Praesepe, nebula 117ff
Professional classes 32, 34
Pu K'ung, monk 273
Purple Crepe Myrtle see Tzu Wei
Purple Palace 322

Qi, Twenty-four, 332

Rat, Years of 338
Regions, Nine 177
Rectangular horoscope format 321ff
Reticulated plate see Lo P'an

sad-al-sud (star) 104
sad-al-malik (star) 105
San Ho, type of Lo P'an see Lo P'an
San Kuo Shu (History of the Three
    Kingdoms) 181
San Ming, Three Kinds of Fate 79

San Yuan, type of Lo P'an see Lo P'an
Saros cycle 219
Saturn, planet 204, 265
Saussure, L de 62
Schlegel, Gustav 84, 112, 187
'Science and Civilisation in China',
    Needham 62
Scythian soothsayers 121
Seasons 27ff, 30ff
Seven Regulators 274
Sexagennial cycle 73, 350
Sexagenary numbers, to find 336ff
Shan, term used in Feng Shui 261
Shan Tung (Eastern Mountain) 185
She T'i ko (techn ical term) 187, 198,
    209
Shepherds, Anatolian 63
Shih see Divination plates
Shih Chi (Historical Records) 180
Shih Ching (Classic of Poetry) 149, 273,
    357ff
Shih Shen (astronomer) 23, 132, 175
Shih Sheng-Han (philosopher) 129
Shuo Kua Ch'uan (I Ching) 46, 47, 64ff
Shu (Chinese Books) 22
Shu Ching 60, 142, 356
Shu Fu, Diplomat, 361
Shun, Emperor 6
Silkworms, House of (Unlucky omen)
    266
Silla, Korea 64
Sixty stems and branches, 350
Si Wan-bi, Astrologer 362
Social classes 32ff
Solar terms, periods, or fortnights
    see Ch'i
Solar year see Year, solar
Solstice 54, 102, 105, 122, 145
Spica (star) 90
'spider's web' horoscope
    format 280ff, 314
Spring see seasons, equinox
Spring and Autumn Annals 22, 60, 357ff
Spring and Autumn Annals of Mr Lu 39
Spring Ox 54
Ssu-ma Ch'ien 16, 23, 180ff
Ssu Ma Tan (Historian) 180
Stein, Aurel 23, 276
Stellar divinities 275
Stems (ten) 58, 72ff
Stem, Day, to find, Table 343

Stem, Month, to find, Table 343
Stems and Branches, Tables of 336ff
Sumeru, Mount 244
Summer see seasons, solstice
Sunday 82
Sunspots 24
Su Sung (horologist) 319

Ta Chi Cheng (book) 272
T'ai Hsuan Ching (book) 55, 310
T'ai P'ing Calendar 369
T'ai Sui 65; see also Great Year
T'ai Tsung, Emperor 64, 69
Ten Stems see Stems
Terdenary cycle 129
Terms see Solar, Planetary, Dial plate
Thai 69, 149
Thirteen–day cycle 129
Thousand Character Essay 275
Tibet, calendar 69
Tien Kuan, Celestial Ministers
    (book) 142
Tortoise 88, 169
Trigrams, eight 47, 48
Tripitaka (sacred books) 273
Tu Mu (poet) 81
Tun Huang 23, 48, 64, 82, 132, 175,
    223, 241, 254, 294
T'ung Fang Shuo, Astrologer 25
Turfan 129
Turkish names for zodiac cycle 63
Twelve animals see Animals, twelve
Twelve Branches see Branches
Twelve indicators, system of
    divination 129
Twilight 14
Tzu Wei (deity) 320
Tzu Wei astrology 320

Unicorn, 364
Ursa Major see Northern Ladle

Vast and Eminent Chronicle 176
Vega (star) 101
Venus (planet) 16, 206, 208, 231, 265
Venus, in Feng Shui 262

Vietnam, substitution of Cat for
    Rabbit 69
    horoscopes 282

Wang Mang (Rebel Emperor) 73
Wang Shuo (meteorologist) 73
Wang Wei (philosopher) 267
Wang Yuan Lu (monk) 276
Water, element see Elements, five
Water Planet see Mercury
Wealth, God of 107
Weaving Girl (star) 149
Weaving Maiden see Ox-boy
Weights and measures, testing of 166,
    171
Wenchang, Queen 69
Western zodiac see zodiac,
    western
Willow 121
Winds, Eight 178
Woman's horoscope 281ff
Wood, element see Element, five
Wood Planet see Jupiter
'World Conception of the Chinese'
    Forke 75
Wu Hsien (astronomer) 132, 175
Wu Ti (Emperor) 175, 180

Yang Hsi (artist) 81
Yang Hsiung (philosopher) 55
Yao Tien (document) 87, 141
Year 50
    Bright and Dark see Li Ch'un
    Great see Great Year
Year Star 192
Yellow Emperor's Classic of Dwellings,
    book 267
Yi Jing, see I Ching
Yueh Ling (Monthly Instructions) 141

Zi Shen, astrologer, 363
Zodiac 15
    Chinese see Animals, twelve;
    ecliptic; celestial equator; solar year
    Western 51, 272, 315

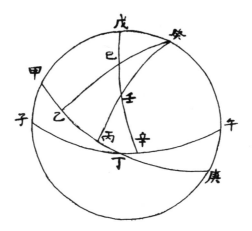